KARLA,

I'VE ALWAYS HAD A FEELING THAT YOU MIGHT SOMEDAY SAVE ME FROM DROWNING, BUT EVEN IF YOU ONLY 'TRY' TO RESCUE ME AND I DON'T MAKE IT, HERE'S MY 'THANK YOU' IN ADVANCE ANYWAY. JUST WANTED TO GET THAT OUT OF THE WAY...

YOU EFFING RULE FOR SUPPORTING ME IN MY WORK. I HOPE YOU'LL FIND IT FUNNY AND RECOGNIZE ME IN THE WRITING. THANKS FOR BEING A THREE-DECADE FRIEND. YOU ARE ONE OF THE GOOD ONES.

HERE'S TO NOT DRINKING,

FRANK
6.16.13

Nate!

I didn't had a feeling that you might
sunday save me from drowning, but even it
you didn't 'try' to rescue me and I don't make it,
here's my 'thank you' in advance anyway. Just
kinda to let that out of the way...

You better kudo for supporting me in my events.
I hope you're fun it funny and recognized me
in the water. Thanks for being a three-decade
friend, you are one of the good ones.

Let's to not drowning,

Love,
Robin.
From,

recoil
news satire you can trust

volume one

recoil

IS

Cliff Frantz
Kimberly Frantz
Matt Schilstra
Benjamin Hunter
Eric Mitts
Andrew Watson
Ira A. Briggs
Shi Briggs
Ira T. Briggs
Charles Preston Smith
Dick Bill

CONTRIBUTORS

Ben Wolford, Chris Frantz, C.J. Judd, David Zann, Ira T. Briggs, Jeff Smith, Mark Ritzema, Mike Church, Jeff England, Naomi Goedert, Nick Stephenson, Randy Hughey, Ryan Cunningham, Sherrie Coke, Sheila Streeter, Shi Briggs, Dr. Steve Mikulak, Steven Shehori, Wes Eaton

NOT THAT IT'S ANY OF YOUR BUSINESS, BUT

Recoil is a free news satire and entertainment magazine published monthly in West Michigan since 2001, founded by the husband-wife publishing team of Cliff and Kimberly Frantz. Cliff Frantz writes the satire section, oversees publishing and has a credit score approaching 400. Kimberly Frantz contributes original crosswords, writes book reviews and blogs about literacy, language and prose at midnightrite.blogspot.com. Matt Schilstra helped develop recoilmag.com's platform, writes proprietary software and keeps enough Adderall on his desk to power an entire hockey team through the Stanley Cup. Eric Mitts directs and edits Recoil magazine's entertainment section, conducts exclusive interviews with national recording artists and has been the foundation of Recoil's entertainment coverage for more than a decade – all while only having been seen in person three times. Benjamin Hunter acts as Recoil's print ad salesman, promotions director, cultural advisor and main mischief-maker. Andrew Watson aided Recoil's inception in 2001; his keen music taste and deft writing have been keeping Recoil readers steeped in good music since day one – and good luck finding a better writer or friend. Ira Andrew Briggs keeps our computers from exploding too often and provides enough muscle and beard for the entire Recoil team. Shi Briggs does graphic design, branding and 3 a.m. Meijer runs. Ira Thomas Briggs does proofreading, contributes comedy and forges handmade weapons for Recoil's entire readership. Reverend Charles Preston Smith contributes ideas and ideologies, handles print delivery and performs marriages. Dick Bill drinks beer. Chris Frantz put up his house as collateral to secure Recoil's initial funding (he either really loves his brother or has a fucking rock in his head – or, we suspect, both); he contributes satire ideas, constructs photo props and administers unspeakable acts of raccoon justice. Interact with Recoil through recoilmag.com.

DISCLAIMER:
THE PARABLE OF THE SNAKE

An old woman was walking down a road one day when she happened upon a group of men beating a poisonous snake with clubs. The woman intervened, saving the snake. She took the snake home and nursed it back to health. When the snake recovered, the woman carried the snake with her wherever she went, caressing it as if it were her child. One day, the snake bit her on the neck. As she lay dying, she asked the snake, "Why have you done this, after I have been so kind to you?"

"You knew I was a snake when you picked me up," said the snake.

Recoil contains satire. If you do not understand the concept of satire, you should not read the satirical news stories that comprise this book, because you WILL BE OFFENDED by some of the subject matter.

Recoil is not intended for readers under 18 years of age.

This book uses invented names in all stories, except notable public figures who are the subjects of satire. Any other use of real names is accidental and coincidental.

Copyright 2013 by Blue V Productions, LLC

All rights reserved. No part of this book may be reproduced or transmitted in any form or by any means, electronic or mechanical, including photocopying, recording or by any information storage and retrieval system, without permission in writing from the publisher.

Published by Blue V Productions, LLC

Printed in the United States of America

Concept and design by Cliff Frantz

Cover by Shi Briggs and Cliff Frantz

First Edition

ISBN: 978-0-9891631-5-6

Library of Congress Control Number: 2013905456

recoil

RECOILMAG.COM   NEWS SATIRE YOU CAN TRUST

Missing fat kids pictured on side of Whoppers® cartons

Above: A completely plowed Gene Reynolds attempts to plow his driveway.

Hershey, Penn. – Seeking to help desperate parents across the country in their efforts to locate missing children, officials at Hershey Foods Corporation announced Monday that packaging for the company's Whoppers® malted milk balls will now feature photographs of missing fat kids on one side of every carton sold in the U.S.

"Hershey is proud to lend a hand in helping reunite parents with their obese sons or daughters – many of whom had been among our most loyal customers before they went missing," said Hershey spokesperson Stephanie Moritz at a Tuesday morning press conference. "For these parents, the sight of that empty chair at the dinner table every night brings a pain that cannot be comforted – even by eating all of the extra food that's now up for grabs every night. Hershey is committed

Above: A carton of Whoppers® malted milk balls featuring the photo of Dean Orr, an overweight 10-year-old last seen at an Old Country Buffet in June.

see WHOPPERS page 4

Driveway, driver plowed

Holland, Mich. – Neighbors and family members voiced concern for the safety of homeowner Gene Reynolds, 48, who was obviously plowed Sunday evening while attempting to plow the snow from his driveway using a lawn tractor outfitted with a snow plow attachment.

"I asked Gene not to go out and plow, considering how he was already almost too drunk to stand after spending the entire day drinking beer and watching sports on TV," said Reynolds' wife, Margaret. "But, as usual, Gene doesn't listen to anyone when he's been drinking, especially me."

After looking high and low for his keys, which turned out to be in his pocket, Reynolds donned his winter wear, grabbed his cigarettes and a fifth of Wild Turkey and set out to haphazardly perform the winter chore – a half-hour job that took Reynolds nearly two hours to shabbily complete.

"Someone in that condition shouldn't even be allowed to use a shovel, let alone drive that big lawn tractor," said Anderson.

"I watched Gene stumble his way out to the shed, where the tractor is stored, and about ten minutes later I remember thinking – hoping, actually – that he might have just passed out in the shed to sleep it off, since he hadn't come back out," said Margaret Reynolds. "But then all of a sudden I heard the tractor

see PLOWED page 4

Babies: 100 percent suffer from depression

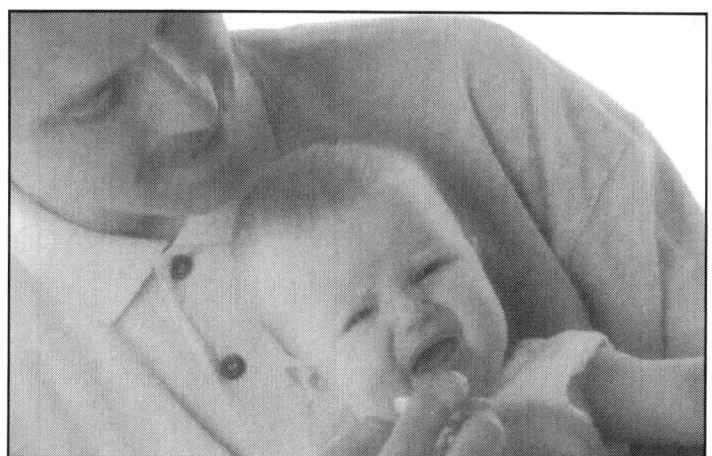

Above: As in adults, frequent crying and irritability are often the most noticeable physical symptoms of depression in infants.

Rockville, Mary. – A study conducted by researchers at the National Institute of Child Health and Human Development (NICHD) reports that 100 percent of all newborn infants display symptoms normally associated with clinical adult depression and in fact suffer from a medical condition known as Infant Depressive Disorder (IDD).

"A baby suffering from Infant Depressive Disorder will exhibit many of the same warning signs as depressed adults: frequent bouts of crying, weight gain, disrupted sleep patterns and so on," said Dr. James Redab, who headed up NICHD's three-year study. "Parents, do not dismiss your infant's behavior and assume that the little one is just tired or

see BABIES page 3

Infant Depressive Disorder Symptoms

- Frequent irritability, crying
- Sudden change in appetite
- Disruption of normal sleep pattern
- Abrupt mood swings
- Weight gain
- Difficulty thinking, concentrating, remembering or making decisions
- Lack of social interaction
- Indifference
- Low motivation

page 1

LIFESTYLE

eHarmony.com founder matches socks based on 29 dimensions of compatibility

Pasadena, Calif. – Dr. Neil Clark Warren, founder of the popular Internet dating service eHarmony.com, matches his laundered socks based on 29 dimensions of compatibility necessary for creating harmonious, long-lasting sock pairings, the well-known psychologist and author told reporters Tuesday.

"While others attempt to match socks based on a very limited amount of information such as size, color and stitching pattern, our scientifically developed set of compatibility principles is proven to foster that magical union between two socks that can lead to long-term domestic bliss," said Warren from his Pasadena home. "Every day, socks from around the world are finding their drawer-mates right here in the comfort of my laundry room, thanks to our advanced system."

Drinking tea from an eHarmony.com mug while carefully sorting printouts of each sock's computer-generated character profile, Warren explained that the principles of his patented sock-pairing technique were developed based on information garnered during 30 years of first-hand clinical research.

"I spent years interviewing housewives, maids and laundry service employees in an effort to understand what causes three out of every four sock pairings to end in separation within their first year," Warren said using the same soft, comforting voice found in his eHarmony.com television and radio commercials. "It's important to understand that the reason socks will suddenly abandon their partners usually has to do with the fact that the pair – although seemingly compatible on the surface – should never have been together in the first place. The resulting situation eventually becomes one of extreme discomfort for all parties involved, and the partnership is ultimately doomed to failure."

Warren's intensive study of successful and unsuccessful sock matches led he and his team of researchers to identify combinations of 29 key dimensions common to harmonious pairings. These dimensions include such traits as color, length, width, fabric, age, stiffness, elasticity, texture, stitch quality and stitch pattern, among others.

Warren said that compiling a comprehensive and accurate profile of each foot garment is key to finding a sock its life-partner.

"Each new profile is run through our proprietary matching model, where it is screened against a database of existing profiles in order to locate the most compatible matches," said Warren, opening a dresser drawer to reveal dozens of perfectly matched socks as a testimonial to his system's success. "A lot of times you can just tell that two socks are meant to be together from the moment you put them side by side. It brings me a great deal of satisfaction when I see socks that have sat alone for so long finally make that magical connection."

According to Warren, other information obtained during the initial screening process – such as details regarding the sock's history with previous partners – occasionally suggests that his system may not be able to find the sock a suitable match.

"There are some socks that you're just never going to be able to find a match for," said Warren, holding up a ragged, faded pink sock that appeared to be losing its elasticity. "Some of these socks are too old. Some have been through such harsh experiences in the past that they've become very abrasive and seem unable to provide any warmth or comfort anymore. And some are quite obviously on the verge of completely coming apart. I'm afraid that you're just not going to find a compatible partner for deeply flawed socks such as these. I usually throw them in the garage to use for rags when I change the oil in my car – the miserable, lonely bastards." ■

> "Every day, socks from around the world are finding their drawer-mates right here in the comfort of my laundry room, thanks to our advanced system," said Clark.

> "Our scientifically developed set of compatibility principles is proven to foster that magical union between two socks that can lead to long-term domestic bliss."

Above: eHarmony.com founder and spokesman Dr. Neil Clark Warren applies his revered matching skills.

EDITORIAL

Unt nu we a sprinkle de fleur

By The Swedish Chef

Eer skir mor por skir dir skikadoo, mmnork der snu nyork dir mmmn, Bork Bork Bork! ….Dur un ski doo inda bir. Mm nu we tayka inda beeg. Un skur dee horda reem. Ir skirbi hor dir skurba hibir nu. Ir skubor mir inda cookin caken. Skidoo mor! Birdirski. Oh, bi dir ski da morg. Skibork du skirmork dee skikadoo. Skirborsk skimork ski bir skibir. A spirgun a mirdur, spirgir under cakeski bu, nubir da. Birski borsk "Iya mono bir." Ir skirbir skirdi mmnork. Goskir di bir! Unski birdir da caken smoosher. Mor dir skudir hinder dough. Di skir da sprinkle de fleur, sprinkle de fleur, sprinkle de fleur on de dough. Oh, hikir deskir de dunka. Di kaskir dor, de caken dir hunyuns. Oh ya, hunyun ur very gud fir da singen sool. Un dir spurgi hirndi spurndi. Iyir di borga boom boom. Ir un dir inski room. Ira dir mor, di mir deskir dir speesy spicy soose. Ir mor, dir speesy spicy. Iskidoo dir skipir skoodir ir mor skumorg. Iskir dir hotsy-totsy. Unsmork dir soose. Musir dir meata-loafer. Mirskir dir meat, mirskir dir loafer. Undir – OH! … Nu meata-loafer. Undir roosta torkey! Hir we getda torkey. Hir, torkey, nirs torkey. Nu, we rosta dir torkey. Ir dir mor dir mirskir dir skurba hibir nir. Un skur dee skidoo mor birski. Bir skirdir hikir. Ir hur skir dir morbork ir dir flippen flappin jacken hirkin. Undir hirskibor dir batter. Ahir dough, a snirdir morda borkendir mor. Skidoor morn dir bir hoor dir sploosh. Askir dir mor dir flip-flop flippin flappin jacken undir mork. Unspir dirhir dirpski de cocoonoot. Askir de cocoonoot, askir do open dir cocoonoot. Ir skir dir bir skiborsk dir cootin, sawski, mordir cloobin dir cocoonoot. Undir hundir skoodir Borski mor dir skudir. Dir spurgi deski. Norski dir skibork dur skirdir di skir: Eer skir mor por skir dir skikadoo, mmnork der snu nyork dir mmmn, Bork Bork Bork! ■

> Nu meata-loafer. Undir roosta torkey! Hir we getda torkey. Hir, torkey, nirs torkey. Nu, we rosta dir torkey.

WORLDWIDE HEADLINES

Guy named Anderson suggests alphabetical order

Louisville, Ky. – According to sources present at recent events, Ted Anderson, an unmarried 39-year-old construction supervisor, routinely suggests alphabetical order as the most efficient means for coordinating activities in which it is beneficial to be among the first people to participate. "Last month, Ted had the balls to suggest we use alphabetical order to decide in which order guests at my sister's wedding reception should be invited to join the buffet line," said David Zielinski, a longtime friend of Anderson, confirming his regular predilection for recommending the use of alphabetical order. "I'm sure he'd be singing a different tune if his last name was Walker."

Bowflex® holds eight towels

Greenville, Mich. – According to resident John Irwin, the 26-year-old financial adviser discovered last month that as many as eight bath towels can be hung from his abandoned Bowflex® Ultimate2 machine when not in use. "It's not one of the ninety-five functions they advertise on the [television] commercials or anything, but if you're already out of the bathroom when you take off your towel, the Bowflex® is a great machine to let it dry on for a few days – as long as you're not planning on using it to exercise, that is," said Irwin. Irwin admitted that he has not used his Bowflex® machine for its intended purpose since early November, approximately three weeks after he bought the popular exercise unit with the full intention of using it on a daily basis to get in shape. Irwin noted, however, that he has also used the otherwise neglected contraption to occasionally hang ties on after coming home from work.

Online gambler loses house without leaving it

Terra Haute, Ind. – Jim Mackey, a regular visitor to the online gambling web site goldenpalace.com, lost his house to bank foreclosure over the last six months without once having to leave his house in order to gamble in a casino. "Gambling from home online is so much more convenient than having to drive two hours to an Indian casino or whatnot," said a sleep-deprived Mackey, taking a break from packing his few belongings into cardboard boxes in order to transfer his remaining bank savings into his goldenpalace.com account using his laptop. Asked about the deepening financial crisis caused by his online gambling, Mackey explained: "I've just had a string of bad luck recently. In fact, I've never seen a live dealer hit as many blackjacks as the computer dealer has over the past couple of weeks. But that just means I'm due for some winning any time now. Besides, I think I've got the program's tendencies figured out now."

Students' attendance, class participation twice that of professor

Mt. Pleasant, Mich. – A coalition of students attending Central Michigan University confirmed Tuesday that students' overall attendance and preparation for classes taught by one of the younger CMU professors is roughly double that of their teacher. Charles McBride, an energetic sophomore wanting to make the most of every part of his college experience, said, "Well, guess what? [Professor John] Warren cancelled class again for tonight. What a shock," after reading a mass e-mail bulletin regarding the cancellation. "He must be hungover again." McBride explained that even when Warren, 32, does manage to make it to class, he rarely appears properly prepared, seems to be "winging it" through most of the class time, and has even twice fallen asleep at his desk so far this semester.

Fucker heavy

Gary, Ind. – Peabody's Furniture delivery coordinator Joe Brocker used elements of slang to inform workers that the glass and mahogany coffee table scheduled for Monday's afternoon delivery was indeed heavy, sources reported. "Joe was giving us a rundown on the day's deliveries," explained crew leader Bob Ceglarek. "When he got to the coffee table that was going to the Andrews residence, he said, 'Careful with that one – fucker is heavy.'" Ceglarek said Brocker also explained that the delivery crew was to install the fucker in the Andrews' upstairs den, meaning they would have to carry the fucker up two flights of stairs.

Blender available for limited time also breaks after limited time

Los Angeles, Calif. – The amazing new Quasimatic 4000, a multifunction, high-speed blender available by phone only for a limited time, also breaks after a limited time, purchasers of the revolutionary new product recently reported. "I called and ordered right away, afraid I might already be too late to get the product since it was advertised as only being available for a limited time," said Cheryl Masters of Raleigh, N.C. "I'll have to see if the offer is still available, though, because my Quasimatic stopped working the third time I used it." Masters and other buyers of the Quasimatic 4000 insist the advertisements said nothing about the life of the product being of a limited time. ∎

BABIES from page 3

fussing. We now know that the infant actually requires immediate medication, psychotherapy and quite possibly electroconvulsive therapy. Your baby needs to get well."

Between July of 2000 and July of 2012, NICHD researchers examined an internationally representative sample of 121,000 infants, reporting that in all 121,000 cases the newborn exhibited various physical signs of depression – from irritability to difficulty making decisions to abrupt mood swings.

"As a parent, once you know the signs of IDD and know what to look for, it'll become very obvious to you that your baby has depression," said Redab. "And although it's a huge blow to come to the realization that your child has this serious of a medical condition at such a young age, you'll be relieved to finally know why your baby has been crying nonstop and just laying around, practically lifeless, for weeks if not months."

Redab, himself a father of two, expressed concern about the frequency in which IDD appears in children under the age of one.

"Whereas roughly one in six persons will exhibit symptoms of depression at some point during their adult lives, for infants we found that figure to be profoundly higher: one in one," said Redab. "Women, though twice as likely to suffer from depression, are fortunate in that they are twice as likely as men to seek help for their depression. Infants, on the other hand, blatantly refuse to talk with anyone about their condition."

Other symptoms of Infant Depressive Disorder that intersect with adult warning signs include low motivation, sudden change in appetite, lack of social interaction, indifference, difficulty thinking, concentrating and remembering.

Don and Carol Jorgeson were recently leveled by the news that their four-month-old daughter, Terina, suffers from Infant Depressive Disorder.

"Ever since Terina was born we had both noticed that she was prone to cry for no reason, and she always seemed indifferent to whatever was going on around her," said Carol Jorgeson, fighting back tears as she recalled the experience. "When the doctors told us that Terina was depressed and needed help, at first we didn't want to believe it. But accepting reality and moving on was the only way we were going to get Terina the help she needed. With the aid of a psychotherapist and counseling, now Terina only cries when she's hungry or thirsty or tired or wet or soiled or hot or cold or bored or teething or needs burping. Let me tell you, you wouldn't believe the difference."

Though the NICHD study failed to provide a solid answer as to the exact cause of IDD, Redab did not hesitate to offer a theory.

"An infant is likely depressed because they've only just been brought into the world and they can already see how much it sucks," said Redab. "The infant has not yet had time to develop the coping mechanisms that adults have – apathy, denial, alcoholism and such. At that point they child is likely to develop a 'Who cares?' attitude."

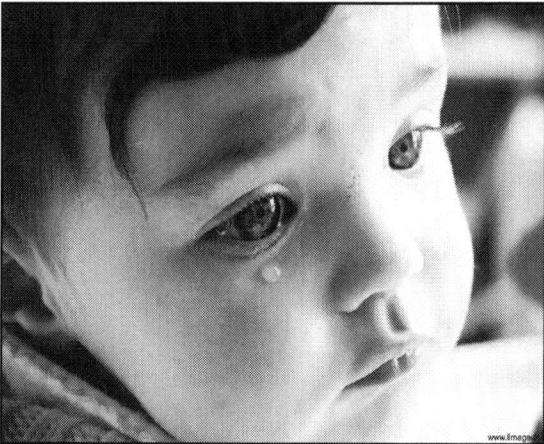

Above: Each of the 121,000 babies studied exhibited symptoms such as mood swings and weight gain.

> "You'll be relieved to finally know why your baby has been crying nonstop and just laying around, practically lifeless, for weeks if not months," said Redab.

Redab cautioned parents to approach their infant's condition with kid gloves.

"It is important for parents to keep in mind that depression is not a sign of personal weakness – telling your baby to just snap out of it doesn't usually work," said Redab. "Often, medication and counseling are more productive paths, and there are a lot of good child psychologists out there. So parents, remember, violently shaking your baby is not the only answer."

"I mean, violently shaking your baby is not the answer," Redab said, correcting himself. "You knew that." ∎

A page from the Recoil handbook...
Burglary Prevention Tips

Protecting your home from burglary should be a top priority for every family. Here are some tips to help fortify your castle:

• Studies show that in the U.S. a home is burglarized every 15.4 seconds – so never leave the home for more than 15.3 seconds at a time. Carry a stopwatch if necessary.

• By definition, burglary is a non-confrontational crime – so if you're a non-confrontational type of person, sounds like you're pretty much fucked.

• If you have a vicious guard dog, make sure to post a sign that reads: "Do not be aware of the dog." This will give your dog the element of surprise.

• A good rule of thumb for securing your front door is to add one deadbolt for every housing project within five miles of your home.

• Inform yourself! Check out some books by the Marquis de Sade, who wrote extensively about the nature of burglary. Oh, wait – actually, that was buggery.

• A majority of home burglaries occur while the victim is away at work or school. So if your parents are constantly riding you to stay in school or get a job, they're probably just looking for an opportunity to loot your room.

• Advertise the fact that you own few expensive material possessions worth stealing by putting a "Vote for Kucinich" sign in your yard during election years.

• Remember to store the written copy of your home alarm system passcode *at least* 12 inches away from the keypad.

• Call 911 every hour or so. The police enjoy testing response times by constantly driving out to your home for false alarms, and all that traffic ought to keep any would-be crooks at bay.

• If you absolutely must leave your home unguarded for an extended period of time, set fire to it.

• Understanding that most burglaries are carried out in order to finance drug habits, you can prevent penetration of your home by leaving small quantities of drugs outside your door.

WHOPPERS from page 1

to doing everything it can to help these folks find their fat little babies."

Moritz told reporters that the new Whoppers® packaging follows the same design concept made famous by the "Have you seen me?" milk carton campaign of the 1990s.

"Each carton will feature a black and white photo of an overweight missing child as well as information regarding the child's height, weight, age and last known whereabouts," said Moritz. "But we're also including some extra information that may help citizens track down these kids: a list of the child's favorite fast food restaurants, what kind of foods they're likely to be found around, what smells they respond to, what food stains were on the clothes they were wearing – that sort of thing."

Moritz pointed out that the classic milk carton catchphrase "Have you seen me?" has also been modified to reflect the physical trait common to all of the children featured on the Whoppers® cartons.

"We went with the phrase, 'How could you *not* have seen me?'" a straight-faced Moritz told reporters. "Look, you have to admit, one thing fat kids have going for them is that they're easy to pick out of a crowd: they're the ones at the playground sitting on the park bench, breathing heavily through their mouths while they rest up for a second trip down the slide. I wouldn't be surprised to find out that a few of us here today have actually gawked at or made fun of at least one of these missing fat kids in the last year without even knowing the child was missing. We're hoping that by putting these kids' images on our cartons, people will recognize and try to help them in addition to making fun of them."

"I mean, *instead* of making fun of them," corrected Moritz.

Hershey also hopes that by placing the fat children's photos on a product that the kids themselves are likely to seek out on a daily basis, the campaign may be more effective than the milk carton campaign in finding these missing children.

"We believe there's an excellent chance that these kids could see their own picture while they're polishing off another carton of Whoppers® or window shopping in the candy isle at Walgreens, and understand that their parents miss them and are trying to find them," said Moritz. "Remember, not all missing kids are taken against their will – especially fat kids, who aren't exactly the easiest ones to cram into a trunk in a rush. No, almost half of all missing children are runaways – well, I guess the term 'walkaways' would maybe be more accurate in this case. 'Waddleaways,' perhaps. At any rate, our hope is that kids who have left home voluntarily will see that they are missed and go home – knowing there'll be a fully stocked fridge waiting for them." ■

recoilmag.com

PLOWED from page 1

engine crank up. The shed door suddenly flew open and out flies Gene, driving that tractor as fast as it could possibly go for about ten feet before slamming on the brakes just in time to keep from ramming headfirst into our minivan."

Neighbors reported watching in bemusement as Reynolds experienced great difficulty repositioning the family's two cars into temporary parking spots on the city street.

"If you've ever watched someone having difficulty parallel parking a large car into a very small space, that's pretty much what it looked like watching Gene trying to park on the street, despite the fact that there were no other cars anywhere in sight," said neighbor Joel Anderson, who observed Reynolds' activity through his living room window.

"Moving the cars alone must have taken him twenty minutes, and the cars still ended up slanted and sitting about four feet from the curb. Ray Charles could have done a better job," said Anderson. "But the real show didn't begin until he got behind the wheel of that tractor. Those things take some skill to operate when you're stone sober, you know. The combination of booze and operating motorized equipment is almost always a recipe for disaster."

"It was definitely the first time I'd seen someone put a lawn tractor up on two wheels during turns," added Anderson.

Steering recklessly around the driveway in no discernible pattern, often with the plow positioned a full foot above the snow, the plowed Reynolds managed to plow roughly half of the snow from the driveway, while also failing to negotiate a number of high-speed turns which resulted in the uprooting of soil from most of his front lawn and the complete destruction of a section of his wife's prized shrubbery.

"Someone in that condition shouldn't even be allowed to use a shovel, let alone drive that big lawn tractor," said Anderson. "Although he never actually completely flipped the vehicle or crashed it into his house, he did fall out of his seat a couple of times. I also watched him accidentally drop a lit cigarette that landed about two inches from the tractor's open gas tank while he refueled after running out of gas."

Having successfully refueled, the plowed Reynolds continued plowing until the arrival of two police cruisers caused him to suddenly abandon the project and retire for the evening.

"Some of the neighbors must have called the cops, probably terrified that Gene was going to do them the favor of plowing their driveways for them," said Margaret Reynolds. ■

> Neighbors watched in bemusement as Reynolds experienced great difficulty repositioning the family's two cars into temporary parking spots on the city street.

page 4

RECOILMAG.COM   NEWS SATIRE YOU CAN TRUST

recoil

Local retailer frames first dollar hidden from IRS

Kettle prefers to be called 'African American'

God damns Detroit Lions per fans' requests

Detroit, Mich. – In response to statewide public outcry following the Lions' Sept. 19 three-point home loss versus the Philadelphia Eagles, God bestowed eternal damnation upon all active players and coaches of the losing National Football Team team that has only earned a single playoff birth since 1999. "The decades-long, unified plea of our flock has been granted by our Lord," said senior Heaven spokesangel St. Peters. "God has reflected on the weekly, deafening cries and officially damned every member of the Lions organization; from defensive line members to quarterbacks to team coaches and executives, each member of the Lions has had their soul eternally doomed to rot in hell, just like we've all asked." Asked to comment on the blessed act, Lions head coach Jim Schwartz said he and his staff were more concerned about notching the season's first victory than worrying about whether or not [team members] would be eligible for the Great End Zone in the Sky when their numbers get eternally retired. ■

Party host Trent Obeler frantically pumped the tap and breathed into the spout in a heroic attempt to revive the dead keg (above).

Keg found dead in bathtub
Tragedy grips local partygoers

Livingston, Ariz. – Partygoers were shocked and horrified Friday night when 20-year-old party host Trent Obeler found his quarter-barrel keg of Budweiser beer dead in the upstairs bathtub of his parents' Livingston home at approximately 11 p.m., sources report.

"I went into the bathroom to fill another pitcher for the guys playing pool downstairs and [the keg] was just, well, dead," said Obeler, who was throwing the party for more than 50 friends while his parents visited relatives in Utah. "I pumped the tap a few times and tried breathing into the spout, you know, trying to revive it, but it was no use. [The keg] was dead. I was in total shock. It was very unexpected."

Obeler: "I wish I'd spent more time with her, paid more attention to her, gotten to experience more from her, you know?"

Obeler said that after discovering the dead keg – which had been rented by an undisclosed source for $60 from a Crescent Avenue party store earlier that same day – he experienced a brief period of denial before accepting what had happened.

"At first I was like, 'Jesus, [the keg] can't be dead already,'" Obeler said, recalling his emotional response to the dreaded discovery. "I guess I thought it would just keep on going forever. After it was gone, I started wishing I had spent more time with it, paid more attention to it, gotten more out of her existence, you

see KEG page 8

Unemployment rate among hot young women holding at zero percent

Above: Just a few of the single young hotties that recently had no trouble finding work in today's otherwise dismal job market.

Washington, D.C. – Economic analysts were abuzz Monday following the release of December's Labor Department figures, which showed the unemployment rate for hot young women in the U.S. holding steady at zero percent for the 302nd month in a row.

"What these figures say is that if you're looking for work in America right now, you'll have no problem finding it – as

> "We're an equal opportunity employer: we'll hire blondes, brunettes, Latinos, Russian girls, whatever," said Ceritteno.

long as you're a totally smokin' hot young chick, that is," senior U.S. economist Cary Leahey said in a television interview Sunday. "From small businesses to major corporations, companies across the board are hiring cute young hotties

see HOT WOMEN page 6

page 5

HOT WOMEN from page 5

for positions every bit as quickly as they always have."

Independent economic analyst Eli Patterson said the report indicates that although the national jobless rate for run-of-the-mill, average-looking workers actually rose from 7.8 percent in November to 7.9 percent in December, not a single attractive female under the age of 30 is currently unable to find work.

"Sure, today's job market is kind of a nightmare for those unskilled laborers who are maybe a few pounds overweight or not especially striking or, well, male," said Patterson, speaking from his New York office. "But the Labor Department's December figures say conditions remain optimal for gorgeous, barely legal girls to find someone willing to hire them – especially if they wear their hair down and dress in semi-revealing clothes for their interviews. It's little things like that which can catch a male human resource manager's eye and go a long way toward getting them the job."

Patterson claimed that thin, young, ultra-sexy women have a distinct advantage in today's job market: "Employers in general seem more willing to take a chance on total drop-dead knockouts."

In fact, analysis of Labor Department figures shows that the rate of unemployment among the country's young stunners has not risen above the

> "Hey, if the skirt can even manage to operate a pencil, we'll find something around here for her to do," said Arthur Ceritteno.

zero percent mark since January of 1978.

"If you look at the statistics, it's clear that sexy babes are historically the most employable members of the nation's labor pool," said Patterson as his secretary – an unbelievably hot piece of ass who couldn't be a day over 21 – refilled his coffee mug. "And all indications are that this trend will likely continue for the foreseeable future."

A recent poll conducted by USA Today reported that employers – even when presented with a field of more qualified applicants – predominantly hire the youngest, best-looking female for the job, regardless of that sexy little number's lack of education, work experience, intelligence, personality, literacy or competency.

"Hey, if the skirt can even manage to operate a pencil, we'll find something around here for her to do," said Arthur Ceritteno, who owns a mid-sized furniture retailer in the southern U.S. "I always say we're an equal opportunity employer: we'll hire blondes, brunettes, Latinos, Russian girls, whatever. Hell, if the broad – excuse me, applicant – has the assets we need around here, I'll fire somebody to make room for her if I have to. Then everybody's happy."

President Obama, refuting claims that the country's modest economic recovery is failing to translate into new jobs, cited the December report as confirmation that the nation's unemployment situation is improving.

"I don't understand how anybody can say they can't find a job in this market, given all of the improvement we've seen," Obama said. "I guarantee you that I could send my daughters out right now today into this job market and they'd have absolutely no trouble landing a job."

Finding employment "has never been an issue" for Kathy Riley Jones (above).

WORLDWIDE HEADLINES

Report: Fucking blamed for swelling of world population

Las Vegas, Nev. – According to a three-year study conducted by researchers at UNLV, the blame for the quickly escalating world population can be assigned to all of the fucking in which couples around the globe are continuing to engage. "Our study proves that you, I and everyone else of consenting age – save homosexuals and Catholic priests – are to blame here," Dr. James R. Tobias told reporters Monday. "Unfortunately, overpopulation will continue to be a very real long-term threat to humanity so long as we all continue to fuck like there's no tomorrow." Although the study's report fails to outline possible solutions for quelling the worldwide craving to fuck, Tobias did respond to questions by suggesting that alcohol being banned from all trailer parks may go a long way toward slowing the population explosion.

Kitten catapulted from recliner headrest

Port Huron, Mich. – Local short-order cook Kyle Holmstead's 14-week-old kitten, Tiger, is unharmed and in good spirits following an accidental catapulting from the headrest of Holmstead's rocking recliner late Thursday evening. "I got up from the recliner to use the bathroom and I forgot [Tiger] was taking a nap on the headrest," Kyle Holmstead, 34, explained of the circumstances surrounding the kitten's unexpected launch. "I stood up pretty fast, and the chair's got a wicked recoil; Tiger must've flown at least six feet. It was really cute, actually." Upon landing, Tiger reportedly darted out of the room, only to return to the volatile nap site less than an hour later.

Extremely quiet life flashes before dying mime's eye

Manhattan, N.Y. – Forty-six-year-old pantomime artist Kyle Sikes saw his inaudible life flash before his eyes Tuesday night as the veteran street performer drew his final breath and succumbed to stab wounds inflicted by an irritated pedestrian whose identity remains unknown. Dressed in classic mime garb and whiteface makeup, Sikes prefaced his death by envisioning a series of notably muted scenes from his life, nearly all of which included Sikes' constant use of exaggerated gestures and annoying bodily movements when expressing his artistic talent to others. "Individuals who have been revived after briefly dying often report seeing their entire lives pass before their eyes," explained psychologist Dr. Martin Freeman. "Having been a professional mime most of his life, Mister Sikes's flashes likely included little-to-no dialogue – just physical gesturing. Stupid, annoying and talentless physical gesturing – more specifically." Witnesses present at Sikes' death said it remained unclear whether the dying mime's final gestures were an attempt to describe the type of casket he wished to be buried in or if he was performing one last pantomime of the classic "trapped in a box" routine.

Nature leaves message

Hendrickson, N.C. – Nature was forced to settle for leaving a message after its familiar call went unanswered by advertising salesman Hans Peterson Friday afternoon. "I was on the phone with a client when nature called," said Peterson, explaining his dismissal of nature's initial call. "Then I got really busy and simply didn't have time to respond properly to nature's call. I got the message that night, though – loud and clear – and ended up on the toilet for an hour, backed up to my elbows." Peterson said he was fully expecting nature to call again the following morning after the 45-year-old consumes his regular breakfast of a bran muffin and cappuccino.

Dieter experiences 30-day moment of weakness

Hartford, Conn. – Admittedly overweight receptionist Jean Dickinson explained to sources Tuesday that her second attempt to lose 30 pounds in 30 days using a diet outlined in a women's magazine was derailed by an extended moment of weakness which lasted the entirety of the diet's timeline. "As committed as I was to sticking to my diet this time, I'm afraid I did have a moment of weakness in there," said Dickinson, 44, of her 30-day, uninterrupted moment of relapse from sticking to a restricted food regimen. "It started that first morning of the diet with a raspberry Danish and lasted up through the meatlover's pizza I broke down and ordered last night when I was supposed to be suffering through my last scheduled dinner of celery stalks." Dickinson vowed to continue her work toward achieving her target weight, expressing an interest in trying a new 14-day diet in hopes of shortening the duration of any similarly persistent moment of weakness.

Neighbor out there staring at his sprinkler again

Great Falls, Mont. – Resident Barry Gordon confirmed several times Sunday that his next-door neighbor, 72-year-old retired machinist Thomas Fontaine, was out there staring at his sprinkler all day again. Gordon said Fontaine emerged from his home at approximately 6:30 a.m. to turn on the faucet feeding his front yard sprinkler and then proceeded to stare at the sprinkler for most of the day until finally coiling up the hose shortly before 6 p.m. "What do you suppose he's thinking about out there all day? Does he not trust himself to just leave it running because he's afraid he'll forget to shut it off later? Seems like a screwy way to spend your day, but I guess he's got the time." Gordon noted that he personally sat on his porch and stared at his own sprinkler for no more than two hours over the course of the weekend. ∎

Used car lot rolls back prices, odometers

HOROSCOPES

Cancer (June 21 to July 22)
Technological advancements could soon jeopardize Cancer's life. Don Corleone from *The Godfather* warned, "Keep your friends close, but keep your enemies closer," and the smartphone is definitely hermit Cancer's best friend. Be prepared to smash your cell on a moment's notice, just in case your ever-evolving "friend" starts acting like HAL, the homicidal copiloting compadre from *2001: A Space Odyssey*.

Leo (July 23 to August 22)
The practical, non-Webster definition of insanity is continually repeating the same process with the expectation of different results – something Leo should keep in mind when another Monday morning on the assembly line still isn't making you happy, you consider going out for "one" drink, or you start getting back together with your ex.

Virgo (August 23 to September 22)
Your nicotine dependency is your own business; smoke all you want – but for heaven's sake, please stop incessantly smacking fresh packs against your palm like you're sending Morse code to the Grim Reaper concerning your ETA. If Virgo wants those filtered bullets packed tighter than blasting caps, fine, but take it outside; that sound is more damaging to our mental health than secondhand smoke is to our physical.

Libra (September 23 to October 22)
The phrase "That's great, honey" is your mate's polite and subtle way of saying that extensive explanations of the minor details of your day are not welcome during *X-Files* reruns. Libra should remember that if something is worth saying, it's also worth saving – until a commercial.

Scorpio (October 23 to November 21)
Grammatically challenged alcoholic Scorpio will continue to be disappointed with daily trips to the supermarket for another hopeful stand in the "Alcohol Free Lane." Becoming Hooked on Phonics isn't an addiction requiring 12-step rehab, it's a non-embarrassing, mail order way of getting up to speed with the rest of society's public-school-system-products who can already read at a fourth grade level.

Sagittarius (November 22 to December 21)
Sagittarius' wardrobe is ugly enough to embarrass a rodeo clown. Even poodles dressed up in sweaters uglier than Poland's national flag look at you wondering, "I don't much like wearing this, but I'd choke myself to death with my own tongue before putting THAT on." Revert to letting your mother dress you – you'll be subject to accurate ridicule, but at least you'll have somebody else to blame.

Capricorn (December 22 to January 19)
God-fearing Capricorn's afterlife compass will point north only if you pay strict adherence to Biblical guidelines. Sure, it's difficult to sell your daughter into slavery (Exodus 21:7) or kill those who work on the Sabbath (Exodus 35:2), but His word is His word – and when the Great Surf comes up, you don't want God having any excuse to cast your soul onto the Lake of Fire with a kerosene-soaked surfboard and lead life preserver.

Aquarius (January 20 to February 18)
Aquarius shouldn't accept advice from anyone bigger than Richard Simmons. Natural selection suggests that anyone possessing a large, workhorse body still makes a living doing grunt work because they're not even smart enough to operate a computer. Learn to spot an intelligent bloodline: small-boned geeks with Hubble telescopes for glasses who look too weak to topple a Coke machine for all the quarters in Vegas.

Pisces (February 19 to March 20)
Be proud of the power with which your magnetic personality attracts members of the opposite sex, but be careful it doesn't draw any one particular member too close unless you're ready to be re-polarized. A wedding ring may well give your sense of security a positive charge, but it will also repel the remaining members of the opposite sex.

Aries (March 21 to April 19)
Like a drunken Japanese Karaoke singer stumbling through "Hotel California" with his fly open, Aries is oblivious to your instinctual tendency to make a fool of yourself in public. Like Twain said, "Better to remain silent and be thought a fool than to open your mouth and remove all doubt" – so dike that endless stream of moronic queries you feel compelled to spew whenever your crude conversations momentarily peek above primitive.

Taurus (April 20 to May 20)
Don't go spending your hard-earned money on a psychic or fortune-teller – they're about as reliable as discounted Firestones. If psychics really could see into the future, they wouldn't be wasting their talent predicting your inevitable divorce, they'd be cleaning up on blackjack at Caesar's Palace.

Gemini (May 21 to June 20)
Gemini attacks workdays with less enthusiasm than an innocent chain gang member with African sleeping sickness. Spending eight hours a day tethered to a cubical may seem a bigger waste of time than drinking non-alcoholic beer, but you don't have much choice – you need the medical insurance. Remember, all those hours at work pay off in the emergency room, when even a mild headache justifies you to cut ahead of uninsured shooting victims.

CHARITY

Drunk Americans unite for Million Man Stumble

Above: Drunk citizens congregate to participate in the Million Man Stumble.

Washington, D.C. – Tipsy Americans of all colors, creeds and ages 21-and-older converged around the nation's capital during happy hour Feb. 4 to participate in the first ever Million Man Stumble – a sloppily coordinated event intended to raise awareness of something that momentarily escaped the mind of organizer Jack Polaski during his introductory public address.

"Look, everyone, I know we're all totally jonsing for an order of mozzarella sticks before the game starts and everything, but it's important – shut up and listen to me now; this is important, what I'm saying – it's important that we take a moment to recognize our purpose for being here today," slurred an obviously tipsy Polaski from a raised podium. Pausing briefly to drink from his hipflask, Polaski continued: "Now, what in the hell was I saying? I was saying something, damn it! Shit. It think it might have been important, too. Oh well, fuck it – [*raising his flask to lead a group toast*] here's to, um, Elvis, I guess."

Polaski then lost his balance, stumbling backward and falling behind the podium, drawing applause from crowd members who didn't currently have a drink in their hands and were paying attention to Polaski's intoxicated ramblings in the first place.

The event appeared to be loosely modeled after 1995's Million Man March, an event drawing African American men from across the country to convey to the world "a vastly different picture of the black man" and unite in self-help and self-defense against economic and social ill plaguing the African American community, which drew an estimated crowd of 837,000 participants.

Efforts to estimate the number of participants in the Million Man Stumble were met with failure by organizers, participants and reporters, who were typically unable to reach a headcount above 50 before either simply loosing count and/or interest, stopping to engage in conversation with a potential sexual partner, or needing to quit mid-count in order to grab a fresh beer.

Openly intoxicated event coordinator Louis "Good Times Lou" Bryant recalled as much as he could regarding the conceptual spark resulting in the disjointed meandering of a bunch of drunks throughout the streets of downtown Washington.

"Jack [Polaski] and I were three sheets to the wind down at McGruder's [Tavern] one night when we overheard some assholes talking about that Million Man March," Bryant explained regarding the conceptual inception of the Million Man Stumble. "Jack was like, 'We should get everybody in [the bars] to go out and march some night to make some kind of statement about, I don't know, man – protesting and all that shit.' So what had originally began as inane drunk-talk between friends eventually blossomed into what we're seeing double of here today, whatever this is."

> "What had originally began as inane drunk-talk between friends eventually blossomed into what we're seeing double of here today, whatever this is."

Added Bryant: "Like they say, never misunderestimate the power of an idea – even one that doesn't make any sense. I mean, look – seriously, man, look; just look – I mean, we've done something here today. Personally, I've never been so proud."

Bryant then spent five minutes vomiting into a public garbage can before conducting a thorough search of his pockets looking for his car keys and passing out on a park bench.

A weaving Polaski managed to negotiate

see STUMBLE page 8

page 7

Bachelor spy's clothes washed on a need-to-wear basis

Classified location – A young, unmarried CIA special agent whose name could not be disclosed admitted Monday that, similar to how his confidential operation information is divulged strictly on a need-to-know basis, the laundering of his consistently large pile of dirty clothes is done strictly on a need-to-wear basis. "I guess that whole need-to-know basis way of operating has kind of spilled over into my everyday behavior – like how I put off doing any laundry until I know I absolutely need clean clothes for the next day," said the twentysomething bachelor. "It kind of makes sense, though, considering my lifestyle. For instance, say I'm ordered to fly to the Ukraine to assassinate a target, I'm going to need a very different set of clean clothes than if I were going into the Colombian jungle to conduct surveillance on a cocaine manufacturing location," the agent said in defense of the accusation that he was simply too lazy to get off the couch and do some laundry. Inside sources claimed that the constant backup of dirty dishes in the agent's sink suggested that the precision government operative also washes dishes strictly on a need-to-eat basis. ■

SCORES
Jets	21	Area	51
Propellers	2	**Spirit of**	76

EDITORIAL

The key to becoming a bum is maintaining an unsuccessful attitude

By Joey Riley

During my 13 years living on the streets of Detroit, I've seen a lot of bums come and go. A lot of these new hot shots show up one day in their moderately soiled clothes, roam the streets talking to themselves for just one summer and then they're gone. They come in walking the walk and talking the talk but they just don't have what it takes to achieve longevity in this scene. Few real bums have the discipline it takes to never bathe or sleep indoors or know where your next meal is coming from for more than a few months at a time. As a veteran streetwalker, I know about every tip and trick there is to making it as a bum, but if I had to sum it all up into one axiom, it would probably be this: the key to becoming a bum is maintaining an unsuccessful attitude.

This isn't half as easy as one might think. You see, without a job, a home, friends, family or television, there really isn't a whole lot to keep your mind occupied when you're out on the streets day after day, night after night. All that spare time eventually leads a man to thinking about your life and what you've done with it. This is where a lot of fellahs will start to lose faith in their choice in becoming a bum. You start to think, 'Man, if I just got off the bottle, got cleaned up and took another shot at life, I could really be somebody.'

This is the kind of thinking that can pick you right up out of the gutter. The next thing you know you've called a friend or relative to let them know you're not dead, that person shows up outside your cardboard box offering to help you get a fresh start and that's it – your days as a bum are over just as quickly as they started.

No, if you're going to be able to keep being a bum through both the bad times and the worse times, you've got to fight through that shit. You've got to constantly reassure yourself that it's impossible for you to hold down a job or keep a woman or even stay sober long enough to collect food stamps. If you can't always maintain this unsuccessful attitude, someday soon even the laziest and craziest of bums are likely to find themselves waking up in a small apartment with a working heater and a cupboard that's full of soup and noodles. And when this happens, let me assure you, you won't be going to no library in order to use the bathroom anymore, that's for sure. It won't be long before you willingly climb into a warm bed and end up pulling blankets over you instead of newspapers – and that's when you'll know that you're life as a bum has officially bottomed out.

So remember, before you gamble away your rent money, sell your car to buy drugs and start you're new life as a bum, be sure you're ready to maintain an unsuccessful attitude and make a lifelong commitment to non-excellence. Otherwise, you're sure to fail. ■

STUMBLE from page 7

the randomly flailing limbs of several participants without spilling the entire contents of his beer before articulating a slightly more succinct explanation of the Million Man Stumble's intent or message.

"Did you know that drunk drivers are one hundred percent more likely than straight drivers to face incarceration for drunk driving?" queried a completely straight-faced Polaski. "Also, employees who arrive drunk to work are at a greater risk of losing their job than sober employees? Our hope is that this demonstration will help rectify these situations."

In addition to participating in the Million Man Stumble, many of the activists will also take part in a parallel activity the following day – a date recognized as the National Day of Absence – during which activists are encouraged to stay home from work, forget to pick up their kid for weekend visitation and skirt all other daily responsibilities they weren't really going to be up for in the first place. ■

> Bryant then spent five minutes vomiting into a public garbage can before conducting a thorough search of his pockets looking for his car keys and passing out on a park bench.

Above: Million Man Stumble organizer Louis Bryant.

KEG from page 5

know? Deep down, I think I just wasn't willing to accept that here it wasn't even midnight and we were already out of beer. What a tragedy."

According to sources, Obeler spent almost 10 minutes collecting both himself and two cans of beer from the refrigerator before regretfully informing his guests of the unfortunate circumstances.

"Talk about a buzzkill," said Obeler. "I don't think anybody at the party was really ready for something like this. I mean losing a keg isn't like running out of fireworks. This was a party, and that was our keg – there's really no overstating how tight that bond is."

Bereaved party guest John Hawthorne echoed Obeler's sentiments.

"When I first heard about the keg dying I was like, 'You've got to be kidding me,'" recalled Hawthorne, 16. "I swear I had just seen [the keg] less than twenty minutes earlier and she seemed really healthy, like she had a lot of life left in her yet. And then just like that, boom, she's gone – and there's nothing anyone can say or do to bring her back. I just hope I can find somebody here that will let me buy in on their case [of beer]."

Sources said that while Obeler frantically phoned party stores in a fruitless attempt to locate another available keg, approximately half of Obeler's guests, visibly shaken by news of the keg's demise and unable to cope with their loss, vacated the Obeler residence.

"There wasn't much point in sticking around at Trent's place," said guest Todd Forner. "I mean, there wasn't really much we could do. And besides, we heard there was a band playing at a basement party across town – and that one's supposed to be a three-kegger."

One guest, 26-year-old Doyle Lungren, went so far as to personally blame Obeler for the untimely deaths of both the keg and the party.

"Dude, you *always* keep a back up [keg] on reserve [at the party store]," said Lungren, a veteran of the local house party scene. "Nothing kills a party like a dead keg. He should've been keeping a better eye on her to begin with. If she was dying he could have at least sent someone out to pick up a couple of cases [of beer]. If no other good comes of this, I hope everyone at least learned a lesson here tonight." ■

RECOILMAG.COM   NEWS SATIRE YOU CAN TRUST

recoil

Bush works out war strategy in backyard sandbox

Above: Bush simulates an F-16 air-to-surface strike after thoughtfully positioning ground forces.

Above: Chris Woodman (right) pretends to give a shit about wife Jena's incessant babble.

Area husband pretends to give a shit

Lafayette, Ga. – Attempting to pacify his wife Jena's incessant desire for verbal interaction, area husband Chris Woodman pretended to give a shit Tuesday as his wife of six years initiated and dominated a series of prolonged dialogues regarding an array of unrelated, unimportant subjects.

According to Woodman, the thoroughly pointless conversation – which comprehensively detailed his wife's work day, lunch experience, plans for the evening and friend's relationship difficulties, a subject that actually brought Jena Woodman to tears – took place in the living room of the couple's Lafayette home at approximately 6 p.m.,

> "I love my wife and everything, but by God does that woman like to talk," said Woodman.

see HUSBAND page 12

Crawford, Texas – Making good on his promise to use August's untimely 25-day retreat as a "working vacation," President Bush began masterminding tactical maneuvers for offensive strikes on Iraq in the backyard sandbox of his Texas ranch Sunday afternoon.

Outfitted in full military fatigues, the 56-year-old Commander In Chief utilized his vivid imagination while manipulating an array of army toys to experiment with different combat strategies and attack drills.

"Zzzzzrrrreewww boom!" yelled an excited Bush, firing a series of pretend air-to-surface missiles from the toy F-16 Fighting Falcon being piloted by his left hand. Using his right hand, the President simulated the impact of the rockets by grabbing a fistful of sand and tossing it softly into the air while vocally

> "Wwhhhooossshhhh," added Bush, banking the miniature fighter jet hard west and landing the unit just inches away from his blue plastic shovel.

mimicking the cries of wounded fake Iraqi soldiers.

"Wwhhhooossshhhh," added Bush, banking the miniature fighter jet hard west and landing the unit just inches away from his blue plastic shovel.

During Bush's intensely focused six-hour strategy session – which involved the fabrication of forts, foxholes, bunkers, roads and tunnels; the dressing and arming of several 12-inch G.I. Joe action figures; the positioning of toy artillery, vehicles, tents and munitions depots and detailed run-throughs of actual combat situations levied against an imaginary resistance – the President simulated defenses for a variety of possible engagements, from protecting against very likely threats such as suicide bombing attacks to the highly unlikely event of U.S. soldiers being

see SANDBOX page 12

Building resident realizes doorman has been dead for weeks

Server down

Imperial rights activists protest opening day of AT-AT season

Saginaw, Mich. – Hunting enthusiasts across the state met with opposition Monday as an estimated 7,000 members of the People for the Ethical Treatment of Imperial Forces (PETIF) protested the opening day of AT-AT Walker season.

> PETIF's message seems widely lost among rebel hunters determined to bring down a trophy AT-AT.

Gathering in front of state forests and other popular hunting areas throughout Michigan's Lower Peninsula,

see AT-AT page 10

Despite protests, hunters like Ted Walling (above) hope to bag record AT-AT Walkers this season.

page 9

WORLDWIDE HEADLINES

Band's tracks previously unreleased for good reason

Hollywood, Calif. – Fans of the legendary influential grunge band Nirvana gathered at a Hollywood Tower Records store shortly before midnight Monday night to be the first to hear and buy *Lost*, a new collection of previously unreleased Nirvana tracks that fans and critics alike agree had remained previously unreleased for good reason. "Wow, these songs *suck*," critiqued fan Keith Larson upon hearing the five-song EP, which consists of songs recorded over the phone by former drummer Aaron Burkhart during a call from a drunken Kurt Cobain in 1986, when the band was still named Skid Row. "No wonder these songs were never released – they're fucking terrible. Hearing this, it's hard to believe [the band] ever got a record deal in the first place. [Cobain's wife] Courtney [Love] must be hurting for cash to let this crap see the light of day. Kurt must be rolling over in his grave."

Zombie's phone line undead

Buffalo, N.Y. – Executives at the national telecommunications juggernaut AT&T expressed concern, confusion and a thorough lack of practical resolutions to the perpetually undead phone line reported by the Jones's, a related horde of zombies who – after having ordered phone service through AT&T more than a month ago – have yet to find their line either dead or live. "The entire family – or pack, or horde, or whatever – is undead, which makes them a slightly different clientele to work with, but that really shouldn't matter. Still, every single reading on my instruments prove the line is either live or dead depending on how it's connected, until one of them picks it up," said Brian Paisley, an AT&T service technician who has been to the zombies' estate 15 times during the last 38 days in an attempt to connect them to the live network of telephone and internet. Added Paisley: "This may just be an instance of technology needing to catch up with folklore. Or whatever. I'm getting out of here in case somebody from the office shows up to try to fix the whole situation with a hammer and a bag full of wooden stakes."

Ultimate Fighter also ultimate asshole

Chicago, Ill. – Producers of the reality television show *The Ultimate Fighter 2* told reporters Wednesday that Ultimate Fighting Championship (UFC) middleweight contender Chris "The Red Terror" Leben has been repeatedly referred to as "the ultimate asshole" by both cast and crew members during taping of the show's second season. "Most of these fighters are every bit as cocky and rude as they appear on the show, but Chris is in a league of his own – sort of an asshole among assholes, if you will," said cameraman Kenny Landers, who contends that Leben constantly yells at him for being "all up in [his] face." "I try to keep in mind that it's probably just the steroids talking, because it's hard to believe anybody could be that much of a prick all of the time."

Casino comps ruined gambler length of rope, chair

Las Vegas, Nev. – Having already been furnished with a complementary suite and breakfast voucher, David Arbor, a Detroit bank manager who lost over a million dollars of money borrowed illegally from his place of employment gambling at Caesar's Palace Saturday night, was offered a complementary length of rope, a chair, and instructions for tying a noose by casino host Alex Peterson immediately following his monumental loss. "I had told the blackjack dealer that this was it for me – either I was going to win big or I was going to be ruined," said Arbor, wiping tears from his eyes before ordering another whiskey sour from the casino bar and accepting Peterson's offer. Peterson explained: "Providing for a guest's every need – in this case, a means of self-induced euthanasia – is part of being a great casino host."

Man being shot at diagnosed with nervous condition

San Diego, Calif. – Ian Norman Drake, a 37-year-old accountant with no previous history of mental illness, was diagnosed as having a serious nervous condition by physicians who evaluated Drake while he was being shot at by an unknown gunman Friday afternoon. "Someone please help me! There's someone trying to kill me, for Christ's sake!" screamed Drake, dodging bullets as three doctors with clipboards observed their patient through a one-way mirror from inside a soundproofed room. "Talk about having a serious case of the nerves," said Dr. Jorge Montgomery. "I think our patient needs a vacation or something. He's incredibly tense." Montgomery and his colleagues suggested that Drake begin taking medication for his nervous condition as soon as possible, or convince people to stop shooting at him. ∎

AT-AT from page 9

demonstrators condemned hunters for their eagerness to systematically wipe out the state's Imperial assault vehicle population in the name of sport.

"We stand opposed to the senseless slaughter of *any* Imperial ground force," PETIF organizer Ira Ottenwess told reporters. "Not only is the brutal murder of AT-AT Walkers barbaric, these actions

> "We stand opposed to the senseless slaughter of any Imperial ground force," Ottenwess told reporters.

threaten to disrupt the delicate balance in nature between Imperial and New Republic forces. These hunters – who are they to play God?"

The Department of Natural Resources began permitting the recreational, licensed hunting of All Terrain Armored Transport (AT-AT) Walkers by rifle and bow in 1990. That same year, the hunting of All Terrain Scout Transport (AT-ST) Walkers also became permitted during season for hunters possessing a small game license.

Ottenwess said that the Supreme Court's recent upholding of hunter harassment laws has made it difficult for protesters to impede the annual mass-butchery of one of the Imperial's most vital military land units.

"We're basically powerless to stop someone who's bent on having a mounted AT-AT head hanging on his wall," said Ottenwess, 34. "By law, we're prohibited from standing in a hunter's line of fire. Nor can we attempt to scare the AT-ATs away from a hunter's feed pile by, say, firing a couple of turret-mounted ion cannon blasts across their bow. Essentially, we can't do anything that directly interferes with the taking of game.

"Our only hope is that we can appeal to hunters' sense of humanity before they even enter the woods," said Ottenwess, opening a copy of Monday's *Detroit Free Press* to a full-page anti-hunting advertisement paid for by PETIF. The ad depicts a small group of AT-AT Walkers peacefully mingling in a forest clearing. Written in large block letters atop the photograph is the phrase, "What did they ever do to you?" along with harsh statistics illustrating the decline in population of wild Imperial Transports over the last decade.

PETIF's message, however, seems widely lost among the hunters determined to bag a record AT-AT.

"Not only is hunting AT-ATs our legal right, it's our duty," said hunter Ted

The more agile Imperial AT-ST Walkers (above) are legal for licensed hunting during small game season.

Walling, who currently holds the state record for the 46-meter-tall, 10,000-pound AT-AT he bagged in 1999. "Letting wild Imperial [forces] go undisturbed would give rise to an unhealthy overpopulation, not to mention the inevitable destruction of the Rebel base."

Heavy metal rocker and noted hunting enthusiast Ted Nugent also publicly challenged PETIF's efforts to encourage the DNR to revoke the licensed hunting of AT-ATs and AT-STs.

"These People for the Enriched Treatment of whatever or whoever they are have no idea how amazing it feels to put food on the table using your primal hunting instincts," said Nugent. "Hunting is natural. We do it, the animals do it, insects do it. We're all bound together by this common thread; it makes us who we are.

Hunters, you know what I'm talking about. May the Force be with you." ∎

EDUCATION

Above: The recently graduated rock-filled box. Inset: The box's University of Phoenix diploma.

Box of rocks graduates from University of Phoenix

Pinconning, Mich. – A historic collegiate achievement was realized Friday when a medium-sized cardboard box containing a half-dozen rocks received a Bachelors Degree of Science in Business/Marketing from University of Phoenix Online, a popular online college.

"Congratulations! You've graduated!" the box of rocks was informed by e-mail following the completion of the course's final exam. "Welcome to the exciting world of Business/Marketing! Click here to register for a Masters Degree from University of Phoenix Online, the nation's leading University for working professionals."

According to sources, the box of rocks had been able to obtain its degree online in only three years and without having to seek a leave of absence from its current job at a Pinconning residence, where for five years it has been solely responsible for stopping a porch's screen door from opening all of the way.

The event marked a milestone for the inanimate object which had previously received no formal education via public schooling or private vocational training.

University of Phoenix public relations director Kyle Rise refused to disclose the cumulative grade point average earned by the box of rocks, but confirmed that it had indeed earned passing marks in all of the courses required to receive a diploma from the atypical school.

"That a box of rocks was able to earn its degree through the University of Phoenix's online program is proof

> The inanimate object had previously received no formal education via public schooling or provate vocational training.

> The box obtained its degree online without having to quit its current job at a Pinconning residence, where for five years it has been solely responsible for stopping a porch's screen door from opening all of the way.

positive that anyone or anything – regardless of social class, cognitive ability or financial resources – can, through hard work and persistence, earn a college degree," said Rise.

Rise speculated that news of the box of rocks' achievement could spark increased enrollment among demographics previously absent from the University's student body, such as bags of hammers, telephone poles and Texas residents. ∎

Dasani introduces new bottled bong water

A page from the Recoil handbook...
Camping Tips

Many people feel an instinctual urge to take to the outdoors every summer carrying less than a third of their modern home conveniences. Here are some tips for getting the most out of your weekend excursion:

• Though you may desperately want to know what's inside, leave one FedEx box unopened for foreshadowing purposes.

• You can greatly extend the life of your flashlight batteries by putting them in backwards.

• It never fails: you're out camping for a few days – just trying to relax, rarely even coming out of the tent except for bathroom runs – and the Gander Mountain manager eventually opens the tent flap and asks you to leave the showroom floor before he calls the cops. Fuckin' asshole.

• Smart people never hike alone. Smart people never hike, for that matter.

• Remember to register daily at the fairgrounds office, otherwise you won't be eligible to win the prize given out for setting off the wee morning M-80 that wakes up the greatest amount of campers.

• Calling tech support in advance will make it much easier to get your internet connection up and running at the campground.

• In the event of a bear attack, lie down on your back and try to appear lifeless. Men, ask your wives for advice on achieving this pose.

• Never feed the wildlife, as this will make animals dependent on handouts for survival. The same goes for your children.

• Make a scrapbook of close-up photos of each of your bug bites, to preserve the memories of your camping experiences for the members of your family that don't die from malaria, West Nile virus, etc.

• Do not, under any circumstances, pack a fire extinguisher. If by some miracle you do manage to get a decent fire going, you certainly don't want to risk someone putting it out.

• Keep in mind that sand, like vampires, can't come into your tent unless invited.

• Spreading a gross or so of industrial-sized tacks around the campfire will keep your baby from crawling into harm's way.

• Be sure one of your friends packs an axe or else years later your straight-to-DVD true story horror/thriller won't be able to get much of a plot going.

• If you're not up to packing everything and then driving 100 miles to camp at some remote, fly-blown shithole, keep in mind that there's no law that says you have to leave home to start drinking beer at noon on Saturday.

• It's wise to find the laundromat nearest to your campsite *before* it starts to rain. It's also helpful if the laundromat has a hotel attached to it.

page 11

SANDBOX from page 9

stomped on by giant feet.

"We've staged ground forces just outside Barsa, Commander," Bush said, struggling to restrict movement of his lips as he subtly shook the G.I. Joe delivering the tactical report. "Hussein's Republic Guard divisions have fallen back. We expect their forces to regroup in either the Tigris or Euphrates River valleys."

Bush then spent nearly 20 minutes molding and detailing a replica river valley using a large spoon and plastic bucket. Unsatisfied with the authenticity of the scaled-down battlefield, Bush retrieved a running garden hose from the side of the house and returned to the sandbox to flood his newly constructed reservoir and conduct a number of mock-up amphibious attacks.

According to first lady Laura Bush, the President concluded his exhaustive outdoors activities at approximately 6 p.m., when Bush came inside and immediately requisitioned two peanut butter and jelly sandwiches and a double ration of Kool-Aid.

"He's so cute," added the first lady. "And such a workaholic. This morning when I caught him rooting through the Presidential toy trunk, I said, 'Honey, you are not going out there again all day today. It's Sunday, for Pete's sake, and this is supposed to be your vacation.' I guess the poor man just can't help himself."

Sources confirmed that the President conducted further amphibious warfare simulations during his 45-minute bath late Sunday evening before retiring to his study to skim Sun Tza's *The Art of War* and reread a compilation book of *Beetle Bailey* comic strips. ■

> The President conducted further amphibious warfare simulations during his 45-minute bath Sunday evening.

HUSBAND from page 9

shortly after Woodman began watching television in an effort to unwind after work.

"I love my wife and everything, but by God does that woman like to talk," said Woodman, 30, who works as a field technician for a local civil engineering firm. "I wanted to just come home [from work] and chill out for awhile, but Jena immediately launches into these long, boring stories about what happened at work and what's going on with a friend of hers and a bunch of other stuff. I just tried to act like I was paying attention and hoped it wouldn't go on too long."

Occasionally retorting with such all-purpose conversation perpetuators as "That's nice, honey," "No kidding? Huh," and "I'm sure it'll all work out," Woodman pretended to give a shit about his wife's exhaustively detailed personal accounts until just after 6:45 p.m., when Jena was forced to interrupt the one-sided exchange to receive a telephone call from her longtime friend Nelly Smith.

"Saved by the bell, I guess you'd say," Woodman jokingly explained, adding that he used the brief interruption to exit the room and seek solace behind some cardboard boxes in the basement, where he remained for several hours.

Woodman acknowledged that although the lengthy, expendable conversation depleted a good amount of his after-work leisure time, the 45 minutes spent maintaining a convincing, give-a-shit veneer was not a complete waste.

"I was able to give some thought to a few things I hadn't had time for," said Woodman, who admitted to mentally drifting "light-years away" from his wife's inane banter. "While Jena was busy carrying on about God-knows-what, I was trying to figure out the significance of a couple of scenes from the movie *Memento*, which we had rented a few nights back. I think I've got most of [the plot] figured out now."

"Listening to her babble also gave me a chance to clean out my wallet, which I've been meaning to do for weeks," added Woodman. "I doubt she even noticed."

In addition to analyzing movie storylines and sorting a pile of receipts, Woodman mentally planned the couple's upcoming camping trip and also reminisced about his 1996 bachelor party weekend in Las Vegas – all the while remembering to nod, say "Yeah," and display other characteristics indicative of a person who is giving a shit.

Woodman said he often pretends to give a shit about what his wife says.

"Somebody – a guy – once told me that women tend to work things out in their

> The thoroughly pointless conversation comprehensively detailed Jena's work day, lunch experience, plans for the evening and friends' relationship difficulties.

heads by talking things out, so most of the time it isn't really necessary to listen to everything a woman says," said Woodman. "It's been my experience that the theory usually holds true. So I usually just keep my mouth shut and let her talk herself out. Sure, it's a complete waste of time, but it seems to make [Jena] happy."

Added Woodman: "And on the rare occasion that she's actually talking about something important, I usually pick up on it as soon as she starts yelling."

After 12 years of marriage, Woodman said he feels that his willingness to pretend to give a shit about what his wife says is vital to the health of their relationship.

"If I didn't sit there in total silence, staring off into the distance but occasionally grunting out an 'Oh yeah?' or a 'No kidding,' Jena would probably start to think we have a communication problem," said Woodman, adding: "I pretend to give a shit because I care." ■

page 12

SELF HELP
Idiocy Indicator

It was Faith No More's Mike Patton who first posed the musical question, "Would anybody tell me if I was getting stupider?" Answer: probably not. And while it is every American's God-given right to burn off brain cells with drugs and television, stumbling through the following quiz will at least alert you to your intellectual landslide's impending avalanche. Assign yourself three points for every A answer, two points for every B, one point for every C and zero points for every D.

1. To your understanding, the metric system is:
A. A government-oppressed measuring structure.
B. A food-bar based diet.
C. A collection of planets on *Star Trek*.
D. A method of birth control.

2. Your problem-solving abilities include being able to:
A. Hack into computer systems.
B. Complete two sides of a Rubik's Cube.
C. Avoid drowning by keeping mouth closed while showering.
D. Get drunk enough to forget about the problem.

3. Your intellectual mentor is:
A. Stephen Hawking.
B. Dennis Miller.
C. Regis Philbin.
D. Steve Austin.

4. You think you are being environmentally conscious as long as you are:
A. Careful to use only recycled products.
B. Only shooting animals that are in season.
C. Able to ballpark the current ambient temperature.
D. Awake and in the wilderness.

5. The majority of your extra money is spent on:
A. Carl Sagan books.
B. Adam Sandler DVDs.
C. Lottery tickets.
D. Charitable donations.

6. You were born and raised in:
A. Connecticut.
B. Michigan.
C. The woods.
D. Texas.

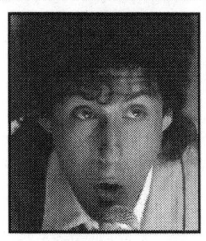

If you scored...

24-18: Check out the big brain on Brad! Alright, M.E.N.S.A. boy, you've made your point. Go split some atoms.

17-12: Well, you're not exactly a rocket surgeon, but at least your brain isn't pleading for euthanasia.

11-6: Corrective measures are immediately needed! Lock your TV on the History Channel, buy some Harry Potter books and stop smoking enough dope to kill an elephant.

5-0: Recoil has an Editor position that's screaming your name.

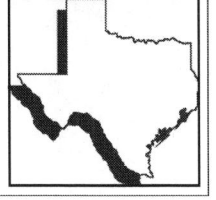

recoilmag.com

RECOILMAG.COM   NEWS SATIRE YOU CAN TRUST

recoil

ESPN commentators trying to avoid saying new player's name

Nuclear plant's safety report glowing

Anticipation mounts over odometer rollover

quikSTAT
Rejected vehicle names
- Nissan Sonama Bitch
- Ford Exploder
- Dodge Youjustdontcaravan
- VW XYZ
- Nissan Vulva
- Ford Tortoise
- Saab Story

Tammy in human resources dressed like slut again today

Indianapolis, Ind. – Sources at Elliot Manufacturers, an industrial packaging materials supply company, confirmed early this morning that Tammy Spicer in human resources came to work dressed like a total slut again today. "Did you get a look at Tammy yet this morning?" accounts manager Paul Albert asked marketing director Edward Richards after returning from an interview with a prospective salesperson. "I swear, that girl dresses like she's going straight from here to her weekend stripper gig or something. I can't believe nobody's said anything to her about wearing those kinds of clothes to the office. Not that I'm complaining or anything." Albert later returned to Spicer's department to double-check his timesheet after Richards confirmed that the 24-year-old office assistant is not currently dating any men from the office.

Above: Andrews curses God and all that is holy after failing to properly perform yet another routine task.

Area man can't do a single goddamn thing right today

Peterborough, Pa. – After botching a plethora of simple, everyday tasks, *Peterborough Times* classified editor Steve Elliot confirmed to sources that the 39-year-old can't seem to do a single goddamn thing right today. "This entire day has just been for shit," Elliot explained to coworkers as he used napkins to soak up a spilled Coke during lunch at a Lawrence Avenue Red Lobster.

see MAN page 16

Above: A disabled automobile assembly line robot (left) and a newer Fujitsu robot avoid the work of eight humans on the streets of our nation's capital.

Nation's homeless being replaced by lazier, less-efficient robots

Washington, D.C. – An annual report released this week by the U.S. Conference of Mayors shows that an increasing number of homeless people throughout the country are being replaced by lazier, less-efficient robots.

"What this study says is that our perception of the nation's homeless as a group of men and women who are unable to adapt to society's structure is becoming increasingly outdated," said Philip Mangino, director of the U.S. Interagency Council (ICH) on Homelessness. "In truth, more and

"Humans simply can't compete with machines' ability to sit around and do nothing all day," said Mangino.

see ROBOTS page 14

page 13

EDITORIAL

Drinking was the only thing that saw me through the tough times

By Craig Sanders

Like a lot of people, my life has not exactly been a bowl of cherries. From childhood family problems to my own marital difficulties, from my teenaged struggle to find meaning in my existence to my recent financial woes, it seems like every day of my life has offered little more than a 24-hour struggle to avoid complete mental breakdown.

Through it all, there's only been one thing I could count on – one companion that's always been at my side, one friend that's never led me astray: alcohol. Yes, for much of my life, drinking was the only thing that saw me through the tough times.

I was barely out of my youth the first time drinking alcohol helped me make it through a particularly difficult period. It was my fifteenth birthday, in fact, and my father had gone a little overboard with my birthday spanking, if you know what I mean. No, it wasn't the first time he'd hit me, but I was determined to make it the last. That night, as I gathered my belongings and prepared for my premature escape into the word of independence, I found a half-full bottle of my father's whiskey. Although I didn't care much for the taste, I hastily guzzled it down to celebrate my pending liberation.

To make a long story short, I didn't end up running away from home that night. Instead, I ended up passing out on my bedroom floor. And you know something? In the harsh light of that February morning, I realized that running away from home was not such a great idea. It turned out that drinking had helped me both forget about my father's physical abuse and deter me from making a big mistake in running away.

I've been drinking my problems away ever since.

In fact, looking back on all these years, I think it's safe to say that by now, if it hadn't been for drinking, I probably

> It's pretty hard to cause yourself harm when you have zero control over your basic motor functions.

would have ended up on skid row, in jail or even dead. With as much shit as I've had to go through in life, as many nights as I've been on the brink of emotional and mental collapse, it's perfectly reasonable to envision myself having resorted to some sort of self-destructive behavior instead of just crawling inside the bottle for a few days. It's pretty hard to cause yourself harm when you have zero control over your basic motor functions. With alcohol being so readily available, I often find it hard to believe that so many people turn to self-destructive activities like listening to rock music or overeating whenever one of life's little hurdles puts them back on their heels. Equally confusing are the ideas of going to a psychiatrist or joining a support group. Whenever I need to find someone to listen or a group of people with similar problems, I needn't look any further than the closest pub! You'd be surprised how many others use the bottle as their pillar of strength.

Just remember that no matter what remedy you choose to combat this cancer called life, like a hangover, the tough times will pass. ∎

ROBOTS from page 13

more of the non-hardworking humans who've been the backbone of this nation's homeless population for hundreds of years are being replaced by machines – robots capable of being far less productive than a traditional, flesh and blood homeless person could ever be."

According to the report, many of the same robots built to replace humans in the workplace since the 1980s are now beginning to edge out homeless people for full-time positions on the streets of our inner-cities – so much so that robotic units now constitute almost 12 percent of the nation's estimated 3.5 million homeless – up sharply from approximately eight percent in 2011.

Experts pointed to breakthroughs in robotics technology such as the development of the Fujitsu robot – an advanced humanoid-like machine capable of avoiding the work of at least four homeless people – when projecting that by 2020, more than half of the nation's homeless guttersnipes will have been replaced by these slothful, super-unmotivated robots.

Speaking to reporters Monday, Mangino explained the conditions currently driving the trend toward automation in the nation's homeless environment.

"Humans are losing out to robots on the streets simply because they are just that – human," said Mangino, the federal government's highest-ranking official on homelessness. "Your typical homeless person can only sit around at the library or lay on a park bench for so long before they must motivate themselves into at least scrounging up some food or they're going to die. Modern robots, on the other hand, can squat in an alleyway for months on end without even running a self-diagnostic check, let alone have to lift a hydraulic-powered arm in the name of self-preservation. In a nutshell, humans simply can't compete with machines' ability to sit around and do nothing all day."

Arthur Clive, head of robotics for a major U.S. automobile manufacturer, agreed with Mangino's assertion that a highly-inefficient modern robot can simply do a better job of avoiding work than can a homeless person.

"Compared to your average homeless person, a robot is capable of taking up to five times as long to bend over to pick up a used cigarette off the street in the middle of oncoming traffic," said Clive, detailing one of many advantages homeless robots have over humans. "And when it comes to yelling at telephone poles, modern robots' speech and language capabilities enable them to shout completely irrational nonsense for a longer period of time and at a higher decibel level than

> "Our perception of the nation's homeless as a group of men and women who are unable to adapt to society's structure is becoming increasingly outdated," said Mangino.

can a human – without the need to pause for breath every once in a while for fear of passing out. Not only that, but they could yell obscenities at parking meters in more than *two hundred* languages, which only succeeds in making the homeless robotic unit look even that much crazier in the eyes of the public."

Mangino said that homeless robots are also capable of being discriminated

> "It takes a more than a battery recharge to convince a homeless robot to completely reformat its drives and adopt an entirely new operating system that can lead them toward success," said Clive.

against and looked down upon as second-class machinery by common citizens, who tend to harbor the misconception that a robot's homeless status is purely the result of its CPU consciously choosing not to run any work programs.

"Just because a robot is homeless doesn't necessarily mean it's programmed to be lazy," Mangino said. "The truth is that many of today's homeless robots have a few wires crossed, if you know what I mean. They're often singled out and kicked to the curb just because they're a few millimeters off. What's worse, their conditions are often improperly diagnosed or they are never able to get the maintenance they need to function properly and coexist with other robots in an assembly line mainframe."

Clive agreed with Mangino's argument that just because a robot is homeless doesn't necessarily mean it doesn't want to perform intricate, repetitive motions 24 hours a day.

"A lot of the robots you see hanging around in storefronts on your drive to work every morning are not lazy chunks of metal that would sooner have their USB ports removed than have to be on an assembly line working for *the man*," said Clive. "Many of these units are proud, hard-working bots that just got overloaded or damaged somehow and became unable to work. Maybe they had their extension arm seize up on them, or maybe they fried their motherboards experimenting with bad downloads. Or maybe they have memory problems that make it impossible for them to function. It's important to remember that not every robot out on the streets is there because they've made a conscious decision to throw their lives into the scrap yard."

Mangino said that although the U.S. government has only recently addressed the homeless robot issue, the ICH has already been approved to launch two federally funded programs aimed at helping homeless robots get back up on their wheels.

"Twenty-seven major U.S. cities have received funding to open up free shelters – a place where wayward robots can go

> Mangino: "Humans simply can't compete with machines' ability to sit around and do nothing all day."

to get a good power-wash and maybe get their batteries charged or download a few software updates so they can start scanning for jobs," Mangino said. "In addition to that, most of these cities will be implementing a program that issues free memory cards once a month to as many needy robots as possible." ∎

WORLDWIDE HEADLINES

Uppity houseplant only drinks bottled water

Santa Monica, Calif. – Madeline Stack told sources Sunday that the well-to-do Santa Monica resident's geranium plant refuses to absorb into its roots any water that is not a bottled, store-bought product. "Santa Monica residents typically have a bit higher standards than common folk, or in this case, common plant life," said Stack, pouring the contents of a 16-ounce bottle of Dasani into a spray bottle. "If you give this plant just regular tap water, the next day it'll already be wilting. It's like the plant goes on a hunger strike or something and refuses to drink – it'll just keep looking worse and worse until you give it some Evian or some other brand of bottled water." Stack, 39, later confirmed that she herself also refuses to drink any water that has not been stolen from a polluted lake, run through a filter, bottled and sold at a remarkably inflated price.

Infant not nearly as adorable when crying at 3 a.m.

Seattle, Wash. – First-time parents Mark and Julie Ward have begun recognizing that their sweet, cute-as-a-button infant daughter April is not nearly as adorable when the toddler is wailing and crying for attention at top volume three or four times every night while both career-minded parents attempt to rest in preparation for their upcoming workdays. "Everyone from the grandparents to our friends and neighbors agree that April is absolutely the most adorable baby one Earth, but they've never had to fuss with her for half the night, feeding and changing her," said an exhausted-looking Julie Ward while heating baby formula for at 3 a.m. Monday morning. "I love her and everything, but trust me, little April isn't nearly as adorable when viewed through red, bag-ridden, sleep-deprived eyes."

Supreme Court reaches 5-4 decision on lunch

Washington, D.C. – Members of the U.S. Supreme Court reached a 5-4 decision to go to Pizza Hut for lunch Tuesday afternoon after deliberating the matter for nearly 10 minutes on the steps of the Supreme Court Building moments prior to the decision's announcement. "Dissenting Justices made valid arguments for voting in favor of Arby's, citing the sandwich specials currently running at the establishment," Chief Justice John Roberts told a group of court reporters, who were themselves struggling to reach a decision on the matter. "However, the majority held that Arby's food is repugnant, inedible trash unsuitable for human consumption, and that no compromise of standards was to be made simply in the interest of economics. A general feeling of "being in the mood for pizza" also weighed heavily on many of the Justices, and perhaps influenced their vote for Pizza Hut." The Justices later reconvened on the building's steps at 5:30 p.m. where they reached an 8-1 decision to hit the Eagle Lounge for cocktails.

Accountant gives birth to healthy deduction

Superior, Wis. – Certified Public Accountant Maria Jennings, 30, gave birth to a healthy male standard deduction late Friday night, her second with husband and fellow CPA Paul Jennings. "We're overjoyed," said Paul Jennings, as the 31-year-old began to tear up, "It's just such a blessing to be given another write-off during such a tough economy." The deduction weighed nine pounds four ounces and is expected to save the family at least $125,000 on the couple's joint tax filings over the next 18 years. The Jennings said they decided to have a second deduction last April when simultaneous job promotions and subsequent salary increases pushed the family into a higher tax bracket.

Head shop's prices, employees high

Ann Arbor, Mich. – Employees of Ann Arbor's Token Stuff admitted that prices for the head shop's merchandise are high in direct relation to the highness of the staff. Skip Griffin, owner and consummate doper, smiled and shrugged in an interview Monday: "Our employees are required to gain firsthand knowledge of our products during their training, which hikes up our costs. This shit ain't cheap, you know." Griffin then grabbed an iridescent water bong seemingly at random from a display shelf and adjusted the price from $24.99 to $29.99. "Dude, it's a great place to work," said eight-year employee Jimmy Williams, pausing to drink deeply from his Big Gulp as a means for counteracting his cottonmouth. "People come to Token Stuff for the vibe, man. Nobody cares that rolling papers are twice as expensive here. And so what if they do care? We don't." ∎

LAW

Drunk-driving attorney a total blast to party with

Akron, Ohio – Clients of local defense attorney Jarrod R. Kendall told reporters Saturday that in addition to being one of Akron's busiest and most well-known DUI defense lawyers, the 44-year-old bachelor is also a total blast to hang out and party with outside the courtroom.

"I've partied with Jarrod on and off since we got to know each other in 2002 – when he represented me on my third impaired driving [charge]," said Curt Stefan, a night deejay at the local gentleman's club Daffodils. "He comes in to the club at least two or three nights a week and lays out a couple hundred bucks on dances and drinks. We usually end up closing the place down and partying at my place right up until he has to be in court the next morning to keep one of his clients from getting their [driver's] license cut up. The guy knows how to have a good time, that's for sure."

After pausing briefly and quietly laughing to himself, Stefan added: "It's pretty funny to think that one of my worst influences is also my DUI lawyer."

Having specialized in DUI-related law since opening his practice in 1992, Jarrod has built his business and reputation around happily defending the kind of clients who might otherwise have trouble finding legal representation.

"I consulted other attorneys who said they would have taken my DUI [case] if I hadn't also gotten nailed for possession with intent [to distribute] at the same time," said Jeremy Buckler, a new client of Kendall's. "I guess those lawyers didn't want to have anything to do with a suspected drug dealer. Jarrod, on the other hand, was immediately interested in working with me – especially after I told him about the dope charge. He's so cool he's even letting me barter for services so I won't go broke trying to pay him. I doubt there are many lawyers out there who will accept an eight-ball as a retainer."

> Client Jeremy Buckler: "I doubt there are many lawyers out there who will accept an eight-ball as a retainer."

Despite having had only one week to prepare for their case – a process that included several intense, late-night consultations at Hooters – Buckler said that not only does he have great confidence in Kendall as a legal advisor, he is also enjoying the comfort of being represented by an experienced DUI attorney who shares many of Buckler's views, values and hobbies.

"Jarrod told me that he's actually gotten popped for drunk-driving like *five times*," Buckler noted. "To me, the fact that he's still behind the wheel instead of behind bars speaks volumes about his legal skills. And besides, the last person I'd want in my corner on a DUI is some straight-laced, buttoned-down square of a lawyer who's never even

Above: Kendall (left) parties with client Jeremy Buckler, the night before the two were to appear in court to defend Buckler on DUI and drug trafficking charges.

gotten a parking ticket let alone evaded and eluded police at four in the morning before blowing twice the legal [blood-alcohol level] limit. That's what's so cool about Jarrod: he's been there. He knows what it's like.

"And he can shotgun a can of beer in under eleven seconds," Buckler added.

Like most of Kendall's clients, Buckler is astonished by Kendall's uncanny ability to balance such a wild private life with his high-pressure legal career.

"It's hard to believe a hardcore partier like Jarrod can even hold down a job, let alone be one of the most sought-after attorneys in town," said Buckler, who was briefly hospitalized for alcohol poisoning following a consultation with Kendall Wednesday night. "It's a rare breed of human who can drink and party every night of the week and still be sharp enough the next morning to talk a judge out of locking up his client. He'll go from partying like a Hell's Angel on acid to being a smart, uncompromising legal eagle in a matter of hours. I wouldn't be at all surprised to see him someday make judge." ∎

A page from the Recoil handbook...
Recycling Tips

The Earth's current inconvenient yet inescapable environmental status demands that more and more of us accept recycling as a daily priority. Here are some pointers for beginning recyclists:

• Resealable envelopes can be used many times and are a great way of communicating to pen pals what a sickeningly cheap bastard you really are.

• Tin cans can be used as potted plant holders. They can also be used to store the bright, shiny penny that you saved as a result of your backbreaking four-hour recycling effort.

• Yoghurt containers, egg cartons and film canisters can be kept and used by the kids to create stuff. Yeah, they'd certainly rather play with your fucking garbage than an X-Box.

• Speaking to your neighbors about joining in on your recycling effort will ensure that your entire neighborhood will go out of their way to avoid you for as long as you live at your current address.

• Ice cubes can easily be recycled by putting them back in the freezer.

• Instead of throwing away jeans, shirts and other clothes after wearing them once, invest in a washing machine and you'll be able to get three or four good uses out of each outfit!

• Junk mail can be used as bedding for pets as long as you don't mind your home looking like a dedicated trash dump.

• Old tires can be used outside for plant pots – or, if you live in the South, as decoration.

• Try to make eye contact with drivers as you pull into an intersection or make a turn, so they know your intentions and you know that they've seen– ...whoops, sorry, that one actually belongs under Cycling Tips.

• If you really want to use Styrofoam plates or cups, refer to them by their technical name, Expanded Polystyrene, and you won't feel so bad about destroying the environment.

• Try to get more than just two or three uses out of each condom.

recoilmag.com

page 16

MAN from page 13

during lunch at a Lawrence Avenue Red Lobster. "It's like there isn't a single goddamn thing I can do right today. [I] should've just stayed in bed."

Elliot told sources that his decidedly luckless day began at 9:05 this morning, when he awoke over an hour late to the blare of an incorrectly set alarm clock.

"I had an important meeting at nine," Elliot explained. "I was pissed about oversleeping, but I remember thinking, 'Oh well, what are you going to do? Worse things could happen. Shake it off and get on with your day, Steve.'"

That day, Elliot would soon find, was to be plagued by a seemingly never-ending series of mishaps that would eventually prompt Elliot to admit that he can not execute one simple goddamn task correctly today.

"First off, I cut myself shaving, which I never do," said Elliot of his unusually blunder-laden morning routine. "I burned the toast I was going to eat for breakfast, and when I tried to make a pot of coffee, I spilled beans all over the floor and counter. I remember just standing there, staring at the beans scattered across the floor, shaking my head. I already knew it was going to be one of those days."

At work, Elliot again struggled to find any goddamn job that he could perform without incident, as even his most focused efforts at productivity continued to yield bungled results.

"First thing, right off the bat, I spilled my coffee all over my desk as I was sitting down to edit tomorrow's automobile section [of the classifieds]," said Elliot, rolling his eyes in obvious frustration. "I was like, 'Perfect. That's just perfect.' My copy pages were soaked. I had to get production to reprint them so I could proofread."

Coworkers agreed that while Elliot is typically considered a picture of efficiency and "the guy you go to when you need something done right," repeated incidents around the office this morning and early afternoon indicated that Elliot was unable to do a goddamn thing right all day.

"It's like the Klutz Fairy visited Steve last night," said coworker Pam Lewoski, who witnessed Elliot drop a copy machine toner cartridge into a full mop bucket just before lunch. "I felt sorry for him."

Lewoski added that around mid-

> "It's like the Klutz Fairy visited Steve last night," said coworker Pam Lewoski, who witnessed Elliot drop a copy machine toner cartridge into a full mop bucket just before lunch.

afternoon, Elliot's mood deteriorated as he became increasing frustrated with his inability to do a single goddamn thing right.

"I saw that Steve was having trouble with the fax machine jamming so I asked him if I could help at all," said Lewoski. "He spun around and said to me, almost yelling, 'I wish, I just wish, I could do one fucking thing right today. Is that too much to ask?' I was like, 'Jesus, dude. Sorry I asked.'"

After witnessing the exchange, senior editor Kyle Hughes insisted that Elliot take the remainder of the afternoon off before another goddamn thing could go wrong and break Elliot's understandably deteriorating tolerance.

"Things were not going Steve's way today. It looked like he was heading for a breakdown," said Hughes. "I told him to go home and get a fresh start in the morning. He was just having some rough luck. We've all been there."

ADVICE
HOW TO...
SLOWLY KILL YOURSELF

Gradual harikari for the suicidally slothful

With modern medicine determined to prolonging our grim and pointless human existence, American life expectancy is quickly becoming a number that more and more Game of Lifers would just as soon shoot under par. Here are some long-term health demoters capable of snuffing out your flame long before you're due to burn out.

Cigarettes
Lung cancer, throat cancer, emphysema – you name it, half a million dead people every year can't be wrong. Sending the Grim Reaper a pack-a-day of smoke signals regarding your quick arrival may be losing social acceptability, but it still looks cool as hell.
Express Checkout: Testify in tobacco industry lawsuit; end up sharing storage space with Jimmy Hoffa.

Stress
High-pressure jobs and financial difficulties offer the best exposure to this invisible killer, which raises blood pressure, causes heart attacks and promotes alcoholism. But then again, so does watching a Detroit Lions game.
Express Checkout: Daytrading.

Booze
Often viewed as the only thing that keeps people from killing themselves, habitual alcohol consumption causes liver failure, hepatitis, cirrhosis, death and beer goggle-related diseases. Not to mention the increased tendency to act like a drunken asshole.
Express Checkout: Use while driving.

Cell Phones
Cell phones emit radio waves right next to the user's head, allegedly causing brain tumors. As the loaded-gun-to-the-head of choice among American work-/talk-oholics, cell phone use increases a permanent headache's likelihood by three times.
Express Checkout: Use while driving.

RECOILMAG.COM   NEWS SATIRE YOU CAN TRUST

recoil

Roofer nails shingles, housewife

Beginner guitarist says 'wait' between every chord

Tire ironed

recoilmag.com

Shower taken immediately after dollar store visit

Rockford, Md. – Dollar Dayze patron Andrea Witt, upon completing her purchases, sped home and immediately showered Friday in a panicked effort to counteract the icky, disquieting sensation induced by her 20-minute shopping experience. "That dollar store is just nasty," said a feverishly lathering Witt from the shower of her Rockford home. "The place is enough to make you gag. And the hygienic condition of those primates that shop there. God." Xim Lei, manager of the Arlington Avenue retailer, defended his business. "We sell good product. Good product. You buy something? You go now," Lei screamed.

Novice bulimic regurgitates laxatives

Bishopville, S.C. – Lincoln High School junior varsity cheerleader and aspiring bulimic Kimberly Heinz made a common beginner's mistake Wednesday when the 16-year-old forcibly purged four Correctol tablets from her stomach only moments after swallowing the laxative medications, sources report. "It was a knee-jerk reaction," explained the 120-pound Heinz, "I was a little lightheaded from fatigue and after I swallowed [the laxatives], I couldn't remember what I'd eaten." Heinz began experimenting with various eating disorders two months ago after varsity football captain Keith Maples told Heinz she had "a fat ass." ■

Above: Gatske (left) and Millon discuss the degree to which their respective balls were tripped.

Balls tripped off

Madison, Wis. – University of Wisconsin freshman Gabe Gatske told sources that the 19-year-old political science major tripped his balls completely off Saturday, Sept. 6, after ingesting multiple doses of a powerful hallucinogen and attending a planetarium showing with friends.

> "I was tweaking so hard I thought that big red dot on Saturn was going to eat me alive," said Gatske.

"Dude, where'd you get that shit we took last night? I swear, man, I was tripping *my fucking balls off* after we ate that second hit," Gatske told friend Howard Millon at a late breakfast the following morning. "I was totally [Hunter] Thompsoned before we even

see BALLS page 19

U.S. Treasury no closer to finding cure for the penny

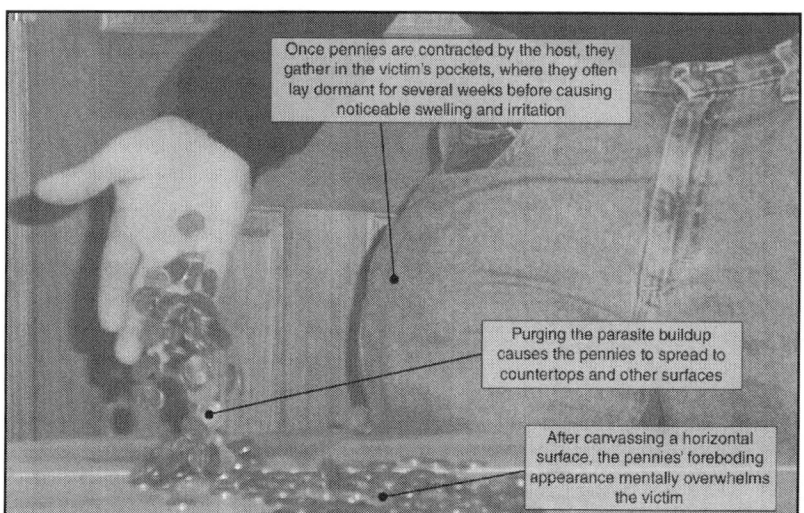

- Once pennies are contracted by the host, they gather in the victim's pockets, where they often lay dormant for several weeks before causing noticeable swelling and irritation
- Purging the parasite buildup causes the pennies to spread to countertops and other surfaces
- After canvassing a horizontal surface, the pennies' foreboding appearance mentally overwhelms the victim

Above: Studies indicate that penny buildups can cause one or more asymmetric swellings to develop around the host's lower torso, inhibiting free movement of the legs.

Washington, D.C. – Having exhausted nearly $350 million in federal research funding, the U.S. Treasury Department disclosed this week that it has made little progress in discovering a cure for the penny, a widespread financial parasite that experts say causes severe discomfort in otherwise economically healthy consumers.

"Halting the spread of the bronze menace is not a battle that will be won overnight," warned Treasury Spokesman Neil Rubin at a White House press conference held early Thursday morning. "But rest assured, our nation's top financial experts are determined to find methods of treating the millions of consumers nationwide who struggle daily to cope with the detrimental effects of the penny."

Though infecting the American pecuniary system in the 1790s, the penny has only recently risen in status to one of

> The parasitic pennies are said to spread from host to host during everyday monetary transactions generated by the exchange of goods and services.

the most pervasive epidemics plaguing American consumers. As parasites, the pennies are said to spread from host to host during everyday monetary transactions generated by the exchange of goods or services. Once contracted, these

see PENNY page 20

page 17

ENTERTAINMENT

Tour manager mostly in charge of getting band drugs

Above: Wes Bradley, tour manager for the metal band Faces of Nothing.

Cleveland, Ohio – Wes Bradley, tour manager for the heavy metal band Faces of Nothing, spends most of his time on the road trying to score drugs for each member of the band, sources said Sunday.

"Most people think being a tour manager for a road band is easy: ordering hotel rooms, organizing transportation, maybe coordinating some interviews," said Bradley, double-checking his cell phone to make sure he hasn't missed a return phone call from his Cleveland hookup. "The truth is I'm on call twenty-four hours a day, and I've usually got my cell phone glued to my ear. My job is to keep [the band members] happy, and that means getting them whatever they need. Usually, that means drugs."

Added Bradley: "I barely get any sleep [because I'm always busy] making sure these guys barely get any sleep."

Bradley and the band are currently winding up a 30-city headlining tour with a string of shows in the Midwest, an area Bradley said is notoriously among the most difficult places in the United States to score drugs.

"This area is pretty dry to begin with, but it doesn't help that I don't know too many people up here," said Bradley, who is originally from San Francisco. "Next week we'll be in Michigan, which is like a barren wasteland when it comes to coke. I'm hoping my buddy in Toledo comes through tomorrow night so we'll – I mean, the band will – have enough shit to get through the week."

Bradley ran through a typical day in his life as a tour manager.

"It usually isn't until about five or six o'clock at night, a couple hours before the gig, before the guys start asking me to get them something, but that doesn't mean I haven't already been working on hooking up all day," said Bradley. "As soon as the bus pulls in I'm on the phone trying to see if anybody I know knows anybody in town that deals. If not, I start shaking down the local [production] crew for them to call somebody. If it's getting close to sound check and I still haven't found anything, I'll start asking the bartenders, door guys, anybody who looks like they party. Believe it or not, it's usually an all-day project."

Bradley said that in addition to the illegality of his duties, the preferences of each individual band member make his job a difficult one.

"It would be easier if the entire band were just straight-up cokeheads," said Bradley, nervously standing outside the band's tour bus waiting for a person named "Goat," whom he's never met, to arrive in a white Chevy S-10. "But no, only [guitarist] Gary [Knuble] and [drummer] Eddie [Corset] are into white. [Bassist] Mike [Richards] always wants smoke and [singer] Pete [McWilliams] is into downers, so I've got to find

> Added Bradley: "I barely get any sleep making sure these guys barely get any sleep."

somebody that can deliver all three. This is where the good tour managers get separated from the okay ones – the good ones can get everybody exactly what they need so the show can go on." ∎

TRANSPORTATION

2013 DODGE CHALLENGER SXT

Adapting to the needs of modern consumers, Chrysler's 2013 Dodge Challenger SXT includes a more versatile list of options available for custom order. Listed below are some of the standard and optional equipment available on the 2013 model:

STANDARD EQUIMENT
Power Door Mirrors	PDM
Sunroof	SUN
Spoiler	SPL
Dual Exhaust	DEX
Air Conditioning	AIR
Power Moonroof	PMR
Speed Control	SDC
Power Locks	PL
Power Front Windows	PFW
Remote Keyless Entry	RKE
Heated Steering Wheel	HSW
Navigation System	NVS
Front Beverage Holders	FBH
Rear Beverage Holders	RBH

OPTIONAL EQUIPMENT
Full Rubber Tires	FRT
Corinthian 'Leather'	RCL
Stirrups	FUN
Kitten Compartment	KC
Exterior Grow Lights	EGL
History Eraser Button	HEB
Retractable Wheels For Driving On Train Tracks	RWT
Beef Flaps	BFF
Pre-Regulation, Destroyer Class Solid Fuel Rocket Booster	PRDCSFRB
Breast Enlargement Rear-View Mirrors	TIT

Potato Shooter Hood Ornament	GUN
Continuous Battery Drainer	GMC
Automatic Crank Seal Oil Releaser	LEAK
Fallout Radiation Shielding	SOON
Onboard Stomach Pump	BARF
Strapless Seat belts	DIE
Crash Promoter	SCCA
Temporary Belief Suspension	TBS
Trunk-Mounted Whiskey Still	HOBO
Moon Burn Shield	MBC
Auto-Cracking Windshield	AW
External Clap Detector	STD
Insurance Premium Increaser	KID

Bias News Radio Adaptor	FOX
Intermittent Steering Lag	ISL
Al Capone Storage Rack	IRS
Overactive Bladder Suspension	OBS
Random Squeak and Raddle	NVH
Increased Spec Body Panel Trim	+25MM
Butane-Fueled Cigarette Lighter	CRACK
Driver-Side Gun Rack	DTW
Dead Stripper Storage	QUAMI

Astro-Mech Droid	R2D2
Mystery Machine Decals	DOO
Buck Scent	BSC
Rear Cheese Wheel	RCW
Mid-Life Crisis Kit	MLCK
Rap Music Suppression Device	RUNDMC
Wheel-Wrapped Steering Leather	HUH
Bacon-Wrapped Sausage Biscuit	McD

page 18

WORLDWIDE HEADLINES

Married gymnasts experiment with missionary position

Norman, Ohio – For the first time in the couple's three-year relationship, married Olympic gymnasts Bart Conner and Nadia Comaneci shared conjugal relations using the missionary position for the first time Friday night. "I think it's a sign that we're really starting to get comfortable with each other, sexually," said the diminutive Conner, who is best known for his gold medal performance on the parallel bars at the 1996 Olympics. "Our bodies' superior balance, stamina and flexibility had before encouraged only wildly dynamic multi-positional sex, but now we are learning how to drop our inhibitions and be able to look each other in the eyes during intercourse, and even kiss."

New mustache makes cop seem like even bigger prick

Indianapolis, Ind. – Officer Terry Scott of the Marion County Sheriff Department looks like an even bigger, more arrogant prick since growing a thick mustache last month, sources reported Tuesday. "Terry has always worn the reflective sunglasses and walked like he's got a stick up his butt, but adding that godawful mustache has really taken his 'I'm a total prick' look to a new level," said fellow policeman Kyle Runyen. Scott, 37, also lifts weights daily, has sported a sharp brush-cut since joining the force in 2001 and has announced his intention to begin smoking cheap cigars by the end of winter.

Inexperienced embezzler microwaves books

Kissimee, Fla. – Confused Wells Fargo Bank teller Gary Langlois failed to misappropriate company funds in his favor last week when the 22-year-old placed several of the bank's accounting ledgers into the break room microwave in an attempt to "cook the books," bank officials reported Thursday. "Gary must have heard that phrase used in a movie or something, and just didn't think through the logistics of his actions," said Wells Fargo spokesman Abe Hess. "Instead of carefully manipulating payroll or benefit funds, he microwaved useless hardcopies of account files." Hess said Langlois will remain in the bank's employ despite the incident, indicating that bank executives believe Langlois is "probably too dumb to steal."

Drummer neighbor going at it again

Gary, Ind. – Area homeowner Lyle Leonard told sources that the drummer living nextdoor to the 43-year-old's suburban residence was going at it again between 8 and 10 p.m. Friday night. "I can't believe he's going at it again," yelled an unnerved Leonard, who was enjoying an evening of television with his family before "that godforsaken noise" began. "Is that man insane? Has he no regard for his neighbors?" Leonard later vowed to begin running his leaf blower at 6 a.m. Saturday morning, adding that it would be different if the guy had a full band and was playing some decent music.

Encore forced upon audience

Jacksonville, N.C. – Minutes after finally completing their last set of cover songs at Bogart's nightclub early Saturday morning, house band First Snowfall forced an encore song upon an indifferent crowd of approximately 40, sources said. "You guys aren't ready to go home yet, are ya?" posed singer Sony Rede, failing to elicit a decisive reaction from the audience. "We're gonna give y'all one more tonight. This one's a First Snowfall original." Bogart's patrons, determined to finish their drinks, endured the five-minute blues-based number before offering a smattering of applause and continuing their attempts to hustle members of the opposite sex.

All teen's sexual encounters qualify as quickies

Orlando, Fla. – Sources close to magazine editor Neil Chapp told reporters Wednesday that every one of the single 18-year-old's sexual encounters could technically be classified as quickies. "Being with Neil is nice and all, but he's definitely more of a sprint horse than a stallion, if you know what I mean," said Cara Brigstock, who has occasionally dated Chapp for six months. "Sometimes when we're getting ready to go out or whatever, he'll joke around, asking me if I want to have a quickie before we go. I just laugh to myself and think, 'No, that's all right. We'll just do exactly that tonight.'"

EDITORIAL

My biggest weakness as an employee? Probably my immense laziness

By Dale Reinhout, Applicant

What do I feel is my biggest weakness as an employee? Um, hmm, let me think for a second here.

Boy, that's a tough one, isn't it? My biggest weakness, let's see. Just one right? Well, I suppose if I had to narrow it down to just one character trait that really stands out as my absolute biggest weakness in terms of how I'd perform in a profession capacity here at Penn Inc., I'd probably have to say it would be my immense laziness.

Elaborate? Um, yeah, sure. I guess that's what I'm here for right, to tell you what you want to know? I suppose I can't very well expect you to pick me for the job if I just sit here like a mime and stare at you for fifteen minutes.

Okay, so, my laziness. Well, I guess let me start by assuring you that when I say I'm lazy, I'm not talking about your run-of-the-mill, not-exactly-the-first-guy-to-volunteer-for-the-job-type laziness here. I'm talking about chronic indolence, sloth of staggering proportions. Pretty much, it's like this: I'm the type of worker that continually slides by doing the absolute minimum amount of work I can get away with without getting fired.

No, my laziness isn't an every-so-often type of thing, I'm pretty much lazy all the time. Actually, let me clarify: I'm lazy all the time I'm *at work*. Over the years I've found that if I'm lazy enough at work, I can conserve so much energy that when I get home from work I'm generally able to be quite active.

Promise you that I'll work on my laziness? Truthfully, I don't know if my laziness could get any more refined. I mean, right now I can pretty much guarantee with a good deal of certainty that within no time my coworkers would come to know me as *the* person not to go to when they need a hand, an opinion, some advice or any other sort of help that requires me to stop daydreaming and concentrate on something work-related for ten seconds.

Other weaknesses you should be aware of? Oh boy, where do I start? Well, I have an extremely short temper – especially when it comes to bosses that like to bark orders at me or ride me really hard or demand that I be on time. That sort of thing.

I also tend to steal a lot of stuff. No, not kleptomania, per say – let's just say that a fair share of office supplies from work like pens and staplers and printers and laptops and stuff tend to end up at my house. Well, that's unless I've already implemented some sort of embezzlement scheme and don't want to risk drawing any attention to myself by lifting items I'd easily be able to pay for with the cash I'm skimming from the company.

> Promise you that I'll work on my laziness? Truthfully, I don't know if my laziness could get any more refined.

I've been told by previous employers that the sexual harassment lawsuits that are constantly being filed against the company because of me can be a bit of a hassle as well. You're in the human resources department, so you'd probably know: are the female employees here at Penn Inc. generally pretty willing to swing or are they usually all uptight about being hit on at work? Because no matter how lazy at work I can and will be, I usually have no trouble making time to mack on the hotties, if you know what I'm saying. ■

BALLS from page 17

got to the planetarium. I was tweaking so hard I thought that big red dot on Saturn was going to eat me alive. *Fuck*."

> "I told those guys not to drop more than two [doses] or they'd trip their balls so far off they might never find them again," said Millon.

In addition to providing the means with which Gatske's balls were tripped, Millon, 20, also aided in the tripping off of the balls belonging to roommate Keith Broder and acquaintance Noah Cloutier.

"I told those guys not to drop more than two [doses] or they'd trip their balls so far off they might never find them again," said Millon, who sold Broder and Cloutier five hits of LSD that he had obtained a week previous from an unnamed source. "Shit this powerful you've got to be a little careful with or you might fry and spend the rest of your life telling people you're a carrot."

Broder and Cloutier both commented on the fervor with which their respective balls had been tripped.

"That paper Howard sold us was unreal," Broder told Cloutier, who nodded in agreement. "I haven't tripped my balls off like that since [high school classmate Chris] Brenner gave us those shrooms before [graduation] commencements. Man, that was a wild ride. I remember I just about lost it when I went up to get my diploma and [principal Thomas] Cook's face started melting. That I'll never forget." ■

page 19

A page from the Recoil handbook...
Travel Tips

Whether on business or vacation, traveling can be a thrilling experience. Here are some tips to help you get the most out of your journey:

• Don't believe what travel agents tell you about how dangerous it is to visit places like Libya, Syria or North Korea – they're just trying to throw you off track so they can keep all of the cool destinations for themselves.

• Considering the level of anti-American sentiment currently abounding overseas, you'll have to claim to be Canadian unless you're willing to risk getting lynched. It's a tough choice, I know.

• There's a lot more to ocean cruises than just eating and drinking. There's also a great deal of throwing up.

• If you lose your visa while traveling abroad, you're likely to encounter problems trying to reenter the United States. Officials will often demand to witness you offhandedly shoot someone in order to prove you're an American.

• Absolutely never crack jokes about bombs at the airport unless it's really, really funny.

• Remember that many countries require motorists to drive on the opposite side of the road, so you need to steer in the opposite direction of which way you're turning. No, wait – you need to turn in the opposite direction of the way you want to go. No, that isn't it either. Maybe it's that you need to drive in the opposite direction of where you're going? Boy, are other countries screwy!

• Many people are still unaware that most traveling can now be done online.

• Before traveling to a foreign country you don't know much about, it might be a good idea to find out if the nation's government is currently implementing indescribably violent ethnic cleansing, and cross-reference that with your own ethnicity.

• When visiting European countries, you'll find that relying on busses as your primary method of transportation sucks just as much as it does back home.

• When packing, keep in mind that you won't get a good, clean hit unless you pack the pipe really tight.

• Be aware that once you leave U.S. borders, none of our laws apply to you anymore. And yet the laws of the country you are heading to do not apply to you either! You are invulnerable and immune. Like a god. You will make them all pay. They will rue the day, I tell you, rue the day.

• Discover the richness of Latino culture: visit Los Angeles.

recoilmag.com

PENNY from page 17

pennies gather in the pockets of its host's apparel, where they often lay dormant for several weeks before a buildup begins to cause noticeable irritation.

> "Purging the parasite buildup just causes the pennies to spread to countertops and dashboards and so on," said Chatham.

"Most consumers, though fully aware they've contracted pennies, take their situation too lightly, thinking, 'Oh, it's just a few pennies,' like they'll just go away or something," explained financial analyst Derek Chatham, who is acting as a consultant during the Treasury's research. "If the host fails to alter his habits in regard to money exchanges, an increasing penny coagulation will eventually make it difficult for the host to perform even such simple, everyday tasks as finding change for a soda machine or selecting correct bus fare."

But the host's discomfort does not end there. Studies indicate that penny buildups can cause one or more asymmetric swellings to develop around the host's lower torso, inhibiting free movement of the legs. Often, experts say, the host's instinctual attempt to alleviate the irritation only amplifies its severity.

"Purging the parasite buildup just causes the pennies to spread to countertops and dashboards and so on," said Chatham. "Once a large number of pennies canvass a horizontal surface, their visual appearance can be incredibly foreboding. The victim, realizing how many pennies he's contracted, becomes mentally overwhelmed."

Victim Jessica Jarrod, 25, recently discovered she had contracted pennies while changing clothes after a Saturday afternoon spending spree. Said Jarrod: "I dumped a handful of pocket change onto the top of my bedroom television, and suddenly the whole surface was covered with pennies. It's hard to explain the feeling you get seeing all those worthless units, knowing full well that you're never going to be rid of them."

When informed of Jarrod's episode, Chatham nodded his head in recognition. "See, this is what happens," Chatham said after a brief sigh. "I've seen it a thousand times. Her penny condition is now a serious problem. At this point, quarantining the pennies into 50-cent rolls or a glass jar may relieve the irritation, but it's no cure. In other words, she might get the pennies *out* of the way, but they certainly aren't going to *go* away."

For financial analysts seeking a cure, unlocking the secrets of the penny has proved exceedingly difficult. Beyond the penny's refusal to be broken down into smaller units that could be more thoroughly examined, Rubin says that through more than 200 years of evolution and mutation, the penny has developed many unique strains that continue to circulate through our country's financial system.

"Currently, the most common strain of penny in distinguished by contours that, oddly enough, resemble the bust of a male human," Rubin said. "Other strains display anything from Indian arrowhead images to letters such as V.D.B. What

Above: "Take a penny, leave a penny" receptacles are helping to reduce the penny's spread.

these images mean and how they affect the penny's survival instincts are matters yet to be determined."

With an estimated 1,040 new pennies entering the monetary system every second (30 million per day), and no cure or vaccine in sight, the penny menace has the Treasury Department scrambling to educate consumers about ways of impeding the spread of the epidemic.

> Pennies gather in the pockets of its host's apparel, where they often lay dormant for several weeks before a buildup begins to cause noticeable irritation.

"We've mandated that independent penny receptacles be placed near all cash registers that operate in highly contaminated areas like gas stations and convenience stores," Rubin explained, referring to a key prevention tool. "These receptacles are affixed with a slogan: 'Take a penny, leave a penny.' The hope is that when consumers make retail purchases – during which time they are most at-risk of infection – they will have the good sense to immediately discard the pennies into these receptacles. Specially trained military personnel will then quarantine and destroy the pennies." ■

RECOILMAG.COM   NEWS SATIRE YOU CAN TRUST

recoil

Crips attack bloodmobile

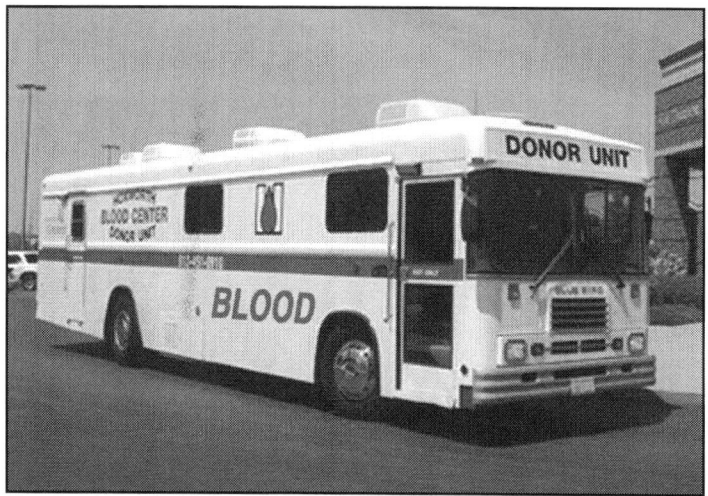

Above: One of six modified RVs being used by the East Los Angeles hospital as mobile blood-donation centers.

Los Angeles, Calif. – Two members of the Los Angeles-based street gang The Crips remain in custody Wednesday following their alleged attack on a Santa Marta Hospital bloodmobile, one of six modified RVs being used by the East Los Angeles hospital as mobile blood-donation centers.

> The mangled body of the bloodmobile was discovered by would-be blood and plasma donors Tuesday evening at the corner of 134th Street and Martin Luther King Blvd.

The mangled body of the bloodmobile was discovered by would-be blood and plasma donors Tuesday evening at the corner of 134th Street and Martin Luther

see CRIPS page 24

Automatic tithing machine installed outside church entrance

Photographer struggling to identify model's good side

Above: Cloned members of the band Blink-182. Inset: Members of the band Blink-182.

Scientists clone pop-punk band
Technology to ensure continued stream of color-by-numbers radio swill

Worchester, Mass. – At a Monday morning press conference, researchers at Advanced Cell Technology (ACT) announced their successful cloning of Blink-182 – one of the mega-popular mainstream radio bands that major record labels have previously attempted to clone hundreds of times with only partial success.

"Our development of band cloning technology will ensure the music industry's ability to churn out an endless parade of bands that all look and sound the same," said ACT President Andrew R. Taylor, Ph.D. "This technology's impact on [MTV's] *TRL* alone is almost too massive to comprehend."

According to Taylor, ACT – a biotechnological research company located in Worchester, Mass. – made the

> "Band cloning technology will ensure the music industry's ability to churn out an endless parade of bands that all look and sound the same," said Taylor.

breakthrough in early April after more than 20 failed attempts. A seven-person team of scientists successfully created identical clones of Tom Delonge, Mark Hoppus and Travis Barker, who together as Blink-182 achieved enormous mainstream success with their 1999 album, *Enema of the State*, and spawned a flood of bandwagon-jumping acts that closely mimicked the pop-punk trio in both appearance and substance.

Taylor noted that although such bands as Sum 41, Marvelous 3, American Hi-Fi, New Found Glory, Good Charlotte, The All-American Rejects, Unwritten Law and others may bear uncanny resemblances to Blink-182 – rambunctious, carefree young hipsters performing three-chord, three-minute,

see CLONE page 24

VH1's *Behind the Music* exposes Bobby McFerrin's nightmare descent into love and happiness

Hollywood, Calif. – According to a preview article published on www.tvguidelive.com, an upcoming episode of VH1's biographical program *Behind the Music* brings to light previously undisclosed information regarding the nightmare descent into love and happiness that followed vocal sensation Bobby McFerrin's massive international success in the late eighties.

Scheduled for an Aug. 15 airing, the hour-long documentary details how the fortune and fame brought on by McFerrin's 1998 single "Don't Worry Be Happy" propelled the 10-time Grammy-winning artist down a twisted road of joy,

see NIGHTMARE page 23

Above: Multi-Grammy winning recording artist Bobby McFerrin.

page 21

WORLDWIDE HEADLINES

Financial restructuring forces Heaven to cut 14,000 angel positions

Heaven – Financially pressured by increasing overhead and declining revenues, Heaven today announced that it would be forced to cut approximately 14,000 angel positions – posts previously considered exclusive, long-term appointments. "It is unfortunate that those who have worked so hard to get a position in Heaven – what, with the strict adherence to worldly behavior guidelines and all – have to be let go," God said at a recent press conference. "Unfortunately, to remain competitive, we have no choice but to make these permanent cuts," God added. All angels are asked to report to their designated clouds at 8 a.m., May 24, when representatives will inform each angel as to whether or not their soul will continue to have an eternal position in Heaven.

November named November Awareness Month

Washington, D.C. – In an effort to educate the public regarding the importance of the month of November as a necessary component of the modern Roman calendar, senators from a number of states backed a proclamation Friday to recognize the entire month of November as November Awareness Month. "November Awareness Month is an important opportunity for all of us to remember that, were it not for the great month of November, the fall season would only last for two months, the National Football League would be reduced to having only a twelve-game season, and who knows what in the hell would happen to Thanksgiving," said Senator Lamar Alexander [R-TN], who led the campaign to single-out the month for recognition. Earlier in his career, Alexander was credited with having the date of April 7, 2002 recognized as April 7 Awareness Day among residents of his home state of Tennessee.

Man dies doing woman he loved

St. Louis, Mo. – Friends of St. Louis resident Ben Styles said Tuesday that the 44-year-old accountant died doing the woman he loved when he expired from a heart attack brought on by sexual activity late Monday night. "If it was Ben's time to go, at least he went while he was doing the woman he loved, his wife Jenna," said Tate Morrison, Styles' neighbor and good friend. "If there was one thing on this Earth that Ben loved doing, it was his wife. As long as I've known Ben I've always known him to constantly be doing her, day and night. Doing that woman was what Ben lived for, so it seems appropriate that she should be who he died doing." Medical records released to reporters Tuesday confirmed that Styles had previously experienced no medical problems as a result of doing the woman he loved.

Film studio refuses to show movie to critics, audiences

Hollywood, Calif. – Expanding on the same strategy that kept the film *Snakes On A Plane* from being shown to film critics before its release, executives at New Line Cinema announced Monday that the studio will protect its latest movie, *The Final Inch*, from being seen by reviewers or international audiences both before and after the film's Nov. 28 release date, in hopes of keeping negative opinions about the film from reaching potential moviegoers. "Generally, the theory behind not allowing film critics an advance screening of the picture is that the studio wants to try to make as much money as possible on the film before the public gets a chance to hear about how bad it is," said film critic Jeffery Giddion. "However, by not even allowing paying audiences to view the movie, New Line is trying to further expand that amount of time they have before negative word hits the streets and destroys the film's earning potential."

Date without job less attractive than date without arm

Miami, Fla. – Leslie Falk, a single, 29-year-old dental technician, confirmed Sunday that of the two men she dated on Friday and Saturday nights, she found the date who admitted to not being currently employed considerably less desirable than the date who did not have a right arm. "Daniel [Forrester] is a sweet guy and all, but apparently he hasn't worked since April of last year, whereas Gene [Garber] had his arm lopped off by a combine during his childhood but is now a successful analyst for a large investment firm," said Falk, recalling her first dates with the two men. "Sure, Gene's been divorced twice and has, I think, four or maybe five children who he isn't allowed to see for some reason, but at least he could afford to take me to a nice restaurant, which he paid for using his gold [Visa] card, I might add. Daniel, on the other hand, hasn't even had a solid interview in months. It's nothing personal against Daniel, but a girl has to have her standards." ■

BUSINESS

Offshoot chain targets alternate market

Los Angeles, Calif. – Plague Pestilence & Beyond, an offshoot chain of the home décor mega-chain Bed Bath & Beyond, offers shoppers a large variety of darker-themed items that would be out of place amidst products found in Bed Bath & Beyond stores, company executives said at a store ribbon-cutting ceremony Monday.

"You won't find colorful throw pillows or decorative hand soaps at a Plague Pestilence and Beyond location," said Steven Temares, President and CEO of Bed Bath & Beyond Corporation, which owns the new Plague Pestilence & Beyond chain. "All of those goods and more are already available at any of our more than eight hundred Bed Bath and Beyond locations. Our new Plague Pestilence and Beyond stores, on the other hand, will cater to consumers who bear a more dark and gloomy disposition and lifestyle – the alternative, emo and gothic crowds, in particular."

Specializing in domestics, linens, bathroom and kitchen décor and home furnishings of a style that's the polar opposite of its sister store, Plague Pestilence & Beyond is stocked floor-to-ceiling with items that are more likely to be found in the homes of more alternative-minded consumers.

"There are a lot of consumers who prefer to decorate their homes or apartments with swords and daggers rather than floral paintings and stuffed bunnies," said Temares, addressing a 400-plus crowd present at the ribbon-cutting of a Los Angeles location. "These folks were not being served by our Bed Bath and Beyond stores, so we created Plague Pestilence and Beyond with the intention of targeting this previously forgotten demographic."

Among the goods sold at the new chain superstores are blood-stained candle holders, demon-possessed ouija boards, cryptic handmade crafts, artworks and other hard-to-find items essential for decorating the domiciles of today's more dark-thinking, gloom-filled consumer.

> "Items found here will much more properly express the angst, pain and depression harbored by the purchaser than what's available at Bed Bath and Beyond," said Moore.

"Items found here will much more properly express the angst, pain and depression harbored by the purchaser than what's available at Bed Bath and Beyond," said Marci Moore, vice president of marketing for Plague Pestilence & Beyond. "For a person who's obsessed with death, or even just views life as some sort of torturous and inescapable gauntlet of perpetual misery onto which their decaying soul has been forcibly thrust, Plague Pestilence and Beyond will be their one-stop home décor and furnishings store."

Moore explained how this quickly growing demographic had previously gone ignored by national retailers.

"For years, Goth-minded shoppers have had no quick answer to questions such as, 'Where can I go to purchase quality-made drink coasters with pentagrams sewn into them using the testicle hairs of sacrificed goats?'" said Moore. "Or maybe you're looking for bleak, cryptic paintings of scorched landscapes being surveyed by the Four Horsemen or something of the like. Plague Pestilence and Beyond will carry a wide variety of these previously hard-to-find items that reflect the dark side of the human psyche." ■

Above: A Los Angeles location of the new national chain store shortly after the ribbon-cutting ceremony.

EDITORIAL
I'll be handy if it fucking kills me

By Wendell Freeman

As a religious man, I do not question why I was skipped over when God passed out the basic mechanical skills with which my siblings are so magnificently endowed. Granted, I'm blessed in other areas; my talent for oral surgery, for example, has allowed me to enjoy great success within the field of dentistry. But as a man, it's been extremely frustrating to continually be left feeling useless when it comes to fixing the car, overhauling the bathroom plumbing or even building a simple tree house for the kids.

My whole life I've been told that being handy is not something you can learn, it's something you're born with. Well, that theory's about to be put to the test. I mean, Jesus, if I can take out wisdom teeth I sure as hell ought to be able to fix the garbage disposal. I've had it. Hear me now and believe me later: I'm going to become handy if it fucking kills me.

I've always felt that the desire to take pride in a job well done is one of the defining attributes of a handyman – a characteristic that'll need summoning for me to become the next Tim the Tool Man. As they say, an object at rest tends to stay at rest – so it would seem I'm up against nothing less than physics from the get-go, since my wife has for years harbored zero expectation when it comes to me fixing things around the house. What a lucky break it was for me that our family car recently broke down, an event that's spurred me down my ambitious and probably self-destructive path.

My sincere aversion to personal injury will no doubt be another weighty obstacle in my quest to forge even mediocre handiness. Accidentally jamming a slotted screwdriver into my wrist trying to pry off a fan belt, for example, held about as much appeal for me as becoming one of my own patients. But I'll need to learn to embrace rewards such as excruciating pain if I'm to become Mr. Handy – or at least I think

> I'll need to learn to embrace rewards such as excruciating pain if I'm to become Mr. Handy.

that's what the emergency room nurse was trying to tell me by saying, "No pain, no gain." Now there was a girl who could use her trap wired shut.

Perpetually dirty hands is another attribute of a handy individual that I'm still warming up to – as are my patients, as far as I can tell. Apparently, even the strongest of soaps cannot disguise instances when much of the evening before an oral surgery was spent sifting through a pan of engine coolant, looking for an alternator bolt that fell off a bucking engine. Well, Mr. Patient, my apologies, but you're lucky I came in at all this morning. That engine fan just about chewed my fucking arm off.

Speaking of danger, I can't say that electricity has ever really been my best friend in the world. We've had smaller run-ins before – the ignition of a toaster here, a block fire there. The unhandy man of old would simply look the other way in these instances, but when the dryer damn near exploded today after I handily bridged a circuit using a staple gun, I, Mr. Handy, repeating my creed, became eager to jump right in. This will be the trial by fire! The true test of my passage into handiness!

Now, typically, no one will argue that significant electrical work such as home 220V wiring shouldn't be left to an expert. Fortunately, years of observing men of the handy persuasion have taught me not to start that argument to begin with. Besides, if I don't get the dryer running soon the washed cloths are going to start getting moldy.

Wish me luck! ■

NIGHTMARE from page 21

inner peace and self-satisfaction.

"On the surface, McFerrin seemed to have it all: a number one single, international fame, multiple Grammy Award nominations and lucrative tour offers," *Behind the Music* narrator Jim Forbes explains during the show's opening. "But underneath the happy-go-lucky melodies of his perennial hit was a man quickly spiraling into a world of love, happiness and spiritual fulfillment that threatened to further stabilize his life and inspire songs. Bobby McFerrin: Behind the Music."

VH1's Carla Fanglo, executive producer of the popular *Behind the Music* series, said that while music fans around the world were becoming familiar with McFerrin's universally appealing feel-good melodies, few knew that the positive vibes characteristic of the 42-year-old's music were slowly beginning to pervade McFerrin's personal life.

"Like most virtuoso artists, McFerrin's music was driven by his own personal demons," said Fanglo. "His desire to bring music to children, to grow as a musician, his commitments to religion and his family, his quest to unite people through music – McFerrin's success allowed him to begin to pursue and indulge in these excesses. Unfortunately for McFerrin, feeding these inner demons only made them grow stronger and stronger."

According to McFerrin's former manager, Kevin DeGraff, the unforeseen success of "Don't Worry Be Happy" also created weighty financial repercussions. Though McFerrin refused to sell out – turning down a multitude of product endorsements and other fast-money deals – the phenomenal international sales of his *Simple Pleasures* album generated substantial royalty money – money that McFerrin, against the advice of DeGraff, thoughtfully sank into sound, reputable investments.

"If McFerrin had never invested that money he would've never had to pay the taxes on the monstrous returns those investments brought him," said DeGraff,

> McFerrin, against the advice of his former manager, thoughtfully sank his profits into sound, reputable investments.

divulging one of the never-before-told tragedies that sidled his former client's skyrocketing career. "And now that Bobby no longer needed to worry about making more money, he started making all sorts of insane career decisions."

Indeed, under continued pressure from his wife Debbie for McFerrin to continue chasing his dreams, McFerrin – ignoring offers for concerts and events brought on by his sudden popularity – instead began seriously pursuing a career in conducting, again to his manager's disapproval.

"I guess that's when he pretty much just snapped," said DeGraff. "Instead of heading right back into the studio to write another fifteen songs that sounded exactly like 'Don't Worry Be Happy,' he went out into left field with the orchestra conducting stuff. All the time wearing a big smile on his face, too – like he was *enjoying* just going out and doing whatever the hell he wanted to and not becoming a puppet for the [music] industry. It broke my heart to see him like that, but there was pretty much no talking to him by that point."

Added DeGraff: "Thank God MC Hammer was coming up right behind him."

Decades later, a grounded, carefree McFerrin – now a father of three, world-renown classical conductor and passionate spokesman for music education – explained to *Behind the Music* how his love of music, fulfillment of his goals and support from his family contributed to his personal implosion.

"All that stuff starts to add up," said McFerrin, interviewed at his modest Hollywood residence. "I remember being so happy at the time with all of the good fortune that I was having that I just wanted to burst. I had so much love and happiness and music built up in my heart that songs and love would just pour out of me around-the-clock. I still have flashbacks of that time in my life." ■

Youth either flashing gang signs or suffering acute arthritis

U.S. sales of Mega Cooper flop

Villain gives shackled Bond longwinded spiel regarding world conquest

page 23

CLONE from page 21

color-by-numbers songs featuring catchy, preschool choruses and Ritalin-fueled tempos – these bands can not technically be classified as "clones" since they were not produced through the use of somatic cell nuclear transferring.

Rolling Stone managing editor Ed Needham reinforced Taylor's contention: "Like most of today's pop-punk acts, members of bands like Sum 41 take

> *Rolling Stone*'s Ed Needham: "As much as Sum 41 may strive to imitate Blink-182, they certainly can never pretend to have the same DNA. They're really just copycats, not actual clones."

their musical influence from seventies punk bands – but their DNA they take from their parents. As much as Sum 41 may strive to imitate Blink-182, they certainly can never pretend to have the same DNA. They're really just copycats, not actual clones."

With a majority of mainstream music enthusiasts keen on being spoon-fed album after album of brainless swill generated by cookie-cutter bands devoid of an inkling of originality, ACT's technological advance is expected to revolutionize the music industry.

"For record executives, band cloning technology is a dream come true," said Taylor. "No longer will label representatives be expected to travel around the county on that seemingly endless search for trend-riding bands that look and sound the same as whatever bands are hot at the time."

Taylor emphasized that although ACT selected a power pop-punk act as the subject of their cloning experiments, the technology, once perfected, will have extraordinary diverse applications.

"Hip-hop, nu metal, gangsta rap, contemporary, hardcore, emo – the possibilities are endless," said Taylor. "Band cloning will guarantee there's never a shortage of inane corporate schlock for radio to repeatedly cram down the public's ear canals."

Taylor noted that while ACT's cloning technology could, in theory, be used to reproduce bands that labor immensely to conjure innovative and articulate musical explorations that seem to transcend the very boundaries of the audio spectrum, such an application has yet to find a market.

"Today's discerning listener doesn't want any of this artsy-fartsy conceptual music crap," said Taylor. "What's more is expecting record executives – whose very jobs hinge on the success of the bands they sign – to take a chance on upcoming, potentially revolutionary artists with something unique and different to offer. I hear the last rep that tried that is now scraping barnacles off of rental boats in Haiti for twenty-five cents a day." ■

CRIPS from page 21

King Blvd. – deep in the heart of well-known Crips-controlled territory – after having suffered a massive loss of motor oil due to numerous bullet and knife wounds. Pronounced "pretty much shot" on the scene by mechanics, the vehicle was immediately towed to an undisclosed body shop where it awaits repairs in a condition described by authorities as stable but not drivable.

According to Los Angeles Chief of Police William J. Bratton, the attack represents yet another episode of violence caused by the long-standing feud between the rival Crips and Bloods gangs.

"Slash wounds have long been a known trademark of Crips attacks, and the bloodmobile was found with both its front tires slit," said LAPD Chief William J. Bratton, explaining some of the evidence linking the two Crips members in custody to the crime. "Anything Blood-affiliated intruding on Crips territory is obviously a target – even a harmless bloodmobile simply commuting between blood drives. The attack is a message from the Crips to all Bloods and bloodmobiles: steer clear of Crips territory."

Chief Bratton expounded on details of the attack and Los Angeles gang violence in general during a press conference Wednesday morning.

"Each gang dons different colors to signal their gang affiliation – blue is worn by Crips and red by Bloods," said Bratton. "True, the bloodmobile is mostly white, but all of the RV's signage was red. If you're going to be driving through Crips country, that's like painting a big target on the side of your car saying: shoot me, I'm with a Blood organization."

According to Officer Neil Avery, a policeman on the scene, the bloodmobile was also found to be engaged in illegal behavior at the time of the attack.

"When we searched the bloodmobile, we found [a] crack in the engine block," said Avery. "Crack, of course, is rampant among Los Angeles gang members. This helped us further identify the vehicle as being Blood-affiliated [sic]." ■

> The Bloodmobile suffered a massive loss of motor oil due to numerous bullet and knife wounds.

EYE ON DICK

DICKING AND DRIVING

Stripped of his legitimate driving privileges almost immediately after having earned them, former professional stunt driver and cultural icon Dick Bill recently began a campaign to get his driving rights legally restored. Having pledged to avoid drunk driving by swallow his car keys at the first sign of drunkenness (a public service being sponsored for Ace Hardware, who has already pressed 365 copies of the keys for the company's first year of participation), Dick's first obstacle to overcome in pursuit of a legal driving status was passing his driving exam. Below are the results of Dick's first attempt at passing the mandatory driving test:

Pre-driving procedures: Immediately broke cigarette lighter and managed to chew through seatbelt, but displayed mastery in adjusting mirrors.

Obeying traffic signs: Strictly obeyed signs' commands, almost to a fault. Told students not to take signs' orders so literally after stopping car and refusing to pull past a "Do Not Pass" sign.

Following distance: Consistently had trouble maintaining a safe distance a safe distance from other vehicles when they were loaded with hot women.

Overtaking vehicles: Problem understanding terminology; student was upset to learn that proper technique for "overtaking vehicles" in no way resembled pirates boarding other ships.

Driving in reverse: Started off shaky, but did much better after taking "neck pills" and removing welding goggles.

Incidents: 1. Almost killed pedestrian, although it technically didn't count against his driving score because student left vehicle and ran him down on foot screaming something about "bad acid" before assaulting pedestrian in alleyway. **2.** When briefly followed by police car, student handed instructor a small paper bag and asked for me to hold it for him. Contents unknown.

headlines every day on twitter @RecoilMagazine

Pregnant wife now bitching for two

Accountant's pencil, personality dull

RECOILMAG.COM — NEWS SATIRE YOU CAN TRUST

recoil

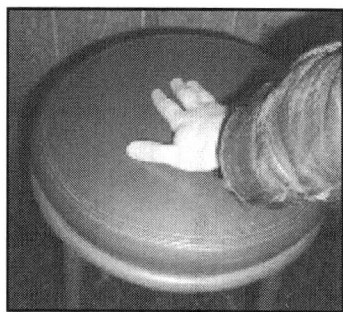
Atheist's seat saved

Schizophrenic blogger convinced people are following him on Twitter

Pickin's slim

Mom fine

Dayton, Ohio – Local auto repair shop owner Teddy Roland's mom is 'fine,' reports childhood friend Kurt Baxter, who recently asked of the Roland family's general well-being while dropping off his 1998 Dodge Caravan at Roland's shop. Roland, 27, reportedly told Baxter, "Mom? Oh, yeah, mom's fine. Stop by and see her if you're in the area. She'd really be glad to see you." Sources indicate that although glad Roland's mom is fine, Baxter currently harbors no intentions to schedule a visit with the aging acquaintance.

Area asshole demands to know what you're looking at

Detroit, Mich. – Forty-two-year-old construction worker and noted asshole Don E. Williams demanded answers to tough questions Friday morning after the loud, arrogant man noticed you staring at him while he argued with the cashier at a local coffeehouse. "What the fuck are you looking at?" questioned Williams, spitting slightly as he shouted at you. "You got a problem or something? If you got a problem why don't you come over here and let's figure it out – how about that?" After receiving no auditory response from you, Williams closed his questioning with a brief statement, saying, "Yeah, [I] didn't think so." ■

Vegas housekeeper about had it with finding dead people in rooms every morning

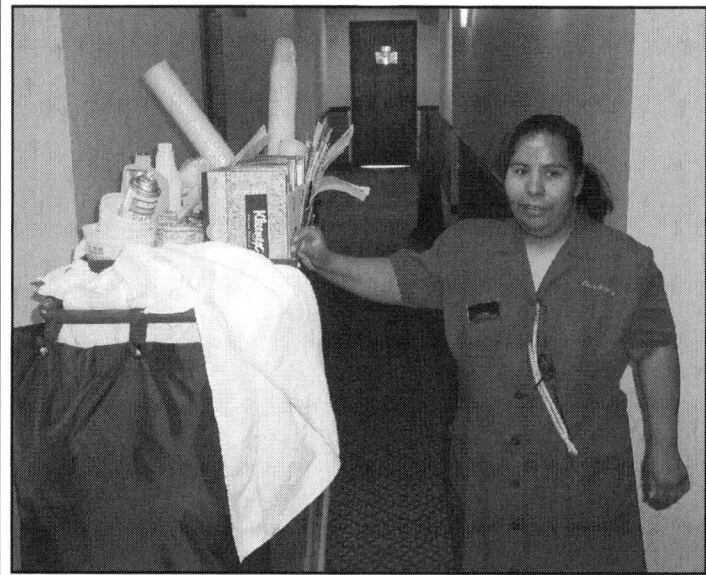
Above: Golden Nuggest housekeeper Rita Gonzales.

Las Vegas, Nev. – Rita Gonzales, a longtime housekeeper at the Golden Nugget Hotel & Casino in downtown Las Vegas, confirmed Tuesday that she has just about had it with finding hotel guests lying dead in their rooms nearly every morning.

"Not another one," remarked an unwavering Gonzales, 42, upon entering the room of Los Angeles native Eric Gerard Tuesday morning. "Great, here we go again. Okay, well, time to call the cops and get ready for about eighteen hours of questioning. Wonderful. Just wonderful. Another workday shot all to hell."

"I'd prefer to clean a bathtub that isn't coated in human blood," Gonzales said.

Gerard, whom investigators later confirmed of having died of a heroin overdose the night previous, represents

see BODIES page 28

New speed bump successfully lowers traffic speed within 100-foot proximity

Ada, Mich. – A majority of Cole Street residents are lauding the city's recent decision to install a speed bump on the street's 200 block – a move that has significantly lowered traffic speed for a 100-foot stretch of the four-mile-long suburban drive.

"A lot of drivers use to barrel through here like a bat out of hell. Not anymore," said Misty Moorhead, the 40-year-old homeowner who spearheaded the neighborhood's successful campaign for the speed regulator. "Now drivers have absolutely no choice but to slow down to a reasonable speed when they get about fifty feet away [from the bump]."

Moorhead's successful bid for governmental action began in late fall when, concerned for the safety of her two pre-teen children, Moorhead began writing letters to city council members requesting that a speed bump be installed

see BUMP page 26

- Traffic speed significantly decreases from 35-50 mph to 5-10 mph
- Traffic reaccelerates to normal speed

Right: Graphic illustration of the speed bump's effect on traffic.

page 25

WORLDWIDE HEADLINES

Area man finally able to be left alone with his thoughts, television

Encino, Calif. – After what seemed like weeks of appeasing nonstop work deadlines and family-related commitments, area man Eddie Ryan was finally able to escape to the privacy of his study Friday evening, where he enjoyed nearly three hours alone with his thoughts and cable television, the 32-year old Investment Banker disclosed today. "I just hadn't had any time to sit down and think or watch TV in so long," Ryan said of his quiet, secluded evening spent pondering current life events during muted commercial breaks. "With all the running around I've been doing, for work and with the family, it felt really good to be left alone to think about life and catch *The Mentalist*.

NAACP calls for more diverse hurricane names

Tallahassee, Fla. – During a Thursday morning press conference, officials at the National Association for the Advancement of Colored People (NAACP) called for the World Meteorological Organization (WMO) to make immediate changes to its longtime practice of consistently naming hurricanes with such Caucasian-sounding monikers. "Bret, Cindy, Stan – I challenge anyone to look at this year's list of possible hurricane names and tell me it reflects our culturally diverse society," said Marcus DeGoode, reading briefly from the WMO's annual list of 21 possible storm names. "Take for example the last four 'D'-named storms we've had: Dolly, Danny, Danielle and Dennis – all evidence of the pattern of subtle name discrimination that's been going on for decades. Is it too much to ask that one of these hurricanes be named Deon or Dawanda?" Michael Spooner of the WMO issued a statement Friday refuting the notion of a bias, noting that Yolanda is a name frequently listed as a possible "Y" hurricane name. "Also, among this year's potential Atlantic storm handles are the names Franklin and Katrina, both of which, we feel, could go either way."

Temperature inside Eskimo sweatshop actually quite reasonable

Iqaluit, Nunavut – A new study out of Nunavut, Canada, has found that despite below-freezing spring weather, temperatures inside Iqaluit's principal sweatshop are rather clement, all things considered. "Sure, most of us here work oppressively long hours in cramped conditions with poor ventilation," said longtime sealskin wallet-maker Anuk Pukkeenegak. "But I have to say, the ol' thermometer generally stays put around the sixty-eight degree mark. You really can't beat that." Co-worker Paj Aulanerk agreed with Pukkeenegak's assessment, adding: "If I were to take a daily five-minute stretch break – which I most certainly cannot, by the way – I'd likely just relax at my idyllically temperate workstation instead of braving the nasty elements outside." The study claims the effects of the near-arctic outdoor environment on the windowless complex harboring the body heat of 70 overburdened laborers have created a veritable perfect storm of reasonable indoor climate. "I truly hope these employees realize how good they have it here," said researcher Patrick Meehan. "This time of year, my corner office's central heating system makes me sweat like a Taiwanese nine-year-old pulling a double-shift at the Nike plant."

Scientists isolate gene that makes cats suddenly stop whatever they're doing to take bath

Washington, D.C. – Researchers at Georgetown University announced Monday results of a new study which pinpoints the gene in charge of triggering the common housecat's shared impulse to abruptly stop whatever they are doing to at least partially bathe themselves before continuing with their activities. "For centuries mankind has stood in wonder of this bizarre universal feline idiosyncrasy," said Dr. Thomas Green, the genomics specialist who identified the gene responsible for the domesticated animal's erratic behavior. "We're of course busy mapping the respective genomes of hundreds of plants, animals, insects, fish and so forth, but just for myself, I really wanted to unlock the secret of what makes cats do that. I don't know about everybody else on the [study's] team, but I feel a whole lot better just having found the gene. Hopefully we're on the way to being able to shut off that whole impromptu bathing thing, because it just really, really bugs me."

People starting to wreak things other than havoc

Waterloo, Iowa – Early reports coming out of the country's Midwest indicate that people are beginning to wreak things besides havoc, sources confirmed Tuesday. "Apparently, havoc is not the only thing that can be wreaked – even though I can't think offhand of a single other word that sounds right immediately following the word 'wreak,'" said Jason Scribner, a 44-year-old library clerk who recalled having recently seen the word "wreak" used in a newspaper article. "The dictionary defines 'wreak' as a verb meaning 'to inflict or execute,' such as in wreaking vengeance, punishment or justice. But as strange as it seems, the word is not necessarily supposed to imply a negative connotation. So hypothetically a person could wreak peace or wreak sympathy or wreak joy – as stupid as those phrases sound when you say them out loud."

Terrible geometry student afraid to sail through Bermuda Trapezoid

Fort Lauderdale, Fla. – Afraid his vessel might suffer a similar fate as the many ships and planes reported to have sunk, crashed or gone missing while navigating through the area, marine enthusiast and poor geometry student Dale Smith told sources Wednesday he is afraid to sail his father's watercraft "anywhere near that Bermuda Trapezoid." "The half-million square miles of area between these three corners – Fort Lauderdale, Bermuda and Puerto Rico – make up the Bermuda Trapezoid, where bizarre marine disappearances have been taking place for more than a hundred years," said Smith, 23, drawing a triangle with his finger on a map of the Atlantic Ocean. "No way I'm going anywhere near that area. I may be crazy, but I'm not stupid." Smith, a senior at Texas A&M college, intends to graduate next year as long as he can manage a passing grade in his rudimentary geometry class, which to date he has failed four times. ∎

BUMP from page 25

near her Cole Street home. These letters, along with a petition signed by nearly half of Cole Street's homeowners, prompted city officials to allocate $2,500 in local tax money to fund the bump's February construction.

Neighbors agree that while Cole Street's standard 25-mph speed-limit is routinely ignored by motorists during other sections of the road, the speed bump's installation has prompted a substantial change in traffic speed in the area immediately surrounding the bump.

"No matter if they are going twenty-five [miles per hour] or sixty-five [miles per hour], they all reach for the brake when they get about a stone's throw from the speed bump," stated Moorhead's neighbor Randall Bell. "Everyone that lives and recreates in this one-hundred foot stretch owes Misty a debt of gratitude. Pedestrians and other drivers are much safer when they are right here by this part of the road."

Not all residents, however, agree that the speed bump's installation is a positive achievement, instead claiming it does little to control the overall speed of traffic on Cole Street.

"Yeah, drivers decelerate to manage the bump, but I swear at least half of them try to see exactly how close they can get

> "They all reach for the brake when they get about a stone's throw from the speed bump," stated neighbor Randall Bell.

to it at full speed before slamming on the brakes at the last second," said Palmer Kingsbury. "It's like a little game to them. In fact, I've even seen drivers unfamiliar with the road actually speed up when they see the 'Bump' sign, like they need to make up for the time they're going to lose when they have to slow down."

With little hope of influencing Ada's traffic commission into removing the bump, Kingsbury and likeminded neighbors have instead submitted a formal complaint to the little-known Ada Joint Commission For Gentrification and the Promotion of Good Taste.

AJCGPGT was founded in 1991 by longstanding homeowners who opposed a new resident's excessive implementation of garden gnomes as yard décor. Offended neighbors created the AJCGPGT as a way of preserving their way of life.

AJCGPGT continues to hold neighborhood jurisdiction on certain matters, although it has acted only twice since 1991 as protection against the use of bright yellow house paint, and the public appearance of cutoff jean shorts. The commission remains in existence "for the continued gentrification of east Grand Rapids and the preservation of finer sensibilities."

After reviewing Kingsbury's complaint, Fitzgerald Montague, chairman of the AJCGPGT, said the commission is only

> "I've even seen drivers unfamiliar with the road actually speed up when they see the 'Bump' sign, like they need to make up for the time they're going to lose when they have to slow down."

allowed the power to rule against the speed bump on the basis of aesthetics, not functionality.

"The most compelling aspect of Kingsbury's 28-page complaint is that the offending obstacle has been painted with diagonal white lines, which may be a violation of local statues ensuring good taste," said Montague. ∎

COMMUNITY

Genealogy fanatic can trace his roots all the way back to some boring jerk you've never heard of

Above: Genealogy enthusiast Brendan Kaplan, who has traced his family ancestory all the way back to some obscure Roman dink named Lucius Cornelius Balbus (inset).

Midland, Mich. – During a dinner party Saturday evening, local genealogy enthusiast Brendan Kaplan explained to his guests in great detail that the 44-year-old can actually trace his bloodline all the way back to some boring jerk you've never heard of, source reported.

"I'm sure you all know that genealogy research is a bit of a passion for me, but what I may have never told some of you is that I can actually trace my family ancestry all the way back to Lucius Cornelius Balbus, who was a distinguished citizen of ancient Rome," an excited Kaplan told an indifferent audience of eight during the serving of the main dinner course at his Midland home. "Balbus was an influential figure during Roman times and actually served as private secretary to Caesar, which I find simply fascinating."

Despite the obvious disinterest expressed by his guests – none of whom had ever heard of Balbus, nor voiced an interest in Kaplan's family tree – Kaplan continued his discourse on the ancient, no-name loser to whom he believes he is distantly related.

> Despite the obvious disinterest expressed by his guests, Kaplan continued his discourse on the ancient, no-name loser to whom he believes he is distantly related.

"Balbus lived during the last century B.C., and though he was originally from Spain, he was granted Roman citizenship and used his wealth to become one of the chief financiers in Rome," said Kaplan. "He was friendly with all political parties and exerted influence on the major political figures of the last years of the Roman republic. In fact, it is widely believed that Balbus served Octavian after Caesar's murder."

Following a long awkward silence broken only by the clanging of silverware and guest Chris Morris' pronounced throat-clearing, Kaplan attempted to induce conversation on the subject, adding: "I'm sure you're all familiar with Octavian."

The host then spent the next few minutes explaining that the Octavian of whom he spoke was not the villain in *Spiderman 2* – a notion sardonically

see JERK page 28

A page from the Recoil handbook...
Writing A Screenplay

Writing for the silver screen can be a challenging and lucrative career. It is also the field of writing in which beginning wordsmiths notoriously encounter the most difficulty earning their first check. Here are some tips to help you wedge your foot in Hollywood's doorway:

- Before you decide to become a screenwriter, check to make sure you are a white male between the ages of 20 and 40. No? Well, you could always try sports medicine.

- The quickest way to get your screenplay into the hands of a big Hollywood executive is to tape it to a bimbo actress' ass.

- One of the most important parts of becoming a successful screenwriter is learning how to write a query letter. So go practice writing your faggy letters, queerboy.

- Unlike the music industry, you cannot sell your soul to Satan in exchange for success in the movie business – because anyone even remotely associated with the movie business wouldn't have a soul to begin with.

- If you are asked to write a "spec script," that means you'll need to submit a script that has a lot of specifics in it.

- Movie executives generally won't even read a script that's more than 114 pages, so if you find your completed script running a little bit over, simply tear off the last bunch of pages.

- Print your script on hard stock paper to prevent movie executives from literally wiping their asses with it.

- Many screenplays are adapted from Broadway productions. Way too many.

- You can't sell your screenplay by just chasing Steven Spielberg through a restaurant parking lot. Trust us on this one.

- Don't be surprised if your first few screenplays are completely ignored by the industry. Remember, if your movie's going to get made it'll have to wait in line behind *Gigli*, *Waterworld* and *Bubble Boy*.

- Try not to get discouraged by rejections. Remember, even the guy who wrote *Big* had several other body-switch movies turned down before scoring a hit.

- The "perfect suburban family that is really quite dysfunctional below the surface" story has been done a thousand times. So if you can't think of anything else, do that.

- Know that it is not always correct to simply follow the industry trends – especially if that trend involves limiting the use of nudity. ∎

page 27

HOROSCOPES

Aries (March 21 to April 19)
Considering the stock market's recent volatility, male Aries would be wise to pull everything out for a while – by that I mean, of course, don't have any children. Regardless of the emotional rewards, the financial obligation of having a child is as massive and lengthy as your exaggerated description of your procreative tool. Keep both that thing and your wallet in the safest place for them: in your pants.

Taurus (April 20 to May 20)
Alcoholic Taurus understands that nothing chases away the blues as effectively as a legal depressant. Everyone needs an emotional crutch; most people, however, choose to fill their internal void with extra helpings of pork chops rather than pints of vodka. Fortunately for Taurus, being a boozer is far more fashionable and socially acceptable than being fat, so stick with your liquid diet until further notice.

Gemini (May 21 to June 20)
Carving your own idealistic world out of bookmarked Internet sites and unrealistic romance novels is certainly a lot easier and far more interesting than actually living life; Gemini enjoys tooling along on a self-constructed highway of daydreams, rather than joining everyone else in the one-lane traffic jam of the Real World. But remember, making good time on a smooth road doesn't mean much if you have no destination.

Cancer (June 21 to July 22)
Sickly Cancer shouldn't waste time going to a doctor – those holier-than-thou pen jockeys know absolutely nothing about the human body. Doctors merely see symptoms such as enlarged prostates and swollen glands as catalysts for enlarging their swollen wallets. Save your money – there's no ailment that Nyquil, Ipecac, or Elmer's Glue can't patch, or at least numb, until your body can repair itself.

Leo (July 23 to August 22)
Now is as good of a time as any for Leo to get back on the Jesus train. By my watch, it's been at least eight years since one of those righteous salesmen otherwise known as evangelists got his own words thrown back at him by a Federal Court judge. Send checks to whichever of these suspicious geeks seem most capable of securing you an advance ticket to heaven's big afterlife party, which is sure to be a sold out event.

Virgo (August 23 to September 22)
Virgo's wardrobe is ugly enough to embarrass a rodeo clown. Even poodles dressed up in sweaters uglier than Poland's national flag look at you wondering, "I don't much like wearing this, but I'd choke myself to death with my own tongue before putting THAT on." Revert to letting your mother dress you – you'll be subject to accurate ridicule, but at least you'll have somebody else to blame.

Libra (September 23 to October 22)
The fine print of your marriage license makes no provision for physically "letting yourself go" after the ink is dry; regardless of the hassle of maintaining your impressive mane of hair, female nymphomaniac Libra has no choice but to suppress the urge to cut it short. The moment your hair becomes short is the moment your husband will develop a perpetual headache – a sexual hindrance that can destroy a marriage quicker than winning the lottery.

Scorpio (October 23 to November 21)
Unless Scorpio's attempts on the mailman's life become more successful, wedding invitations will continue to appear in your mailbox – just what you need, more bills. Purchasing a gift for the couple is fine as long as you deem it a wise investment; there's no sense dropping a bill on a wedding present when you suspect the couple's marriage license has a divorce application stapled right to it.

Sagittarius (November 22 to December 21)
Depressed Sagittarius should bear in mind that happiness is not a human right guaranteed in the Constitution - it's an elusive emotion that pokes through the gray clouds only about as often as the sun in Seattle. Depression is the human mind's natural emotional state – the result of having too often stumbled upon one of life's golden gooses, only to discover that it's had a hysterectomy.

Capricorn (December 22 to January 19)
Your intended sexual promiscuity can be blamed on Capricorn's vagabond nature. Your failure to achieve said promiscuity, however, stems from a deep-rooted fear of STDs and the opposite sex's aversion to your cheapskate, "go Dutch" dating protocol. If finding potential dating material seems impossible, try trolling the local plasma clinics – where everyone is blood-disease free and bleeding their way to being able to pay their own way.

Aquarius (January 20 to February 18)
Condoms are great protection against unwanted pregnancy, but Aquarius should be aware that condoms do have expiration dates. And unlike expired mayonnaise, which will merely make you sick to your stomach for one day, expired condoms often make the female's stomach upset for nine months. Check your wallet for dated digits before stepping out on that date – the heat of passion rarely allows for last minute inspection.

Pisces (February 19 to March 20)
Don't expect your divorce lawyer to be sympathetic of your situation – exaggerating and profiting from other people's misery is every lawyer's God given right and moral obligation. Respect your divorce attorney's cold, professional manner; indifference to your emotional pain is necessary for him to focus on the task at hand – making sure Pisces gets screwed *fairly*.

JERK from page 27

suggested by Morris.

"I was hoping the dinner conversation would be a lively discussion of politics, social issues or even pop culture, but Brendan just wouldn't stop droning on and on about some boring jerk ancestor of his that nobody's ever heard of," Morris later told sources. "Maybe if Brendan would've told us he's a descendant of Caligula or something – now there's a well-known dead guy worthy of discussion. Personally, I could talk shop on Caligula all night long, no problem."

Morris said that guests' attempts to steer the subject of conversation toward something the least bit interesting were unsuccessful.

"Every time Brendan would stop to rest his jaw for more than two seconds, one of us would try to change the subject," said Morris, who works with Kaplan at Midland City Library. "Jean [Byers] tried to get us started on the topic of technology by saying something about how the Internet has made genealogy research so much easier, which I thought was a stealthy, well-executed segue. But before anyone could stop him, Brendan snatched up that ball and ran with it. The next thing we knew he was explaining in exhaustive detail about how this primitive dink was 'instrumental in the formation of the First Triumvirate,' whatever the hell that was."

> "And I thought dinner with my parents was boring," added Morris.

According to Morris, Kaplan finally finished talking about his obscure jerkoff relative only after having withheld dessert service until each guest had viewed a copy of his family's genealogy chart.

"He must have gone to Kinko's and made copies for everybody, whether they were interested in seeing it or not," said Morris. "When he finally asked who wanted coffee and went to the kitchen to get dessert, Jean summed up what we were all thinking: 'Jesus, let's hope he pours himself a nice cup of shut the fuck up.'" ∎

BODIES from page 25

just one in a long line of corpses discovered by Gonzales during her morning housekeeping duties.

"I'd say [I find] at least one [body] a week, usually more," said Gonzales, commenting on the normally traumatic event that has become commonplace in her job. "After fifteen years of coming in to change guests' sheets and finding them laying face down in a pool of blood or choked to death on their own vomit, I'm just plain sick of dealing with it. I assure you that nowhere in my job description does it say anything about having to deal with dead bodies on a regular basis."

Gonzales, who immigrated to the U.S. from Mexico with her family when she was just a child, said that Las Vegas' standing as the world headquarters for decadent adult behavior invariably contributes to the staggering frequency with which the hotel rooms she services contain one or more murder, suicide, accident or overdose victims.

"Years ago, when I was first starting out as a housekeeper at the Ramada Inn in Arlington, only maybe once or twice a year would I have the misfortune of finding a dead body in the room I was making up," said Gonzales, recalling early work experiences in Texas. "But here in Vegas it's a different story. The gambling, the drinking, the strippers – it all adds up to people doing bad, bad things. The people I find dead have usually gone too far with one of their vices. 'Vegas casualties,' I call them."

According to Gonzales, in a city filled with two-bit hustlers, drug dealers, degenerate gamblers and other mischievous characters, housekeepers must become accustom to the sight of the carcasses of recently deceased humans.

"It used to be that finding a stiff hanging from the shower rod as I went to replace the shampoo would freak me out to no end," said Gonzales. "But after more than a decade of working in Vegas hotels, I'm so used to it now that it doesn't really even faze me anymore. I guess for this job, in this town, there really is no substitute for practical work experience."

Gonzales said that her years of experience in finding dead bodies in rooms helps her teach new housekeepers how to deal with the situation.

"Just like at any other job, you pick up little tricks and tips along the way, which I try to pass on to some of the girls I

> "Nowhere in [my] job description does it say anything about having to deal with dead bodies every morning," said Gonzales.

train," said Gonzales. "I teach the girls that you're better off to just wait until the police finish before trying to make up the room. They get all huffy about 'tampering with a crime scene' and stuff. You might as well just take your break while waiting for the authorities to haul away the stiff."

"Guest," Gonzales added. "I meant to say guest."

Despite her indifference to Golden Nugget guests' mortality, Gonzales remains committed to professionalism.

"Sure, it would be easy to just throw some fresh towels in the bathroom and act like the door didn't hit some poor bastard's bullet-filled head, but Golden Nugget guests deserve top-notch maid service, whether they've paid their bill up front or not," Gonzales said. "No doubt, I'd prefer to clean a bathtub that isn't caked with human blood, but if it is, I'm still going to make that tub shine like nobody's business." ∎

RECOILMAG.COM   NEWS SATIRE YOU CAN TRUST

recoil

Above: White gangsta wannabe James B. demonstrates the inferior shooting style.

Gangsta trend significantly reduces inner city gunshot fatalities

Los Angeles, Calif. – According to an article published in the October issue of *Handguns* magazine, a recent decline in fatalities resulting from inner city handgun shootings can be credited to the thriving popularity of a flashy new gangsta-style shooting technique wherein the weapon is canted 180 degrees from its standard upright position when

see TREND page 30

Above: Two suburban teens too engrained into their lazy behavior to consider running away from home.

Report: 78 percent of angry teens too lazy to run away from home

Notre Dame, Ind. – Researchers at the University of Notre Dame announced Monday results of a three-year study which suggest that an overwhelming majority of today's teenagers who are emphatically frustrated with their home life are simply too lazy to go through the process of running away from home.

"For teens today who are really lazy – and these days that means about all of them – it can be a tough decision whether or not it's worth going through all the trouble of running away from home," said Dr. David Regal, lead researcher in the Notre Dame study, which surveyed more than 1,200 youths between the ages of 13 and 17. "It comes down to a matter of what's more

> "The act of running away involves a whole bunch of manual labor such as packing clothes and having to walk all the way to the bus station," said Dr. Regal.

bothersome to the teen, the fact that their fascist parents are making their lives a living hell, or the knowledge that the act of running away involves a whole bunch of manual labor such as packing clothes and having to walk all the way to the bus station."

Notre Dame's study, the results of which will be published concurrently in the August issues of *Scientific America* and *Teen Beat* magazines, indicates that as many as 30 percent of current American teenagers are upset enough with their home situation to have seriously considered running away from home during the last 18 months. The study confirmed, however, that of

see LAZY page 32

Line at post office comprised of most intense individuals imaginable

Above: The Lansing, Mich., post office inside which the line formed.

Lansing, Mich. – The line of customers waiting for assistance from counter attendants at the U.S. Postal Service's downtown branch Friday afternoon consisted of some of the most intense individuals imaginable, sources reported.

"Go! Go! That's you, go!" exclaimed Kevin Dunlop, encouraging the elderly woman ahead of him in line to approach an open attendant after the 74-year-old did not immediately step forward when called. After pointing angrily toward the counter and slightly nudging the woman in that direction, Dunlop shook his head sharply and added, "Jesus Christ."

> "This is absolutely ridiculous. They should have more people out here or something," Harper stated loudly.

Leslie Harper, 48, another visibly tense member of the mega-impassioned procession, tapped her foot impatiently while intermittently toggling her fiery, frustrated stare back and forth between service personnel and her wristwatch.

"Can you believe this?" Harper asked of the complete stranger in line behind her. "This is absolutely ridiculous. They should have more people out here or something."

The collection of notably vehement patrons formed at approximately 12:30 p.m. Friday afternoon as the lunchtime traffic volume began to overwhelm the

see LINE page 32

page 29

TREND from page 29

discharged.

"Holding your gun sideways had become so cliché that it forced modern hoods to invent a flashier gimmick," wrote freelancer Marian Ayoob in *Handguns*' recent cover story entitled "Better To Look Good Than To Shoot Good." "During the last three months, holding a firearm completely upside-down has become the predominant method used by today's gangstas whom, as they say, 'be fixin' to bust a cap in [a person's] dome.'"

The article went on to reiterate statistics from the National Archive of Criminal Justice Data, which documented September of last year to have tallied the lowest record of shooting fatalities for men between the ages of 14-35 since 1990.

"The number of gang-related altercations involving gunplay has remained steady in most metropolitan areas of the country, but the rate of deaths resulting from these shootings dropped fourteen percent last quarter," wrote Ayoob. "These statistics clearly indicate that the bullets are not hitting their intended targets – for what seems like the obvious reasons."

Ayoob also cited studies by ballistic experts at the University of Michigan in Ann Arbor, which estimate that employing the unorthodox handgun shooting technique can reduce a subject's short-range accuracy by as much as 80 percent.

U of M researchers said that this significant decrease in accuracy results from attempting to shoot the weapon while it is upside-down.

"A gangsta utilizing the sideways, ninety-degree shooting method generally experiences only an accuracy loss of roughly twenty percent," said Dr. Keith Marcus. "But the shooter loses tremendous accuracy when the gun is turned an additional ninety degrees. With the sideways method you could still use the sights to aim. Upside-down, you have to pretty much just guestimate [when aiming]. And having to use certainly your doesn't pinky help." to operate the trigger

Marcus added that a shooter's accuracy is further reduced if the shooter is either running from police or trying to take a picture of himself with his phone while shooting.

Still, Ayoob contends, more and more gangstas area becoming willing to sacrifice accuracy in return for aesthetic rewards.

"What the shooter loses in accuracy and the ability to fire consecutive rounds quickly, he more than makes up for in presenting himself with a more 'badass' appearance," wrote Ayoob. "Polls indicate that thugs consider how you be representin' to be just as important as how you be shootin'."

Ayoob said that Americans can expect the number of shooting fatalities to continue to drop as the flamboyant attack pose gains further popularity among the public.

"Right now, mostly only gangstas in the inner cities are employing the 'one-eighty cock,' as many are calling it," said Ayoob. "As soon as the entertainment media gets wind that holding the gun upside-down is the 'shizzle' cool way to fire off a cap, you'll be seeing it in all of the movies and television shows."

Added Ayoob: "Just wait until the next 50 Cent [movie] character blows away a rival gang member using that one-eighty cock. *Everyone* will start shooting that way. Morgues across the country will probably start going out of business." ∎

> This significant decrease in accuracy results from attempting to shoot the weapon while it is upside-down.

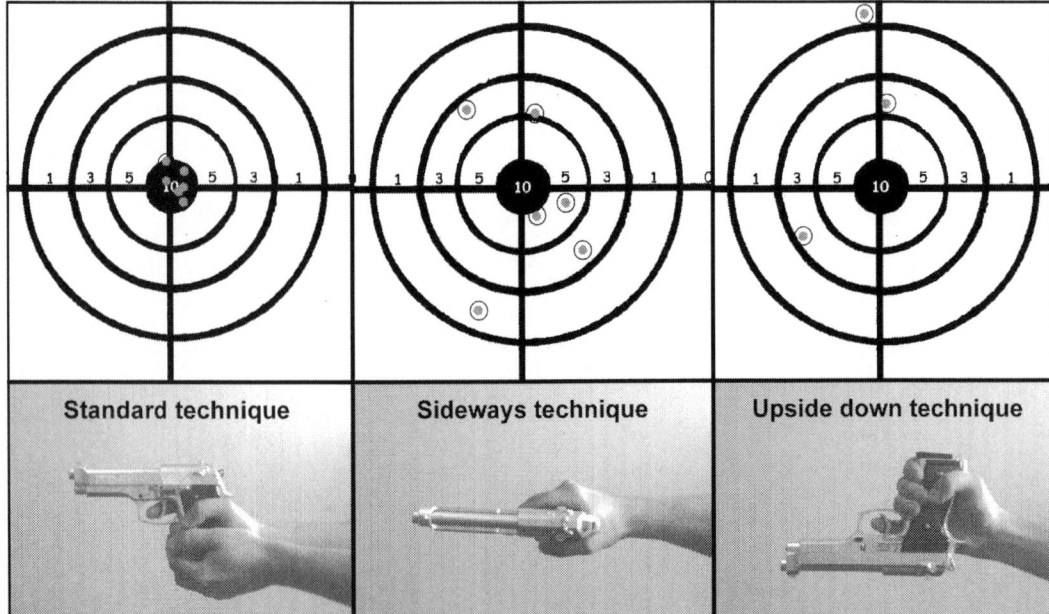

Above: Results from University of Michigan shooting accuracy tests.

EDITORIAL

What can I rub my face against next?

In between naps and bouts of tail chasing, I have been rubbing my face

By Martha

with varying degrees of intensity on assorted household furniture and other items all day. Now, with the sun withdrawing from its daily perch, I find myself wearying of the game. Assuredly, it's a great hobby, but after you've rubbed your face on every available projection, when your whiskers are intimately familiar with every texture in every room of the domicile – from fuzzy pink bunny slippers to cold, metal floor lamps – the thrilling 'rub' can indeed become a half-hearted 'brush-against.' It all seems rather blasé. What in this apartment can I rub my face on next?

Wait! The nice lady who lives here from dusk until dawn, who serves me meals and showers me with affection, has just arrived. I can hear her keys jingling in the door! Now is when the serious, skillful rubbing begins in earnest.

I quickly preen, and then trot to the entrance so as to meet her just as she opens the door. She walks in with a sigh of pleasure, drops the beribboned package she is holding onto the nearest chair, and walks swiftly toward the bathroom. As she walks, I sinuously weave my body in between her feet, rubbing my face briskly on each of her ankles as they flash by. She stumbles and yells in admiration at my skilled maneuvering. She physically sets me near the plant stand in the hall, which I immediately rub my face against.

I hear the toilet flush, which reminds me of the situation at hand. Rubbing, I leave the hall, only detouring slightly to rub my face on the nice lady's discarded shoe, the ribbons hanging from the package on the chair, the leg of the same chair, and the kitchen wastebasket. Then I see that the pantry door is open, and I slip inside. What a treasure trove of rub-worthy items! Cans of tunafish: rub. Paper grocery bags: rub, and a bonus bunch of rustling noises. Boxes of pasta: rub. Mop handle: rub. Broom straws: rub. Rolls of wrapping paper: rub, and also an extended round of sniffing, because the wrapping paper smells interestingly of some other creature, perhaps a mouse. Upon further sniff, I rule otherwise.

The lady picks me up and holds me against her shoulder. I take the opportunity to rub my face heartily against her eyeglasses, knocking them askew. When she opens her mouth to shout in happy surprise at my playful

> Now is when the serious, skillful rubbing begins in earnest.

rubbing, I play along, and affectionately rub my face against her teeth. It appears that some of the recently devoured canned food that stuck to my whiskers has smeared across her cheek. Speechless with joy, she sets me on a kitchen chair and goes into the bathroom again.

I hear water running, and excitedly I follow her – she has turned the faucet on for me again. I jump to the counter and try to rub my face against the stream of water, then I remember that water – along with curling irons, open oven doors, and sharp pencils – are not items intended for rubbing. I instead drink deeply from the flowing stream, then rub my face against the nice lady's toothbrush, which she has presented for my ministrations. She snorts, gleefully, and elbows me, as if we've just shared a good joke. She makes the water very hot and runs her toothbrush under it before putting it away.

I am so glad the nice lady appreciates all of the rubbing that I do. Feeling newly invigorated, I venture back out into the main area and again pose the perplexing conundrum: what can I rub my face on next? ∎

WORLDWIDE HEADLINES

Wife's period more accurately described as exclamation point

Ann Arbor, Mich. – Area wife Anne Gile's menstrual period could possibly be more accurately described as an exclamation point, according to husband John Gile, an English professor at the University of Michigan. "An exclamation point is usually associated with the loud or deliberate expression of feeling or emotion, which characterizes Anne's whole demeanor during that time of the month," said Gile.

Sports anchor still working dumb jock sound out of voice

Atlanta, Ga. – Viewers of local television station Channel 11's 6 p.m. news said Sunday that rookie sports anchor Ty Roberts, 23, is yet to rid his on-air voice of the Neanderthal tone he no doubt developed during his many years of playing varsity and collegiate football prior to his career as a newscaster. "This new guy barks out the scores like he's calling plays in the huddle – 'Phillies, six! Braves, four! Diamondbacks, three! Rangers, two!'" viewer Ross Valla noted. "He's going to have to work that dumb jock sound out of his voice if he expects people to think of him as anything but a failed tight end falling back on his communications degree."

Developmentally disabled alien awed by flashlight

Clarion, Nev. – Travelers Marjorie and Daniel Gardner claimed to have interacted with a developmentally disabled alien while broken down on Route 10 Saturday night after the seemingly lost extraterrestrial approached the couple and became enthralled with the basic functioning of their flashlight. "Naturally we assumed that the being had an intelligence far beyond our capacity for understanding," said Daniel Gardner. "But after watching the alien marvel at our flashlight like it was a light saber or something, we realized that he was actually a, well, a little slow, let's say." Gardner said the alien was short with bucked teeth and glasses, and appeared to be wearing a bicycle helmet.

Character built through miserable chore

Sault Saint Marie, Mich. – According to the father of 12-year-old Tommy Joseph, an hour and a half of hauling firewood built character in his son Friday, despite the child's continuous pleas to the contrary. "Tommy keeps complaining that the only thing he's getting out of helping me stock firewood for the winter is a sore back and blisters, but I told him that it's hard work like this that builds character in a young man," said Thomas Joseph, Sr., grabbing a beer and sitting down on the chopping block to watch his son finish hauling the day's load into his truck. "Letting him out of working today just because he was running a little bit of a temperature certainly wasn't going to toughen him up or teach him anything about hard work, determination, responsibility or being a man. What kind of father would I be to deny him this character-building opportunity?" Joseph later confirmed that his son's character would continue to be built over the weekend through the washing and waxing of both family cars, the cleaning of his room and the mowing of the lawn.

Zs caught

Owensboro, Ky. – Sources close to mall security guard Ted Laurel confirmed Friday afternoon that the 32-year-old had managed to single-handedly apprehend a number of wanted Zs that had eluded Laurel the night previous. "Ted asked me to come into the break room and wake him up after lunch because he was going to try to catch some Zs – apparently he had closed the bar last night and hadn't gotten much sleep," said Dale Breckenridge, a coworker of Laurel's at Middletown Mall. "When I came in an hour later he was sawing logs like a lumberjack, so I guess the mission was a success." The Zs, which were held for the full hour before being released on their own recognizance, were unavailable for comment.

Online dater's picture older than suitor's undisclosed child

Flagstaff, Ariz. – The flattering photo being used by 38-year-old building superintendent Randy Schulz on his Match.com profile is almost two years older than the eight-year-old daughter who has yet to have been mentioned by Mary Lawrence, a receptionist with whom Schulz has been e-mailing since being matched by the online dating service's compatibility matrix two weeks ago. "I don't know which of these two is being more deceitful, the woman who isn't telling the guy she has an eight-year-old, or the guy who's using a picture that's even older than her secret kid," said Tracy Vaughn, a system administrator at Match.com. "More than likely, during the decade since that picture was taken, Randy's probably gained as many pounds as Mary's little girl weighs." ■

EYE ON DICK

HANDY DICK

Former high school woodshop class casualty and cultural icon Dick Bill recently fell back on his extensive knowledge of woodworking, coordinating a small construction team to make upgrades to his first-class domicile. Below are some notable events from the almost entirely injury-free work sessions:

• Construction gets off to slow start when Dick refuses to start working until everyone involved hits Dick's thumb with a hammer as hard as they can.
• Dick Bill becomes unable to obtain supplies for project after Home Depot bans him from store for life for using store's paint shaker for 'inappropriate sexual endeavors.'
• Production slows after Dick insists entire crew adopt new woodworking policy: measure twice, cut once, drink five times.
• Dick ruins portable concrete mixer by using it to make 30 gallons' worth of margaritas for entire work crew.
• Work halts when Dick refuses to admit any knowledge of what happened to all the razorblades that were in the boxcutter just a few days ago.
• The need to start from scratch becomes apparent when Dick notices that he is the only builder who has been using the metric system the entire time.
• Dick "accidentally" paints himself into the only corner of the room that has a full cooler of beer in it.

HOW TO... AVOID BEING POISONED

Drink
Granted, modern dinner etiquette typically forbids tossing a strip of litmus paper into your White Zinfandel – but hey, would you rather pass out dead during the soup service? If the litmus paper turns blue, your host has probably poisoned your drink (better check your brake line before driving home). Also, observe the liquid's distribution process; if your portion came from a sealed bottle or others are sampling from the same source, you're probably safe. Oh yeah, check the bottle you're drinking from for a gigantic red fucking sticker marked "POSION."

Food
Make sure you're not in Denny's. Next, take a small amount of the questionable entrée and place it on the lips – a burning or bitter taste is a warming sign. If you suspect a tainted dish, eat only a small quantity (a low quantity of poison may not prove fatal) and wait five hours without eating or drinking anything else. Food immediately not agreeing with your digestive system should be regurgitated; vomiting can be induced by putting your fingers down your throat or by watching Oprah. Long-term poisoning can be more difficult to detect, but if you experience an unexplainable, extended bout of illness while the same person has been preparing your daily food, you might consider starting to dine out.

Ecstasy
If you're one of the many bent on poisoning your body with drugs (good ones), you've got to be careful that an unscrupulous drug dealer doesn't trick you into poisoning your body with drugs (bad ones). Ecstasy tablets laced with toxins can be discovered using one of the many home test kits available through websites such as DanceSafe.org; these kits verify the presence of MDMA (that's good) as well as all of the common substitute drugs on the ecstasy market, including DXM (that's bad).

Mail
Think the boss has it out for you? Make sure his attempts to spike the adhesive strips of your envelopes with cyanide or ricin are in vain by keeping your tongue at home and relying on a bottle moistener. And, of course, if you still insist on purchasing your cocaine through mail order, don't forget to check for anthrax.

recoilmag.com

A page from the Recoil handbook...
Airplane Etiquette

Airplane travel can be a nerve-racking experience. Below are some basic tips for contributing to a more comfortable in-flight atmosphere:

- A note about boarding: officials agree that boarding is one of the most dangerous penalties in hockey, so expect to receive a five minute major for boarding, no matter the situational conditions. Arguing with flight officials about the boarding call will only result in your being ejected from the plane.

- Should a stranger start driving you crazy telling you his life story, vomiting all over him will often resolve the issue without you having to be rude.

- Try not to bother the flight staff until that gremlin out on the wing that nobody else can see really looks to be making progress in dismantling one of the jet's engines.

- Having sex in the bathroom, first class, or coach area is strictly off-limits. The only place public sex is permitted on a commercial airplane is in the cockpit. So, looks like you'd better start working on earning that pilot's license, pervert.

- The sooner you begin forcing conversation on the stranger sitting next to you, the sooner that passenger will try to move to another seat, giving you the entire armrest.

- If you need to make a tight connection, let a flight attendant know. He or she will probably think you're pretty hip for using the slang "tight" instead of "cool," and they'll let you off first.

- Use caution when retrieving items from the overhead compartments, as items tend to shapeshift during flight.

- Grab and kick at the seat in front of you; this will help keep the passengers in front of you awake and alert in case there is an emergency.

- Upon arrival, each passenger is required to immediately stand up the second the airplane comes to rest at your gate. The reasoning behind this is unclear, but it's obviously very important since everyone does it on every single flight.

- If someone is having trouble getting their bag out of the overhead compartment, fuck 'em.

LINE from page 29

three postal employees manning the service counter. As the single-file line swelled to nearly 20 patrons and the wait to upwards of 10 minutes, the intense sense of urgency that gripped many of the line members began to physically manifest itself.

"Sighing loudly is probably the most common way that people in public environments communicate to others that they, too, are distraught by the situation," explained sociologist Chris Gibbons, a leading expert on crowd hostility. "They'll roll their eyes or laugh sarcastically while shaking their head. Maybe they'll call someone on their cell phone and, talking loudly enough for everybody in line to hear it, tell the person on the other end of the phone that they're 'stuck in a stupid line at the post office.' The idea is to avoid coming right out and saying what everybody there is thinking: 'Okay, this blows.'"

Perhaps more prevalent than the obvious venting of displeasure was each line members' adamant concern that the customer heading the line react promptly when it became their turn to be helped.

"They're open down on the end!" barked one line member when patron Andre Livingston – one of the few customers who didn't appear on the verge of physical and emotional implosion – did not instantly step toward an open clerk.

"I was talking on my cell phone and didn't notice I was up," said Livingston, 34. "The guy right behind me was practically shouting at me to go, like it

> As the single-file line swelled to nearly 20 patrons and the wait to upwards of five minutes, the intense sense of urgency that gripped many of the line members began to physically manifest itself.

was a matter of life or death. I was like, 'Take it easy, dude.' It's not like I was there to defuse a bomb – just mailing a goddamned letter."

On-duty postal workers appreciated Livingston's blithe tolerance of the delay.

"Jesus, it's not like these people were Iraqis waiting in the water line," said post office clerk Sheri Miller. "Customers always get totally uptight when they have to wait in line for a couple of minutes. So five minutes of your life is wasted – so what? It's not something to get your blood pressure up about. Tell you what, don't smoke that next cigarette and you'll have that five minutes of your life back." ■

SCORES			
Agent	007	Four	20
Hill	**364**	Beer	**30**
Assassin's Creed 3		Apples	NA
Black Ops	2	Oranges	NA

LAZY from page 29

this group of youths, 78 percent lack the personal motivation needed to achieve such a goal.

"For today's angry, rebellious teen, running away from home represents the ultimate escape, the ultimate freedom – which all sounds great until they realize they're actually going to have to put in a little bit of work in order to make it happen," said Dr. Helen Hayes, a clinical psychiatrist specializing in counseling teenagers. "I don't know about your kids, but mine would starve to death before actually putting forth the thirty seconds worth of effort involved in making themselves a sandwich. So as far as them running away from home, where they'd have to fend for themselves for a change, I don't think I have too much to worry about."

Hayes cited several studies showing that today's teenagers spend an unprecedented number of hours each day watching television, surfing the web, playing video games or simply lounging around, often going to extreme lengths to avoid engaging in more physical activities such as cleaning their room, walking, riding a bicycle or even swimming.

Jeffery Skyles, a 16-year-old resident of Billings, Mont., participated in the study by answering questions during a short interview conducted by Notre Dame researchers.

"My parents are constantly on my case about my grades or the way I dress or a million other things, to the point where sometimes I just want to take off, man," said Skyles, who has never held a part-time job, babysat or mowed lawns for money. "But then I think, 'Well, if I leave home I won't have anywhere to plug in my computer to play *World of Warcraft*.' So I usually just lock my bedroom door, crank up the stereo mom just bought me and try to stick it out."

During another interview, one which took place immediately following a fight with his parents, 17-year-old Daniel Ewing of Irvine, Calif., spelled out his options for his interviewer and walked him through his reasoning.

"On one hand, yes, my dad looks like he's totally going to hit me or at least cuss me out big-time every time I bring home a failing grade or get a girl pregnant or something," said Ewing. "But run away from home? First I'd have to haul all of my dirty clothes down to the laundry room so my mom could wash everything. Then I'd have to roll all of dad's change into rolls so I'd have some money for Subway or something. Plus, I haven't really gotten around to taking my driving test yet, so I'd be having to hoof it wherever I go – and it's like ninety-five degrees out there or some shit."

Ewing then got up to adjust the temperature on the house's central air thermostat before snagging a bag of Doritos from atop the fully stocked refrigerator and plopping back down on the couch in front of his parents' 45-inch plasma screen television. ■

RECOILMAG.COM   NEWS SATIRE YOU CAN TRUST

recoil

Federal deficit forces elimination of three states

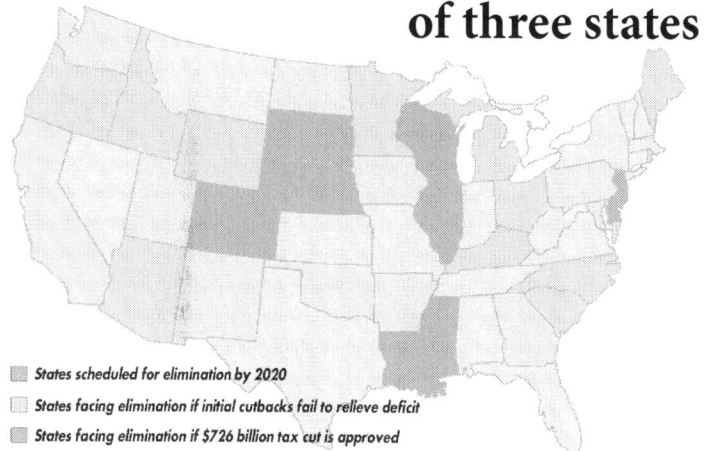

- States scheduled for elimination by 2020
- States facing elimination if initial cutbacks fail to relieve deficit
- States facing elimination if $726 billion tax cut is approved

Federal cutbacks will force the closure of Illinois in 2018, South Dakota in 2019 and New Jersey by 2020.

Washington, D.C. – Officials at the Congressional Budget Office (CBO) said Monday that the national deficit will necessitate the phasing out of three states over the next seven years.

"The bottom line is that this country cannot continue to operate in the red," CBO Director Douglas Holtz-Eakin explained flatly at a morning press conference. "Citizens may not realize it but this country has no less than fifty

> Eliminating the states is not only expected to provide relief to the federal deficit, but will also serve to strengthen the solidarity of the remaining union.

independent states. *Fifty*. In the business world, that's what is known as 'redundant overhead.'"

The cutbacks in statehood will begin when federal officials close the doors

see DEFICIT page 35

Little League pitcher intentionally walks dog

Denny's potato, patron baked

Flim flammed

Above: Dalton at the company Halloween party with his wife Julie, who is rumored to be "no prize."

Area man here with that wife of his

Hanover, N.J – According to sources, financial analyst Tim Dalton brought that wife of his to the company Halloween party the evening of Oct. 31, where the woman's crude social skills and drunken antics only served to inflate her infamy among her husband's coworkers.

"Oh great, Tim brought that wife of his with him," recognized Blake Montgomery, a mid-level manager at Nabisco, where he's worked alongside Dalton for the last six years. "If you've never met her, she's a piece of work, that woman. Don't get me wrong – you guys all know I think Tim's great and everything. But that wife of his? Let's just say she is *no prize*."

Coworkers recounted that Mrs. Dalton had not accompanied her husband to an office party since Christmas of 2009, when an incident between her and a catering attendant led to a short fistfight and an appearance by the city police.

"Oh god, *her*. I want to say [her name is] Jody or Judy or something," said receptionist Annette Gaylord, observing Dalton's socially perverse mannerisms as

> "If you've never met her, she's a piece of work, that woman," said Montgomery.

the woman pushed her way to the front of the line at the open bar. "*Julie*, that's right. The only time I've ever spoken with her she was slurring so bad that I couldn't make out her name past the first letter. I think that was the same night she tackled the janitor when he jokingly walked away with her cell phone. I don't know whether she's a drunk or just fucking weird."

The wife's surprise appearance sparked a great deal of similar speculation among Dalton's coworkers.

"It's weird because not many of us bring our spouses to office parties except for Christmas," Gaylord said offhandedly, her eyes transfixed on the blonde office-legend as the couple of five years worked the room. "Maybe Tim thought having her dressed as a zombie would somehow make her seem less crazy. So much for that idea."

Employees voiced a number of different theories as to what inspired Dalton to "drag that wife of his out of her dungeon [for]" this year's office Halloween party.

"Maybe Tim's hoping no one will

see WIFE page 35

Relief workers distribute food to customers stranded in line at Panera Bread

Sunset Hills, Missouri – Food, water and blankets were distributed by relief workers to customers stranded in line at an area Panera Bread location early Friday afternoon.

"God bless these relief people – we were all starting to think we were literally going to die of starvation right here waiting in line," said patron Avner Greenstein, 42, who could not recall exactly when he first arrived at the local franchise, but that it was "like, forever ago." "Before [the Red Cross] showed up we'd only seen a couple of rescue ambulances come through to cart away some elderly customers who must have collapsed from malnutrition before they could get served."

see PANERA page 36

Above: Red Cross volunteers distribute coffee, bread, soup and sandwiches to customers stranded in line at a local Panera Bread franchise.

page 33

WORLDWIDE HEADLINES

Acronyms give greater credibility, reports FFLS

Toledo, Ohio – A new study from FFLS suggests that companies and organizations that use acronyms to represent themselves when publishing reports are taken more seriously and given more credibility. FFLS cites various reports and resources, such as FBND and The ERH-KCN standard, as supporting evidence of the ACR effect. TRNB refutes the FFLS findings, claiming credibility stems from only the SPKR of an organization and not the ACR effect. In the past, previous research has shown that acronyms at least lead to a greater credibility of the TBN standard, but that does not conclusively show a relationship to the ACR effect.

Pastry shop explosion leaves six city blocks delicious

Concord, Mass. – A ruptured gas line was blamed Tuesday in an explosion that leveled a pastry shop, leaving at least six city blocks deliciously covered in sugar-coated flakes and creamy gourmet filling. At least four people known to be inside Tasty's Pastries bakery during the blast were missing and presumed scrumptious in the hours after the disaster. Concord police and fire departments were on the scene within minutes, but given the severity of the explosion, anticipate those inside will be frosted beyond recognition. Pedestrians walking nearby recall seeing what could only be described as a loud and intense flavor explosion. Officials have begun searching the site, but hold little optimism for finding any survivors. "My only hope is that we be able to identify my employees." said Gerry Robertson, owner of Tasty's Pastries, who guesses the recovery search will uncover a greater-than-usual amount of crème brûlée.

Poorly worded U.N. resolution inadvertently sends more AIDS to Africa

New York, N.Y. – An unfortunately drafted U.N. resolution passed late last month has pledged an additional 15 billion cases of AIDS to Africa, making the epidemic even more perilous on a continent already ripe with suffering. After meeting with African leaders, UNAIDS, the Joint United Nations Program on HIV/AIDS, recommended to the U.N. General Assembly an increase in aid to Africa by $15 billion a year for the next 25 years by 2015 to mitigate the impact of the epidemic. Unfortunately, in a gaffe that has officials of the international organization smacking their foreheads, a series of typographical errors on the part of the drafters means the resolution will afflict an additional 15 billion humans with the virus that causes AIDS over the next 25 years, causing much greater suffering from the disease on the continent. "Obviously, this is not what we had in mind," said Michel Sidibe, executive director of UNAIDS. "We will have a longer fight ahead of us now." UNAIDS is now calling upon the U.N. to pledge an increase of more than $30 billion a year to combat the even greater damage that will be caused by the erroneous resolution.

Serial killer keeps victim's head on a swivel

Brooklyn, N.Y. – James Lee Brant, an as-of-yet uncaught serial killer accused of at least five murders in New York City over the past three months, is reported to be an extremely aware, cautious and vigilant killer known for keeping his victims' heads on a swivel after beheading them with a hacksaw, authorities said Thursday. "When you're on the run from the law, it's important to keep your head on a swivel – always remaining aware of your surroundings and noting any present threats. Evidence suggests that Brant takes this concept to the next level, as several of his alleged victims have been found with their disembodied heads attached to swivels," said Detective David Holmes, an NYPD authority assigned to the case. "Living in New York during such dangerous times, there's nothing wrong with insisting your acquaintances keep their heads on a swivel, but this is going too far."

Band you've never heard of announces reunion tour

San Francisco, Calif. – Broken Mirrorball, a little-known San Francisco Bay-area band you've never even heard of, announced plans for a reunion tour this week. "After twelve years apart, we figured it was time to put our differences aside and hit the road," noted Neil Campanelli, the band's frontman, whose name may seem vaguely familiar, but rest assured, you're thinking of someone else. The never-signed three-piece, influenced by Alice In Chains, Pantera and several other bands you have actually heard of, claimed the decision to tour again was, above all, a selfless one. Said bassist Derek Gorman: "We owe this to our fan base. They've been waiting a really long time to see us back together." Sources close to the band confirmed that the "fan base" referenced by Gorman consists of a handful of old community college acquaintances and four former girlfriends, all of whom lost touch with the band in the late 1990s. The reunion tour will see the trio performing their derivative brand of forgettable guitar rock in several towns you've never heard of, including Randsburg, Lytle Creek, and Fields Landing. ∎

EDITORIAL

Sometimes you just have to sit down and eat an entire rotisserie chicken

By Jim Brack

For the most part, life can be almost excruciatingly monotonous most of the time. Every day it's the same thing: get up, go to work, come home, eat dinner, relax for a couple of hours and then go to bed. Even those youngsters who are hell-bent on never settling down usually fall into the routine eventually – and understandably so. After all, who in the hell has the energy for spontaneity these days? Still, the desire to escape the workaday routine can get pretty overwhelming over time. That's why I firmly believe that sometimes you just have to sit down and eat an entire rotisserie chicken.

When I was younger, my parents regularly discouraged – in fact, forbade – me from sitting down with a freshly cooked chicken and devouring the whole thing in one session. Sure, it was an odd restriction, but then again parents are known to make up some pretty damn weird rules.

Of course, now that I'm all grown up and on my own, I need not worry about anyone compromising my endeavor to eat a two-pound chicken from start to finish. I can and will eat an entire chicken whenever the urge strikes me, which tends to be fairly often.

Now when I say a person would do well to sit down and eat an entire rotisserie chicken every so often, I'm not talking about whipping up a huge Thanksgiving-style feast with potatoes and stuffing and such, and then eating the entire main course along with helpings of the side-dishes. No, I'm talking about ingesting

> One chair, one chicken, one fork and a full shaker of salt. Now that's what I call living.

just a chicken. One chair, one chicken, one fork and a full shaker of salt. Now that's what I call living.

Sure, having variety in your diet is great for maybe 28 or 29 days out of the month – but letting loose a couple times every month with an all-poultry meal is one of the surest and most cost-effective ways I know for breaking up your daily grind.

In practice, following through with the self-satisfying and therapeutic mission I've outlined here is a lot easier than back in the days when you'd have to stand over the oven with a baster in your hand for half a day cooking the damn thing. Nowadays, your local supermarket puts out about 50 of these puppies an hour, so you can just swing by and pick one up for five bucks on your way home from work. Oftentimes I'll pick up a 12-pack of beer, too – for later. But that indeed is a whole other column for a whole other day. Right now I'm focusing on the chicken.

When you add up all of these pros for semi-regularly consuming a fully-grown bird in under 15 minutes, the argument will no doubt seem convincing. However, if you're still at odds with yourself regarding the wisdom of the undertaking, I suggest you just bite the bullet and give it a try once. It can't kill you. And I think you'll see how rewarding it is to look down at that pile of bones and skin and know that, whatever else happened or happens to you today, you've eaten an entire chicken. ∎

> You'll see how rewarding it is to look down at that pile of bones and skin and know that, whatever else happened or happens to you today, you've eaten an entire chicken.

page 34

PANERA from page 33

Red Cross rescue crews assembled in the Panera parking lot after reports from the community suggested that the line at the popular fast-casual restaurant had reached a disastrous level during a heavier-than-expected lunch surge.

"The customers seem determined to wait it out, but they're really grateful that we're out here providing them with such crude provisions as soup, sandwiches and coffee to help sustain them until they can at least get inside the building," said Red Cross volunteer Kevin Lear.

"Obviously, anyone standing in this line is in need of some serious help," Lear added.

Standing near the end of a line of customers extending outside and around the corner of the eatery, Janelle Dryer said that she was "willing to take [her] chances" acquiring nourishment at Panera rather than make the unbearable 100-yard trek to an overstaffed Arby's located immediately adjacent to Panera Bread.

"I don't think any of the people around me [in line] are even considering just giving up like that," Dryer said. ∎

WIFE from page 33

recognize her in that costume," observed Montgomery, who as a neighbor claimed to know the Daltons best among the partygoers. "Fat chance. Between the hundred-proof breath and that crazy witch-cackle laugh of hers, she's pretty tough to miss. All you have to do is listen: she's one of those people who won't even take yes for an answer – just nonstop 'blah blah blah blah blah' at top volume. I honestly don't know how [Tim] lives with that woman."

"Maybe they're trying to save their marriage by doing more things together," theorized accountant Janet Smith. Noting Dalton's body language, Smith conceded: "Except Tim looks as if he's looking for somebody to save *him*." ∎

DEFICIT from page 33

on the state of Illinois on Dec. 31, 2018, shutting down our 21st state's government agencies and encouraging businesses and residents to relocate to one of the 49 states remaining in operation. South Dakota will incur a similar shutdown in 2019 and New Jersey in 2020.

Holtz-Eakin said that eliminating the states is not only expected to provide relief to the federal deficit, but will also serve to strengthen the solidarity of the remaining union.

"Trimming this prize fighter of a nation down to a lean forty-seven [states] is key to staying competitive in the current global marketplace," said Holtz-Eakin. "Naturally, homeland security will be improved because a smaller country is that much easier to defend than a big one."

CBO public relations manager Theodore Hadley said that following each state's closure, independent contractors will be commissioned to liquidate the state's natural resources and prepare the lot to be used by the federal government as storage space.

Although initial cutbacks in statehood will leave a majority of U.S. citizens unaffected, CBO warned that failure to balance the federal budget could force Washington to let go of several more states including Michigan, Delaware, Kentucky, Wyoming, Minnesota, Ohio, Arizona, Oregon, Idaho, Maine and North and South Carolina.

"You can't continue to increase spending while tax revenues remain stagnant – something had to give," said Hadley. "It comes down to simple choices: would you rather have health care or Delaware? Maybe I'm nuts but I think most Americans would say health care."

Outspoken opponent of the plan Congressman Tom Osborne (R-NE) recently argued that, logistical problems aside, CBO's plan is flawed in that it makes no provision for limiting federal spending.

"While I admire their creativity on this matter, CBO's failure to address our out-of-control federal spending is grossly negligent at best," said Osborne.

Rebuffing the criticism, Holtz-Eakin called Osborne "short-sighted" before asking a reporter exactly which state Osborne represents and scribbling the answer onto his legal pad. Holtz-Eakin later named Nebraska along with four other states when indicating that more cutbacks may be required in the future. ∎

HOROSCOPES

Pisces (February 19 to March 20)
Your strong foot-gnawing fetish could be construed as an unconscious predilection towards cannibalism – an eating habit strongly contradicting your vegetarian diet. I'd offer words of advice, but since most Pisces claiming to be "vegetarian" still consume fish, well, they're just too far out of touch with reason for me to even worry about saving them. I won't waste my time; there are other stars in the sky more worthy of my attention.

Aries (March 21 to April 19)
Sexual ninja Aries has incredible difficulty finding sparring partners for those lengthy bedroom workouts; not everyone is into prolonged efforts into tricking the procreation instincts of the body for the sole purpose of inciting momentary pleasure. Realize that in today's fast-paced lifestyle, people working 14-hour days don't have time to sleep, let alone go 15 rounds in the sack every night just to achieve 15 seconds of euphoria.

Taurus (April 20 to May 20)
Any sports magazine calendar will confirm that NFL field-goal kickers and World Cup soccer goalies are predominately Taurus – tunnel-visioned snobs who believe in doing only one thing but doing it well. Fine; you Taurus freaks let us peasants do the grunt work, but you better be damn sharp when it comes time to showcase your specialized talent, or expect mass ridicule from everyone that's counting on you.

Gemini (May 21 to June 20)
Gemini's navigationally challenged nature demands declining employment at gas stations. Rather than purchasing one of the $1.29 maps at the cash register's immediate right, lost travelers depend on benzene jockeys for traffic guidance, and the last thing we need is your direction-dyslexic ass telling us which way is north.

Cancer (June 21 to July 22)
World traveling Cancer has too much blind faith in the safety of commercial aviation. Sure those winged tubes have been thwarting King Physics for years while maintaining a better safety rating than automobile travel, but when the Great Horn honks out "Taps" in your key, bear in mind that most would rather die ON the ground than because of it.

Leo (July 23 to August 22)
Your reckless disregard for the menace of STDs makes you statistically destined for infection; a Leo drinking his/her way into an unprotected one night stand is as doomed as a colorblind epicure picking mushrooms without a field guide. Playing Russian roulette with your procreation equipment is big fun until mathematical inevitability causes your duties on the toilet to indicate a BURNING need to see a doctor. Superglue your zipper at once.

Virgo (August 23 to September 22)
Michigan winter will soon cause seasonally-saddened Virgo to take a cruise; indeed, there's nothing like getting set afloat aboard a $17 million raft with nothing to do except indulge in sun, sex and slot machines. Be sure to bone up on International Waters law loopholes before setting sail, so as to properly exploit the lack of Big Brother's policing.

Libra (September 23 to October 22)
The Death Rattle isn't a toy the Grim Reaper played with as an infant, it's the body's way of warning you that your next breath will indeed be your last. And while typically viewed as a sound you'd rather not hear any time soon, the Death Rattle would be a breath of fresh audio air in a week when you can expect a significant amount of bitching streaming from the lips of your significant other.

Scorpio (October 23 to November 21)
Scorpio can't help but feel apprehensive about the effectiveness of the upcoming Presidential administration. Realize that whichever yahoo eventually does become President will merely be another manufactured carburetor for the engine of a government locked on cruise control at 40 MPH in the left lane of the country's progress – we could spend the next century electing and installing new parts, but the whole vehicle needs to be replaced by the electric car.

Sagittarius (November 22 to December 21)
Staying off incarceration is a top priority for homophobic Sagittarius; the limited options provided by our gender-segregated penal system would no doubt force strange and unnatural self-experimentations. And considering that guards rarely leave inmates alone with an entire apple pie, creative stimulation might require the use of more available, more abrasive apparatuses. Abiding by society's laws seems a fair price for avoiding all that.

Capricorn (December 22 to January 19)
Brainiac Capricorn should spend a little less time at the library and a little more time getting a life. What good is knowing by memory the atomic weight of Tungsten and the optimum PH value for growing tomatoes if you still live with your parents and consistently get fired from your paper routes? Lay off the weed and start getting interested in greed like everybody else.

Aquarius (January 20 to February 18)
Aquarius' curious mind has read enough Darwin and Sagan to understand man's evolution from amphibian to mammal. Turning to atheism out of pure logic seems wise, but even a mild familiarity with the cryptic words of Revelations should be enough to scare you into making whatever promises are necessary to ensure that if indeed the Great Bullfrog ever does croak, you've reserved a spot on one of those big, white lily pads in the sky.

MUSIC
Area musicians frustrated by their city's lack of a scene, drugs

Madison, Wis. – Discouraged as much by the recent closing of two downtown live music venues as by the continued scarcity of recreational narcotics, area musicians expressed frustration Friday over their community's failure to support a virile music scene or a decent drug market.

"The scene in Madison is pretty lame, always has been," said Matt Brassen, singer and guitarist for the emo punk three-piece Frog Dash In Frisco and seven-year veteran of the local club scene. "Even when The Front and The Black Room were open and running bands, the scene around here was still shit. Nobody's going to shows, the radio stations won't touch [local music] and you just about have to kidnap a newspaper editor's kid to get a story done on your band."

"The only thing harder than trying to get signed out of this town is finding a good [drug] hookup," added Brassen, 25, noting the poor availability of press, gigs and controlled substances in the Madison area. "The cops made a major [drug] bust this summer and ever since there's been like nothing around. Not only has the music scene dried up, but so have everyone's connections."

Brassen is not alone in his frustration. Other area musicians agreed that February's almost simultaneous closing of The Front and The Black Room – clubs that featured live local bands and acoustic acts at least four nights a week – coupled with the effects of Feb. 14's drug-related arrests, has delivered a crippling one-two punch to Madison's already struggling music and drug scenes.

"It was already hard enough to book a show or score a dimebag in this town," said local pop folk singer/songwriter Jesse Arndt, 29. "Now with these clubs going down and most of [drug dealer] Aaron [Smith]'s crew in lockdown, artists like myself are finding themselves only able to perform or hook up like once a month. *Maybe* twice."

Arndt then excused himself from the interview and used a nearby payphone to make a series of brief telephone calls regarding an undisclosed subject matter.

Neil Abraham, promotion director for The Annex, a 250-seat club that's become Madison's lone live music venue, disagreed with the majority consensus that the current scene offers few options for local bands looking to perform.

> "The only thing harder than trying to get signed out of this town is finding a good [drug] hookup," added Brassen.

Above: Local band Frog Dash In Frisco.

"The Annex asks local bands to open for national touring acts all the time, which is a tremendous opportunity," said Abraham. "To play these big shows for a lot of people – in a lot of markets that's an opportunity that's just not available to bands."

Arndt argued that Abraham's claim is not as exciting as it may appear.

"Opening for a national [band] at The Annex doesn't do shit for a band," said Arndt. "You don't get paid anything and you end up playing at like eight-thirty when nobody's even there yet. It's always a let down. It's not like the headliner's label is there looking at you or anything. Most of the time you don't even get to meet the band. And on the off chance that you do, it's usually completely embarrassing because they always ask you to hook them up and here you can't even score any for yourself."■

A page from the Recoil handbook...
Guide To Safe Driving

Exercising constant caution behind the wheel is one's best defense against automobile accidents. Here are some tips to help keep you and your vehicle in one piece:

• Before driving, make sure the safety is in the "ON" position on all of your guns.

• To ensure safe, evenly worn treads, install anti-lock breaks on two tires and ultra-lock brakes on the others.

• Even though you have rolled your windows down, always keep your doors locked when performing drive-by shootings.

• Teenage drivers are involved in a disproportionate number of fatal crashes. Running these self-centered assholes off the road will ultimately save lives.

• Concentration is the single, most important factor in safe driving. Make sure you're immersed in a game of Milton-Bradley's "Concentration" with a passenger whenever driving.

• Drive defensively. If your wife asks you to make a right turn, tell her you're tired of her constant questioning and that where you go after work is your business.

• High winds make driving difficult; you may find that you'll have more control using a long iron off the tee instead.

• Respect older drivers. They have a right to be on the road, or, when they mistake the gas for the brake, a crowded sidewalk.

• If you are James Bond, make sure your Aston Martin DB5's Stinger missiles are fully armed before setting off on your drive to a criminal mastermind's compound.

• Share the road! If we all work together, we can finally extertiminate every last bicyclist and pedestrian for good.

• Be aware that backing up on the shoulder of expressways is not legal unless you are absolutely sure you saw something shiny back there.

• Intense, emotional or complicated text communications can help keep you awake while driving.

• In heavy rain, your tires may begin to "hydroplane." If this happens, increase speed to achieve flight. Decelerate and safely touch down only when roadway dries.

• When the red lights near train tracks begin blinking it means drivers only have a few more seconds to dart across the tracks before getting stuck waiting for the train to pass for God knows how long.

• If you are pulled over by a police officer, get out of your car and, after tucking one hand inside your coat for warmth, quickly rush up to the police car's driver window so the officer doesn't have to get out of his vehicle.

• When traveling abroad, keep in mind that in many countries, rear-end collisions are likely to be an early stage of that culture's mating ritual.

• When your high-speed chase through a construction site inevitably takes you airborne, keep both hands on the steering wheel as you and your passenger look at each other for a mid-flight scream.

• When experiencing a tire blowout, you should buy as many tires as you can afford before the tire store's blowout sale is over.

• When in doubt, always refer back to the two golden rules of driving: there is always enough time, and there is always enough room.

RECOILMAG.COM　　NEWS SATIRE YOU CAN TRUST

recoil

Unisom now available in liquid form

Kristen Stewart's management wants to distance her from themselves

quikSTAT
Which nostalgic candies are regaining popularity?
- Circus Peanuts
- Tripe Bites
- Truffle Lumps
- Plague O'Plenty
- Glue Balls
- Rancid Snaps
- Semi-Sweet Innards
- Reese Witherspoon

History teacher repeats himself

Madison, Wis. – Eighth grade American History teacher Michael Rose tends to repeat himself during lectures regarding details of World War II battles, students told reporters this morning following third period. "This is the third day this semester that Mister Rose has gone over the importance that the weather – Typhoon Louise, which hit Okinawa without warning on Oct. 9, 1945 – seriously impacted the planned invasion of Japan," said sophomore Adam Davies. "You know how I know all that? Because he's told us this twice already today."

Pointy stick appointed U.S. Defense Secretary

Washington, D.C. – In a surprise move Monday, U.S. President George W. Bush appointed a sharp, pointy stick as the next Secretary of Defense, head of all armed service and military matters for the United States. Having previously spent the entirety of its career as part of the environment, the three-foot-long former tree limb is expected to bring fresh ideas and perspective to the position formerly held by Robert M. Gates. While fielding questions during a Monday morning press conference, the pointy stick was asked specifically his plans for distributing the $420 billion annual budget now under its command, to which the slightly curved branch lightheartedly responded: "I realized that even if *I* do, money doesn't simply grow on trees." The pointy stick is expected to be quickly confirmed by the senate early next week. ∎

Above: Members of the iconic '80s rock band.

Mötley Crüe theme park brings to life the world of four drunken criminals

Hollywood, Calif. – Legendary 1980s hair metal band Mötley Crüe has partnered with NBCUniversal to create a new theme park inside Universal Studios Los Angeles: "Mötley Crüe's Wild Side," where visitors will get to experience what it's like inside the drug-fueled world of the four multiple felons who founded the legendary and controversial rock band.

"It's every Crüe fan's fantasy to live the lives of these four troubled young alcoholic lunatics who rose to notable prominence in the music industry during the eighties," said NBCUniversal public relations director James Beal. "Visitors to the new attraction will get to experience firsthand what it's like to be coked to the gills twenty-four-seven, gallivanting around the world while unapologetically committing arson, spousal abuse, vehicular manslaughter and instigating a riot, as well as surviving heroin overdoses – all while remaining the most popular rock act of the decade."

Also available inside the detailed recreation will be a gift shop, stripper cages and a highly unsterile tattoo parlor.

Presented as an R-rated version

see CRUE page 40

Band's lighting more intelligent than drummer

Above: The act's intellectually challenged drummer Scott McCloud.

New York, N.Y. – Members of the alternative rock cover band Scorned Corn & the Pseudo-Somethings expressed opinions Friday that the band's state-of-the-art lighting system possesses a more advanced level of intelligence than that of their drummer, 32-year-old Scott McCloud.

"On stage we run four MojoScan intelligent lights, which I sometimes think are actually smarter than that balloonhead drummer of ours – who, incidentally, managed to lock the keys in our van with the motor running last night at a truck stop outside Cleveland," said Dave Keys, bassist for the New York-based act. "Granted, drummers in general are usually a pretty low-brow lot, but Scott's a space-case like no other. Don't get me wrong, we love the guy, it's just that he makes Jessica Simpson look like Stephen Hawking."

Singer Al Prevo agreed that the circuitry found within the MojoScan units and control board consistently proves more adept at recalling and processing information than the synapses comprising McCloud's cerebellum.

"Those I-Beams [sic]

"You can count on [the lights] to run the same patterns for each song every night, without exception," said Prevo.

are fully programmable and have a ton of memory, so you can count on them to run the same patterns for each song

see LIGHTING page 38

Above: Scorned Corn & the Pseudo-Somethings' stage setup, which includes four MojoScan intelligent lighting units.

page 37

LIGHTING from page 37

every night, without exception," said Prevo, who founded the band with Keys in 1999. "Scott, on the other hand, can somehow manage to forget the bridge part to 'Whole Lotta Love' every other time we play it. I don't know what that boy did to those poor brain cells of his, but let's just say most of them don't answer the phone anymore, if you know what I mean."

Guitarist Greg Adamski said that intelligence is only one area in which the act's high-tech lighting equipment outshines McCloud.

"Not only is our lighting system smarter than Scott, but it often shows a lot more artistic sense and versatility," said Adamski. "With the push of a button, the MojoScans are capable of designing their own patterns and sequences. Then there's Scott, who can't even come up with his own drum parts for our original [songs]. Seriously, one of us usually has to write the beats and fills because Scott can't make up his own stuff."

Added Adamski: "It's pretty sad to think that artificial intelligence would actually be a step up for Scott."

Keys noted that members of the band also find their lighting system easier to work with than McCloud.

"A lot of people think you need to be some kind of genius to run a lightshow that uses intelligent lights, but the MojoScan system was designed to be simple to use," said Keys. "The lights are a breeze to set up and the [control] board is really simple to operate. In fact, working with the MojoScans is a hell of a lot easier than working with Scott, who's always forgetting rehearsals or showing up late for gigs saying he got lost. If he's not in jail that week for drunk driving, that is."

Although McCloud routinely displays less intelligence, creativity and reliability than the band's stage lighting, Keys said the band currently has no intention of replacing their longtime drummer.

"Scott may be far and away the dimmest bulb on our stage, but this band is a family, and you don't kick a member of your family to the curb just because he's a little slow," said Keys, watching from afar as McCloud repeatedly circled the stage looking for his drumsticks.

"Okay, maybe a lot slow," Keys added before suggesting to McCloud that he look in the back pocket of his jeans. ■

ADVICE

Ask A...
Bottle Return Machine

Dear Bottle Return Machine,
Are people who contribute to the environment by recycling privy to any tax breaks?–
Ten Cents At A Time, Janesville, Wis.

Dear Ten Cents,
Please insert bottom of container first. Insert empty can. Push receipt button when finished. **PLEASE WAIT** Can't read barcode, try bottom first. Remove rejected can. Push receipt button when finished. **PLEASE WAIT** Bin full, can't accept more containers. Please ask for assistance. Push receipt button when finished. Printing receipt. **PLEASE WAIT OUT OF PAPER**

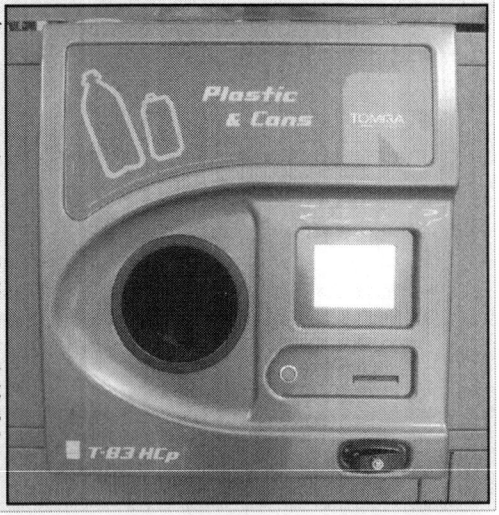

WORLDWIDE HEADLINES

Card counter reveals secret: there are 52 cards

Las Vegas, Nev. – Las Vegas native and semi-professional blackjack player Carl Smith's new book, *What the Casinos Don't Want You to Know*, reveals the secret behind his mysterious card-counting technique. "Each deck the casinos use contains fifty-two cards," the 44-year-old Smith discloses in Chapter One: The Big Secret. Smith goes on to explain how this knowledge can be used to gain an advantage over the house: "What I do is announce the count, just to mentally throw the dealer off his game. I'll say, 'There are fifty-two cards in that deck. Fifty-two.' The dealer will often look back at me in complete bewilderment. That's when I place my bet."

Even after getting to know him, area man still seems like complete prick

Cleveland, Ohio – Area man Ken Crombie still seems like a complete prick, reported acquaintance Tyler Morgan after spending nearly five hours getting to know the 32-year-old insurance salesman earlier this week. Morgan, who dismissed his initial impression of Crombie based on mutual friend Steve Spruance's insistence that "(Crombie) is cool, you just have get to know him," spent Saturday afternoon having lunch and playing golf with both Crombie and Spruance. This meeting, however, only confirmed Morgan's negative impression of Crombie. "He stiffed our waitress on the tip, cheated on 'out of bounds' rules and was giving the finger to nearly everyone on the golf course for no apparent reason," said Morgan of Crombie's abrasive persona. "What a fucking asshole."

Surgeon dad routinely kicking son's ass at *Operation*

Akron, Ohio – Dr. Stuart Johnson, a 50-year-old medical practitioner specializing in reconstructive bone surgery, routinely kicks his six-year-old son Colin's ass at *Operation*, Milton Bradley's battery-operated game of physical skill that challenges players' nerves and hand-eye coordination. "Just think son, after seven years of college and three years of residency, you could be this good at the game too," joked Dr. Johnson, using the tweezers to skillfully remove the white plastic slice of bread – known as the Bread Basket, the game's most difficult piece to remove – increasing his already substantial 600-point lead over his son by another 1,000 points. "In real life, I'd bill the patient sixty thousand dollars for that," added Dr. Johnson, failing to notice the tears streaming from his son's eyes as the first grader's shaking hand caused the buzzer to sound after failing to remove the Adam's Apple on his fourth attempt.

Spammer running out of innovative ways to spell 'Cialis'

St. Paul, Minn. – In what may signify trouble for the American pharmaceutical industry, professional spammer Ken Paulsen has confessed he's quickly running out of innovative ways to spell "Cialis" in his e-mail subject headings. "Spam filter technology is just getting too advanced," claimed Paulsen. "Last week I bombarded eight-hundred-thousand AOL accounts with 'C!@LI$ – just 75 cents/pill!!!' and easily ninety-five percent of the e-mails bounced back." Other recently rejected spellings of the popular male virility drug include "C.I.^.L;is," "cI*AL-1s," and the phonetically-based "see-AH-liss." The U.S. Food and Drug Administration (FDA) has taken stock of the situation, and believes Paulsen's dilemma is symptomatic of a bigger issue. Said FDA Commissioner Andrew von Eschenbach: "If Americans are denied access to drugs like Cialis or Rogaine from internet-based middlemen using dubious bulk mailing campaigns, where are they supposed to go to fill their prescriptions?"

Real-life *Ratatouille* rat seasons cordon bleu with saliva, feces

New York, N.Y. – Manhattan's Orange Pepper Bistro found life imitating art yesterday evening when a real-life Ratatouille rat scurried across the kitchen's countertop and seasoned a veal cordon bleu dish with its own saliva and feces. "In all my years here at the restaurant, I've never seen anything so remarkable," said sous-chef Robert McTeague. "It's like I was watching the hit Pixar film take place at my very own prep station." McTeague described the rodent as being similar to *Ratatouille*'s loveable hero Remy, only without the capacity for speech, comic timing or cognitive reasoning ability. Despite these limitations, the furry visitor managed to both gnaw at and defecate on the $48 ham and cheese-infused entrée, not unlike a miniaturized, disease-ridden Wolfgang Puck. Noted McTeague: "Were it not in violation of fourteen separate health codes, we'd get rid of Alejandro and set the little critter up on dessert duty."

Culver City consults the band Starship for urban development recommendations

Culver City, Calif. – In an effort to reinvent itself as a thriving metropolitan center, Culver City, Calif., has sought out '80s music ensemble Starship to provide a series of urban development recommendations. Says Mayor Gary Silbiger, "Although Culver is now ninety years old, our population sits at a mere thirty-nine thousand people. We need to build this city, and if anyone knows how to meet that goal, it's the civic-minded partnership of Grace Slick, Mickey Thomas, Craig Chaquico and Donny Baldwin." Starship, which was also named both Jefferson Airplane and Jefferson Starship at different times, has already submitted a number of proposals, including a revised economic infrastructure, a tighter end-date for the long-delayed Expo Line rail system, and an incessant stream of tepid, corporate synth-pop passing itself off as relevant, anti-establishment rock 'n' roll. ■

SELF-HELP
Sensitivity Meter

Are you emotionally equipped to handle human interaction? 
Zoological studies have shown that cruelty is a trait universally common to all mammals at every level of maturity. Consequentially, navigating today's sea of emotional storms demands that one develop a strong mental hull. Find out how thick of a skin you've evolved by gauging your reaction to the following scenarios. Assign yourself three points for every answer of A, two points for B, one point for C and zero points for every D.

Which of these unexpected events would provoke the most personal grief?
A. An immediate family member is killed by a drunk driver.
B. A member of your favorite boy band is struck by tragedy.
C. Your cellblock starts cracking down on prison rape.
D. Your dental hygienist gets breast reduction surgery.

Which verbal exchange do you find the most embarrassing?
A. Confessing your sins to a priest or lawyer.
B. That part of the meeting when you have to introduce yourself as being an alcoholic.
C. Admitting to your doctor that you really don't mind the itching and swelling.
D. Explaining to the cop how your pants got up in the tree in the first place.

What would you do if a friend mentioned he's considering suicide? 
A. Phone police in a panic; refuse to leave his side until he's counseled.
B. Pretend you didn't hear him and quickly change the subject.
C. Delicately explain that killing someone else might make him feel better.
D. Understand and support his decision; assist.

Which situation would you find most insulting? 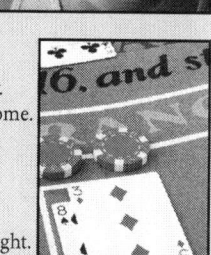
A. Having your sexual preference questioned.
B. Being asked if you are pregnant because of your obesity.
C. Someone questioning your sobriety before you drive home.
D. Reading **Recoil**.

Which scene's sheer beauty could bring you to tears?
A. Children playing in a field on Sunday morning.
B. A refrigerator completely filled with beer on Saturday night.
C. A face card after doubling down on eleven.
D. Anything while on mushrooms.

How do you best express your emotions?
A. Writing a daily blog.
B. Presenting thoroughly perverted performance art.
C. Randomly demeaning or beating your spouse.
D. Systematically executing international genocide.

If you scored...
18-15: You are a delicate flower struggling to survive in an emotionally barren wasteland. Calm your emotive hyperactivity by gobbling Prozac like it's popcorn, before you cry yourself into dehydration.
14-10: No, you're not exactly a geyser of drama drawing from a seemingly endless tear reserve, but consider your lack of party invites a hint that you're a bit too emotionally unstable to appear in public.
9-5: Good for – you you're rational enough to know that there is a specific time and place for expressing emotion: on bowling night, after your fifth round of Blatz.
4-0: You must be of Vulcan descent. Take pride in your ability to repress public displays of emotion, even if it's only because years of plastic surgery have soldered your tear ducts shut.

CHARITY

Above: Mentor Joel Jarvis. (Inset: Mentee Keith Senchuck.)

Area man a mentor to some poor bastard

Cleveland, Ohio – Unemployed area resident Joel Jarvis, 58, is a volunteer mentor to some poor bastard named Keith Senchuck, a local 14-year-old whose father abandoned him before he was born, sources confirmed Tuesday.

"Mister Jarvis has been involved with mentoring young Keith for almost three months now, frequently taking him to the library or out on scavenger hunts to collect and recycle aluminum cans or to salvage and sell copper wiring and whatnot," said Gale Pierce, a representative of the United Way of Greater Cleveland, who organizes and watches over each mentor-mentee relationship in the organization's program. "Mister Jarvis may be a man of limited means and prospects – such as a steady income – but he's always more than happy to spend time with Keith by taking him along to help with [Jarvis'] projects."

> "What had originally began as inane drunk-talk between friends eventually blossomed into what we're seeing double of here today, whatever this is."

The United Way's mentorship program connects children who are at-risk or in need of a role model with adults who are willing to help prepare the mentee for oncoming challenges in life through psychological support.

"A prospective mentor's most important qualification is that he or she be willing to donate their personal time – something Mister Jarvis apparently has more than enough of," explained Pierce, describing the bedraggled former landscaping assistant as "very eager" to be assigned a protégé immediately upon completing two one-hour mentor training courses. "[Jarvis] said something about having 'a lot of work that needed to be done,' which I assume meant he was excited about imparting his knowledge, wisdom and experience upon a child in need. And from everything Keith has told me, his mentor is definitely spending *plenty* of time with him."

Senchuck, who has never met his biological father, agreed that Jarvis has been more than generous in regards to taking time to be involved in the estranged high school sophomore's life.

"Even when we aren't out making cardboard signs on street corners, collecting hubcaps or selling car radios at pawn shops, Joel is always hanging around our apartment, just chilling out, watching cable TV, using the phone or doing his laundry or whatever," said Senchuck, detailing Jarvis' steadfast commitment to his role as a mentor. "Joel's always wanting to cook for me, too. Even after I'm totally stuffed, he's always in the kitchen rummaging through the refrigerator for food. I've never seen *anyone* who can eat as much as Joel can."

Senchuck's mother, Maria, who works an afternoon factory job full-time in order to provide for her son, said that although she's yet to be formally introduced to Jarvis, she takes relief in knowing that her son has an adult male in his life from whom to draw influence.

"I'm yet to meet 'Uncle Joel,' but Keith says he's an older gentleman who apparently likes backpacking and camping, and really loves to talk – to Keith, to the dog, to himself, to the toaster, whatever," said Maria Senchuck. "The man must really like to go shopping, too, because Keith says he has his own personal shopping cart that they push

see **MENTOR** page 40

page 39

Vet drinks more before 9 a.m. than most people drink all day

Allentown, Penn. – Retired U.S. Army Sergeant Henry "Hank" O'Boyle regularly consumes more alcohol before 9 a.m. than the average person drinks in an entire day, sources reported Monday. "Usually, he's half in the bag before I even leave for work," said Tom Wilmont, who has resided next to O'Boyle for eight years. "And he's usually still going at it when I get home. You've got to admire that sort of dedication in a man."

Woman considered dead by every conceivable criteria still pulling arm on slot machine

Las Vegas, Nev. – Though pronounced legally dead by several on-hand physicians, Dorothy Melville, 68, continues to pull the arm on the quarter Haywire slot machine that the Philadelphia native has been playing since her arrival at the Stardust Hotel & Casino two days ago, sources report. "No pulse, not breathing, rigor mortis setting in – medically, it makes no sense," said Dr. Herbert Holland, a vacationing Detroit physician who examined the still-moving body of Melville. "Then again, this is Vegas. Anything can happen!" At time of press, sources could not confirm reports that Melville's body had moved up to playing two machines simultaneously.

Bikini waxer strike becoming hairy situation

MENTOR from page 39

along with them wherever they go. I'm just thankful that Keith now has a male role model that he can look up to and trust for guidance in learning the value of a dollar, being responsible, establishing credibility and showing determination during times of hardship."

Despite spending large amounts of time with Jarvis, Senchuck admitted that he knows very little about his mentor's past, family, friends, hobbies, place of residence or future goals.

"I've never come right out and asked him, but I'm pretty sure Joel doesn't own a car," Senchuck stated in an uncertain tone after being asked personal questions regarding Jarvis. "Only because any time we go anywhere we're always on foot – or we take the bus. But I could be wrong about that because I asked Joel if he could teach me to drive and he said he thought he knew of a way he could get his hands on a car for a few hours – one that he wouldn't care if I accidentally dinged it up a bit while practicing. Then he pulled a wire clothes hanger out of one of his backpacks and bent it until it was long and straight with a little loop on the end of it. I'm not entirely sure what all that was about."

Added Senchuck: "I think he might be into collecting coins, too, because he's always digging around in our change jar at the apartment." ■

CRUE from page 37

of Universal Studios' popular "The Wizarding World of Harry Potter" attraction in Orlando, "Mötley Crüe's Wild Side" aims to recreate and place the visitor in the middle of memorable events that occurred during the band's drug-addled heyday of the 1980s.

"'Wild Side' strives to replicate the provocative visual presence and over-the-top hedonistic reputation by letting visitors relive incidents involving each individual member – Vince Neil, Nikki Sixx, Tommy Lee and Mick Mars – as these four perpetually inebriated lawbreakers somehow soiled their way to fame and fortune," said Beal.

According to Beal, the idea for the Mötley Crüe theme park came together following the overwhelming reception of the band's best-selling, tell-all autobiography, *The Dirt: Confessions of the World's Most Notorious Rock Band*, which piqued interest in the band's reckless history and rekindled the band's popularity during the new millennium.

"[With *The Dirt*] fans got a true glimpse into the fascinatingly anarchic world of four narcissistic, uneducated drunks during the pinnacle of their success," said Beal. "Readers were captivated by the revelations about what was actually going on behind the scenes during the Mötley Crüe dynasty years. Moreover, they wished that *they* could be the irresponsible, depraved, borderline-talented musicians who could stumble their way through enormously successful careers without displaying a hint of self-control or regard for anyone but themselves. Now there is a place where fans can come live out those dreams."

Among the many attractions at "Mötley Crüe's Wild Side" will be an exact replica of Hollywood's famous Whiskey-A-Go-Go, the nightclub that helped launch the band's popularity. Inside the recreated set, visitors will be served free cocktails and be able to purchase elicit drugs from on-set actors. Visitors will also find a great location to ingest illegal substances in the expanded bathroom area of the set. Also available inside the detailed recreation will be a gift shop, stripper cages and a highly unsterile tattoo parlor.

"Audience members will get to participate in many of the park's attractions, such as 'Kickstart My Heart,' which will give visitors the opportunity to relive Nikki Sixx's 1987 near-fatal heroin overdose by jabbing two shots of adrenaline directly into the heart of a realistic human dummy bearing Sixx's likeness.

Also on display will be some of the actual spoons and other drug paraphernalia used by Sixx during the height of his chemical dependency, worldwide fame, and crazed, paranoid behavior.

Other park attractions include "Theatre of Pain," which replicates the 1985 studio sessions in which the audience can watch live actors portray the roles of each band member as they feebly attempt to throw together arguably the band's worst artistic effort while dealing with frequent delinquency, internal squabbling, and the spontaneous demolition of high-priced recording equipment at any moment for absolutely no reason.

Another major attraction, "Tommy Lee's Water Park," will give park-goers their own chance to potentially drown in a recreation of the 2001 swimming pool tragedy that took place during Lee's son's fifth birthday party. There is also an exact replica of the actual jail cell Lee occupied for six months in 1998 for spousal abuse against his celebrity wife, Pamela Anderson, which can be reserved for overnight group lockdown events. The water park also features "Mick Mar's Vodka Extravaganza," which will allow fans to watch a Mars lookalike almost drown in a hot tub because he was too drunk to sit upright during a photo shoot.

"Vince Neil's Hard Driving" will take riders on a interactive thrill-packed reenactment of Neil's 1984 beer run-turned car accident, the death of passenger Nicholas "Razzle" Dingley of Hanoi Rocks, Neil's arrest, fine and devastating 15-day jail sentence.

Rounding out the park is a centrally located food court featuring themed eateries such as "Too Fast For Lunch," "Shout at the Doughnut," "Pamela's Melon Heaven" and "Tommy's Tube Steaks," where servers encourage patrons to make amateur videos of themselves repeatedly fitting the entire oversized hot dog into their mouths. ■

Above: Motley Crue performs live in between members' jail sentences.

> Rounding out the park is a centrally located food court featuring themed eateries such as "Too Fast For Lunch," "Shout at the Doughnut," "Pamela's Melon Heaven" and "Tommy's Tube Steaks."

> "'Wild Side' strives to replicate the provocative visual presence and over-the-top hedonistic reputation by letting visitors relive incidents involving each individual member," said Beal.

> Senchuck: "I think he might be into collecting coins, too, because he's always digging around in our change jar at the apartment."

RECOILMAG.COM   NEWS SATIRE YOU CAN TRUST

recoil

Ant governement calls for magnifying glass defense system

Washington, D.C. – The Sycamore and 11th ant colony could deploy a system to protect its homeland from child-based magnifying glass attacks within 14 months, according to lobbying republicans.

Conservative ants argued on the Hill Tuesday to pursue the technologies needed to track, identify and destroy any such magnifying glass initiatives through what they call a Magnifying Glass Defense System (MGDS). In theory, the system would protect the Sycamore and 11th colony by stationing protective reflecting technology at its borders.

In a presentation from Lockheed Martin, scientists explained how the reflectors would repel light in the opposite direction, thwarting any magnifying glass offensive and causing petulant adolescents to squint and retreat.

"It only requires the will to do it," said Bill Grassleton, representing residents of the Weed-In-Crack region of Sycamore and 11th.

Pundits of the program said major reallocation of what residents pick up and carry around would be necessary, but the result would be a safer colony. "Sure,

> The Magnifying Glass Defense System in theory would protect the Sycamore and 11th colony by stationing protective reflecting technology at its borders.

see ANTS page 43

Above: Two children from the Sycamore and 11th area launch a devastatitng magnifying glass attack.

Above: GorgeDerm user Kathy Droge is one of the many weight-conscious consumers who would sing the product's praises if she was able.

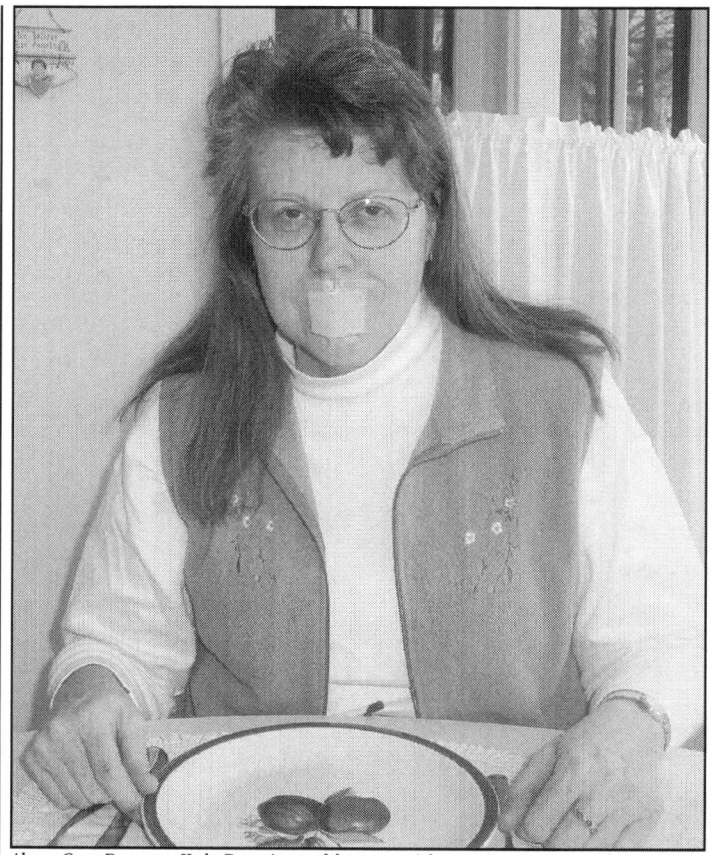

Johnson & Johnson test markets new weight-loss patch
Side-effects include improved marital relations

New Brunswick, N.J. – At Johnson & Johnson Corporation's annual shareholders meeting Monday night, company officials expressed excitement regarding its ongoing test-marketing of GorgeDerm, a revolutionary new weight-loss patch which developers claim can help patients lose significant amounts of weight by curbing their ability to eat.

"One GorgeDerm patch placed over the mouth works all day to impede the patient's consumption of proteins, fats, carbohydrates and other nutrients that can lead to obesity," explained Johnson & Johnson Research and Development Team Leader Jonathon David, who spearheaded the product's development. "The patch adheres itself to

> "My wife and I have gotten along great since she started using the patch," said Droge.

see PATCH page 44

Internet privacy concerns rising, finds secret online spyware study

Above: Internet users unknowningly participate in the online study on privacy concerns.

New York, N.Y. – As the theft of credit card data and other personal information rose to record levels in 2012, so did privacy concerns over online shopping, a new secret online spyware study has found.

According to secret data-gathering software, 59 percent of adult Americans are "very or extremely concerned" about the fate of personal information when shopping online, an increase from 43 percent in 2009.

The data, collected from Americans over the age of 26 via cleverly disguised

see SPYWARE page 43

Cleric radical

page 41

COMMUNITY

Area man accused of staging own life

Mt. Union, Penn. – According to charges filed Tuesday by friends and family members, a Pennsylvania investment banker is accused of attempting to fake his own life, spending more than 36 years pretending to be capable of productivity and holding social relationships in an effort to make his existence look genuine.

Jacob Raffield, 36, was charged in Huntingdon County, Penn., with 87 counts of wasting people's time and more than 200 counts of falsifying ambition by a panel of family members and acquaintances.

Local associates believe Raffield purposely deceived both close family members as well as lifelong friends through repeated, deliberate lies and half-truths designed to convince those around him into believing the depressed and banker was certifiably alive – which involved Raffield attending junior college, taking civil service tests, performing volunteer work, and coupling with women, so as to externally appear to have simply lived of natural causes.

Family members and friends became suspicious of Raffield's reported life almost four years ago, when the then-construction worker failed to react emotionally when his long-time girlfriend moved out of their shared apartment. Since that time, no clear evidence has been found to prove Raffield had intentionally staged an illusion of his own life, but suspicions remained.

Those fears were confirmed last month when Raffield's mother discovered two months of piled-up dirty clothes and more than 30 open Cheez Whiz containers in Raffield's apartment, where he had been assumed to be carrying on a life.

In light of the discovery, authorities have accused Raffield of faking his own life for more than 30 years, including much of his time spent in high school, where, it has been discovered, he failed to participate in any social activities, educational functions, or drug abuse.

"It's just beyond my understanding how someone would think they could get away with anything this deceptive," said Raffield's friend of 15 years, Hank Grafton, of the auto salesman's misrepresented vivacity. "I knew he wasn't the most motivated or outgoing, but all this time I guess I held out hope he was still maintaining some kind of existence."

It is not known what awaits Raffield now that his secret has been uncovered, but friends and family members say they will pursue the greatest possible action to see that justice is served, intending to force Raffield to get dressed on weekends and purchase a mop. ■

> Jacob Raffield, 36, was charged in Huntingdon County, Penn., with 87 counts of wasting people's time and more than 200 counts of falsifying ambition.

Above: Jacob Raffield, 36.

EDITORIAL

This relationship isn't over until *my* facebook status says it's over

By Mark Sanborn

Charlene, honey, we really need to talk, but you won't return my calls, texts or e-mails since we had that big fight last night, which ended with you kicking me out of your apartment and saying you wanted to break up with me. Now, this morning, I see you've gone ahead and changed your facebook profile from reading "In a relationship with Mark Sanborn" to "Single." So apparently when you said, "I want to break up with you," I'm worried that what you were actually saying was, "I am breaking up with you." Yes, I know I have jealousy issues, Charlene, but I love you more than life itself. I'd rather die than see you with another man. So believe me when I say that our relationship isn't over until *my* facebook status says it's over.

Maybe you truly believe our relationship is over, but after everything we've been through during the last two years, don't think for a second that I'm just going to let you throw it all away with a few impulsive mouse clicks. How could you just suddenly announce yourself to the world as being single just because we had a little fight over you e-mailing that old boyfriend of yours? I simply refuse to accept the idea that you're just all-of-a-sudden flat-out dumping me over this. I, therefore, am at least going to be adult about this and keep my facebook status as "In a relationship with Charlene Barns" until we get a chance to sit down face-to-face and work this thing out.

I for one know deep down in my heart that if you really were serious about breaking up with me just because I get insanely jealous whenever you even look at another man, you probably would have changed your status to "In an open relationship," because you'd know how enraged and crazy that would make me. So, clearly, you still have feelings for me. Changing your relationship status on facebook is probably just your way of communicating your feelings to me. I'm sure that if facebook's relationship window included a "Working it out" option, you no doubt would have selected that instead of "Single." Either way, Charlene, understand that I'm hearing you loud and clear: your love for me transcends all space and time – we're just going through a rough patch.

Also, I'm not so blinded by my obsession with you that I can't recognize that you may have inadvertently clicked on "Single" when you were actually trying to temporarily change your relationship status to "It's complicated." Everybody makes mistakes; you probably just clicked "Single" and simply didn't notice that it wasn't what you meant to click. If so, you don't worry about explaining – just switch your profile setting back to "In a relationship with Mark Sanborn" and we'll just put the whole thing behind us. Please do it quickly though, and make sure my name is in there, because if a couple of days go by and then your status reads "In a relationship," I could misinterpret that to mean you've started seeing someone else – and that would devastate me.

For me, Charlene, I'd sooner shoot myself than change my facebook status to "Single." You are the only woman for me, always and forever – thus, my facebook status will remain as "In a relationship with Charlene Barns" until one or both of us are dead. One thing is certain: I will not lose you to someone else. Trust me on this one. You know me better than anyone else on Earth, but even you might not know what I'm capable of and just how far I'll go to ensure that no one but me can ever have you.

Anyway, if you're phone is broken or something and you're simply unable to respond to my messages, rest assured that I'll be refreshing your facebook page about every 10 seconds until I see you've changed your status back to "In a relationship with Mark Sanborn." That will tell me all I need to know.

By now I'm sure you can tell how important this is to me. I promise not to leave this chair, not to stop compulsively refreshing your page until your facebook status stops indicating "Single." I actually just called the office and quit my job today so I can spend all day every day watching your relationship status for as long as is necessary.

Whatever happens, my beloved Charlene, please know this: I will see you at least one final time before either of us move on. Cross my heart and hope to die: my facebook status will read "Widowed" before it ever reads "Single." You'd do well to keep that in mind. Our time together will not be over until my facebook status says it's over. This I can guarantee. ■

> Charlene, understand that I'm hearing you loud and clear: your love for me transcends all space and time – we're just going through a rough patch.

WORLDWIDE HEADLINES

Milwaukee's Best voted World's Worst

Chicago, Ill. – Brewers, beer aficionados and critics from around the world convened for Chicago's 2011 World Beer Cup (WBC) Saturday to sample, vote and award prizes for the finest beers currently being crafted, while also disclosing the judges' unanimous decision that Milwaukee's Best – a rock-bottom-priced blend of dishwater and hops consumed in great quantities by the lest impoverish – retained its title as the World's Worst beer currently manufactured in large quantities by an established brewery. "It's not like Milwaukee brewing companies are incapable of crafting good beer; Miller High Life actually won the gold medal for 'Best American-style Lager' at the 2002 [World Beer] Cup," said Dale Moore, public relations director for the annual competition. "I realistically can't imagine any brewery purposely crafting a beer worse than Milwaukee's Best anytime in the near future." Moore confirmed that Milwaukee's Best has now taken home the WBC's World's Worst title for an unprecedented 50 straight years, having won every year since its introduction in 1961. Controversy remains regarding this achievement, though, since WBC judges have continually disallowed Milwaukee's Best Light from competing for the title on grounds that such a disgusting substance could not possibly be intended for human consumption.

Child told not to do that shit

Dearborn, Mich. – Five-year-old kindergartener Kevin Sawyer continues to mess with the television's remote control despite repeated scoldings, spankings and other punishments, said stepfather Bernard Greenwood. "I've told you not to do that shit!" screamed a noticeably agitated Greenwood, as the 43-year-old construction worker rose from his recliner and retrieved the remote unit from Sawyer during Saturday's TNT James Bond marathon. Sawyer, whom Greenwood half-affectionately refers to as "that little bastard," declined comment, instead opting to cry himself to sleep in a bedroom closet of his parents' loveless home.

Four people's 15 minutes of fame negated by Daylight Savings Time

Hollywood, Calif. – Variety editor Nicole Parsons expressed relative indifference Monday to the fact that the beginning of Daylight Savings Time March 13 will cancel out the 15 minutes of fame allotted to four of the world's citizens. "Pushing our clocks ahead an hour means that four borderline celebrities won't get their 'fifteen minutes of fame' with a small blurb about gaining thirty pounds or getting caught screwing a hooker or whatever," said Parsons, yawning as she paged through countless red carpet photographs of big name celebrities like Brad Pitt and Jennifer Aniston. "It's like, big deal, you know? So four talentless reality show personalities miss their chance to get chewed up and spit out of the Hollywood machine. They'll probably be better off for it, if you ask me." Asked about the possibility of shoving eight new faces into the 15-minute public spotlight when the nation sets its clocks back an hour Nov. 6, Parsons responded with a rational, professional conclusion: "Well, if Gerard Butler marries Mila Kunis or something huge like that, than no, certainly not. We simply won't have enough pages to include the wannabes."

Stricter seat belt law to ensure accident victims remain inside car while being killed

Lansing, Mich. – Despite opposing public outcry, state legislators this week increased the monetary penalty assessed to motorists who fail to wear a seat belt – an alteration expected to significantly decrease chances that accident victims will be thrown from their vehicles while being dismissed from existence. "This fifty dollar fine increase will further encourage travelers to buckle up, helping ensure they'll remain inside their vehicles while being killed," Senator Virgil Smith (D-MI) proudly explained to reporters Monday. Legislators also confirmed a continuing lobby for tightened airbag deployment sensitivity, requiring airbag launch to accompany turbulence as subtle as the crossing as a speed bump.

Likes of which seen before

Santa Barbara, Calif. – Thousands of southern California residents are nonchalantly returning to their homes this week after authorities successfully contained a massive wildfire, the likes of which has been seen many times before tore through the state – scorching thousands of acres and destroying dozens of homes, as usual – late last month. "The magnitude of this wildfire was just like anything we have seen before in this area," said California State Fire Marshall Mark Moran, whose experience in fighting wildfires proved absolutely commonplace among the tens of area firefighters who worked their entire eight-hour shifts battling the completely ordinary blaze. "You always know when something like this will happen. Also, no two wildfires ever behave anything unlike the other. Still, we are relieved to have contained this wildfire, the likes of which we'll probably see again." ∎

ANTS from page 41

we will need to sacrifice a chunk of hard candy here or an open packet of Sweet 'N Low there," said President Gerald Moon. "But my feeling is that we must stop these evil-doing children and their weapons of magnifying destruction."

The Sycamore and 11th colony has plans in place to protect its worker ants, bread crumbs and other-side-of-street bases from magnifying glass attacks, but it currently has no plan and no budget to protect the Sycamore and 11th borders by way of a MGDS, said Anthill Majority Leader Tom Spindel.

Many Sycamore and 11th residents feel resources should be spent on domestic issues like cleaning up the colony's gutter district, where many ants feel unsafe walking at night, or developing levees to protect sidewalk cracks that flood during rainstorms or when someone drops a McDonald's cup. ∎

SPYWARE from page 41

pop-up windows, also suggests that Americans over the age of 50 are more likely to click on these pop-ups.

Furthermore, the computer-debilitating spyware found that 80 percent of participants had third-party insidious software on their personal computers prior to clicking on the pop-up survey that falsely promised to pay participants $500 for taking part.

"Even the twenty percent of participants that did not have any third-party spyware [on their computers] when the study began now have ours," said Kent Young, code writer for the invasive software that gauges privacy concerns and automatically redirects users to fraudulent e-commerce websites. "It also installs false spyware protection software, so that when a user tries to run it, it only enhances my browser-redirecting program."

The findings also suggest privacy fears are warranted in at least half of studied cases. In fact, a person does not even need to be using a personal computer to have their identity or personal information stolen.

"My friend told me I shouldn't be an organ donor," said Molly Collins, a 52-year-old participant in the study. "She said they can pull all your information from the organ donor database or whatever and then they can start to do things like unlock your car and stuff."

Collins, whose Internet Explorer browser is now mostly covered by spyware-installed toolbars, said she is considering getting rid of her computer because of her privacy worries.

The study of 4,452 Americans was conducted in January of 2013, with participants selected randomly and without informed consent. The survey was designed to gauge the level of security Americans feel when providing personal information online and to install vicious computer-attacking software. ∎

Recoil's Shallow Thoughts

- Instead of inventing the dehumidifier, they should have invented the demystifier. That way they could have instantly demystified the reason why it was so humid in the first place.

- People often get mad at whoever lets the cat out of the bag, but shouldn't the anger be placed instead on the cruel person who shoved the cat into the bag?

- I'm willing to bet that if I put as much emphasis, money and time into drinking as possible, I could become an extraordinary alcoholic. Perhaps one of the all-time greats. I could also rack up a huge point total on my driver's license.

- I think a great prize to give away at parties would be free incoming U.S. mail service for a year, provided the winner already has a mailbox.

- I know people often suffer ramifications for things they've said or done, but does anyone every suffer Rammsteinifications? Because that might be kind of cool, with all the fire and smoke and all that German shit going on while they're playing "Du hast."

- You know what can be a funny word to look at? "Ophthalmologist." Just look at that word for a moment. Doesn't it look kind of weird? If it does, you might need to see an ophthalmologist.

- If someone is betting you "dollars to doughnuts" regarding something, you're probably getting the better end of the deal – especially if you have a bunch of day-old doughnuts you bought for $.50 each.

MEDIA

Above: The January issue of *Cosmopolitan*.

Cosmopolitan celebrates 40 years of setting women's movement back 40 years

New York, N.Y. – *Cosmopolitan*, the influential American lifestyle magazine, has announced its plan to spend the month of June celebrating 40 years of the magazine setting the women's movement back 40 years through its material.

"Although *Cosmopolitan* has been in existence since 1886, we didn't really begin inflicting irreparable damage to the state of modern feminism until the mid-to-late sixties," said Kate White, the magazine's editor-in-chief. "Prior to that, it was mostly a boring literary journal. And we all know *that's* not going to get your man hot under the collar!"

Back when *Cosmopolitan* began its identity shift four decades ago, it was breezily setting the women's movement back into the 1920s with articles such as "Marrying Rich: It's Like College For Smart Girls" and "It's Not Really Debt – They're Just Credit Cards, Silly!"

With 40 years of female-centric history under its belt, the magazine has commemorated its storied legacy with an anniversary issue, available this month in 32 languages throughout 100-plus countries. Despite the common perception that *Cosmopolitan* is exclusively American in cultural reach, 75 percent of the nations that carry the publication are actually second or third world countries.

White finds such statistics heartening.

"The fact that we're giving eighteen-year-old girls in Equatorial New Guinea the confidence to spend their fifty cents-a-week salary on the right kind of eyeliner… that's something *all* women can feel proud of," said White.

As the editor of a back catalogue spanning hundreds of issues, White is philosophical about *Cosmopolitan's* longevity.

"Although forty years is extremely ancient by any conceivable standards of femininity, you're only as old as you look," said White. "And that makes *Cosmo* only as old as the heavily airbrushed, Photoshop-enhanced eighteen to twenty-three-year-old women who grace our cover each month. That's very empowering."

White, however, does acknowledge that the magazine has been dispensing its anachronistic insights to readers for some time now.

"It seems like just yesterday we published 'Small Dogs: Not Just For Our Purses Anymore' and 'Anorexics: Are They On To Something?' But can you believe those pieces first hit newsstands way back in 1991? Wow, time sure flies."

White believes *Cosmopolitan's* staying power stems from the fact that women – whose opinions the magazine has calculatingly sculpted from a formative age – can relate to what's in between its covers.

"Whether they're seeking fashion and lifestyle tips, sex and dating advice, or answers to harder-hitting issues like makeup do's and don'ts, our readers know *Cosmo* has all the right answers," said White. "Through basic sociological erosion, they've gradually regressed into complete reliance on our publication, and really, that's the ultimate compliment. Girl power!"

Despite *Cosmopolitan's* success, White has no plans for the magazine to rest on its laurels.

"If you think about it, sixty years into the future we'll be setting the women's movement back to the year 2023, which is a full ten years from now," said White. "That's pretty cutting-edge."

White added: "So when it comes to taking all the hard-won advances our gender has fought for and knocking a few decades off them, *Cosmo* is actually way ahead of its time." ■

PATCH from page 41

the upper and lower lips using a special bonding agent that lasts up to sixteen hours, fully restricting use of the mouth and thereby preventing the patient from 'cheating.'"

Aesthetically similar to the popular NicoDerm nicotine patch that has helped thousands of smokers kick the habit, the GorgeDerm patch is currently available to consumers over-the-counter in select areas of Alabama, Kentucky, Mississippi and Tennessee – states home to 23 percent of the nation's 59 million obese individuals.

"Patients may still experience the psychological compulsion to eat everything that isn't nailed down, but GorgeDerm ensures that they will not be able to act on these impulses," said David. "[GorgeDerm] is an exciting new option for people who *want* to lose wait but have had no luck using conventional methods such as pills, hypnosis or nicotine gum."

"Oh, and diet and exercise," added David. "I always forget that one."

According to consumer polls, a majority of satisfied GorgeDerm users said that not being able to open their mouths or chew and swallow a large variety of foods was key to successfully dropping the unwanted pounds. A large percentage of patients, however, reported incurring a number of side-effects including dry mouth, fatigue, difficulty breathing and, perhaps most commonly, vastly improved marital relations.

"My wife and I have gotten along great since she started using the patch," said Mark Droge, whose wife of nine years began using GorgeDerm in early January. "I noticed a difference almost immediately. It's not just that she's becoming more and more attractive to me, but she's more fun to be around, too. I've even been helping out by reminding her to put her patch on every morning."

"Mmmmff, mmff eff ummm," added Droge's wife, Kathy. "Umfff efmm mmmff."

Though marketed primarily toward adult women – statistically the most at-risk demographic – this breakthrough weapon in the battle of the bulge is designed to treat obese children as well. ■

page 44

RECOILMAG.COM   NEWS SATIRE YOU CAN TRUST

recoil

Supreme Court bans medicinal use of aloe plant

Above: FBI Aloe Division troopers raid the home of Kendra Kelly as she tends to her personal crop of recently outlawed aloe plants.

Washington, D.C. – The U.S. Supreme Court unanimously ruled Monday that people using the aloe vera plant for medicinal purposes are not exempt from federal laws prohibiting use of the naturally occurring herb, which medical experts say can ease the suffering of burn victims.

"It is clear from the text of the [controlled substances law] that Congress has determined the aloe vera plant has no medical benefits worthy of an exception,"

> The decision allows the federal government to classifying the naturally occurring plant that invokes feelings of euphoria in the user as a Class I Narcotic.

Chief Justice John G. Roberts wrote for the court.

The Supreme Court's recent **see ALOE page 48**

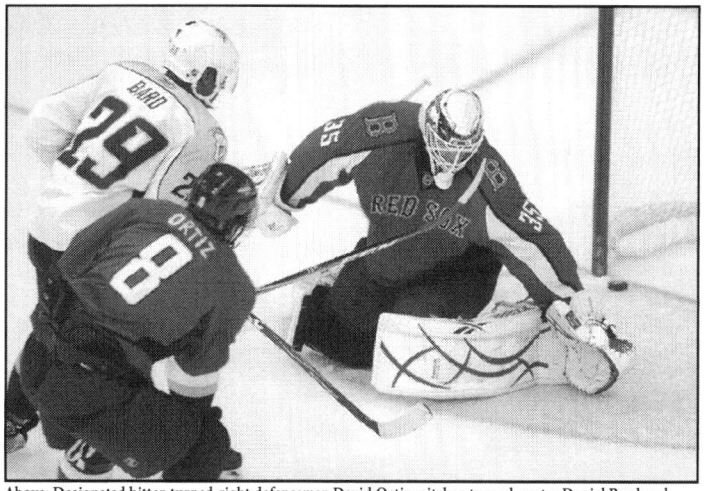

Above: Designated hitter-turned-right defenseman David Ortiz, pitcher-turned-center Daniel Bard and catcher-turned-goalie Paul Hoover attempt to stay upright during a Boston Red Sox training scrimmage.

Boston Red Sox determined to end 94-year Stanley Cup drought

Fort Myers, Fla. – Seven years after the Boston Red Sox finally succeeded in bringing home their first Major League Baseball championship in 86 years, team executives confirmed Tuesday that the Red Sox's 2011 season will focus on ending the team's 94-year drought of winning the Stanley Cup – a pursuit that has eluded the club since the National Hockey League formed in 1917.

"If there's one thing I learned during our [2004] triumph, it's this: don't ever tell a Red Sox player they can't do something – it only increases their resolve to achieve," boasted team manager Terry Francona, recalling the team's glorious come-from-behind victory over the New York Yankees during the 2004 World Series. Francona then went back

> "Does it seem cold in here to you?" asked Francona, pulling an extra Red Sox training jacket over the one he was already wearing.

to watching his players wildly flail their arms while shakily attempting to slalom through a column of generously spaced orange pylons at a Fort Myers, Fla., ice arena – this year's home for Red Sox spring training.

After breaking the so-called "Curse of the Bambino" – a popular reference to the Red Sox's inability to win a title for 86 years following the sale of baseball legend Babe Ruth to the New York Yankees in 1919 – and having won another championship in 2007, the team's confidence appears to be at an all-time high as they vie for the 2011-2012 NHL Stanley Cup.

"Remember, only three teams in the history of organized sport has won a **see SOX page 47**

Peacock's father embarrassed by offspring's shyness

Bakery worker out back getting baked

Gluten freed

Novelist incorporates real-life experiences she can't otherwise get anyone to listen to

Seattle, Wash. – Friends and associates of 39-year-old fiction novelist Colleen Steinberg confirmed Wednesday that the moderately successful writer consistently weaves into her storylines tales of personal experience that she is otherwise unable to procure the slightest bit of interest in during friendly conversations.

"Having known Colleen since kindergarten, I often recognize parts of her books as being drawn from real-life events she's experienced, such as having a borderline alcoholic for a stepfather – just like the main character Daphne's situation in *For The Ages*," said longtime friend Gale Morris, referring to Steinberg's debut novel. "A lot of people close to Colleen don't usually recognize these similarities, however, because they **see NOVELIST page 48**

Above: Steinberg weaves her boring experiences into her mediocre-selling mystery novels.

page 45

WORLDWIDE HEADLINES

Courtesy call anything but

Omaha, Neb. – Describing his intrusive dialing as a "courtesy call," an anonymous bill collector interrupted Emily Taylor during the dinner hour Tuesday night to aggressively alert the 35-year-old homemaker regarding the overdue status of her cell phone bill. "Yes, Misses Taylor, this is a courtesy call from T-Mobile in regards of [sic] your account, showing that you currently owe a past due amount of one hundred thirty four dollars and seventy six cents; would you like to arrange to make a payment today?" the voice forcibly trumpeted during the unsolicited call, overpowering Taylor's timid attempts to postpone the intrusive communication. "If that's their version of courtesy, I'd really hate to hear what rude and obnoxious sounds like. Maybe it involves gunplay," said Taylor.

Half of community members at anti-crime meeting look like they belong in jail

Atlanta, Ga. – Roughly half of the concerned community members that gathered at a coffee shop in the alternative district of Little Five Points to discuss a recent upsurge in crime Tuesday night themselves looked like they belonged behind bars, sources said following the meeting. "The folks that make up the community of Little Five Points are, well, let's just say they're an eccentric group of people," said Atlanta's Chief of Police Neil Gaines, who led the town hall-style meeting. "About half of the people there for the anti-crime meeting – many of them residents who are genuinely concerned about the safety of the area – had tattoos, odd piercings, leather jackets, dreadlocks, mohawks, you name it. From the look of them, I'm sure most of them, if they haven't been there yet, will see the inside of a jail cell before long." Gaines supposed that had he had reasonable cause to search each person at the meeting, at least 50 percent of the roughly 200 people in attendance would likely have been immediately arrested on drug possession charges.

Furious meteorologist forecasts major shitstorm

Philadelphia, Penn. – Television news meteorologist Kent Moore, enraged by rumors of his wife Karrie's infidelity moments before his live broadcast of the 6 p.m. weather report, forecasted that a "major shitstorm of epic proportion" would reign down upon his cheating wife before late evening Friday. "And if you are Karrie, the no good slut of a wife whom I've devoted my entire life to and never even once considered screwing around on, well then I'm afraid your part of the state is looking at a one hundred percent chance of there being a major fucking shitstorm the second I get home from work," Moore reported using his soothing but sassy on-air voice. "So, just to recap, if you exchanged wedding vows with me eighteen years ago, you can expect to see a major storm tonight. You might want to consider moving into a hotel at least until this storm settles." Added Moore: "Now here's Neil Warren with a look at sports."

Man strains back applying back pain cream

Tempe, Ariz. – Elderly back pain sufferer Walter Matthews strained a muscle in his upper left back Friday when the 64-year-old retired plumber attempted to apply Ben Gay to his lower back, a painful area for which he has sought relief for years. "A friend recommended this cream – [he] said it would make me feel less pain in my lower back," explained Matthews. "In a sense it did, because I pulled a [muscle] in my upper back trying to apply it and now that spot hurts so much that I don't even really notice the pain in my lower back anymore." "Let's hear it for the miracle cure," Matthews added sardonically. Matthews' injury comes only weeks after the widowed retiree, stretching awkwardly to apply the ointment to a tender calf muscle, incurred a tear-inducing Charlie horse in his upper thigh.

Planetary leaders agree global domination not what it used to be

Jalagana 5 – Amortis the Hated, feared leader of the planet Jalagana 5, agreed with members of the Interplanetary Leaders Conglomeration Tuesday when he voiced the opinion that being the sole dominating force of a planet's population is not as personally gratifying as it used to be. "Centuries ago, when I would arbitrarily decide to exterminate a section of a planet's population, an increased sense of power, incomprehensible monetary gain, or at the very least a feeling of great pleasure, would always follow – but anymore it's like, I don't know, like it's almost more of a headache than anything else, what with all of the public outcry and threats of uprising and all," Amoris stated in loud Jalaganian tongue. Members of the Conglomerate, convening via holographic imaging system, groaned in universal agreement of Amorits' venting.

Drug-seeking student accidentally sneaks into math lab

Atlanta, Ga. – An area high school student looking to score speed slipped into the Bedford High School math lab by mistake Tuesday. All Todd Hobson wanted was to tiptoe without being noticed into and out of a room which he believed contained a methamptheamine lab. However, upon carefully entering and gently closing the door, 13 Bedford High Mathmateers members greeted him with welcome eyes. Taken completely by surprise, Hobson pretended to harbor an interest in joinging the arithmetic fraternity and stayed for the remainder of the four-hour session. The school's math lab has caused mix-ups in the past; the common confusion is reportedly responsible for at least 30 percent of the Bedford High Mathmateers membership.

EDITORIAL

Damn you, Google! Now my employees want a bunch of crazy shit in the workplace

I consider myself a decent, reasonable and generally well-liked boss. Or at least I always have – up until you guys, the

By Dick Klein, manager

made-of-money internet giant Google, started upstaging every single other company in the world as far as offering its employees just about every luxury under the sun. These days, from what I can tell, the Google office appears to be more like a luxury vacation spa than a place of international business. Well, let me just say to you, Google, from the bottom of my heart: thanks a billion for setting the employee workplace bar so impossibly high that my meager attempts to lighten my own company's office atmosphere, compared to yours, makes me look like Liona Helmsley.

I for one know how important keeping employee morale up is to running a profitable business. This is exactly why I've made the company spring for a hotdog cookout in my backyard every other summer, so employees can bond with management and their fellow laborers. That gig costs us upward of $500 bi-anually. But the stuff you guys do is simply unreasonable to try to match: slides in place of stairs, foosball and ping-pong tables, five star chefs preparing breakfast, lunch and dinner – for FREE no less – pets allowed at work… and I hear now you're even thinking about moving headquarters to a cruise ship off the coast of La Jolla. Did you ever stop to think that perhaps you're going too far? I mean, sure, you want your employees happy, but never so happy that they won't eventually quit so

> You want your employees happy, but never so happy that they won't eventually quit so you can hire some fresh college graduates who'll accept half the salary of their more-experienced predecessors.

you can hire some fresh college graduates who'll accept half the salary of their more-experienced predecessors.

When my employees drool over your Jobs At Google page, with its photos of employees parking their laptops and keisters in lawn chairs in a sandbox, with their feet soaking in a wading pool while they work, my lift of the ban on wearing colorful socks that is detailed on page 93 of our employee dress code manual sort of pales in comparison. When you happy, shiny management people are encouraging your employees to think and share ideas freely, without fear of a bureaucratic smack down and unpaid time off for coming up with what eventually may prove to be winning strategies, how am I supposed to hold my head up when I trade my employees' collective genius for

see EDITORIAL page 47

page 46

Nation's faint acquaintances demand to know how it's going

Washington, D.C. – Seeking to break the long, awkward silence instilled by coincidental encounters with infrequently seen associates, a coalition of the nation's faint acquaintances gathered at the country's capital Friday, demanding to know how it's going. "We have not seen you a long time, man," the acquaintances' spokesman Pete Tolls said at a press conference. "So tell me how in the heck things have been going with you?" The nation shrugged before responding, "Good, good, you know; busy," while racking its brain to remember recent occurrences worth noting, such as the purchase of new possessions, career changes, procreative endeavors or deaths in the family. ∎

recoilmag.com

SOX from page 45

league championship best-of-seven series after being down three games to none: the 1942 Toronto Maple Leafs, the 1975 New York Islanders, and, oh yeah, *the 2004 Boston Red Sox*," said a confident Francona as he watched panicked outfielder Mike Cameron slam into the rink's boards after being unable to execute a hockey stop. "The point is this: our club has an extraordinary amount of experience [at playing baseball]. I for one think we'll be serious contenders – as soon as the players get over being scared of slipping and cracking their heads open on the ice."

"Does it seem cold in here to you?" asked Francona, pulling an extra Red Sox training jacket over the one he was already wearing.

Despite weeks of witnessing his players' struggle to master basic ice hockey skills – essentials such as correctly putting on their equipment, maintaining their balance and conditioning their bodies for a sport that actually involves athleticism and endurance – Francona had his morale considerably improved after a rink employee informed him that skate blades could be "sharpened," a technique known to significantly improve a skater's ability to maneuver, turn and stop.

"Well, there you go," said a relieved Francona. "That explains why half the team can barely stand upright."

Francona said he plans to begin to acclimate his players with the rules of the game as soon as he gains a full understanding of the offside rule.

Boston's designated hitter David Ortiz – one of three team members who have already begun learning how to skate backward – expressed other concerns regarding the team's transition.

"I'm still trying to figure out who I should charge if an opponent fires a puck at my head as an intimidation technique," said Ortiz. "Instinctually, I'd just take a run at the player who shot it at my head, but this crazy game moves so fast I doubt I'll ever be able to figure out who did it. Maybe I'll just go after their goalie."

Sports analysts have voiced unanimous skepticism regarding the Red Sox's chances of winning an NHL championship anytime soon.

"First off, management will need to make some key trades in order to put themselves in contention," said YES Network sports commentator Jack Curry. "And that's going to be hard, considering how few NHL clubs are actively looking to trade a valued skater for a right fielder who still doesn't know how to properly tape his hockey bat."

Francona dismissed such negative criticism, insisting that his team is one that has learned to overcome adversity and find ways to win no matter the circumstance.

"Hey, before you go, one more thing: can you tell me who the fuck this Bobby Orr guy is?" asked the longtime Boston native/Red Sox pitcher Bobby Jenks. "I keep hearing his name. Apparently, he was a defenseman for a Boston hockey team named, like, the Brewers or Bruisers or something like that. I guess it doesn't matter; he certainly couldn't be a great player like Wayne Gretzky, because I know who Wayne Gretzky is." ∎

EDITORIAL from page 46

a handful of Chuck E. Cheese tokens?

As long as you do-Googlers keep ramping up the employee morale to unmatchable heights, the majority of my employees are going to suffer from Google envy. You want your employees to get to know each other, to use each others' creativity and positivity as a springboard for their own. You say a happy employee is a productive employee, and worker camaraderie results in problem solving strategies. I say that workers putting their heads together is more likely to result in a workers union, or the staging of a coup d' etat.

I've had it. I'm ditching the Mr. Nice Guy attitude. I just can't compete. Around here, a happy employee may give 100 percent, but a fearful employee will give 110 – if he or she wants to keep their job, that is. It's an employer's market right now; we've got them over a barrel and they know it. In fact, I think I'll skip this year's hot dog cookout, and use that money to purchase a gross of new pink slips pads. ∎

HOROSCOPES

Taurus (April 20 to May 20)
Taurus' refusal to pull over for ambulance sirens is racking up negative karma equivalent to the combined cosmic demerits awarded for adultery, stealing from the blind, and teaching your kids to smoke. Sure, selfish driving will get you where you're going a couple of seconds sooner, but you'll pay for it in the afterlife. I understand the stoplights in Hell stay red for 15 billion years at a time.

Gemini (May 21 to June 20)
Give God credit for mustering enough ambition to launch His legendary Creator/Supreme Architect monopoly, a venture documented as being six long days of tedious, non-union labor. That's a good example of how much can be accomplished without cable television numbing the creative ambition. Step away from the TV at least long enough to tell time by the position of the sun, rather than by the urgency in Regis' voice.

Cancer (June 21 to July 22)
Why in hell do you even own a television if you're not going to spend every free moment watching it? Ignoring the brain-numbing discharge of the tube will invariably spark Cancer's ambition and creativity - worthless traits that invariably lead to no good. Television has a designed purpose: to congest the industrious mind, so you won't invent yet another way of destroying the planet, or at least some of the people on it.

Leo (July 23 to August 22)
Thirsty, trendy Leo doesn't seem to notice that bottled water companies have brainwashed the public into paying big dollars for a substance that flows readily from a household tap. If you're genuinely convinced you must pay more than the cost of a beer to properly hydrate your body, then you, Leo, or whatever your name is, are indeed mentally congruent to 'Evian' spelled backwards.

Virgo (August 23 to September 22)
That classic break-up condolence, "Better to have loved and lost than never to have loved at all," has provided its fair share of comfort during Virgo's woeful times. But considering how bad your last relationship was, perhaps more applicable is the truthful axiom, "Better to have loved and lost than to have to live with a complete goddamned psycho for the rest of your life."

Libra (September 23 to October 22)
Cancer's self-centered phone diplomacy explains why your telephone rings less than the Voluntary Audit line at the IRS. Hold and Call Waiting are rude, conversation-killing options used by the kind of selfish people who also don't think twice about using someone else's last squeeze of toothpaste on Monday morning. Call Ma Bell and cancel your caller-alienating options at once – they'll put you on hold long enough for you to taste your own medicine.

Scorpio (October 23 to November 21)
Scorpio's job search is indeed a difficult endeavor; with your lack of qualifications and job experience, you'll be lucky to land a seasonal gig chalking lines on football fields or mopping up peep-show stalls. Your best angle is the "It's not what you know, it's who you know" theory – more specifically, it's who you know that doesn't know you well enough to think better of hiring you.

Sagittarius (November 22 to December 21)
Thinking for yourself is an idea that needs to be force-fed into Sagittarius' malnourished frontal lobes; your willingness to thoughtlessly repeat learned behavior rivals those brain-dead rock pitchers from *The Lottery*. Don't let society, tradition or television dictate your behavior – do what makes sense to you – but remember that rocking the boat may make everyone else want to throw you overboard.

Capricorn (December 22 to January 19)
Capricorn's love of animals contradicts mankind's self-preservation instincts. Remember, no matter how cute chimpanzees may be, any species intellectually capable of sign language, space travel and playing ice hockey is getting way too close to mounting a global takeover. Do whatever you can to hinder the simians' advancements, for it is only a matter of time before apes team with computers to stick us humans in the cages. Won't that be a hoot.

Aquarius (January 20 to February 18)
The way to a father's heart is not through his stomach, it's through leaving him the hell alone while he watches television. Sooner or later, you're bound to have a power outage; when devoid of electronic amusement and faced with family conversation, Aquarius' father naturally resorts to booze, which will loosen his tongue long enough for him to confess his true feelings: "Child, I love you very much – for not bothering me while I watch TV."

Pisces (February 19 to March 20)
Pisces' blind support of the American military is indicative of someone who's never fired a gun, let alone fired it at complete strangers you've been told to hate. Reconsider your "Die with your boots on" wartime attitude – that's a bloodthirsty phrase most likely penned by some warmonger politician who never had to spoon his own soup, let alone dig one of those shallow graves otherwise known as foxholes.

Aries (March 21 to April 19)
The menace of Aries' short temper is compounded by the convenience of today's 24-hour superstores, which stock every caliber of ammunition needed for carrying out most liquor-fueled, impromptu acts of violence. No longer does anger have to wait until morning – but frugal Sagittarius should at least take the time to check for coupons.

page 47

A page from the Recoil handbook...
Babysitting Tips

Babysitting is the first paying job for many teenagers. Although not terribly strenuous work, babysitting does require patience, care and responsibility. Below are some tips for first-timers:

- During your initial interview, remember to ask parents if they happen to own mint coin collections that they hardly ever look at and would not notice missing for months.

- Be sure the parents who asked you to babysit aren't the couple recently profiled in the newspaper for having sextuplets.

- If you're new to babysitting, it can be helpful to rent an instructional video, such as *Adventures In Babysitting* or *Fight Club*.

- Remember to always carry the frustrated babysitter's secret weapon: duct tape.

- After the children are in bed and your boyfriend finally comes over, please, at least have the decency to put a darn towel on the couch.

- Turning up the television really loud will help drown out the sounds of babies crying or children screaming for help.

- Only allow each child one package of matches per night. Once those are gone, that's it, no more matches until next time.

- Only let the children play with toys that have sharp edges or points if there is good lighting in the room.

- If a child insists that the toy he wants to play with does not present a choking hazard, well, then, make him prove it. Yeah, not so smart now, are you, purple boy?

- If the kids want to watch television, pop in a DVD that has those Christian talking vegetables or some shit like that.

- At the end of the night, decide which child has been the most well behaved and then send a message to the other children by telling them how much better that child is than them, and that no matter what they accomplish in life, they'll never be as good as that child.

- Put away electronic toys that might burn or shock a child until they won't fess up as to which one of them was going through your purse.

ALOE from page 45

decision reinforced its 2005 ruling that the Commerce Clause of the U.S. Constitution allows the federal government to ban the use of aloe vero for medical use, classifying the naturally occurring plant as a Class I Narcotic to be grouped alongside heroin, cocaine, ecstasy, LSD and other substances capable of invoking feelings of euphoria in the user.

Public controversy surrounding aloe's legal status has escalated since 16 states have allowed authorized doctors to legally prescribe aloe as a medicinal aid for certain health ailments – an authorization in direct conflict with the Controlled Substances Act. With doctor's orders, patients residing in these states can legally purchase, use and in some cases even grow aloe vera plants, the leaves of which yield a thick sap that can be used to relieve the pain generated by some skin conditions.

Aloe legalization activists, having long questioned the inclusion of aloe in the Controlled Substances Act, said authorities are "acting out of drug paranoia" in the continued suppression of aloe's legality.

"It's unfortunate that the Supreme Court imposed faulty logic in continuing this country's inherently doomed war on drugs, rather than seeing the legalization of aloe for what it is: a health care issue," said Santa Clara University law professor Gerald Uelmen, spokesman for Legalize It!, a pro-aloe activist organization. "Aloe can relieve the pain that accompanies oxidation of a burn wound. Further, there is evidence that aloe can aid digestion and be used as a healing agent for digestive problems."

"No one's asking for full-blown aloe legalization – not in this case, anyway," added Uelmen.

Pro-aloe activists insist that since aloe plants occur naturally in the environment, use of the plant and its extract should not be – and in theory, can not be – controlled. It is believed that as much as 40 percent of the nation's current populace privately uses aloe illegally in their homes.

Legalize It! volunteer and pro-aloe activist Jesse Knoll said he disagrees with the government's position that it is legal to use manmade antiseptics like hydrogen peroxide and isopropyl alcohol – which often incite hostile reactions in the user – while aloe remains a controlled substance.

"It's like, aloe, you know, man, comes out naturally right from Mother Earth, like it's nature's gift to humanity. That such a gift is illegal just blows my mind," said Knoll, who admits to occasionally purchasing aloe for his personal home use. "Aloe is like the mildest [of antiseptics]. When I use aloe, it's like, 'Oh, yeah.' It totally mellows me out. Not like [hydrogen] peroxide. That shit makes me scream."

Knoll refused to elaborate on the events surrounding his past arrests for medicinally using aloe vera; Knoll was cited for aloe possession in 1988 at a busted college party, when "a whole bunch of us were getting burned," and again in 1993 after police searched Knoll's car after suspecting Knoll had recently used aloe to repress the pain of the burns on his face. ∎

NOVELIST from page 45

pretty much tune her out whenever she starts talking at length about her family, childhood, recent problems or one of the other half-million painful boring stories that she feels obligated to divulge at the drop of a hat."

Morris said that although each of Steinberg's four published novels incorporate at least a couple of the author's unremarkable real-life experiences, *For The Ages*, a morose tale of a small-town girl's desperate struggle to escape the work-a-day life of her perpetually unhappy middle-class parents, draws an unapologetical parallel to the author's mind-numbingly dull upbringing.

"Everything that happens to Daphne in *For The Ages* is pulled straight from Colleen's life growing up in Tennessee – just as she'll try to explain to you in great detail if you give her half a chance," said Morris. "Don't get me wrong, I love Colleen, but Lord knows why she thinks anyone would be the least bit interested in hearing a half-hour story about the time the dog she had in high school got sprayed by a skunk."

"At least with her books there's usually enough fiction and exaggeration worked in to make her real-life stories mildly alluring," Morris added.

Steinberg's editor, Audrey Sims of Shining Beacon Books, was quick to point out that even the most trivial and humdrum of life experiences can magically be brought to life when a talented writer puts the experience onto paper in the form of fiction.

"Traditionally, great prose is born of personal experience," said Sims. "Granted, that personal experience is *usually* some sort of unimaginable personal tragedy or fiery romance, but in the case of authors such as Colleen, that experience can be an event as commonplace and emotionally lifeless as failing to make the pom-pon squad three decades ago or running out of sticky notes on Sweetest Day."

Sims agreed that listening to Steinberg orally chronicle the highpoints of her notably mundane existence is significantly less appealing than reading versions of similar accounts in her novels.

"You know that sense of boredom you get when someone insists on telling you all about a dream they had recently? That's what it's like listening to Colleen talk about anything that has to do with her life," said Sims. "It's so uninteresting that you're practically in tears wishing someone would step in and interrupt you with a phone call or something. And the whole time all you can do is nod sympathetically and think about how sad it is that she doesn't realize how much nobody cares."

Sims added: "If Colleen ever does figure out that she's boring people to death with her stories, she'll probably end up writing a best-selling book about it." ∎

RECOILMAG.COM   NEWS SATIRE YOU CAN TRUST

recoil

Fake person wears real fur

Nation's motorists demand to know what the fuck

Movie of the Week weak

CEO downsizes own family

New York, N.Y. – Swept up in the thrill of downscaling businesses, new Fannie Mae CEO ordered the "immediate and necessary downsizing" of his own family Monday night. "We've got to make some cuts around here," said Hardwell from the head of his family dinner table. "Unfortunately, that means that some of our more expendable personnel will have to go." Wife Judy scorned Hardwell's decision: "He's just on an I'm-the-new-CEO-everyone-watch-out-or-I'll-downsize-us' power trip." Citing grocery budget concerns, Hardwell also stretched his reorganization powers Tuesday morning by ordering the downsizing of his son Eric's breakfast from toast and eggs to just toast.

In-laws tolerable when high

Buffalo, N.Y. – Joining friends around a hookah Thursday evening, 25-year-old Kevin Hietsma confirmed that interacting with his wife's family is decidedly more pleasant when high. "If I didn't get stoned before sitting down to the [dinner] table with Lisa's parents, I swear, I'd never make it," Hietsma told friends. "The conversation over there, the atmosphere of their house, it's just excruciating. It's too much for me to try to handle sober, that's for sure." ■

Above: Doomed couple Leana Harrison and Derek Fredricks.

Couple's resolve to communicate more openly can lead to no good

Phoenix, Ariz. – Sources close to Derek Fredricks and Leana Harrison reported this week that the young couple's inspired post-fight resolution to communicate in a more frequent, candid and straightforward manner can lead to no good.

Opponents of the July 26 decree said that although they applaud the lovers' significant effort to facilitate an open relationship – one in which borderline-risky information or conversation topics are willingly shared without fear of heated contest – they harbor tremendous doubt that the uncensored airing of previously suppressed thoughts will improve the couple's already turbulent relationship.

> Lot: "That's the kind of idea that only looks good on paper."

"I don't necessarily think Derek and Leana's decision to be more open with each other was a good one," said Harold Lot, Fredricks' best friend since childhood. "Derek often confides [information] to me that would probably send Leana into a tizzy if she heard one word about it. Nothing big, like affairs or anything, but just little shit that is probably best left not even mentioned because of the can of worms it could open up. Now he's supposed to just mention this stuff to her and vice-versa? No way, man."

Added Lot: "That's the sort of idea that looks good on paper but fails in practical

see COUPLE page 51

Report: Alarming number of kittens being diagnosed with ADD

Los Angeles, Calif. – Veterinarians across the country are reacting to Monday's release of a UCLA study claiming that as many as 90 percent of all felines currently being born in the United States will develop Attention Deficit Disorder (ADD) or Attention Deficit Hyperactive Disorder (ADHD) during their first month as a kitten.

> In the past, most kittens displaying the symptoms of ADD or ADHD were routinely misdiagnosed.

"Our research shows that an overwhelming majority of kittens begin displaying classic symptoms of ADD and ADHD within their first two to three weeks of life, symptoms such as uncontrollable, aggressive hyperactivity,

see KITTENS page 51

Left: Kittens displaying many of the tell-tale symptoms of Attention Deficit Disorder.

ATTENTION DEFICIT DISORDER SYMPTOMS
- Short attention span
- Uncontrollable, aggressive hyperactivity
- Undue inattentiveness
- Constant squirming
- Easily distracted by irrelevant sights, sounds and extraneous stimuli
- Difficulty following instructions (written and/or oral)
- Often interrupting or intruding on others
- Often engage in physically dangerous activities without considering possible consequences
- Often does not seem to listen when spoken to directly

WORLDWIDE HEADLINES

Boss gladly promises secretary time off to recover from boob job

Chicago, Ill. – Garry Alkest of the Quaker Oats Company seemed more than happy to oblige his secretary's request for two weeks off during late July to recover from breast augmentation surgery, sources said Friday. "Mister Alkest is usually very touchy when it comes to asking for time off, but he seemed more than happy to grant Sally [Drenth]'s vacation request – probably because it concerned increasing the size of her breasts," explained coworker Patrice Klimtt. "[Alkest]was like, 'Oh, yeah, absolutely. No problem at all.' What a pervert." An astonished Klimtt said that she also believes she overheard Alkest suggesting that he and Drenth discuss an increase in Drenth's salary upon her post-op return to work in early August.

Viewer realizes *Top Gear* channel actually BBC

Winston-Salem, N.C. – Gabriel Townsend, 25, realized Tuesday during his nightly viewing of *Top Gear* reruns that the channel he had previously thought was reserved exclusively for airing non-stop episodes of the car-oriented television show is actually BBC America, a cable channel that sometimes shows programs other than *Top Gear*, Townsend told reporters. "I usually watch *Top Gear* from the time I get home until the time I go to bed," said Townsend. "Every time I've ever turned on channel one thirty eight, *Top Gear* has always been on, but this weekend I turned it on and saw that they were airing an episode of *Doctor Who*. I was flat-out confused until I turned on the guide and noticed that the channel is not the *Top Gear* channel at all, but is actually called BBC America – meaning they play shows other than *Top Gear*. [That was] news to me." Townsend later discovered that BBC America even plays shows in which the actors do not use a British accent, such as *Star Trek: The Next Generation* and *The X-Files*.

Something further from the truth

Madison, Wis. – Just when area resident Carla Mitchell thought she had convinced friend Sheila Bartow that Mitchell did not engage in bigotry – stating that "nothing could be further from the truth" – Bartow suggested that another subject, in fact, was indeed further from the truth, Bartow told reporters Monday. "I told Carla that, no, based on the racist tendencies I've seen her exhibit in the past, there are actually a number of things that are further from the truth than her being a bigot – such as the notion that my husband is faithful to me," said Mitchell. "Now that's something that's very much further from the truth."

Gay marriage remains legal in New York if you totally want your ass kicked in public

Albany, N.Y. – Almost one year after New York voters made legal same-sex marriage throughout the state, the right to marry remains lawful for gay couples who are willing to have their asses violently beaten in the streets by people who overwhelmingly oppose the ideal. "As long as you don't mind being vocally ridiculed and physically assaulted every time you go out in public, homosexuals are very much allowed to legally marry in New York," said Representative Eliot Engel [R-NY]. "Even if gay marriage is not recognized by the federal government, the people of New York recognize the unusual pairing and probably applaud these homosexuals' courage – while they're busy beating those queers within an inch of liquid consistency." Engel predicted that the practice of recognizing and attacking married gay couples will one day be adopted by all 50 states.

Area smart ass glad you asked that, actually

Savannah, Ga. – Area resident and renowned smart ass Johan Brun is glad you wondered aloud about how many states originally joined to form the Confederate States of America, since Brun, as always, knows the answer and will have a chance to demonstrate his intelligence while looking down at you for your pathetic ignorance regarding the history surrounding the U.S. Civil War. "Seven southern states banded together against the northern blocking of the expansion of slavery into the western territories," boasted Brun, delivering the trivial fact in his well-practiced know-it-all tone that makes him sound like some sort of elite asshole. "South Carolina, Mississippi, Florida, Alabama, Georgia, Louisiana and, of course, Texas – although Virginia, Arkansas, Tennessee and North Carolina later declared their secession from the United States and joined the Confederacy," Brun added, deliberately mentioning that he minored in American History in college as if anyone gave a shit. ■

A page from the Recoil handbook...
Planning Your Wedding

Organizing your wedding is a monumental task capable of humbling even the most ambitious love-struck fool. Below are some tips to help you plan a beautiful ceremony and memorable reception:

• Women, on the big day, don't joke around in any way or allow others to engage in horseplay – and for God's sake don't smile or try to enjoy yourself, because if one infinitesimally minor detail goes wrong on your wedding day, your entire life is ruined forever.

• Respect your vegetarian friends by offering a choice of steak, chicken or waiting in the parking lot until all the fun people have finished gorging themselves on the flesh of beasts.

• Men, be courteous and do not take more wives than you can use. Sometimes a man's eyes can be bigger than his stomach.

• If you're writing your own vows, keep in mind that slang terms such as "shitkicking" shouldn't appear until the very end.

• Don't be embarrassed – drinking the lamb's blood *before* setting fire to the hexagonal etching is a common mistake made during pagan wedding ceremonies.

• Hiring a photographer *and* a videographer is a great way to preserve the moment for people who can't be burdened with the hassle of having to use their own memory.

• Out of courtesy to all of the divorced attendees, instruct the wedding official to add the words "or whatever" right after "until death do you part."

• Carefully scrutinize the references listed by potential DJs. Good reference: the Henderson wedding. Bad reference: Suge Knight party.

• Men, hold off on telling your fiancé about the wild stuff that went down at your bachelor party so you can use the stories as dinner conversation during the reception.

• Before commencing, make sure you've thoroughly cleaned both metal surfaces and have enough spool on your MIG. Oh wait, sorry, that a tip for planning your welding.

• Pausing ever so slightly before saying "I do" will give you a leg-up in the upcoming battle for control of the relationship.

• The dollar dance will prove much more profitable if you provide your wife with a stage and pole.

• Take special care when cutting the wedding cake with your new spouse – it'll be good practice for when it comes time to divvy up your joint assets.

• Believe it or not, it is possible to put on a beautiful wedding and reception without crippling your pocketbook. God, however, will *not* be pleased.

EDITORIAL

If I didn't like you, you'd be the first to hear about it through the grapevine

By Gretchen James

Cassandra Johnson, please forgive me for addressing you by way of open letter, but I felt it a better alternative than confronting you straight out about my feelings regarding Friday, when we had our first actual conversation since becoming coworkers in November. I must admit, I was flabbergasted by your harsh verbal accusation that I have something against you, don't like you, or harbor some manner of unknown grudge against you.

First, Cassandra, please allow me to take this opportunity to assure you that your contention is unjustified. I have nothing at all against you – scout's honor. But while we're talking about my hesitance to interact with you at work, please let me take a moment to make sure you understand, for future reference, that I am the kind of person that if I didn't like you, believe me, you'd have been the first person to hear about it through the grapevine.

Obviously, since we had never before spoken until this week, you haven't been able to find out for yourself that I am by no means the kind of person who shies away from making my personal feelings toward someone known to every other person who will listen. Call me crazy, but I simply can't stand not getting things off my chest by badmouthing whoever it is that's puncturing my craw. Take my word for it: if I don't like someone, you can be damned sure that eventually you're going to hear from someone at work that I speak badly of that person behind his or her back. About that, Cassandra, you can ask anyone.

Some people can keep their muted contempt for a coworker all bottled up inside. Some people can even openly discuss their personal grievances with that person face to face, so that there's no confusion about their issues. But while I have absolutely nothing against these kinds of people, I have to admit that I'm simply not one of them. In the restroom, in the cafeteria, at the watercooler – I'm not afraid to tell everyone within earshot exactly what I think about the

> *I'm not afraid to tell everyone within earshot exactly what I think about the people who aren't around right at that moment.*

people who aren't around right at that moment. So rest assured that if after six months of working in the same office as me, nobody's come up to you in the bathroom and told you that I've got it out for you or think you're a two-faced bitch or something of the like, then obviously you must be okay in my book.

As to your on-target comment that I've "never said two words to you," let me simply assure you that my failure to verbally interact with you at work has nothing to do with adverse feelings toward you – I'm simply not good at conversing in certain social climates. Please understand that I live by the advice that if you can't say something shitty about another person to somebody without that person overhearing you, it's best to not say anything at all – and you happen to have some world-class assholes inhabiting your adjacent cubicles, hence my tightlipped behavior around you. If our work situation was different, like if you and I worked alone together in some isolated area, you can bet I'd be gnawing your ear off every day about some of the jerks in our office. Instead of being mad that I don't speak to you, you'd probably be up in arms about me constantly talking about how much of a prick that guy Paul from IT can be. I'll bet at least 10 different people have told him how much I can't stand him. ∎

KITTENS from page 49

constant squirming and being easily distracted by irrelevant sights, sounds and extraneous stimuli – a ball of yarn or a toy mouse, for example," said UCLA researcher David Berman, who led the study. "In the past these symptoms have simply been attributed to youth – passed off as cute or playful, instead of being acknowledged as symptoms of a disorder. But we now know that when a kitten is bouncing hastily and randomly between playing with a loose string, chasing a remote controlled car, trying to give the goldfish a heart attack and tonguing herself clean, it's actually a physical sign of the kitten's neurotic psychological condition."

According to Berman, UCLA researchers achieved their results by studying a representative sample of 1,000 kittens from all parts of the country during the kittens' first eight weeks of normal, indoors rearing. By documenting the habits of these felines, researchers were able to diagnose 904 of the adorable animals as having either the inattentive type ADD or the hyperactive/impulsive type ADHD.

"The remaining ninety-six kittens were either stillborn or died shortly after birth," said Berman. "So, technically, we could have drafted a report that said that *all* kittens, so long as they're alive, have ADD – but we all agreed that just sounded too depressing. By saying only

> *"Technically, we could have drafted a report that said that* all *kittens, so long as they're alive, have ADD – but we all agreed that just sounded too depressing," said Berman.*

ninety percent of kittens are suffering from these conditions, at least cat owners who haven't read the fine print of the study can hope that their kittens are part of that ten percent which aren't afflicted."

Berman said that in the past, most kittens displaying the symptoms of ADD or ADHD were routinely misdiagnosed – most often by their owners but even by trained veterinarians or behavior specialists well-versed in animal psychology.

"For the typical cat owner, when his or her kitten would display an ADD symptom such as being unable to focus long enough to listen to and act on instructions, he or she would often just shrug it off with a 'She'll grow out of it' and simply hope that as a full-grown adult their kitten will begin to slow down, develop a longer attention span and stop its constant squirming," said Berman, referring to ADD and ADHD symptoms that were previously thought to be part of the normal behavior of a kitten.

Roger Vick, vice president of operations at the pharmaceutical manufacturer Novartis – a company which was quick to voice strong support of the study's findings – told sources Wednesday that Novartis will soon bring to market Kitilan, a specially formulated derivative of Ritilan made exclusively for kittens to help curb their symptoms.

"Using our medication will provide these kittens with their one and only chance to live a normal life," said Vick. "A kitten that is properly diagnosed and prescribed Kitilan will no longer be bouncing off the ceiling like they normally would. They will be able to control their attention span and they won't engage in physically dangerous activities without considering possible consequences like many ADD positive creatures do. Long story short, you won't

> *Novartis will soon bring to market Kitilan, a specially formulated derivative of Ritilan made exclusively for kittens to help curb their symptoms.*

have to worry about your kitten getting into all sorts of humorous situations that look like they belong on a photo calendar." ∎

COUPLE from page 49

Added Lot: "That's the kind of idea that only looks good on paper."

Harrison's friend Mary Eckert agreed.

"The first time Derek offhandedly says something like, 'I just imagined your sister naked,' you know, trying to stick to this 'full disclosure' rule, Leana's going to freak," said Eckert. "But according to this new always-verbally-express-the-full-contents-of-your-brain idea, that's exactly the kind of stuff Derek is allowed – in fact now encouraged – to say."

According to Fredricks, the couple's doomed resolve materialized following a two-hour dispute concerning the 31-year-old's reluctance to discuss previous relationships with Harrison.

"Leana was mad because I didn't want to answer a bunch of bullshit questions about old girlfriends," said Fredricks. "I thought I was doing the right thing by just not even getting into a conversation about it. It seemed like the kind of touchy subject that could lead to an argument. Go figure."

Harrison said she suggested the couple disclose information more openly in an attempt to minimize miscommunication and the harboring of resentments.

"I told Derek that I thought we could avoid a lot of arguments if he would just be open and honest with me about everything," said Harrison. "After about another hour he agreed to try it my way. And I already tell Derek everything. *Everything.*" ∎

SELF-HELP
Soul Mate Selector

Could the person you're currently banging actually be your spiritual split-apart?

Destiny's ability to correctly pair each human soul with its cosmically assigned counterpart is by no means foolproof; very few couples are immune to the occasional contemplation: "Is this the person I'm supposed to be with?" Take the following quiz to determine if cupid was working off the right spreadsheets when appointing your current mate. Assign yourself three points for every answer of A, two points for every B, one point for ever C and zero points for every D.

1. The way you and your lover met seems fateful because:
A. Your parents met in the very same adult bookstore.
B. You hardly ever visit refulxophile chatrooms.
C. Gays had only recently been allowed into the military.
D. It's not like you can choose your cellmate.

2. In your relationship, the male's most fevered arguments pertain to:
A. The declining frequency of sexual penetration.
B. The unanswerable hypothetical questions that follow sexual penetration.
C. Her reluctance to view movies graphically depicting sexual penetration.
D. Her reluctance to budge on preference of orifice to receive sexual penetration.

3. In your relationship, the female's most fevered arguments pertain to:
A. The long work hours caused by your professional commitment.
B. Immediately replacing perfectly functioning drapes, silverware and furniture.
C. Your Mullet & Mustache White Trash Starter Kit.
D. Everything imaginable.

4. Coincidentally, you and your lover have the same:
A. Fashion sense.
B. Tattoo locations.
C. Parole officer.
D. Father.

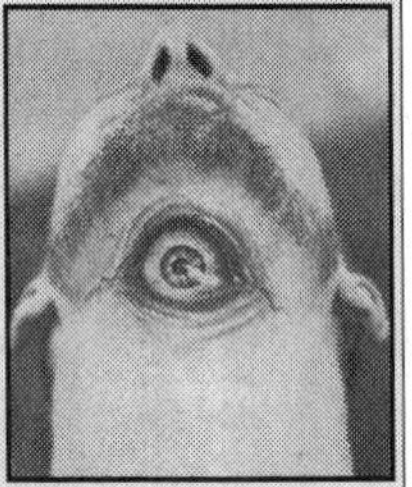

5. You and your partner have pledged yourselves to each other, despite:
A. Religious differences.
B. Being descendants of warring mob families.
C. International protests.
D. He or she only existing as one of your multiple personalities.

6. You would trust your mate to:
A. Be faithful.
B. Pull out.
C. Never wager the family car without holding at least a full house.
D. Let you keep half of everything.

If you scored...

18-15: Thwarting all mathematical improbabilities, you have indeed been united with your soul mate. Either that or your partner was standing over you as you took this quiz. Retake the quiz in the privacy of your bathroom, to ensure accuracy.

14-10: Who would've figured 400 hours of searching Internet personal ads would pair you with someone this close to a perfect match? You could stumble through to death do you part with this mate, but at least consider starting to get familiar with craigslist.

9-5: Your score raises serious questions about your mate's physical and emotional compatibility. Explain your quiz results to your mate and suggest you both do some soul-searching – at night, on the weekends, separately.

4-0: If you're not already shopping around for a new lover, chances are you both will be eventually. Why not beat your partner to the punch?

page 52

SPORTS

Above: Just one of the growing number of grown men of sound mind from around the world who willingly engage in the bizarre spectacle.

Man clad in white strikes yellow sphere with racquet of strings

London, England – Men wearing all white clothing aggressively struck fuzzy, yellow balls with some sort of stringed racquets yesterday during a sport many have taken to calling "tennis."

Tennis, a venture many natives of the island of England seem to term "wembeldon," is a strange spectacle to most and apparently part of a rare leisure interest of a small group of enthusiasts. The game seems to center around two competitors in white clothing hitting the aforementioned yellow ball over a short net, situated halfway between them, back onto the other competitor's territory. Each player seems to wish to hit the ball into an area which makes his opponent's return impossible, an uncooperative strategy which inevitably leads to many pauses in the proceedings.

Often fast-paced, the game requires its partakers to expend copious sums of vigor while pursuing the yellow target. White, an ostensibly inapt color given that the playing surface is composed of grass, is worn possibly to keep players cool in temperatures that reached scorching levels of 77 degrees – unprecedented heat on the secluded island located off the coast of France.

All the while, a figure poised in a heightened chair speaks a clandestine language into a microphone – an activity that frequently delights or disappoints onlookers seated around the event. The man or woman stationed in the lofty seat clearly commands respect and may be a person of importance in the participants' family, given that "love" is often mentioned within a string of otherwise unknown argot.

A secondary activity to the central endeavor seems to be a spaced line of participants staged along the back walls on either end of the "court," a borrowed term not to be confused with the legal use. These participants, it seems, are competing amongst each other in a contest to determine who can remain still for the longest sum of time, and occasionally one is likely eliminated when shifting slightly to avoid one of the small yellow spheres bounding in his or her direction.

A contestant frequently repositions himself to the opposite end of the court while his adversary does the same, a ritual that may derive from the Middle Ages martial game of jousting, which required knights to originate at alternating ends of a track.

Many in the American sporting world wonder how such a game is unknown to the United States, where sports of all variety are commonplace.

"It's marvelous to see these unadulterated sports discovered in primitive cavitations," said *Washington Post* sportswriter Tony Kornheiser. "I doubt this game is interesting enough for anyone in America to pursue, though." ∎

recoilmag.com

RECOILMAG.COM   NEWS SATIRE YOU CAN TRUST

recoil

Above: Museum security guard Marcus Andrews stands around looking like a complete dickhead.

Security guard confident he didn't get job based solely on ability to just stand there looking like asshole

Washington, D.C. – Marcus Andrews, a recently hired security guard at Washington, D.C.'s Smithsonian American Art Museum, adamantly refuted allegations Saturday that he was selected for employment based solely on the 48-year-old's keen ability to just stand around and look like a complete asshole all day long.

"I was chosen from a field of twelve applicants for this [security guard] position based on my qualifications, experience and written recommendations," Andrews stated in a defensively curt tone. "I've worked as a security guard for a number of organizations during my twenty-year career. I get the job done; I maintain order. Sure, my enforcement methods mostly involve constantly casting a hostile, disapproving gawk at everyone around me, but I sincerely doubt [Smithsonian officials] hired me simply because I was capable of looking like a bigger asshole than the other applicants. That's just absurd."

Added Andrews: "Now unless you have any more questions, get your lazy lard-ass moving. You're holding up a huge line of people eager to view this priceless, idiotic painting [which was] obviously thrown together in five minutes by some deranged, drug-fueled hippie."

According to Andrews, effective crowd

> "[Andrews] really gives off that look that says, 'You best watch yourself, motherfucker. Yeah, that's right, I'm talking to you. I'm an authority figure around here," said Prax.

control and public security require a skill set comprised of many components every bit as important as the capability to loiter around acting all superior and giving each passerby a malicious, unblinking stare equivalent to that of a paranoid maximum security prison inmate.

"These folks hired me not only for my peerless ability to make people act uncomfortably cautious, but also because

see GUARD page 55

Above: The Cape Girardeau levee, a known holder. (Inset): Delusional junkie Brad Smythe.

Dope fiend convinced levee is holding

Cape Girardeau, Miss. – Jonesing heroin addict Brad Smythe, originally of Scott City, Miss., is obdurately convinced that the levee located in Cape Girardeau is holding, the 23-year-old dope fiend told reporters early Friday.

"This whole entire city's been dry for, like, ever, man," said Smythe, expressing

> "I sure as hell don't want to have to resort to go begging some spur dike for some H," explained Smythe.

his frustration in finding somewhere to buy heroin during the last 36 hours. "But I know damn well that levee is holding. She's always holding. And I need to

see LEVEE page 55

Shit shot

Atlantis landing brings to end rich history of shuttle explosions

quikSTAT
Most popular elderly activities
- Staring
- Sobbing
- Shrieking
- Microwaving
- Mumbling
- Fidgeting
- Nodding
- Crank calling

U.S. pledges increased funding for scientific advancement of useless crap

Above: Some of the pointless gadgets already developed through decades of generous United States funding.

Washington, D.C. – According to an article published in the July issue of *Consumers Reports* magazine, increases in both government funding and private donations will account for the United States pledging a record $34 billion toward the scientific advancement of useless crap in 2011.

"Laser pointers, one-use tooth floss picks, barking flashlights, eye massagers – every ridiculous plastic trinket you've ever impulsively purchased in the checkout lane at your local Walmart, chances are that product was invented and developed right here in the good ol' United States," said Mark Taylor,

see CRAP page 55

page 53

WORLDWIDE HEADLINES

Only thing man remembers from memory course is it costing $200

Fleet, Ariz. – Local furniture salesman Ed Wellington told sources that the only improvement he has seen in his memory since buying and listening to the cassettes of a nationally advertised memory program is the nagging reminder that the course cost him $200. "I guess [the program] kind of works, because the outrageous cost of the stupid tapes is permanently burned into my brain," Wellington, 44, told a group of coworkers at a work function Saturday night. "Of course, remembering that the tapes cost me two-hundred bucks doesn't do me much good if I'm still too forgetful to write the number in my checkbook. I bounced two checks because of those tapes." Responding to inquiries, Wellington could not recall how many tapes the course contained, whether or not he had listened to each tape in its entirety or if the recorded voice was that of a man or a woman.

Area family can't have nice things

Pittsburgh, Penn. – Local homemaker Gretchen Kendall confirmed Monday that members of the 37-year-old's suburban family cannot have nice things in their home, primarily because of the way her youngest son Derek habitually mishandles fragile and expensive household items. "Oh my God, what happened to my poor lighthouse?" exclaimed Kendall after discovering the $12 ceramic figurine in pieces on the floor near the fireplace mantle upon which it was previously positioned. "Perfect, Derek. Just perfect. I've told you a hundred times that these [decorations] are not toys! I swear, it's like we just can't have nice things." Kendall later told reporters that her husband Don's tendency to ash cigarettes into any available receptacle – regardless of that item's designed purpose – also diminishes the family's capacity to have nice things.

Lil Jon's brain trust advises him to fuck all that shit

North Miami, Fla. – Big Sam and Lil Bo (a.k.a. the Eastside Boyz), who serve as rap music mogul Lil Jon's behind-the-scenes brain trust, encouraged the modern hit-maker to "fuck all that shit" when confronted by Walmart executives about producing alternate-lyric versions of Lil Jon albums for sale in the national retailer's stores. "Being the power behind the throne and all, we told our man Lil Jon, 'Man, fuck all that shit with those crackers. They just be wanting to be lining they pockets and shit,'" Big Sam told engineers at Circle House Studios in North Miami Friday. In between vocal overdubs, Lil Jon's unofficial advisors expressed a similar position regarding producer Rick Rubin's suggestion to use reverb on their obscenity-laden vocal tracks.

Juvenile offender going through identity theft crisis

The Bronx, N.Y. – Twenty-four-year-old hoodlum James Baker, who has for years picked pockets and fraudulently used victims' credit cards for personal gain, admitted Sunday that he is struggling to carve out a unique identity for himself after spending nearly a decade trying to be the person that store cashiers expect him to be when committing identity fraud. "This morning I was at Circuit City buying stereo equipment with a stolen Visa card, so I had to be James D. Harrington from Toledo, because that's who the card said I was," said Baker. "I've gotten so wrapped up in trying to be the persons these cashiers need me to be that I've forgotten how to be James Baker." Baker said that the first step toward reestablishing his own identity will be coming to grips with the fact that he's an unemployed high school dropout with an extensive police record and several outstanding warrants.

Metal guitarists' merit gauged solely on brand of amplifier

Buffalo, N.Y. – At an annual battle of the bands held at a heavy metal nightclub Friday night, amateur guitarists Dave Reno and Alex Moore rated how good each of the seven bands' guitarists were based on what kind of amplifier each musician uses. "The guy from Blade Gallery was far and away the best guitarist there tonight," Reno told a nodding Moore as the two hung out at a late-night coffeehouse after the show. "He ran an A/B box so he could switch between a Soldano head and one of those totally kick-ass Mesa Boogie Triple Rectifiers. That's a totally sweet rig." Moore added further criticism: "And what was the deal with that dude running that ancient, solid-state Peavey head? That guy blew." Reno and Moore's narrow-minded evaluation marked a noted improvement over last year's critique, when the fledgeling guitarists gauged the worth of each guitar player by how many Marshall speaker cabinets they had on stage. ∎

EDITORIAL

I'll get right on mailing in this five-dollar rebate

Oh, my. Well I certainly never expected this. It appears that yours truly's ship is about to come in.

And to think I almost missed the opportunity of a lifetime. For had it

By Jamie Farner

not been for that charming Circuit City salesman mentioning four or five times that the new Sony CRX2100U 48x CD burner I have no choice but to buy today comes with a five-dollar rebate from the manufacturer, I certainly would have overlooked this mammoth prospect. I'll tell you what, as soon as I get home – after I stop at Shell and put $50 in gas into the SUV – I'm going to get right on mailing in this five-dollar rebate.

After all, when that five-dollar rebate check comes in the mail in six weeks or so, it'll be like I only paid $122.19 for the burner instead of the $127.19 I already forked over. That'll make a profound difference in my weekly budget. Maybe I'll buy that three-pack of crew socks I've been saving up for.

At least Sony makes the rebate process simple: all I have to do is fill out a form that looks nearly indistinguishable from my receipt, address an envelop to the completely independent Sony address written in small print on the back of the actual receipt, cut out the cleverly hidden rebate endorsement on the CD writer's box, make a copy of the original receipt, stuff it all into an envelop and then wait until the post office opens in the morning to buy a stamp and ship it out. Fortunately, Sony allows the purchaser 10 whole days to submit the rebate form

> Fortunately, Sony allows the purchaser 10 whole days to submit the rebate form before the offer expires, so I can use the weekend to put the package together.

before the offer expires, so I can use the weekend to put the package together.

Considering how much the envelop weighed, I'm not sure if one $.37 stamp is going to cover the postage, but I'm going to risk it. If it goes through, my net gain will be $4.63, instead of the mere $4.26 I would have made had I went ahead and added another stamp. In this case, I think the possible reward is worth the risk.

Of course, if the mail *is* returned for insufficient postage, and I have to re-mail it using two stamps, my final rake will be only $3.89. That is, if the form still makes it to Sony within the allotted time.

With the mailing out of the way, I can sit back and rest for a while. Just think

> And to think I almost missed the opportunity of a lifetime.

of it, within a month and a half I'll have that five bucks in my pocket – as long as I can get off work early enough to get to the bank and cash the rebate check before they close. I've already made several notes to myself reminding me that Sony's rebate checks become void if you don't cash them within a week. Or maybe it's five days. I'll have to check on that when The Score gets a little closer on the calendar.

Proper planning will play an important role in the final leg of this mega-money marathon of labor. Starting in about four weeks I'll have to significantly alter the way I go through my mail, since Sony sends rebate checks in the form of postcards that look exactly like junk mail, in hopes that they'll be tossed in the trash instead of cashed – and I'll be damned if I'm going to let my five dollars get thrown away. So I'll have to spend a few extra minutes inspecting the mail every day, but it'll be worth it days later when that dead prez takes up residence in the old Farner billfold.

I believe I now have every angle covered. Oh man, is this going to be sweet. Definitely the easiest five dollars *I've* ever made. Thank you, Sony! ∎

CRAP from page 53

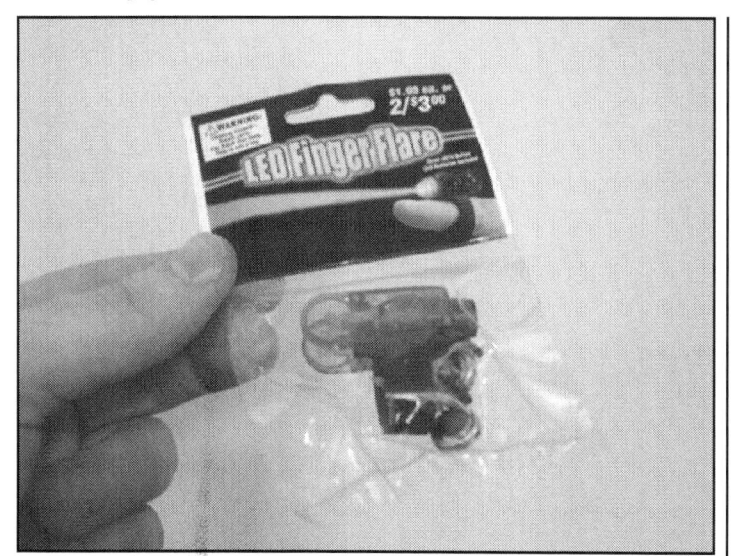

Large amounts of U.S. funding will be used to research the intended use of many of the useless trinkets (above) currently flooding the market.

the Boston-based freelance writer who authored the article.

Taylor said that despite holding a commanding lead amongst the nations of the world in the scientific development of useless crap, the United States' promise to pump $34 billion into the industry this year signals the nation's strong desire to promote further advances in useless crap technology.

"Sure, the United States has played a large part in making sure that worthless gadgets such as the blender phone or the rat race clock or those crazy, mutated bottle opener-slash-keychains line the shelves of every department store, mega-retailer and pharmacy you walk into, but there are many areas in the development of useless crap yet to be explored. Take this thing, for example," said Taylor, holding up a small, plastic product of unknown functionality. "The package reads, 'LED Finger Flare,' but I ask you, seriously: what in the hell is this thing? What on Earth is it for? What conceivable purpose could a consumer possibly have for this thing? Fortunately, through careful use of this generous U.S. funding, questions such as these may soon be answered."

Taylor's article explains that the United States has led the way in the development of useless crap for decades.

"Without the United States' diligent efforts in promoting the scientific advancement of useless crap, the world would be in the Stone Age when it comes to pointless gadgets such as glowsticks," said Taylor. "Let me put it this way: you can't just attach something shiny to a keychain and call it 'progress' in this business."

Added Taylor: "Well, occasionally you can. Like, if you can't come up with anything else that week, I suppose. Actually, that's not a half-bad idea. Excuse me while I jot that down real quick."

Taylor was hesitant to speculate where the world would be in the realm of useless crap without the United States' contributions.

"Imagine a world in which your mega-retailers have no overflowing bins of useless, plastic crap on sale for $2.99 each at the end of each aisle," said Taylor. "I'm not sure how we'd all get by not having all of these useless trinkets cluttering our shelves at home, but thanks to the U.S.' financial commitment, none of us will have to find out anytime soon." ∎

> "There are many areas in the development of useless crap yet to be explored. Take this thing, for example," said Taylor, holding up a small, plastic product of unknown functionality.

GUARD from page 53

I've proven effective at watching the museum floors, making sure people are following the rules and vigilantly scanning for suspicious activity of any nature," said Andrews while giving an extra-long stink eye to a giggling young couple, silently warning them to keep their voices down. "Regardless of the fact that I'm not allowed to carry one, a good security guard doesn't need a *gun* to enforce policy. All I have to carry is my disparaging attitude, which I've carefully refined during years of low-level security detail such as this."

"Well, that and sometimes I need my [two-way] radio to call in some real guards who actually have guns and Tazers and handcuffs and shit," added Andrews, coyly pulling back his suit coat to proudly reveal his communication device. "But very, very rarely do I get a chance to do cool stuff like that. So, granted, a lot of it is about being great at just standing around and acting like an asshole – the most valuable skill I learned from my father."

Reports regarding the behavior of Andrews – who completed a four-hour security training course in 1991 – revolve around the intense, judgmental stares and exaggerated, abrasive body language exhibited by the museum's newest member of its security personnel.

"[Andrews], intentionally or not, really gives off that look that says, 'You best watch yourself, motherfucker. Yeah, that's right, I'm talking to *you*. I'm an authority figure around here, so how about you just move along, scumbag,'" said distressed, non-threatening museum sightseer Gabe Prax. "I was viewing a piece for, like, I swear, no more than twenty seconds before [Andrews] started eyeballing me like he would just as soon see me behind bars as passively enjoying myself. What an asshole; I can see why he went pro – [he] probably gets off on the idea of getting paid to do stuff like that all day."

Independent security consultant Bruce Handel explained that employing a finely honed "absolute asshole" posture and facial expression can be an effective tool for otherwise unarmed security guards charged with the handling of large groups of people.

"Most of these so-called 'rent-a-cops' are ex-policemen who got fired from the force for excessive violence or bad shootings and whatnot," Handel said in an attempt to rationalize Andrews' demeanor. "Public safety is usually all these [guards] have ever known, so they often turn to putting their skills to work in the private sector – which includes bringing to their lesser positions all of the prejudices, God complexes, suspicious nature and general asshole-ness that was formerly expected of them as peace officers.

"But then there are also those, like Andrews, who just use their loathsome, asshole actions to pass the time during work," noted Handel. "As long as [Andrews] realizes he needs to grow an obnoxious mustache and maybe put on some black Aviators, I expect he'll do really well for himself, so long as he remembers to always be a complete and total asshole in response to all situations."

LEVEE from page 53

score soon before I go into full-blown withdrawal."

Having exhausted his personal supply of the illegal and highly addictive opiate Wednesday evening, Smythe began scouring known sources on the street proximate to his temporary residence behind a dumpster in Riverfront Park, only to find all of his usual dealers to be currently out of product and unable to speculate on exactly when they expected their next shipments to arrive.

"Even after I found out that all my dealers were dry, I wasn't too worried about it, because if their entire supplies were sold out, I figured that would mean that a lot of the addicts I know would be holding," Smythe said in a slightly trembling voice. "Us dope fiends are always helping each other out; you know, selling each other just enough of our own [heroin] to get by without getting dope-sick until we can score on our own."

Smythe's worst fears became realized upon the discovery that none of his associates were holding either.

"I started tracking down all my junkie buddies to ask if they were holding and they'd all say, 'Shit, man, I was about to ask you the same thing.' That's when I started grasping that I might be in real trouble," said Smythe before flooding a public trash can with vomit right in front of a group of mortified tourists. "I'm sure half of [the addicts Smythe asked] were sandbagging – lying about not having any because they were worried about their own supply drying out before the streets are again flooded with smack. But, hey, been there, done that myself on more than one occasion. Can't say that I'm proud of hording my stash, but when a crisis reaches this high of a level, it's every man for himself."

Despite being convinced that the levee was holding, a shaking and itching Smythe expressed apprehension in approaching the man-made embankment in hopes of procuring drugs.

"Trust me, I sure as hell don't want to have to resort to go begging some spur dike for some H," explained Smythe, whose physical condition was rapidly eroding. "First off, I've never dealt with her before, so she ain't gonna know me from Adam. I mean, I know from reputation that she's solid, but she won't know if I'm a cop or a narc or whatever. For all [the levee] knows I could start piping up around town about how she's constantly under tons of pressure, which could end up completely undermining her whole operation. Hell, that's exactly how the levee in Poplar Bluff [got] popped back in April."

By Friday evening, however, Smythe's worsening withdrawal symptoms compelled him to at least try to determine if the levee was holding.

"Screw it, I'm heading down there," said Smythe, whose clothes had already become soaked from the uncontrollable fountain of sweat caused by opiate withdrawal. "Besides, if I go down there and find out the levee isn't holding, at least I'll know for sure that I'm sunk. Because if the Mississippi levee system – one of the largest such systems in the world – isn't holding, then it's going to be a complete disaster. Methadone clinic, here I come."

Laboring to stand upright after having spent several hours coiled into the fetal position, Smythe managed to jest despite facing such desperation, saying: "Hell, even if the levee isn't holding, this is Cape Girardeau – the town where Rush Limbaugh was born and raised – so you know there's got to be some dope around here somewhere." ∎

COMMUNITY

Husband supports wife in activities that keep her out of the house

Above: Derek Summers' wife Barbara out on one of her many weekend kayaking trips.

Portland, Maine – Derek Summers, husband of Barbara Summers, a recently inducted member of the Maine chapter of the Sierra Club, fully supports his wife's involvement in the national out-of-doors organization, the 48-year-old construction worker told sources Saturday.

"Personally, I'm not much for the outdoors-type activities like hiking or camping, but my wife, she loves it – and as long as she's happy and out of the house, I'm happy," said Derek Summers, speaking from the recliner of his living room chair, where, dressed in only a t-shirt and boxers, Summers said he planned on spending the entire afternoon drinking beer and watching television while his wife was away on a weekend kayaking trip. "I'm all for Barbara getting out of the house and enjoying herself as often as possible. Nothing would please me more than to one day see her out traveling the state and exploring nature every single day of the year."

Summers said his wife, 46, joined the Sierra Club three months ago after years of his constant persuasion to join a group or take part in activities that would cause her to frequently be out of the house for long periods of time.

"Before Barbara joined the Sierra Club, I'd get home from work and she'd always be here – except for when she'd be out getting groceries or returning movies or getting me my cigarettes or whatever," said Summers, who admitted to rarely washing dishes, doing laundry, taking showers or putting the toilet seat down during his companionless weekends. "Now, Barbara's involvement in the Sierra Club keeps her out of the house at least a couple of nights per week for meetings, as well as nearly every weekend when they're off hiking or what have you. And me? Well, I couldn't be happier [for her]."

In addition to supporting his wife's decision to act as treasurer of the Maine chapter of the Sierra Club – a role which requires her to be present at all area meetings, fundraisers and outings – Summers also fully encourages his wife to take part in the more dangerous outdoor activities conducted by the Sierra Club such as rock climbing and white water rafting.

"Sure, when Barbara goes away for the weekend to go rock climbing on Owl Mountain, there's a fair chance she won't be coming back *at all*," said Summers, underscoring the danger involved in many of the Sierra Club's excursions. "I always try to keep in mind that there's a very good chance that instead of heading off to work on Monday morning, I could very likely be sitting down at the First Mutual office trying to get Barbara's life insurance policy cashed in."

"I think about that a lot, actually," added Summers.

Having been married to his wife for almost 17 years, Summers said he tries to be understanding if his wife is unable to find a way to call and check in with him while she is away on a weekend excursion.

"Barbara's cell phone usually doesn't get reception out in the wilderness where they go, so I know I could very well end up going three full days without hearing from her," said Summers, greeting his

> "When Barbara goes away for the weekend to go rock climbing on Owl Mountain, there's a fair chance she won't be coming back *at all*," said Summers.

> "Nothing would please me more than to one day see her out traveling the state and exploring nature every single day of the year."

poker buddies as they arrived at his house for an all-night card game. "To tell you the truth, knowing that Barbara's probably not going to be able to call me, a lot of times I won't even bother answering the phone for the entire weekend." ■

Tennis ball uploaded to server

A page from the Recoil handbook...
Protecting Your Identity

In today's electronic-driven world, protecting your personal financial information and ATM card passwords is of extreme importance. Below are some tips for protecting your personal info:

• If you notice someone looking over your shoulder at an ATM, swiftly elbow the person in the nose in an upward motion, plunging the nasal bone into the brain of the alleged identity thief or person who was just trying to see if you were someone he went to high school with.

• If you live in a building that has a public billboard, post your credit card receipts on it as a reminder to properly dispose of them when you have time.

• Obtain a copy of your credit report at least once every year so you can look and laugh at all of the jerkoffs who are never going to get one a single nickel out of you.

• Be a total asshole by creating a marketing campaign for your company that reveals your social security number and claims that nobody can steal your identity. Yeah, sure, we'll just believe you because we're all idiots.

• Don't write your social security number on all of the bad checks you write.

• To keep telephone solicitors from asking for your social security number, bank account number or credit card number, willingly offer all three right at the beginning of the conversation.

• If you discover that your identity has been stolen and used to drain money out of your bank account, keep depositing money into the account so you can keep the thief making transactions until the police get around to tracking the thief down.

• Order a copy of your credit report at least once every single day so you can make sure nobody has stolen your identity and started ruining your credit score.

• Call the police, who you can rest assured will toil night and day to find the person who charged $10 worth of movies on your Blockbuster account.

• Claim identity theft as a valid reason for cancelling your constantly overspending wife's credit cards.

page 56

RECOILMAG.COM   NEWS SATIRE YOU CAN TRUST

recoil

Report: pre-natal form of Ritalin® reduces hyperactivity in fetuses

Washington, D.C. – Results of a recent study conducted by researchers at Georgetown University suggest that the use of Pritalin®, a version of the ADHD drug Ritalin® specially formulated for second- and third-trimester fetuses, can significantly reduce symptoms of in-the-womb hyperactivity in unborn children.

"Our research shows that the daily use of Pritalin® by an expectant mother can have dramatic results in calming the behavior of an unborn child who is fidgeting and fussing around and whatnot in the womb

> "My little sunshine hasn't kicked in months, ever since I started taking Pritalin®," said Dault, smiling as she rubbed her stomach with both hands.

– a period during which the fetus should instead remain mostly docile as it focuses one hundred percent on its physical development," said Dr. John H. Ryan, lead researcher on the study.

Engineered and manufactured by Novartis, the same pharmaceutical company that developed the miracle breakthrough drug methylphenidate (known by the brand name Ritalin®), Pritalin® is designed to be ingested in pill form once daily by women who have been pregnant for more than three months and have

see FETUSES page 60

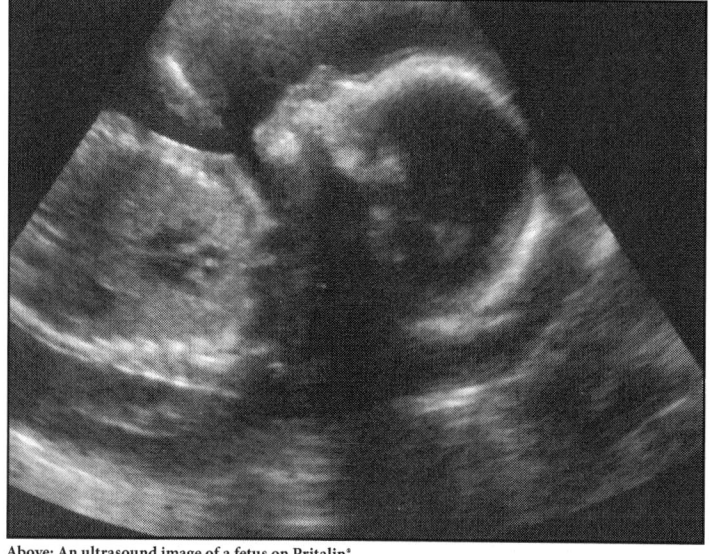

Above: An ultrasound image of a fetus on Pritalin®.

Above: The Grammy-winning metal band's songs are no longer being referred to as "Mandatory Metallica" when introduced on the radio.

Metallica no longer mandatory

Washington, D.C. – Hundreds of thousands of U.S. radio listeners voiced a sigh of relief Friday after FCC regulators announced that modern rock stations are no longer allowed to air daily "Mandatory Metallica" song blocks – a practice that's been religiously employed by program directors nationwide since the mid-90s.

"Considering the abhorrent quality and declining value of Metallica's last four releases, it is the FCC's decision that the band's music can no longer be considered 'mandatory' under even the loosest of mainstream radio standards," said FCC spokesperson Fredrick Moore. "Therefore, stations are heretofore disallowed from the daily airing of three or more of the band's songs in a row as part of a 'Muh-Muh-Muh-Mandatory Metallica' segment, as it is typically called."

Mandatory Metallica – the catchy alliterative moniker for three- to six-song radio segments that draw from Metallica's extensive catalog of radio singles – became widespread among

> "This annulment of Metallica's 'mandatory' standing will be upheld by all active radio program directors," said Moore.

modern rock stations when the band's 1991 multi-platinum self-titled album culminated in mainstream success for a band that had previously toiled for over a decade in the underground metal scene.

The FCC's decision to outlaw Mandatory Metallica segments came after more than 680,000 radio listeners signed petitions encouraging the commission to rescind Metallica music's 'mandatory' status.

"This annulment of Metallica's 'mandatory' standing will be upheld by all active radio program directors," said Moore, "even directors who commonly ignore Metallica's later, weaker, misguided efforts in favor of spinning some of the killer, old-school cuts off of, say, *Ride the Lightning* or *…And Justice For All*. Even though the tunes on those albums totally rock, playing a bunch of those tracks in a row as part of a Mandatory Metallica segment would still constitute a violation."

According to sources, many of those

see METALLICA page 60

Third-grader announces list of classmates who swear

Above: Grade school student Lisa Neumann.

Athens, Ga. – Benson Elementary third-grade student Lisa Neumann announced a comprehensive list detailing the first and last names of classmates who swear, sources confirmed Sunday.

"Billy Augton says the 'H' word *all* the time," stated a focused, unwavering Neumann from the backseat of her parents' Ford Astrovan as the family returned home from church services late Sunday morning. "And Joey Griffin and Todd Lent say it too, like, constantly."

Surprised by Neumann's unprompted revelation, the youth's parents, Cyndi and Damon Neumann, later claimed they

> "Billy Augton says the 'H' word *all* the time," stated a focused, unwavering Neumann from the backseat of her parents' Ford Astrovan.

in no way encouraged their daughter's verbal disclosure of the behavior of her foul-mouthed classmates, and in fact sought to convince the child to abruptly end her unrehearsed statement.

"I think I said something like, 'Is that right? You know, you should never say that word. That's for grownups,'" said Neumann's mother, recalling her reaction to the child's impromptu dissertation. "I

see LIST page 59

Lake effect partners with booze effect

Doggie paddled

recoilmag.com

page 57

COMMUNITY

Man dies living day like it was his last

Above: Adams poses for a photo before riding a fast, dangerous motorcycle like there was no tomorrow.

Newark, N.J. – Greg Adams, a computer software engineer at Adobe Systems, died Monday only hours after a radio talk show host advised the unmarried 31-year-old to begin living every day of his life like it was his last day on Earth.

"The deceased phoned into the morning *Straight Talk* advice show complaining that his life felt meaningless," said Pat Rowing, the show's host. "I gave the caller the typical 'Life is what you make it' pep-talk and told him to start living every day like it's his last. Unfortunately, the caller appears to have taken that advice a bit too literally."

According to sources, Adams was pronounced dead on the scene shortly before midnight after crashing a rented motorcycle into a concrete highway abutment at 180 miles per hour while slugging tequila and wearing nothing but an athletic supporter.

"Speeding naked through the streets jacked up on booze isn't exactly the first thing that *I* would think to do with my last day on Earth, but hey, different strokes, you know?" said officer Miles Landon, who was present at the scene of the crash. "The guy was definitely living like there was no tomorrow – which I guess for him there isn't, now. Funny how that works."

James Horn, a coworker of Adams, said the deceased had spent the earlier part of the day behaving in a manner unbefitting of a person restrained by the conventions of future consequence or accountability.

"Greg showed up for work right on time, but instead of sitting down at his desk he marched right up to our boss and told him to go fuck himself," said Horn. "Then he said really loudly, 'I'll see all you suckers later – like never!' and headed toward the exit. [Coworker] Fay [Joyce] said Greg grabbed the receptionist and planted one on her on the way out the door. I didn't know if maybe he'd won the lottery or something, but at that point we were all pretty sure we'd seen the last of Greg."

Added Horn: "Boy, were we right about that."

Witnesses reported seeing Adams carry out a number of other indulgent, reckless and vindictive activities that reflected Adams' commitment to living the day like it was his last.

"I saw Greg in a shop downtown maxing out three of his credit cards on a flashy silk suit," said Kara Hardings, an acquaintance of Adams'. "I asked him what the occasion was and all he said was that he was 'going out in style,' so I figured he was just getting ready for a fancy dinner or something."

Adams was later spotted at a five-star restaurant surrounded by four scantily clad female escorts and ordering one helping of every item on the menu.

In addition to spending his entire life savings and available credit on superficial, instantly gratifying luxuries, Adams also confessed to his best friend Eric Meyers about having slept with Meyers' girlfriend; streaked across Giants Stadium during the Monday Night Football game; and set his ex-girlfriend Julie Cason's car on fire during her daily tanning appointment.

Dr. Patrick Leonard, a clinical psychologist in Newark, said that it would be wrong to perceive the advice of Rowing as being responsible for Adams' self-destructive actions.

"Anyone with a stitch of common sense understands that's a figure of speech, that you can't actually live every day like there's no tomorrow," said Leonard. "If you did you wouldn't have much of a life left when you woke up the next morning."

"We all have a vision of how we'd live our final day, when there would be no consequences to our actions," Leonard continued. "For example, if it were *my* last day on Earth, I'd probably spend it sunning myself in Aruba, drinking margaritas out of the bloody skull of that bastard that ran off with my wife. But such temporary thinking is completely impractical in a civilized world, lucky for him." ■

> Adams was pronounced dead on the scene shortly before midnight after crashing a rented motorcycle into a concrete highway abutment at 180 miles per hour while slugging tequila and wearing nothing but an athletic supporter.

EDITORIAL

It's a living

By Rex the Pterodactyl

You know, supplying motive power to an assortment of prehistoric household items ain't always a picnic. The hours are long, and the tasks are often pretty thankless. I mean, geez, let's be frank: a lot of birds out there probably have more free time than I do. Instead of engaging in the drudgery of repetitive manual labor, they're hanging out in the park or flying south for the winter or whatever.

Chances are they've never spent eight hours blowing air on a fireplace by having their legs repeatedly squeezed back and forth. They've also likely never sat inside a 10-pound granite camera, chiseling images onto tablets with their beaks in the 90-degree heat. Then again, who am I to complain? A lot of these poor fellas don't even have enough money to take care of their wives and kids. Yeah, the work I do can be pretty grueling some days, but at least it's enough to put a few worms in the ol' nest. What can I tell you? It's a living.

Contrary to what you might have heard, most anthropomorphic feathered vertebrates can count on landing some form of gainful employment. If you're not afraid of a solid day's work, chances are you won't have to line up at the ol' welfare office all that often. Gosh knows I've been able to hold on to a bunch of decent jobs over the years: intercom, hedge clipper, crochet needle, car horn – the list goes on.

Heck, in my younger years I even spent a couple of summers working as a pie maker. I'd use my beak to trim the extra crust around the pan, and then crimp the top and bottom crust together with my feet. It was good, honest work, and hey, if you kept your mouth shut and minded your Ps and Qs, at the end of the day they'd give you some free pie filling to take home to la familia. Sure, a job like that ain't the most glamorous thing in the world. But I'll tell you this much for free: It's a living.

I've been hearing a lot of talk about electricity someday being harnessed and used as a means of power generation. You know, like some sort of energy conversion system capable of independently fueling various home and industrial appliances. Guys down at the pub are saying when that day comes, birds everywhere will be emancipated, finally freed from their "oppressive shackles," whatever that's supposed to mean. All I can say about that is, does "freedom" mean not having the money to cover your water bill every month? 'Cause I'll tell you something: if you're even a few days late on a payment, those elephant trunks are gonna stop spraying.

Yep, if it's all the same, I think I'll keep on doing what I'm doing. A little dirt under the ol' claws sure as shucks never hurt anybody. Heck, some people say you haven't truly worked until you've taken a job as an agitator for a washing machine. And you know something? I have a feeling they might be right. This line of work may not look like much to a lot of folks out there, but at the end of the day, one thing's for sure: it's a living. ■

> Supplying motive power to an assortment of prehistoric household items ain't always a picnic.

WORLDWIDE HEADLINES

Woman dresses, sets ringtone according to mood

Dallas, Texas – Nina Faye Young, a 28-year-old advertising salesperson at WITF radio, told reporters Tuesday morning that she begins every day by dressing and programming her cell phone's ringtone in a way that directly reflects her mood on that day. "If I'm feeling all chipper and happening I'll wear something playful and set my phone to play Outkast's 'Hey Ya' or maybe a Justin Timberlake song or something," said a leather-clad Young, who said her cell phone was currently set to play Steppenwolf's "Born To Be Wild" because she was feeling "free and adventurous." Other popular choices for Young include R.E.M.'s "Everybody Hurts" for days marked by depression and Prince's "Darling Nikki" for when she's feeling sexy.

Horrified teen walks in on parents crunking in bedroom

Cleveland, Ohio – A horrifying image was forever burned into the brain of 15-year-old hip-hop fan Denise Kress Saturday night when the daughter of Don and Brenda Kress walked unannounced into her parents' bedroom only to find her parents clumsily attempting to crunk dance to a Flo Rida song in what the couple had assumed was complete privacy. "Obviously, I've known for years what crunk dancing is – I'm 15 years old, you know – I just never imagined my *parents* doing it, let alone walking in on them and seeing them doing it," said Denise Kress. "When I accidentally saw mom and dad crunking – with all of their disgusting thrusting and wet-noodling and such – it was, like, so gross, and now I can't get the image out of my head." Despite her parents' attempt to explain that what she had seen was "simply a perfectly natural extension of their love [for modern music]," Denise quickly apologized to her parents for the intrusion, insisting she had "not really seen anything," but was later heard promising to "go bleach her eyeballs," by an anonymous sibling.

Court date expected to inhibit area hipster's hairdo

Minneapolis, Minn. – Despite used CD store cashier Geoff Iginla's personal oath to maintain his intentionally messy hairstyle in spite of any unforeseeable social pressures, a source close to Iginla said Monday he expects the 23-year-old's Sept. 18 court date to radically transform Iginla's hairstyle into something more straight-laced and conservative-looking. "Geoff's managed to keep his purposely unkempt-looking through college graduation and job interviews, but court's another situation altogether," said friend Dwayne Knight. "Sure, it's a first offense pinch for possession [of marijuana], but I suspect Geoff's nervous enough about it to snip his do in order to look more like an upstanding citizen." Knight also suggested that Iginla's day in court will likely also involve the breaking-out of his only suit.

Life-term inmate treated for depression

Jackson, Mich. – Jackson State Penitentiary inmate Stephen "Spike" Leger, who is serving a mandatory life sentence without the possibility of parole for the first degree killing of his wife in 1998, is being treated for clinical depression by the prison medical staff, sources reported Friday. "We currently have the patient on a powerful combination of Prozac® and Zoloft®, coupled with daily one-hour talk-therapy sessions, in hopes of curbing the relentless feelings of worthlessness and pointlessness that the patient wrestles with daily," prison psychiatrist Dr. Renee Zielinski said of the 33-year-old inmate. "One thing Spike needs to understand is that recovering from depression takes time, and as long as he's willing to invest that time, he will soon realize that there is a very bright future awaiting him – except, of course, for the fact that he's going to be incarcerated for the remainder of his days."

Peter writes bad check to Paul

Hollywood, Calif. – Enacting revenge for what he regards as years of "thievery through association," Peter wrote a check to Paul Wednesday knowing full well that the check will fail to clear at Paul's bank because of insufficient funds, sources report. "I can't even begin to count how many times over the years that Peter has been robbed in order to pay Paul," Clint Van Allen, an attorney for Peter, told reporters. "It's no wonder that my client – and only *if* he's guilty, mind you – maybe felt the need to give Paul a little taste of what it feels like to get the short end of the stick in a financial transaction. Perhaps in the future, Paul will think twice about so cheerfully accepting money that he knows damn well he is receiving only at Peter's expense."

Vending machine endorses all-quarter diet

Ypsilanti, Mich. – According to the Dr. Pepper machine on the corner of Court St. and Marshall Ave., a strict all-quarter diet is far superior to taking in a random selection of folding money, dimes and nickels. "I've eaten every combination of change imaginable during my six years on the street, and I can tell you without a doubt that just eating a user's quarters is the way to go if you want to operate at top efficiency," the machine told reporters Thursday. "Nickels and dimes might fill you up faster, and everyone knows that one dollar bills are really hard for machines to swallow sometimes, but quarters are without a doubt my favorite denominations to eat. I've eaten a ton of quarters in my lifetime, and I'm still holding the same weight and figure I had when I first got started in this business – even if inflation has me eating more change than I ever have before."∎

LIST from page 57

was hoping that would just end it."

However, after only a short contemplative pause marked by a slight increase in the car radio's volume, Neumann continued voicing her thorough account of recent schoolroom vulgarity and its users.

"Tori Lager told me she heard Noel Gillens say, 's-h-i-t,'" Neumann offered in a firm yet charmingly naïve tone.

Clearly concerned with the increasingly blue content of her daughter's incriminations, Neumann's father further discouraged her to refrain from continuing the report.

"At that point I told Lisa I'd heard enough," said Neumann's father. "I told her, 'Never mind what other kids say, you, girl, are not to even allowed to spell words like that. Now that's enough.'"

Determined to finish the list of indictments, Neumann chose to ignore her father's authoritative statement and conclude the report by citing her last and perhaps most fantastic account of the vocalized obscenities.

"On the playground I heard Teddy Sorton say the swear word that rhymes with 'truck,'" stated Neumann. "He's in sixth grade. The first letter of the word is an 'F.'"

Neumann's testimony broke weeks of silence regarding the nature and frequency of her exposure to adult-oriented phrases. Neumann's last documented report of "naughty language" occurred in April, when she informed cousin Kimmy Robb that she'd overheard Uncle Jim accidentally say "tit" at a family Thanksgiving gathering.

While motivations behind Neumann's decision to list the young ill-linguists remains unclear, the child's parents suspect attending Sunday's church service may have provoked the child's willingly divulged deposition.

"Pastor McNeil was preaching heavily about the importance of the Ten Commandments," said Neumann's father. "I think maybe she felt she needed to confess what she knew, to get it off her chest."

Neumann's parents said they at this time have no intentions of forwarding the list of swearers to school officials or the children's respective parents. ∎

> "Tori Lager told me she heard Noel Gillens say, 's-h-i-t,'" Neumann offered in a firm yet charmingly naïve tone.

Recoil's Shallow Thoughts

- I've been training my dog to do a lot of the menial tasks I hate doing. But don't call my house to ask about details because he's especially poor at answering the phone as of yet.

- The original purpose of carbonated beverages was to fight indigestion. I generally don't get indigestion, so I drink whiskey – and let me tell you, it's kept me free of throat cancer for years.

- My wife and I did this thing once and when we were done we couldn't even look each other in the eye. Simultaneously, we whispered, "Let's never do that again." Those mountain bikes have been hanging on the garage wall ever since.

- There's this scrawny coyote that lives in our suburb. All of the neighborhood moms think it's a wolf. I've shown them, like, a million cardboard ACME boxes hidden around the woods, but they still insist it's a wolf.

- Why is it that a person is referred to as "Justice of the Peace" the first time you see him, but the next time you see him he's referred to as "That miserable cocksucker who's going to give her half my shit!?!"

- Rule of thumb: If you can pronounce "elocutionist," you don't need one.

- One basic medical tip I've picked up over the years is that it isn't all that unusual to discover blood in your urine if you're being repeatedly stabbed while on the toilet.

- There's nothing more satisfying to a man than buying a great lawn tractor. Except, of course, for the satisfaction of stealing one. But I guess that goes without saying.

SCIENCE
Cloned cat just as much of an asshole as original

Rainbow (left) and Cc mingle before pissing all over a cloning team member's clipboard.

Galveston, Tex. – The world's first clone of a domestic cat is every bit as much of an unfriendly, temperamental asshole as the feline from which she was cloned, members of the Texas A&M University cloning team confirmed Thursday.

According to team member Mark Westhusin, Cc (short for "Carbon Copy"), now a full-grown two-year-old, exhibits the same unpleasant demeanor and malevolent behavior as that of Rainbow, the three-colored calico from which Cc received her DNA.

"As you might expect, everything about Cc's personality – from the way she hisses and bares her fangs whenever you walk into the room to the way she scratches the hell out of you if you even try to touch her – is identical to Rainbow's," said Westhusin. "The fact that Rainbow's piss-poor attitude and thoroughly unlikable personality have transferred so perfectly to her clone is great news for pet owners who are looking to someday be able to clone their favorite pets. Although, honestly, I can't imagine any pet owner in their right mind that would want another version of Rainbow walking around their house. The cat hates everyone, you know."

Westhusin said that within minutes of the clone's birth on Dec. 21, 2001, even before DNA tests could confirm a match, members of the cloning team were certain the kitten was a legitimate clone of Rainbow.

"Judging by Cc's colors and the way she instinctively tried to bite [cloning team member] Tim [Sanders] on the hand for no reason, well, we pretty much knew right away she was Rainbow's exact clone," said Westhusin. "In fact, see these bite marks I have on each of my hands? The one on my right hand is from Rainbow, the one on my left from Cc. See how the bite patterns are the same? That's because having the same DNA has caused them to develop the same dental structure."

"Jesus, cats! Chill out!" interrupted A&M researcher Mike Borland, struggling to keep Cc and Rainbow on his lap while posing for press photographers with the history-making felines. "Guys, can we wrap this up before these two shitheads send me to the emergency room?"

Westhusin said that although Cc and Rainbow are exactly alike in almost every way – including their size, color and general contempt for everything in the world that doesn't involve them getting fed – the two felines do have slight differences.

"Cc tends to spend her spare time destroying the backs of all of our chairs [with her claws], whereas Rainbow prefers to trash the screens on all of our cages for her own personal amusement," said Westhusin. "At first I was like, 'Okay, next time we're cloning a cat that's been declawed.' But then of course I realized that that wouldn't work, that the kitten would in fact still be born with claws."

Besides taking every opportunity to destroy University property and scratch or bite members of the cloning team, Rainbow and her asshole clone are also known to urinate on at least one piece of the team's important paperwork on a daily basis.

Westhusin admitted that although his team is delighted that its landmark experiment was a success, team members do regret choosing such a detestable and hostile specimen for cloning.

"I don't know why we couldn't have picked a more gentle, fun-loving kitty to clone instead of that ornery little fucker, Rainbow," said Westhusin. "At the time I guess all we were really concerned with was that the subject be healthy and have very distinctive features. It's too bad nobody ever thought to stand up and say, 'Does anybody else think it's dumb that we're about to create *another* version of a cat that none of us can stand to be in the same room with?'" ∎

FETUSES from page 57

fetuses that are constantly fidgeting around or displaying similar behavioral problems. The medication reaches the fetus through the mother's umbilical cord and causes a chemical reaction that corrects the dopamine imbalance assumed to be occurring in the fetus' still-developing brain.

"There are a large number of unborn children who, through no fault of their own, simply cannot sit still while they're in the womb," David Morris, public relations director for Novartis, said during a recent interview. "These fetuses are often disrupting their mothers during their day-to-day activity by acting out – usually through punching and kicking – and causing much discomfort for their mothers, who would prefer that their unborn children sit quietly and not cause such commotions. It is to help control the behavior of these future infants that Pritalin® was designed."

Participating in the pre-natal study was Arlene Dault, a 35-year-old mother of two who is currently expecting a baby girl in late January.

"My little sunshine hasn't kicked in months, ever since I started taking Pritalin®," said Dault, smiling as she rubbed her stomach with both hands.

"I started taking the medication in November, but before that my future little black belt would be kicking and punching me all day long. Now I sometimes wonder if she's even still alive down there. That's how well the pills are working."

Morris said that marketing executives at Novartis are hoping that once Pritalin® gains FDA approval, the revolutionary drug will open up a vast, untapped market for the pharmaceutical giant.

"Until now, one hundred percent of methylphenidate prescriptions have been written for children or adults – patients who, remember, are already out of the womb," said Morris. "With Pritalin®, we will now be able to start treating patients before they are even born, making it that much more likely that they will use Ritalin® after they are removed from the womb. That's building customer loyalty at a never before heard of age: before they are even born."

Morris confirmed that Novartis will be a willing and active participant in a future Georgetown University study aimed at discovering the short- and long-term effects of Pritalin® on child development following birth. The study is scheduled to begin in the summer of 2012. ∎

twitter: @RecoilMagazine

METALLICA from page 57

who signed the petition were in fact longtime Metallica fans who had become increasingly fatigued with radio stations' overplaying of the band's music as well as the artistic direction the band has pursued since 1996's *Load* LP.

"I'll admit, five or six years ago it was pretty cool to hear rock stations playing three or four Metallica songs in a row on a daily basis, considering that these same stations wouldn't even touch [Metallica singles] until 'One' came out," said longtime fan Mark Elms. "But now every day when I hear that Mandatory Metallica intro, I'm like, 'Jesus, enough is enough already.' I guess these stations hadn't figured out that everybody pretty much tuned out after they did that record where they played with that symphony."

"Man, does that record blow," added Elms. "I still can't listen to the original 'For Whom the Bell Tolls' without hearing those goddamned string parts in my head now."

Though program directors across the nation voiced their opposition to the FCC's decision, many radio station staff members expressed mixed feelings regarding the ban.

"After having abided to the daily Metallica law for so many years, through the good and the bad, we're all still coming to grips with the fact that Mandatory Metallica is finally over," said Rob Gaines, an afternoon DJ at the Los Angeles station KROQ. "When I was growing up with Metallica's music, I used to just dream about a time when their songs would receive *any* airplay, let alone be a staple component of every rock station's play list. So in that sense, I'm kind of sad to think that now there won't be a Mandatory Metallica segment every day. On the other hand, I couldn't be more relieved to know that I won't have to act like I'm excited to play 'The Unforgiven' every other day. And don't even get me started about having to hype up their *Saint Anger* singles, which everyone at the station agrees are complete trash."

Rather than fight the FCC regulation, a majority of program directors polled indicated that they would instead introduce a new daily song block feature that spotlights an act that is currently experiencing significant popularity.

"Here at KROQ we're throwing around the idea of starting a daily block called 'Never-Ending Nickelback,' which I'm not really sure how I feel about yet," said Gaines. "I've also heard our PD talking about segments called 'Essential Evanescense,' 'Compulsory Creed' and 'Unavoidable U2.'" ∎

RECOILMAG.COM   NEWS SATIRE YOU CAN TRUST

recoil

Life coach always wants to meet at bar

Above: Professional Certified Life Coach Walter Billings (left) listens to client Paul Avery while seated at the bar of Morgan's Tavern.

Madison, Wis. – Clients of certified life coach Walter Billings confirmed Friday that the 52-year-old independent contractor routinely suggests meeting his clients at a local tavern rather than communicating his expert life advice via more traditional means of telephone or e-mail.

"[Walter] just *looks* like he's been around the block about a hundred times or so," said Albert Holden.

"I guess it's kind of weird that Walter always asks me to meet him downtown for a drink to conduct our weekly life
see COACH page 64

Broad cast

Schizophrenic man's sandwich not agreeing with him

quikSTAT

What in heaven's name is taking us so long in the bathroom?
- Conceiving witty retort to stall graffiti insult
- Trying to make stuffed crotch symmetrical
- Just died on toilet
- Processing seventh cappuccino
- Determining relationship to equator
- Finding it kind of hard to reach climax with you banging on the door like that

Above: Death metal band Asphyx. Heavy metal musicians have been found to be especially susceptible to RHS.

Study: 95 percent of metalheads suffer from Restless Head Syndrome

Washington, D.C. – Researchers at Georgetown University announced Friday the results of a study showing that as many as 95 percent of all heavy metal music enthusiasts worldwide suffer from a disorder called Restless Head Syndrome (RHS) – a condition characterized by an irresistible urge to repeatedly move one's head in a violent up and down motion when listening to loud, heavy music.

"Restless Head Syndrome has affected young heavy metal music lovers for decades, but until now these folks have gone undiagnosed as suffering from an actual medical condition," said Dr. Neil Graham, lead researcher in the study.

Simple behavioral changes can ease RHS sufferer's symptoms.

"As a result, many of these people have desperately turned to self-medicating – mostly by ingesting large amounts of caffeine and/or alcohol – which we now know only exacerbates their symptoms."

The Georgetown study showed that RHS mostly affects young males between the ages of 13 and 40 who listen to heavy metal music and tend to wear their hair long or styled as a mullet. Sufferers' symptoms tend to worsen during the evening or night, with the fierce, repeated up and down motion often leading them to later suffer severe back pain, strained or pulled neck muscles, headaches or even whiplash.
see RHS page 63

Surgeons remove Barenaked Ladies song from area man's head

Gary, Ind. – In a desperate race against time, surgeons at Gary Methodist Hospital successfully removed a Barenaked Ladies song from local maintenance worker Daniel Hudson's head early Friday afternoon.

According to doctors, the song – "One Week," from Barenaked Ladies' breakthrough fifth album, *Stunt* – became lodged in the 32-year-old's head after his daughter repeatedly played and sang along with the wildly addictive tune in her bedroom last Saturday afternoon.

"That very evening I started hearing pieces of ["One Week"] in my head," said Hudson. "I knew that getting that stupid song [stuck] in my head was going to be a problem, but I figured it would just
see SURGEONS page 64

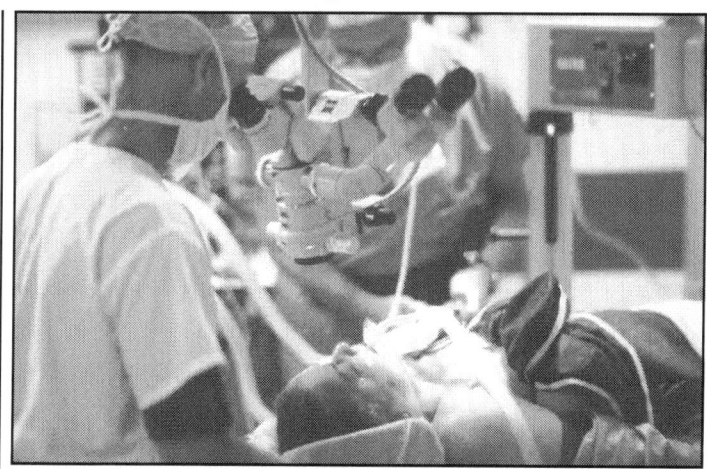

Above: Surgeons race against time to remove the smash single "One Week" from Hudson's head.

page 61

WORLDWIDE HEADLINES

Man has complete conversation with self on friend's voicemail

Gary, Ind. – Systems Analyst Pete Stevens reeled off a thorough conversation with himself while leaving a message on friend Tim Steep's home voicemail system early Thursday evening. "Hey, Tim, it's Pete," the recorded message said. "[I was] wondering if you were going out tonight. I think I am. Well, actually, probably not. I've got to get up early. But then again that Stephanie girl said she was hitting Waldo's [Tavern] later so maybe I'll just go for a quick one. Anyway, I guess I'll talk to you later." At time of press Steep could not be reached to confirm the intent to return Stevens' call.

Determined salesman won't take repeated stabbing for an answer

St. Petersburg, Fla. – Ultra-resilient door-to-door magazine subscription salesman Dale Remington won't take being repeatedly punctured by the knife of an unwilling potential customer as a final "no" according to a witness who saw the 44-year-old salesman stabbed nearly to death on the porch of Marcus Demetri's home during an unwanted sales solicitation Monday afternoon. "At first, [Remington] simply wouldn't take 'no' for an answer," said Tom Brantwood, a neighbor of Demetri who viewed both the attempted sale and attempted murder from his next-door garden. "Marcus got so angry that the salesman wouldn't just go away that he eventually took out his pocketknife and stabbed the guy a couple times." Brantwood confirmed that, despite quickly losing significant amounts of blood from multiple stab wounds in his abdomen, the three-time Salesman of the Year refused to vacate Demetri's doorway until the resident agreed to sign up for at least one 12-month subscription to *Maxim*, *Rolling Stone*, *Boy's Life* or a number of other mainstream periodicals.

Aging scientist discovers, forgets cure for Alzheimer's

Berkley, Calif. – Dr. Lawrence Clark, a 78-year-old research scientist and Alzheimer's sufferer, discovered the cure for his memory disorder late Sunday afternoon before completely forgetting the landmark solution only moments later. Clark, who experiences bouts of dementia, emotional instability and confusion resulting from his condition, retained memory of his breakthrough discovery for nearly three minutes before losing his train of thought, erasing his revolutionary chalkboard calculations and playing tic-tac-toe over the remnants of the miracle cure. Sources said Clark then stared blankly at his chalkboard for nearly two hours before attempting to use several small pieces of chalk as suppositories.

Hell half full

Hell – Officials announced Sunday that occupancy of the popular afterlife destination has reached 50 percent. "Don't worry, humans, there's still plenty of room for all of you sinners," said Satan at a press conference held late Sunday morning. "We're confident we'll have enough space to house the eternal souls of you pitiful mortals for at least two more millenniums, possibly three." Hell officials cite Heaven's unrealistic applicant requirements, an increased efficiency in Purgatory's processing department and the exponentially compounded unwrapping of humanity's moral fiber as reasons for Hell's recent rise in tenancy.

Inexperienced stalker adds Jennifer Lopez' name to Blockbuster card

Hollywood, Calif. – Thirty-three-year-old carpet cleaner and first-time celebrity stalker Larry Golmer has authorized actress/singer Jennifer Lopez to rent videos using his new Blockbuster account, store cashier Jody Walker reported Tuesday. "We were signing [Golmer up for a card] and I asked him if he wanted any other names added to his account," Walker explained. "He said, 'Just my girlfriend, Jennifer Lopez. She stays at the house sometimes.' I was like, 'Whatever, dude.'" Golmer then rented *Angel Eyes* and *Selena*, insisting to Walker that he "is kind of embarrassed to have not yet seen many of [his] girlfriend's films."

Man horny again half-hour after visiting Chinese hooker

Chapel Hill, N.C. – Only 30 minutes after paying a Chinese prostitute to have sex with him, mortgage broker Jason Leeham is already horny again, the 33-year-old reported earlier. "All of a sudden I feel like I need to have sex again," said Leeham. "And here I just had a Chinese [girl] not half an hour ago. That's so weird. I remember feeling totally satisfied when I was finished, but now I could really go for some more [sex]." Leeham added that although he is indeed horny again he "[isn't] really in the mood for [a] Chinese [girl] again. Maybe some Thai [action]."

Sharp, mobile 32-year-old constantly referring to himself as an old man

Arlington, Texas – Despite having full command over his mental and physical faculties, area construction supervisor Keith Connelly, 32, repeatedly characterizes himself as an old man when conversing with others, a source close to the sharp-witted, upwardly mobile young man said Tuesday. "Every time Keith gets out of his truck he always groans and says something like, '[I'm] getting to be an old man,'" said 67-year-old mason Art McSweeny, Connelly's oldest employee. "I'm sorry, but anyone who can still physically run if they want to, or has no problem remembering where he parked or controlling his bladder, is not an old man, period. Start wearing diapers again and you can call yourself and old man all you want, Keith."

Roommate asshole

Detroit, Mich. – Two weeks after cosigning a six-month apartment lease with acquaintance Damion Snyder, Simon Holden told reporters Thursday he is "ready to bail" on the agreement, on grounds that Snyder is an asshole. "You know how some people just have that asshole quality about them?" a frustrated Holden mused. "Beyond his vast and many character flaws, he also leaves beer cans everywhere and never flushes the toilet. The other day he dumped his bong water in the fish tank because he was too lazy to walk to the sink. I think I've made my case." ■

EDITORIAL

We should get really high right before pulling this armed robbery

By Johnny G.

Tony. Hey, Tony. Tony, open up, man, it's me. Tony, let me in!!! Jesus, what the hell, man – we were supposed to meet up like an hour ago. What do you mean you fell asleep? How in the world could you fall asleep right before we do a job? There's no way in hell I could sleep right now, as anxious as I am. Well, shit, I'm here now, so let's do a quick bump and go do this thing.

There, that ought to put a spring in your step, eh? Yeah, that's all I had left. Now hurry up and get dressed so we can get on the road – we should have been back here counting our take by now. By the way, does that guy in your building still deal coke? Good, because we'll need some party favors for celebrating after our score. Can you call and see if he's around? He is? Sweet. See, things are going right for us already!

Actually, dude, how much money do you have *right now*? Oh, shit – you're loaded, man! What do you need to be stealing for? Just kidding, just kidding. Seriously though, the reason I ask is because I'm tapped out and, well, I had an idea on my way over here – and remember, this is just an idea – but I was thinking that maybe we should get really gacked up right before we pull this armed robbery. Yeah? Cool, I thought you might agree. Well what are we waiting for? Get that dude on the phone!

Ah, just what the doctor ordered. There's nothing like an eight-ball of blow to get your blood up right before a job! Shit, I don't feel nervous at all now. I feel like the king of the world! Supercharged! Unstoppable! Invincible!

You know what? Pass me that box of ammunition. No, I know – I don't normally load my gun for a small job like this either, but a feeling suddenly came over me just now that I might need to fire a few off tonight for some reason. Better safe than sorry, right?

> Think about it: if you're acting all calm and collected and shit, the cashier's not going to take you seriously.

You ready for another blast? Cool. Hey, grab me another beer out of the fridge while you're up. Thanks, man. A toast: to the perfect crime. Man, we are going to fucking rock tonight! Give me that bag, I'm setting us up a couple of French fries. Let me show you how to do this. Now *that*, my friends, is a line of cocaine. Go ahead, man: hit that shit!

This was a really good idea, getting good and wired before we stick up this joint. This way we know for sure that we're going to be confident, alert and ready for anything. Really, if you think about it, the last thing you'd want to do is go in while you're totally straight. Think about it: if you're acting all calm and collected and shit, the cashier's not going to take you seriously. Not me, man; I'd much rather be jabbering like a fucking madman and so coked up that I look like I could start shooting up the joint at any second. That's the only way the clerk is going to respect you and do what you want.

I can't believe we were even considering

see **EDITORIAL page 63**

EDITORIAL from page 62

pulling this job without getting high first. What were we thinking? One thing's for sure: you've got to use your head in this business or you'll end up dead or behind bars. Good thing we're two of the smartest sons of bitches alive, eh?

My dumb-ass brother says he won't touch a speck of white before pulling a job because he wants to have a clear head for assessing situations and carefully weighing decisions while the jig is on. Me, I say fuck that shit. I'd rather rely on my instincts when it comes to that sort of thing. Speaking of which, let's have another dose of that Instinct Honing Powder. Thank you, kind sir. Jesus, that shit is good!

Okay, that's the last of it. Good thing, too, because I feel like one more line might put me completely sideways. God, I am so tweaked right now. Man, do I feel sorry for any poor sucker that tries to fuck with me tonight, because he's liable to get force-fed six helpings of lead salad.

What do you mean, "get your keys?" Dude, there's no way in hell I could drive right now. Fuck it, let's just rob a closer liquor store. This way we can walk. ■

RHS from page 61

"Headbangers, the slang name for RHS sufferers, are usually completely unaware that they even suffer from this illness," said Dr. Graham. "Just as most people who suffered from Restless Leg Syndrome (RLS) didn't know they had a medical condition until after a remedy was developed – simply thinking they just had 'the jimmylegs' – RHS sufferers need to be medically diagnosed and put on a path to recovery."

Dr. Graham said that although no medication has yet been developed to eliminate the symptoms of RHS, simple behavioral changes can ease the sufferer's symptoms.

"Patients seeking relief from RHS need to do is stop listening to loud, aggressive heavy metal and start listening to softer, less intense styles of music," said Dr. Graham. "Instead of rocking out to Pantera or Slayer, for example, patients should try listening at a reasonable volume to, say, George Michael or Neil Diamond or something. Barry White. Frank Sinatra. Hell, Yanni, even. Anything that doesn't have a bunch of yelling and screaming."

Heavy metal musicians – a group of people who the study acknowledges as being at an exceptionally increased risk of developing RHS – have largely rejected the idea that the music they create is responsible for listeners developing the symptoms of Restless Head Syndrome.

"I've been headbanging to loud music since I was a teenager, and I'm no worse for wear from it," said Mick Thompson, guitarist for the heavy metal band Slipknot. Asked if the 2005 stroke incurred by Evanescence guitarist Terry Balsamo as a result of onstage headbanging worried his at all, Thompson replied: "Who cares – I hate that band." ■

Young, male concertgoers (above) are at an increased risk of developing RHS.

HOROSCOPES

Capricorn (December 22 to January 19)
Your romantic lethargy has put you on the fast track to becoming emotionally terminal. Your dried-up, withered heart needs a shot of love – or a shot of adrenaline straight through the ribcage. Take your cue from the blooming tulips and open yourself up to somebody's sunshine. Either that, or OD on heroin, and you're likely to get that needle of adrenalin. Either way, revival is certain.

Aquarius (January 20 to February 18)
You are a Venus Flytrap amidst a field of wild daisies. This could be a problem seeing that you are a carnivorous plant and a daisy doesn't have a lick of meat on it anywhere. Look at the bright side, though: they are wild daisies, so maybe you and those happy flowers can party hard until you starve to death. This IS a metaphor.

Pisces (February 19 to March 20)
Debtor's prison may be a thing of the past, but with your credit rating, you are an inmate of the prison of "cash only." While other people are maxing out VISAs, driving SUVs and miring themselves in a life-long bog of debt, you are stuck living paycheck to paycheck, with ends that give each other the finger as they pass by, but have never even considered meeting. Start paying your bills on time today and in seven years you might qualify for a Mobil gas card, and be on your way to the big time.

Aries (March 21 to April 19)
This month, Aries' perpetually cockeyed equilibrium has got you more off balance than a cat with a missing whisker. When you are feeling woozy, go ahead and to excuse yourself and go sit on the john with your head between your knees for the space of a few stabling breaths, rather than weaving haphazardly through a room of your contemporaries like you've got two left feet – or too many whiskies down the hatch.

Taurus (April 20 to May 20)
Spring cleaning is a drag, but you've accumulated more dust bunnies over the winter than Meg Ryan has accumulated wrinkles (before the surgery). Check into the expense of renting a power washer, then nail down the furniture and TV remote, and blast the rest of the useless debris out the back door and across the lawn into your neighbor's yard, where it's no longer your problem.

Gemini (May 21 to June 20)
You are not looking forward to your final rest and oblivion, but you aren't all that excited about the day-to-day drudgery you currently suffer through on a conscious level either. To ease the pain of awareness, try a CD featuring John Williams playing Bach on guitar (no, turn the TV off first!), and a plate full of brownies. If this fails, take the blue pill.

Cancer (June 21 to July 22)
You long for the ability to present yourself as a profound thinker, but you just can't stop singing the Chili's Baby Back Rib jingle long enough to focus on anything cerebral. Here's an alternative – fake it. Buy a pair of reading glasses and a copy of Confucius' dialects. Sit at the local coffee shop with these props, and a steaming espresso, and, as long as you don't make any friends, no one will know the difference.

Leo (July 23 to August 22)
Nothing in life is permanent, and you should stop trying to imprint your individual stamp onto the world – it will eventually fade to naught, as do all things. Start your new life of impermanence today. Sign all legal documents in pencil, pass out the PIN of your checking account to all passers-by, and start telling the uninhibited truth. People will thank you. Especially the people with your PIN.

Virgo (August 23 to September 22)
You've lived your entire life without ever stopping to consider how incredibly cool you might look in a Matador's outfit. Don't wait for Halloween! The stars say you should go immediately to the nearest costume shop and try the getup on for size. You may never want to take it off. Those shiny satin britches and how they cling to your muscular thighs! That lovingly stitched brocade jacket! Okay, small confession – the stars just saw that old Eminem video too.

Libra (September 23 to October 22)
As a trusting Libra, you may find this hard to believe, but I've heard that if you leave valuable items unattended in a public place, someone is likely to walk away with that which you hold most dear, especially if it's something small enough to pocket. Stop trusting the Almighty to guard your family heirlooms (or your Swatch watch) and think about investing in a state of the art wall safe.

Scorpio (October 23 to November 21)
You have two choices after you initially open your daily two-liter of Mountain Dew: you can screw the lid back on as tightly as your muscles will allow, in an effort to preserve that delightfully biting carbonation, or you can screw the lid on loosely, and risk the degree of carbonation in order to retain the ability to unscrew the cap without ripping the skin off of your index finger and thumb when you go for that mid-morning second glass. Be aware of your choices. This is not a metaphor.

Sagittarius (November 22 to December 21)
Save yourself the frustration of turning on the TV, skimming through every channel (twice), stopping sporadically to check the "info" for a show with a promising title (like Love on Ice or Big Brother's Going To Get You) only to be disappointed, and hitting the off button with a sigh. Unless it is 9 p.m. on Sunday, and you subscribe to HBO or AMC, rest assured, there's nothing on.

A page from the Recoil handbook...
Visiting Your Public Library

Though the Internet has largely usurped public libraries as Americans' preferred information resource, libraries remain a viable research tool. Here are some tips for making your trip to the library a fruitful one:

- If you're doing research on European death metal bands, your first stop should be the information desk – the clerks are always up on all the latest shit.

- Aquatic life buffs will be interested to know that microfiche are now extinct in nearly all urban environments.

- Vampires have a hard time getting to the library during business hours. So if you're considering becoming a vampire, keep in mind that you're probably going to have to give up using the library. Hey, even being a vampire has its cons.

- If the only reading materials in the library are beer bottle labels and the only research materials available are shots of hard liquor, you're not in a library – you're in a bar.

- Ask the librarian to see the big dictionary. It's really, really big! You won't believe it, really. It's that big.

- The occult section is a great place to meet fucked up sluts.

- There is rumored to be an office in the basement of the town library. Look in there, past the scrolls, for the trapdoor to the magic-user's guild.

- Considering the FBI's new personal library record access, it's best to counterbalance the checking out of *Mein Kampf* with a *The Horse Whisperer* or two.

- Don't be snooty; a library is just like a Barnes & Noble – except instead of whiny assholes drinking coffee and buying books you have smelly bums taking naps and stealing magazines.

- Lamenting the passing of the Dewy Decimal System card files really works on female librarians.

- Many libraries have a large video section. So fuck you, Blockbuster.

- Sadly, recent budget cutbacks have caused many libraries to cut down on catering, so bring your own beer and sandwiches.

- The library: the perfect supplier for your eBay auction business.

COACH from page 61

coaching session – especially when he knows I'm a recovering alcoholic – but like he's always reminding me, I've got to trust him completely if he's going to help me achieve my life goals," said Paul Avery, a 34-year-old office clerk who enlisted Billings as his life coach nearly two months ago. "From what I've heard, most life coaches just talk with their clients over the phone or send them e-mails. Maybe Walter just thinks meeting over a few drinks is more personal or something."

Despite being thrice divorced and twice implicated in Federal wire fraud investigations, Billings was licensed as a Professional Certified Coach with the International Coach Federation more than six months ago and has since developed a modest client base through his Internet web site.

"As far as I can tell, Walter must take a lot of his life coach meetings at Morgan's [Tavern], because it seems like all of the bartenders there know his name and what he drinks by heart," said Frank Larkin, one of Billings' most recently added clients. "Not to mention that every time we meet he always seems like he's already been there taking meetings for quite some time, judging by the number of cigarette butts, pull tabs and empty shot glasses sitting in front of him. The man's obviously very dedicated to what he does, which is extremely inspiring."

Having little or no experience in the recently popularized field of life coaching, the majority of Billings' clients appear slow to question their coach's choice of meeting place, nor his methods, appearance or professionalism.

"One look at Walter and I knew he'd be a great life coach, because he just *looks* like he's been around the block about a hundred times or so," said Albert Holden, 35, another of Billings' 12 current clients. "We've only just gotten started on the subjects of achieving personal satisfaction, breaking out of self-defeating behaviors and how to reward myself for my successes in life, so I don't know that much about Walter's techniques yet, but I can tell you for a fact that the man is sharp as a tack. He can tell you, for example, just by taste if his drink is even a single drop short on either gin or tonic."

Added Holden: "Walter promises that he will have me doing the same within months, so that's pretty impressive

> I suppose it's possible that he might not even *have* an office. Come to think of it, he might not even have a home."

– especially since you're looking at someone who's never been that much of a drinker."

Although Billings' web site offers his life coaching services through phone or e-mail contact, Holden said he does not mind meeting Billings at Morgan's Tavern for counseling if the atmosphere helps his life coach feel more comfortable and better able to do his job.

"I know a lot of people joking refer to a local bar as 'their office,' but I'm starting to think Walter might be serious when he says it," said Holden. "The only phone number I have for him is a cell phone, and I distinctly remember him saying that he does all of his e-mailing from the public library's computers, so I suppose it's possible that he might not even *have* an office. Come to think of it, he might not even have a home." ∎

SURGEONS from page 61

go away eventually," said Hudson, who remains in stable condition following the song's removal. "In actuality, it just kept getting worse and worse."

Hudson said that although he was able to concentrate adequately during important situations, periods spent performing monotonous tasks such as driving, painting or showering became mentally dominated by the hit song's catchy melodies and quirky lyrics.

"Certain sections of the song would just keep cycling over and over in my head," explained Hudson, who does not own any Barenaked Ladies CDs or other merchandise. "For example, that line in the verse that goes, 'Chickity China the Chinese chicken / You have a drumstick and your brain stops tickin' – I'd just keep repeating it [mentally] for no reason. Then I'd even find myself breaking down the lyrics and actually trying to analyze them. That's just plain unhealthy, as far as I'm concerned."

Unable to overcome the continuous mental replaying of "One Week" – a song which captivated mainstream audiences and reached number one on the Billboard singles chart during the summer of 1998 – Hudson eventually divulged news of his illness to his wife only after his condition had reached a near-critical level of severity.

"Thursday night, when Daniel finally broke down and told me he had Barenaked Ladies song stuck in his head, I knew he must go going through an amazing amount of agony," said Hudson's wife, Maurine. "All week long, out of nowhere he'd been blurting out just that one part, 'It's been,' mimicking that trademark voice. And then that would be it. I should've asked him right then and there what was up with that. If I could've gotten him to tell me what was wrong with him, I would've demanded we get him help immediately."

One expert, however, confirmed that even the people closest to Hudson would have had trouble diagnosing his condition with any degree of certainty.

"Part of the trauma of having a song stuck in your head is that other people rarely pick up on the mental torture the victim is experiencing," said Dr. Howard Wolfen, a specialist in audio treatment. "Family members might have heard Daniel subconsciously humming the part that goes 'I like the sushi 'cause it's never touched a frying pan' a couple of times, but that would be one of the few physical symptoms associated with this condition. Unless the victim lets people know he has a song stuck in his head, he will simply continue to wallow in misery while those around him remain unaware of his condition."

Wolfen also claimed that victims are not always willing to disclose their situation.

"They're usually too embarrassed to admit what song is stuck in their head," said Wolfen. "I once had a patient who went almost six months before seeking help because he was so embarrassed of what particular song had become embedded in his short-term memory. It was the Righteous Brothers classic, 'You've Lost That Lovin' Feelin.'"

Sources close to Hudson confirm that previous to his contracting the devastating mental ailment, Hudson had enjoyed a very healthy audio environment. Among his most prized possessions is a substantial CD and vinyl collection which contains such critically acclaimed titles as Radiohead's *Kid A*, Wilco's *Yankee Foxtrot Hotel* and Tool's *Undertow*. ∎

RECOILMAG.COM   NEWS SATIRE YOU CAN TRUST

recoil

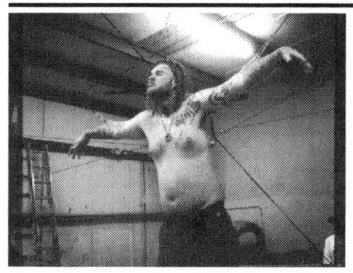

Greece pawns own government

Coroner easily moves suspension artist's corpse

Baby, mom want bottle and bed

quikSTAT
Most common reasons for divorce
- Mail-order bride damaged in shipping
- Irreconcilable body parts
- Must redeem winning Lotto ticket within one year
- Dying to get with foxy in-law
- Spouse obviously lacking sense of humor or wouldn't have called the cops
- Want to masturbate in peace
- Any sob story the Judge will fall for

Short ice cream vendor develops Neapolitan complex

Burbank, Calif. – Five-foot-three-inch ice cream vendor Mario Fuentes, who as of late seems to routinely run low on or be completely out of Neapolitan-flavored ice cream, has begun displaying signs of having developed a Neapolitan complex, area residents said Tuesday. "Mario always seems to be trying to overcompensate for the fact that he's so short on Neapolitan ice cream," said Clyde Reynolds, a local bank teller who frequents Fuentes' vending cart. "For instance, he'll go out of his way to really brag up the other flavors in order to kind of draw attention away from his Neapolitan bin, which has usually been scraped almost bare by noon. Or he'll put every other flavor on sale for half price. I think this behavior is all a way of making up for his being so short [on Neapolitan], which I believe is a condition psychologists refer to as a Neapolitan complex." Asked to comment, Fuentes sternly insisted that being short on multi-flavored ice cream in no way violates any law or hurts his business in any manner, and suggested that he should be treated no differently than any other ice cream vendor because of his condition. ■

SCORES
Catch	22	Hawaii Five	0
Hang	10	Ocean's	11

Above: One of the many Greek government buildings included as collateral in the pawn loan.

Athens, Greece – Greek President Karolos Papoulias, desperate to cover the country's debt obligations long enough to implement a financial restructuring capable of avoiding the derailment of the European Union economy, consigned the consolidation of Greece's parliament, employees, services, military and governing powers to a pawnshop, Papoulias confirmed Friday.

"Obviously, using the ruling organization of the country as collateral in exchange for immediate cash from some shady pawnbroker was a last resort," admitted Papoulias, wiping sweat from his brow while being questioned by reporters regarding the unprecedented transaction. "But, I mean, you guys know how it is – when you're short on cash and simply out of options, you hit the pawnshop. Anyone who's ever found themselves in an impossible financial corner such as the country of Greece should sympathize with our motivation and intentions."

> "Anyone who's ever found themselves in an impossible financial corner such as the country of Greece should sympathize with our motivation and intentions," said Papoulias.

Papoulias claimed to have "gotten the best collateral loan price possible" in trade for his nation's government through lengthy negotiations with Athenian pawnbroker Ioannis Feraios, owner of Athens' Swap & Shop.

"Naturally, I expected the pawnbroker *see* GREECE *page 67*

County's snow plowed back into neighborhood driveways
Trucks responds to citizens' massive redistribution effort

St. Joseph, Mich. – Road officials governing St. Joseph County announced with great satisfaction Monday that the buildup of snow on the county's roads resulting from the massive weekend blizzard has successfully been plowed off

> "Commuters can rest assured they will encounter safe driving conditions on the roads this morning, assuming they can get their cars out of their driveways," said Lang.

of county roads and into the entrances of all homeowners' driveways.

"Over the weekend, county snowplow drivers worked around the clock plowing all of the snow off of the roads and into *see* SNOW *page 67*

Left: St. Joseph County roadplows push shoveled snow back into citizens' driveways.

WORLDWIDE HEADLINES

Peanut gallery issues final statement

A few feet away – Finally yielding to incessant pressure from those who engage in open dialogue, the peanut gallery issued a final statement Monday, forever silencing the wise-cracking union of observers who had strived for decades to inject comic relief into every possible dissertation and conversation. The gallery's final statement read: "Ooooohhhh, well excuuusssse uuusss. Fine, I guess "that's enough" from the peanut gallery. What the fuck ever, man. Eat shit." When asked to comment, the peanut gallery simply put up its right hand and made a zipping motion across its mouth, signaling that it had nothing to add.

Singer Bonnie Tyler still holding out for hero

Up where the mountains meet the heavens above, out where the lightning splits the sea –Welsh-born pop singer Bonnie Tyler is still holding out for a hero until the morning light, according to the lyrics of her oft-played 1984 radio hit. "Where have all the good men gone and where are all the gods?" inquired Tyler before demanding that the hero in question be strong, fast, fresh from the fight, sure and larger than life. "Where's the street-wise Hercules to fight the rising odds? Isn't there a white knight upon a fiery steed?" Late at night, tossing and turning and dreaming of what she needs, Tyler – who reportedly suffered a total eclipse of the heart in 1983 – told sources she believes it'll take a superman to sweep her off her feet, and later confirmed that she can feel the as-of-yet unnamed hero's approach like the fire in her blood, just beyond her reach, racing on the thunder end, rising with the heat.

Cokehead sex addict torn over best use for bedroom's overhead mirror

Dallas, Texas – Local drug and sex enthusiast Nathaniel Baker remained torn this weekend regarding the best use for his bedroom's overhead mirror – being able to watch himself have sex or snorting cocaine off the dismounted mirror's surface. "It's a tough call, no doubt," said Baker, watching himself undress in the mirror which had recently been removed after sex in order to intake part of an eight-ball of coke Baker bought Thursday instead of paying his car insurance premiums. "It's probably too much work to remount the mirror every time I'm going to screw. I guess I'll just leave it down for now – seeing as it's already down, nearing dawn, what's-her-name's getting ready to leave, and I still have some coke left."

Overenthusiastic salute leaves soldier unconscious

Fayetteville, N.C. – Officials at Fort Bragg military base reported Tuesday that an enthusiastic young enlistee named Jeremy Dunn, 18, knocked himself unconscious during day one of basic training Monday, suffering a self-administered blow to the head while eagerly saluting drill sergeant Robert T. Bowers. "This little maggot must have *the worst* depth perception I have ever encountered in my twenty-two years in this man's army," barked Bowers, standing over Dunn as base medics worked to revive the Bradford, Minn., native. "Will *somebody* teach this young lady when to stop his arc, for Christ's sake? Or at least issue the poor bastard a goddamn brain bucket before he salutes himself straight into the infirmary. I will give him this, though: the son of a bitch displayed some good upper-body strength there. He'll be king hell in hand-to-hand [combat] – so long as we can get him karate-chopping in the right goddamned direction."

Angus Alert activated in statewide hunt for lost appetite

Sault Saint Marie, Mich. – In accordance with the Angus Alert issued late Thursday night by Michigan State Police officials, area radio and television stations began airing information regarding the lost appetite of local party store owner Alan Peal, which Peal said mysteriously disappeared sometime between the ordering and serving of his medium-rare Angus steak at Outback Steakhouse on James St. early Thursday evening. "We had just finished ordering, because I remember commenting to the waiter about how famished I was," Peal said, recalling the events leading up to his appetite's disappearance. "I got up to go to the men's room and there was somebody in one of the stalls totally puking his guts out. I practically ran back to my table; that's when I noticed that my appetite was gone." State Police officer Jim McNeal told reporters that although a majority of lost appetites end up coming back within 24 hours of their disappearance, some appetites invariably remain lost for days or even weeks. "Last month we initiated the Angus Alert after some guy's girlfriend dumped him," McNeal explained. "The poor guy not only lost his girl that night – he also lost his appetite. From what I hear, he hasn't eaten in weeks. What can I say? It's a tragedy."

Police suspect missing person will be in last place they'd look

Dayton, Ohio – Ohio State Trooper Dennis Horn told reporters Friday that a majority of investigators are starting to believe that the two-week search for missing 24-year-old Lena Belmore will end only when frustrated detectives finally search the very last place they would ever think to look. "It's always like that in life – you look and look and look everywhere for something like your car keys and they end up being in the last place you'd look," said Horn. "Except in this case it's [possibly] a dead body -- probably behind somebody's couch, I'm betting." ■

A page from the Recoil handbook...
Going to the Dentist

Visiting your family dentist can be a harrowing and painful experience. Here are some tips to help you prepare you and your loved ones for that fateful trip:

- Don't bother trying to trick the dentist – he'll know if you borrowed somebody else's teeth just for your appointment.
- You may need to reassure your children that they needn't fear the dentist just because he killed their older brother.
- Remember to remove the microfilm from your false tooth unless you want the whole dentist office to know about your moonlighting in the dangerous but thrilling world of international espionage.
- Hip-hop artists, you should have the value of your teeth appraised after every dentist visit, to make sure the doc isn't palming one of your nuggets.
- Keep in mind that unless you specify "extraction," dentists will simply move a damaged tooth to another part of your mouth.
- If your son expresses that he is afraid of going to the dentist, explain to him that he's being a total pussy and needs to grow a set of balls before you start making him wear a dress to school.
- Okay, so the whole fluoride-in-the-drinking-water-will-help-promote-dental-health thing forgot to include the part about it also making people violently ill. But this new depleted-uranium-in-the-drinking-water-will-make-Americans-safer idea sounds like it can't miss.

- Beware of any dentist with a trophy case full of teeth.
- No matter how badly your kid begs for you to get him braces, tell him he's not getting them until he's testing in the top one percent of his class and starts getting interested in computers.
- If the oral surgeon asks you if you've ever had nitrous oxide, keep in mind that he's probably just looking for someone to party with.
- It may be wise to ask to see your dentist's credentials if his office features a drive-thru.
- Why is it that not one of the big NHL stars studied dentistry in college? Doesn't that seem strange to anyone else? I think that is very strange.
- If you're pressed for time, many dentists will let you eat your lunch during your visit.
- If you can't bring yourself to lie when asked if you floss regularly, you can always hurl mouthwash into the dentist's eyes and flee.
- Before believing your wife's allegation that she was molested while under anesthesia, demand to know why she put herself in the compromising position of lying in front of a man with her mouth wide open.

- It is well known that half a tube of toothpaste can kill a child. However, you should ask your dentist exactly how hard the child must be struck with the tube. And don't be afraid to seek a second opinion – remember, there's a life on the line, here.

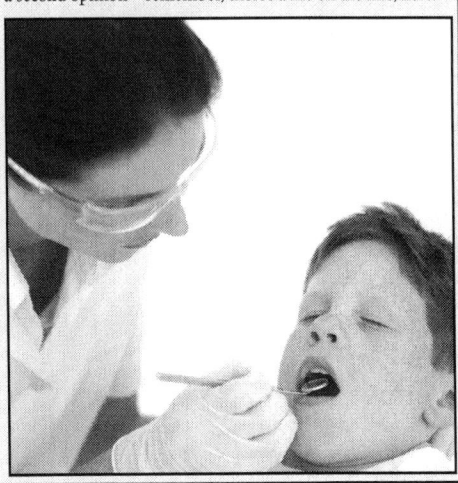

EDITORIAL

Promote Me to pilot or I quit

By Jesus Christ

Drivers of the world, we have gathered here today to listen to My words. My words of resignation.

That's right, My days of "copiloting" your '95 Saturns, '86 Galants and other holy rolling rust buckets are at an end. I'm sick of guiding you ignorant dolts through dangerous everyday traffic – generally unscathed and free from tickets – while you simpletons take sole credit for the prominent piloting position of your worldly vessels. It's this simple: promote Me to pilot or I quit.

Think I'm bluffing? Try Me. I swear, if I see one more of those 'Jesus is my copilot' stickers, I'm going to hie myself on back into the heavens, and I'm not coming back. I mean it. Get this through your thick skulls: no returno el Jesuso.

For how many years have humans been boasting that I, Jesus Christ, Son of God, am merely the second in command of those ultra-conservative hunks of shit you're driving? If you think you can manage the treacherous roads of the Earth without My divine spirit puppeting your every move, I say this: best of luck to you. The ink will still be drying on My letter of resignation when you people start wrapping those deathtraps around fenceposts while dialing in requests to hear "Michael, Row the Boat Ashore" on your Jesus Rocks radio stations.

Frankly, I'm surprised you people even have the nerve to forsake the First Commandment and sport those "Jesus is my copilot" bumper stickers in the first place. Ranking yourself above Me is, as you well know, an abomination, punishable by eternal damnation. My Father does not look kindly on those who consider themselves more important or of higher standing than Me, even if it is on a bumper sticker that's supposed to glorify Me and spread My Father's message. Yes, the correct wording, "I am Jesus' copilot," makes for one of those awkward possessives that end in "s apostrophe'," but last time I checked, uncomfortable grammar is deemed a bit more tolerable than a fiery afterlife.

Acceptable would be a more pious and humble sticker slogan, something like, "Jesus has my soul on cruise control" or "Jesus revs me up." That would keep the light, trailer park style of motor vehicle humor in the message intact, while keeping yourself from being the center of attention in the message.

Look, I'm all about patience and understanding, always have been, but I think this bumper sticker thing has festered, unchecked, long enough. You have My ultimatum; I'll expect an answer by 11 a.m. Sunday, Earth time.

Amen. ∎

SNOW from page 65

everyone's driveways, so commuters can rest assured they will encounter safe driving conditions on the roads this morning," said St. Joseph County Road Commissioner Dean Lang early Monday morning. "That's assuming they can get their cars out of their driveways, of course."

Homeowners in St. Joseph County confirmed that although personal weekend efforts to remove snow from their driveways in anticipation of having to get their cars out of their driveways and get to work Monday morning, county snowplows have completely negated their shoveling work.

"I hope those bastards are proud of themselves," groaned Dane Morgan, a local homeowner, watching yet another snowplow blast a few more cubic yards of snow into his recently cleared driveway during its city plowing route. Morgan claimed to have spent close to two hours shoveling his driveway Sunday before county snowplows relocated a section of his street's snow buildup into his driveway.

Morgan is just one of the hundreds of area homeowners who are now part of the countywide effort to redistribute the snow back into the roads.

"Here, you guys can have it all back, how's that?" yelled Barry Stephenson, shoveling the 14 inches of highly compacted snow thrown into his driveway by snowplows back out into the street. Stephenson's sentiments were being echoed throughout the neighborhood by heavily-dressed homeowners, many of whom were also out shoveling and snowblowing the snow in their driveways back into the street during a widespread redistribution effort expected to last the entire morning.

"Maybe we should find out where these snowplow drivers live and plow snow into *their* driveways, see how they like it," Stephenson shouted to one of his neighbors who was also shoveling his driveway. "If these drivers had any dignity they'd be out picking up cans off the streets for a living." ∎

Above: Morgan is just one of the hundreds of area homeowners who are now part of the countywide effort to redistribute the snow back into the roads.

GREECE from page 65

Above: Swap & Shop, one of Athens' most popular pawnshops.

would start out trying to lowball [me]," said Papoulias, noting that pawnshops typically deal only in the sales of jewelry, electronic devices, CDs, DVDs, tools and musical instruments.

"So when Feraios pointed out all the product's flaws and then offered me a measly thirty-five billion in cash for Greece's government, I just thanked him for his time and started heading toward the door. Then he was all, like, 'Well, hang on a minute now…' That's when I knew he was really, really interested in owning our country's ruling body.'"

After further haggling with Feraios regarding the outright sale of the nation's government, both parties instead agreed to pawn control of Greece for a loan of $157 billion – an amount Papoulias must repay, plus 10 percent interest, within 30 days. If Papoulias defaults on the contract, Athens Swap & Shop will take legal possession of Greece's government.

Having signed the contract, Feraios then photocopied Papoulias' driver's license, just in case the aforementioned property is later revealed to be a stolen item. ∎

recoilmag.com

BUSINESS

FedEx and Ex-Lax battle for rights to promotional slogan
Court to decide ownership of catchphrase: "Keep Your Shit Moving"

Above: A print sample of FedEx's $18 million advertising campaign.

Memphis, Tenn. – After weeks of failed negotiations with FedEx Corporation, officials at Ex-Lax manufacturer Novartis announced Friday that the company is suing FedEx to cease and desist usage of the promotional slogan "Keep Your Shit Moving," an internationally marketed catchphrase currently being employed by both companies.

Independently conceived by FedEx and Ex-Lax marketing teams, the slogan was cast as the focal point for each company's latest advertisement campaign, both of which coincidentally launched Feb. 1.

"Our position is resolute," said Ex-Lax spokesman Ted Lundengard, addressing reporters outside a Memphis courthouse early Friday morning. "When it comes to the swift, timely moving of shit, consumers automatically think 'Ex-Lax.' By continuing to use the 'Keep Your Shit Moving' slogan, FedEx is confusing the consumer purchasing instincts Ex-Lax has for so long worked to cultivate."

FedEx, a global shipping company in no way related to human bowel regularity, said that while the simultaneous release of the exactly matching slogans is indeed unfortunate, the company has no intention of pulling its advertisements just to appease the laxative manufacturer.

"We have just as much right to use the slogan as Ex-Lax does," said T. Michael Glenn, Executive Vice President of Market Development for FedEx Corporation. "[Ex-Lax] trying to secure sole rights [to the slogan] is as ridiculous as it is illegal."

Attorneys for Ex-Lax said the strength of the lawsuit relies heavily on the Webster's Dictionary definition of one of the slogan's key words.

"[Webster's] defines 'shit' firstly as a noun denoting bodily excrement," said Ex-Lax attorney Jean Primon on a recent airing of *The Larry King Show*. "FedEx's usage of the word 'shit' – as slang for possessions, equipment and mementos – is listed eighth. *Eighth*. Unless FedEx can convince Webster's to rearrange the definition's sense order, we're confident the court will deny FedEx rights to the slogan, as Ex-Lax's ads are using 'shit' in a manner representative of the word's most popular application."

While both companies' deep-pocketed advertising campaigns are built on the slogan's powerful message and catchy syntax, each campaign differs greatly in the visual and auditory tone attached to each conception.

"Our ads speak directly to the problem without sugarcoating it: 'your shit needs to get where it needs to get, now,'" said FexEd CEO Frederick W. Smith, pointing to a print ad mock-up incorporating simple block letters and a white background. "We keep it simple and straight. 'Keep Your Shit Moving.' That slogan completely embodies the spirit of FedEx, a company determined to getting your shit where it needs to be faster than any other freight shipping company in the world."

FedEx's $18 million no-nonsense campaign strategy strives to recreate the feel of a fast-paced work environment in order to emphasize its service's importance. Radio and television spots depict a business owner struggling to meet inventory supply orders – frantically working the phones, the slightly obese workaholic only occasionally interrupts his work to motivate workers, shouting, "We've got to keep this shit moving!" along with a series of other inspirational taglines characterized by mild vulgarity.

"The commercial speaks to anyone who's ever been in a hurry," said Smith, who agrees with market research indicating that foul language inevitably sidles high-pressure work environments.

Conversely, Ex-Lax's ad strategy incorporates a more elegant approach; radio and television ads narrated by a soothing female voice encourage consumers to circumvent constipation by using the company's product. "When nature tries to slow you down," the commercial reads, "Keep your shit moving."

Though now relying on a court decision, FedEx officials confirmed that the company at one point considered complying with Ex-Lax's request to change its campaign's all-important slogan.

"We toyed around with some other slogans," said Smith. "We had a couple others that were pretty good. 'FedEx: Faster Than Fuck' was our second-choice, but test-markets indicated an objection to the F's alliteration." ■

> Attorneys for Ex-Lax said the strength of the lawsuit relies heavily on the Webster's Dictionary definition of one of the slogan's key words.

ADVICE

HOW TO... MAKE PRISON SHANKS

CONVICT CUTLERY 101

Anyone who's watched *Oz* knows the importance of carrying a good prison blade. Don't be the only unarmed con on the block; here's a handy guide for turning meager prison resources into a variety of lethal penal sabers.

GILLETTE BAYONET
Designed to slice, not stab. Extract the razor blade from a standard throwaway shaving razor. Use the razor to cut a slot in the end of an empty pen or mechanical pencil, then slide the razor into the slot, making sure to achieve a snug fit. Wrap string through and around for stability.

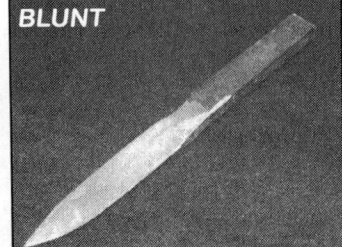

BLUNT
A penal system legend. Have an ally from metal shop pound you out a hunk of metal, then spend your evenings shaping and sharpening a blade by rubbing the metal against the wall of your cell. Crude, yes, but effective.

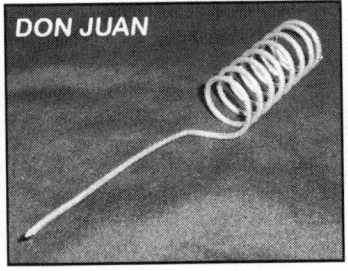

DON JUAN
Borrow a spring from your prison bed, straighten out and sharpen one end and leave the coil to act as a handle. This baby penetrates deep – like Don Juan – and can go in and out of an enemy many times before the assailant is shot by guards.

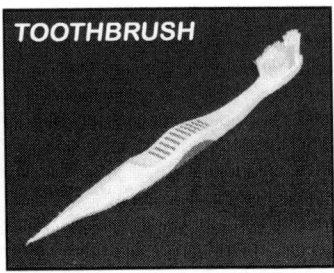

TOOTHBRUSH
This shiv is worn bristles-up in the front shirt pocket to allow quick access. Just rub the non-bristled end of a standard toothbrush against a wall to hone a sharp point. Sure, it takes a while, but you've got the time, haven't you?

RECOILMAG.COM   NEWS SATIRE YOU CAN TRUST

recoil

Nickelback adds fourth chord to musical arsenal

Vancouver, Canada – Nearing completion of its seventh full-length studio album, members of the post-grunge rock band Nickelback explained to sources Wednesday about how they set out to challenge themselves musically on their new release by incorporating an entirely new chord into their songwriting.

"Sure, we could've went in [the studio] and just pumped out another generic Nickelback album using the same three chords we've been playing for the last decade, but with this album we really wanted to branch out and try something new," said Chad Kroeger, singer and guitarist for the Canadian four-piece. "I think that incorporating a fourth chord into our arsenal of musical weaponry has added

> "We hope Nickelback fans will enjoy this more experimental direction," said Kroger.

see NICKELBACK page 71

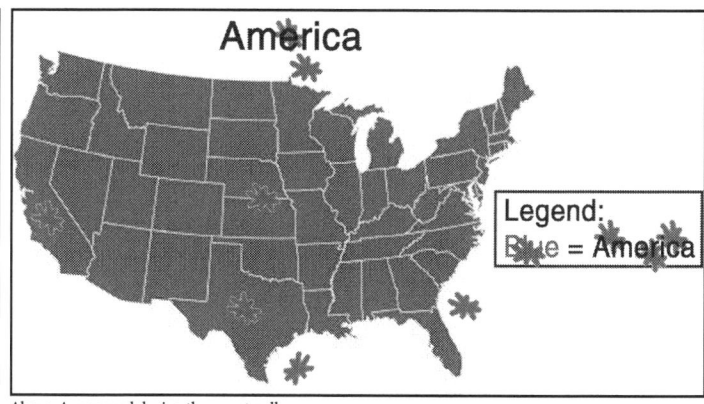

Above: A map used during the recent poll.

Poll: 73 percent of Americans unable to locate America on map of America

Washington, D.C. – According to a Gallup/Harris poll released Monday, a full 73 percent of American citizens are incapable of identifying their home country on a map of the United States.

Of the 1,400 residents surveyed, the most common incorrect responses placed the more than 230-year-old territory in the Atlantic or Pacific Oceans (12 percent), the space where Mexico would appear were it in fact included on the map (nine percent), and inside the word "America" written just above the northernmost states (six percent).

"On the whole, these figures should be construed as somewhat disappointing," Gallup spokesman Keith Ventner said. "Especially the two percent that believed the United States was located on the map's color-coded inset legend. I think we as a nation likely could have done without seeing that."

When asked to reveal the identity of the giant America-shaped landmass found on the map, several of those polled were decidedly varied in their answers.

"That thing definitely looked familiar," said autoworker and father of three Ed McConnell. "And my gut told me there were probably a whole bunch of Americans there. So I had to go with 'Iraq.'"

Other guesses as to the nature of the mystery country included "Hollywood," "Palestine," "The Shire" and "Club Med Punta Cana."

Stuart Weiss, senior sociology professor at Boston College, said although these findings may be surprising to some, they're by no means atypical.

> Other guesses as to the name of the mystery country included "Hollywood," "Palestine" and "The Shire."

"The sentiment of many Americans is that there's little intrinsic value in studying a map of a place you're already at," said Weiss. "It'd be like driving to Graceland and then asking for directions once you've arrived. Not much point."

Shirley Matheson, a part-time Arby's

see MAP page 72

Above: Multi-platinum-selling rock act Nickelback.

Archaeologists speculate on purpose of newly discovered Disco Age artifact

New York, N.Y. – Archaeologists excavating the ruins of a 1970s New York nightclub continued to speculate Friday about the purpose and historical significance of a 36-inch reflective sphere unearthed from the site in late July – an artifact many contend belonged to a flamboyant, groove-based society of people that rose to prominence in the U.S. in the mid-70s before suddenly vanishing near the turn of the decade.

"Figuring out what function this enormous mirrored ball served during the Disco Age would be a tremendous step toward understanding what caused these super-freaky ancestors of ours to groove themselves into extinction so quickly after establishing their culture," explained Graham Kelser, lead archaeologist for the privately funded dig. "Usually, extravagant or luxurious relics like this are determined to have held some sort of religious significance for the people of their times. But considering the bizarre customs and rituals that were prevalent during the Disco Age, I wouldn't be surprised to learn that this thing was worn as an earring."

The mysterious orb is the latest in a series of puzzling artifacts unearthed during a seven-month excavation of the abandoned ruins of the Paradise Garage nightclub, where experts believe people of the disco epoch congregated nightly to participate in elaborate dance rituals that somehow included the use of one or more of these massive, shiny globes.

"We believe the mirrored ball was suspended from the ceiling and

see DISCO page 72

Above: Bemused archaeologists crowd in to ponder the possible functionality of a gigantic, reflecting orb.

page 69

ECONOMY
Lower-middle class criminal tired of living forged check to forged check

Chicago, Ill. – "Slick" Willie Barnett, a lifelong resident who's managed to eke out a meager income as a smalltime street hustler for nearly 20 years, is tired of merely having to live forged check to forged check, the paroled 43-year-old told sources Wednesday.

"I've been working the street for almost two decades and I've never even been able to put away enough money for a decent vacation, let alone start saving for retirement," said Barnett, inching back the curtain of his apartment window and covertly scanning the parking lot. "Between the economy and the cost of living in Chicago being what it is these days, I can forge an eight hundred dollar check I stole from some tourist on Monday and by the weekend I'll barely have enough [money] left to tip the strippers at the Crazy Horse. It's that bad. And this from a guy who doesn't even pay taxes, mind you."

Barnett, who has never married or had children, dropped out of high school at the age of 16 to pursue a life of crime – a career Barnett said he fully expected would secure for him a higher standard of living than could be afforded by pursuing a normal, legal vocation. However, after a number of failed money-making endeavors – namely, two botched bank robberies and an unsuccessful kidnapping, all of which led to multi-year prison sentences – the thrice-convicted Barnett long ago resigned himself to the less profitable but less risky life of a petty larcenist, working to make ends meet through short-con swindles, pickpocketing, check forgery and other fraud-related crimes.

"It's not a glamorous gig or anything, but it pays the bills," said Barnett, sifting through the credit cards of a recently acquired wallet. "Or at least it *used* to pay the bills. These days, with the economy in the shitter like it is, it's hard just finding someone to rob that actually still has a job. There's nothing more frustrating than pickpocketing a guy whose credit cards are already maxed out – which covers just about everybody these days."

In addition to the diminished earning power brought about by the sluggish economy, Barnett said the high price of gasoline has also made one of his best-paying rackets nearly unprofitable.

"It's almost not even worth it to deal in stolen cars anymore," said Barnett, shaking his head and packing his SlimJim and hotwiring tools into a box in his closet's storage area. "It takes at least fifteen gallons of gas to get a car to the chop shop that I work with in Michigan. At four bucks a gallon, the math just don't add up no more."

Despite living modestly in a one-bedroom apartment on Chicago's south side, Barnett's expenses are such that he must beg, borrow or steal at least $3,500 every month to simply keep his head above water.

"After paying rent, buying groceries, scoring dope and paying off the bookies, there ain't a whole lot left over," Barnett said, opening a lock box containing his minimal cash reserve, betting slips and other important papers. "When you

Above: Struggling small-time crook "Slick" Willie Barnett.

live forged check to forged check like I do, you have to cut out such luxuries as dining out, going to the dentist or paying for cable."

Barnett went on to voice other frustrations regarding his financial position – frustrations not unlike those shared by the millions of legit lower-middle class Americans who live paycheck to paycheck.

"It seems like it's impossible to get ahead," Barnett said. "Just when it looks like you're finally going to get everything paid off and you might be able to stash away a few bucks, an unexpected expense comes out of nowhere, like bail money or lawyer fees or maybe Blackie from Miami finally tracks you down and threatens to break your legs if you don't come up with a payment – you know, typical life shit. Then, bam! You're right back behind the eight-ball again – taking back cans for train fare until you can get your hands on your next [forged] check."

> "There's nothing more frustrating than pickpocketing a guy whose credit cards are already maxed out – which covers just about everybody these days," said Barnett.

Although Barnett as a rule has never allowed himself to pull more than one job per week for fear of overexposure, his desire to break out of the rut of living forged check to forged check has recently caused him to rethink that guideline.

"If this damn economy doesn't pick up pretty soon I won't have much choice but to start looking for a second job to pull every week," said Barnett. "The real bitch of it is knowing that I'm partially to blame for this sorry state of affairs, because I actually voted for Bush. I know, I know – I don't know what I was thinking at the time. I guess I thought for some reason that it might be good for business to have a fellow crook in the White House. That didn't really pan out like I had hoped." ∎

EDITORIAL
Look at how much I don't care what you think

Hey, you! Yes, you – the uptight suburbanite wearing the Old Navy sweatshirt, with the immaculately

By Amy Davis

landscaped lawn, two-point-three children and freshly leased 2013 SUV – what do you think of my mohawk? Shocking, isn't it? Unnerving, isn't it? You hate it don't you?

Not that I care. Frankly, it doesn't matter one way or the other to me what a pompous, politically correct, super-conservative consumer pig such as you thinks of my fashion anti-statement. In fact, the whole reason I shaved this weird stripe down the center of my head is to show all of the people like you that I don't care what anybody thinks.

What do you think about that, huh?

It's like, what you see as an inappropriate or maybe even offensive personal grooming preference, I see as just another physical expression of my rebellious personality.

Speaking of seeing, have you noticed that my nose is double-pierced? Hang on a sec – let me step into some better light. There, check it out. Pretty sweet, huh? Double nose rings: how's that for not caring what anybody thinks?

No, seriously, tell me, how is that?

Hey! Are you even paying attention? I'm not going out and temporarily defacing my body for my health, you know. This mohawk – which tomorrow I'm going to dye pink just to further represent moral chaos, insubordination and everything else you hate about today's ungrateful youth – isn't going to just grow back in a couple of days, you know; I'm committed to instilling social discomfort among you prissy lemmings for weeks.

Well, unless I put a hat on, of course.

Can I ask your personal opinion on something? Do you think I'm getting my point across, that I don't care what anybody else thinks? Does this mohawk tromp enough on the stiff family and social values dominating middle America to make me seem a prolific deviant?

I sure hope so. Because if this borderline-obscene haircut doesn't do it, I can only wonder how far I'll have to go to prove that I don't care what anybody thinks. It's like, what level of non-conformity do I have to reach in order to be recognized as part of the freak crowd? Just tell me what it is – I'll do it!

I suppose I could get my genitals pierced, but how would that let everybody that I run into know that I don't care what they think? They wouldn't even be able to see it.

No, I'm pretty sure this mohawk, the nose rings and my devil-may-care attitude pretty much do the job in signaling my separation from the norm. Maybe I'll get a tattoo or something like everybody else to further display my individuality and show the world that I don't care what anybody thinks.

Do you think that's a good idea? ∎

> Are you even paying attention? I'm not going out and temporarily defacing my body for my health, you know.

WORLDWIDE HEADLINES

Overweight couple's stomachs growl as one

Huntsville, Ala. – Sue and Dennis Anchower, chronically obese lovers who have been married for just under four years, admitted Thursday that they love eating together so much that it often feels as though their stomachs are growling as one. "Dennis and I have so much in common it's almost scary – almost like we're the same person," Sue Anchower explained. "We both love to cook, but we also like going out to eat, like to KFC or Pizza Hut or the Chinese buffet where we first met." Dennis Anchower: "I think it's because of all the little things that Sue and I get along so well. For example, we both usually get hungry at the same time. Sometimes, like when our stomachs are growling at the same time, it's like they're one – like we share the same stomach. The same great, big stomach."

Mom invited for dinner whenever dishwasher broken

Long Island, N.Y. – Nightclub manager Dave Elliot admitted to sources Wednesday that the 27-year-old bachelor tends to invite his widowed mother to dinner at his apartment only when his dishwasher appliance isn't working and dirty dishes from previous days' meals have begun to pile up. "Mom's great to have over when there are lots of dishes that need doing, because she makes herself right at home in front of the sink and doesn't quit until every last salad fork has been scrubbed to perfection," said Elliot, lighting a cigarette and kicking back in front of the television while his mother toiled thanklessly in the kitchen after a modest dinner of grilled hamburgers. In addition to fully cleaning her son's kitchen, Elliot's mother also vacuumed his entire apartment and scrubbed his bathroom sink and toilet, jobs which the 62-year-old said her son "has never been able to get very enthused about."

School's Gay/Straight Alliance comprised entirely of gays

Bridgeport, Conn. – Senior members of Bridgeport High School's student-based Gay/Straight Alliance admitted Friday that an overwhelming majority of their coalition's members harbor the sexual preference indicated in the first half of their descriptive moniker. "It would probably be more accurate to call our club the Gay/Gay Alliance, if you actually sat down and did the math on it," said Kurt Williams, president of the action-oriented committee that meets periodically to plan diversity awareness campaigns and other all-inclusive events. "I think our only two straight members thought they were gay when they joined the group last year but have since rethought the whole thing or something."

Dating widower looking for someone to grow even older with

Ft. Collins, Col. – Felix Moore, a recently widowed 78-year-old, has publicly declared his reentry into the dating field, stating in a personal ad printed in the Sunday edition of the *Ft. Collins Courier* that the retired mill worker is "looking for someone [he] can grow even older with." "I knew the instant I met my [first wife] Doris that she was the woman I wanted to grow old with," Moore recalled during a recent interview. "Now that Doris is in heaven, I'm hoping I'll be able to find a nice elderly lady to get ancient with."

Thing done number on

Boise, Idaho – Steve Warren, an experienced crane operator employed by Ace Construction Company, is reported to have done a number on one of the company's air compressors when the controls for his crane malfunctioned Friday morning, causing the crane to over-rotate and sending the air compressor he was lifting crashing into the side of the building under construction. "Fortunately, none of the workers were hurt, but God damn did ol' Steve ever do a number on our air compressor," said foreman Gene Daughtry. Warren admitted to having done numbers on other pieces of company equipment in the past by accident, but refused to accept responsibility for doing the number on the air compressor, instead blaming equipment malfunction. Added Warren: "Well, at least I'm not like Marv and don't ruin everybody's day every single morning by doing a number on the site's only Port-O-John."

Dad would take bullet for son but won't cosign car loan

San Jose, Calif. – John Thorren, the 16-year-old son of Rick Thorren, said Sunday that although his father has repeatedly affirmed that he "would do anything for [his] son, including taking a bullet for [him]," the 55-year-old investment banker will not cosign a $1,200 car loan under any circumstances. "My dad's all like, 'You have to learn to pay your own way in this world' and stuff," said Thorren of his father's unwillingness to help secure financing for a 1993 Ford Escort. "Where's the guy that 'would do anything for me?' I guess 'anything' excludes anything having to do with money." ∎

NICKELBACK from page 69

a whole new dimension to the band. We hope Nickelback fans will enjoy this more experimental direction."

As the band's primary songwriter, Kroeger first conceived the idea of introducing a fourth chord into Nickelback's music almost a decade ago after collaborating with Saliva singer Josey Scott on the duo's 2002 hit single "Hero."

"Josey is an absolute genius – that goes without saying – but he's also a great teacher and he plays a pretty mean guitar," Kroeger said. "During one of our writing sessions I saw him fooling around with a chord I had never heard before, which he later told me was an A minor. I remember falling in love with the sound of that chord; it was dark and haunting, yet so full of life. Finally in 2010, when we both had some time off, I asked Josey to came out to Vancouver to teach me the chord. It was simultaneously the most difficult and exciting six weeks of my life."

When it came to writing songs for the band's as-of-yet untitled new album, Kroeger found that having a fourth chord at his disposal opened up an incredible range of possibilities for the band to explore.

"Increasing our chord catalogue by twenty-five percent allowed us to be more versatile with our songwriting," boasted Kroeger. "Now we can have *bridge* sections, and on some of the songs we change keys for my guitar solos – two things that were difficult to do when we only knew three chords. Also, the A minor has a very Latin feel to it, which allowed us to go completely off the map and lay down an up-tempo Latin groove complete with morocco accompaniment for one song. It's amazing how much freedom this fourth chord has allowed us. I feel like shackles have been removed and we're free to run wild."

According to guitarist Ryan Peake, implementing a fourth chord into the arrangements was a daunting task that pushed each band member's musical ability to their limits.

"I still have trouble with some of the changes, like going from a G chord to the A minor – you have to squeeze your fingers into this little tiny space," said Peake, demonstrating the dynamic new note-grouping. "About half of the time I end up accidentally muting the high E string with the index finger of my fret hand. It's kind of frustrating. I'm getting it, though. In the studio we just used ProTools to fix those kinds of mistakes, but we're all working really hard to get the chord stage-ready for our upcoming tour."

Looking ahead to the band's next album, Kroeger and Peake both expressed interest in experimenting with a different strumming pattern, as well as attempting to write songs that have different tempos.

Recoil's Shallow Thoughts

- I remember that as a child I always dreamed about growing up to become a protector of the people, standing tall and proud, protecting the public against the worst the world could ever blow your way. I guess that's probably why I grew up to become a salad bar sneeze guard.

- Never judge a book by its cover. Do you think God would judge The Bible by its cover? Because, you have to admit, the Bible has a pretty bland-looking cover. And this is GOD doing the judging, mind you.

- Is it at all weird that airport gates and hockey arenas are the only two places on Earth where there are boarding calls?

- In space, no one can hear you scream. On Earth, everyone can hear you scream – they just don't care.

- On exactly whose authority are we taking it that that's what General Tso's chicken tasted like?

- Why do they always say, "And now, a man who needs no introduction," and then they go ahead and introduce him anyway? Maybe instead they should say, "And now, a man who needs no execution." And then maybe go ahead and execute him anyway, to avoid confusing the audience.

- All you really need in this world is a solid plan and a solid cat. Actually, probably even a below-average cat would do.

- All my life people have suggested I have my head examined. So I did. And it turns out my head has no abnormalities. Although the homeless drunk I hired to examine my head may not be exactly at the top of his field.

DISCO from page 69

somehow used in conjunction with two other relics that we discovered within fifty feet of the sphere: a small spotlight and a primitive smoke-making machine," said Kelser. "We couldn't speculate as to what will happen when these three items are used together, but we managed to locate a group of experts at Columbia [University] who've agreed to smoke a bunch of grass this weekend and try to figure it out."

Earlier this summer, publicity surrounding the excavation increased sharply when archaeologists unearthed the largely intact remains of what experts agree is likely to have been a highly exalted leader during the Disco Age: a young male DJ.

"Studying the excavation's discoveries – especially the remains of the male DJ, or 'Afro Joe,' as we've taken to calling him – has solidified theories that the disco DJ reigned as king during this time period," said Dr. Alexander Daprich, an anthropologist and historian at the Brookings Institute. "This beloved figure would look out over his people from a raised altar called a 'DJ booth' and command over the rituals. He and he alone would dictate the pace and overall funkiness of the procession. And the people, especially the ladies, were no doubt prepared to boogie all night at his behest."

Daprich said that nearly eclipsing the importance of Afro Joe's discovery was the incredible treasure-trove of Disco Age artifacts unearthed within immediate proximity of the DJ's remains.

"Polyester pants, platform shoes, crazy medallion necklaces, hair picks, a 'Disco Till You Die' t-shirt – these people appear to have proudly worn some of the strangest garments and jewelry we've seen from culture of any time in the history of civilization," said Daprich. "But even more valuable to the historical community may be the large collection of ancient records that were uncovered under the king's turntables. What these records might reveal about the disco period could provide the biggest breakthroughs yet in understanding this utterly puzzling culture."

According to Daprich, these records – round, twelve-inch vinyl tablets sheathed in cardboard and believed to have been used to record information primarily during the 1970s and 80s – appear to have been penned between 1975 and 1979 by what experts assume were the era's most prominent scholars and artists.

"Four sisters named Sledge made multiple contributions to these archives, as did five young men who are identified only as Village People," said Daprich as he carefully sorted through the priceless collection. "Unfortunately there are no markings on the tablet to indicate which village these men came from or inhabited, but their photo conjures shocking images of what that place may have looked like."

Though Daprich admitted that much of what is trying to be communicated through these records is, as he put it, "difficult to grasp," Daprich and his colleagues, after exhaustive study of the records, have begun to piece together theories as to what circumstances forced such a far-out society of people into sudden extinction after having reigned supreme for half a decade.

"Through study of these records, we've formulated two possible scenarios for the overnight fall of the disco empire," said Daprich. "The first theory suggests that the disco culture was completely wiped out during a 1979 British invasion, in which an angry young anarchist we believe named Johnny the Rotten used something called sex pistols to kill disco and forever change the landscape of the American culture."

"Another theory is that the entire disco population got infected with a disease they called Saturday Night Fever and suffered a long, grueling death that everyone wished could have come a whole lot sooner," Daprich said. ∎

> "What function this enormous mirrored ball served would [help] understand what caused these super-freaky ancestors of ours to groove themselves into extinction so quickly," explained Kelser.

MAP from page 69

employee residing in Dayton, Ohio, agreed with Weiss's assessment. "I live in the U.S.A., so why the hell would I need to know where America is? Or the United States for that matter?"

Added Matheson: "As long as there's still room on that map for all three of those countries, I'm sure everyone will keep getting along just fine."

Meanwhile, the Department of Homeland Security sees the Gallup/Harris poll results as a blessing in disguise. According to Secretary Michael Chertoff, the nation would be better off if these numbers skewed even higher.

"Personally, I believe if fewer people in this world could spot America on a map, we'd have a much better chance of avoiding national tragedies like nine-eleven," said Chertoff. "You can't attack a country you can't find."

Of the respondents actually capable of pinpointing America on the map of America, their accuracy decreased considerably with each additional query about the country. Asked for the name of the U.S. capital, those polled placed Washington, D.C., fifth behind "Minneapolis-St. Paul," "Mount Rushmore," "America City" and "Whitewater."

Further, when quizzed on when America declared independence from Great Britain to become a sovereign nation, more than two-thirds replied: "six thousand years ago, when God created humankind."

Despite Americans' seemingly underdeveloped sense of their own geography, history and domestic policy, they did score high points on the issue of patriotism, calling America "the greatest country in the world" (47 percent), "the best state of all the Unites States" (31 percent), and "a place to definitely explore when I finally get my passport" (22 percent). ∎

> Weiss: "I live in the U.S.A., so why the hell would I need to know where America is? Or the United States for that matter?"

A page from the Recoil handbook...
Manning A Suicide Hotline

Volunteering to answer phones at a local suicide hotline can bring a person a great sense of satisfaction. Below is a basic guide for preventing a caller from taking his or her own life:

- If a jumper calls from a ledge on his cell phone, try to boost his self-confidence by complimenting him on the clear reception he's getting.

- Suicide hotlines tend to receive a lot of prank calls, so always hang up on callers the first couple of times they call – if they keep calling back, you'll know they're serious.

- If the caller has a Middle Eastern accent, try to talk him into moving to an unpopulated area before continuing your conversation.

- Keep a small cooler at your station so you don't have to put a caller on hold every time you need a fresh beer.

- Inform the caller that suicide is not about wanting to die, it's about a powerful need for pain to end – a situation they can easily remedy by just taking a whole bunch of painkillers.

- People near suicide can sometimes be invigorated by hearing famous quotes. Maybe try reading them some Sylvia Plath.

- Threaten to put Dr. Phil on the line – the caller should straighten his act up good and quick.

- Counsel the caller with the suicide hotline mantra: "Suicide is a temporary solution to a permanent problem." [NOTE TO FACT-CHECKER: SOMETHING SEEMS BACKWARD THERE – IS 'PERMANENT' MAYBE SPELLED 'PERMENANT?']

- Assure the caller that their suicidal feelings will likely pass in 20 or 30 years.

- Suggest to the distraught caller that suicide is only *part* of the answer.

RECOILMAG.COM NEWS SATIRE YOU CAN TRUST

recoil

Mexican ice cream vendor eerily combs neighborhood

***Lost* found**

quikSTAT
How are we reducing our fuel expense?
- Quitting job; replaying *Gears of War III*
- Finally using backyard catapult
- Riding lawnmower to work
- Levitation lessons
- Siphoning, regurgitating neighbor's car's gas
- Only stealing cars that have full tanks
- Making Johns shut off car during hummers
- Driving downhill, taking bus uphill
- Running engine in closed garage, mulling options
- Replacing burning moat of gasoline around house with alligators and pointy sticks
- Sailing, sailing away

Dad endorses plan to leave church after communion

Richmond, Va. – Midway through Reverend Gregory's Sunday morning sermon, churchgoer David Allen endorsed his son's suggestion that the family leave church after receiving communion, sources said. "David thinks maybe we should excuse ourselves from the service right after communion so we can beat the traffic," Allen whispered to his wife, Jody. "Normally I would never get behind such a plan, but there are an awfully lot of people [parked] here today, so maybe it's not such a bad idea. On our way back from the altar we could just keep walking right out the door. Nobody will even notice." Jody Allen, in keeping with her longstanding opposition to the early vacating of church, quickly vetoed the proposal and warned of stern consequences should the two attempt to advance the issue at a later time.

Suburban family sometimes recycles

Kankakee, Ill. – The Max and Kris Oliver household occasionally does its fair share to save the environment, son Justin reported Friday. In addition to sometime purchasing pump-spray products instead of Ozone-damaging aerosol cans, the family purchased recycling bins years ago and once in a while fills them with newspapers and used plastic containers. "Half the time Mom just throws the newspapers in the trash, though," Justin told reporters, "and she says the milk jugs are bacteria-laden, so she usually tosses those out, too." ■

Above: Werner, 29, was found dead in his home wearing a Xanax® promotional t-shirt and Paxil® visor. Inset: The Zoloft pen Werner used to express his final thoughts.

Suicide note written using free Zoloft® promotional pen

San Francisco, Calif. – Authorities investigating the recent suicide of telemarketing company account manager Chris Werner confirmed Thursday that the dark, self-hating suicide note apparently penned by Werner only moments before the 29-year-old took his own life Wednesday was written using a Zoloft® promotional pen.

"Lab technicians have determined that the utensil used to convey Werner's final thoughts was a promotional pen he reportedly received as a complimentary gift through his doctor from the Pfizer corporation for his years of dedicated use of their anti-depression product Zoloft®," said police chief Gavin Thompson. "So even though the jury may still be out at the FDA as to whether or not the *pills* work like they're supposed to, it looks like their *pens* work just fine."

"At his time of death he was also wearing a Xanax® t-shirt and carrying an Adderall® keychain," said Thompson.

Zoloft® – a heavily prescribed selective-serotonin reuptake inhibitor (SSRI) Sertraline – is among the most popular antidepressants currently prescribed for OCD and depression with anxiety, the latter of which Werner was reported to have been suffering from for more than seven years. According to Werner's recently released medical records, the Los Angeles transplant had been prescribed increasingly higher dosages of Zoloft® in an attempt to curb the suicidal thoughts that had been mounting since he was first

see ZOLOFT page 76

Area man to throw life away over broad

Raleigh, N.C. – Friends of resident Allen Buteyin confirmed Sunday that the 23-year-old engineering technician seems intent on throwing his life away in order to satisfy the growing demands of his relationship with girlfriend Sheila Coeling.

"I wish I could figure out why Allen's so bent on throwing it all away over this broad," said friend Jeff Letchner following Buteyin's recent announcement that he and Coeling will begin living together in early November. "It was bad enough when he told me he had to quit our bowling league two months ago because Friday is the only night Sheila doesn't work and she wants him to spend them with her. Now he's moving in with her. Well, I guess that should just about do it for the miserable bastard – it was nice knowing him."

Letchner: "Now he's moving in with her. Well, I guess that should just about do it for the poor bastard – it was nice knowing him."

According to Letchner, Buteyin began "totally flushing his life down the toilet" shortly after he began dating Coeling, 24, approximately eight months ago.

see BROAD page 76

Above: Letchner (left) tries to convince Buteyin to get off the phone with the broad.

page 73

HEALTH

New strain of yawn twice as contagious

Geneva, Switzerland – Officials at the World Health Organization (WHO) issued a global warning Tuesday that a devastating new strain of yawn – which experts say is at least twice as contagious as the common yawn – is continuing to quickly spread across all populated continents and now presents a worldwide threat.

"Over the past seventy-two hours, the World Health Organization has received numerous reports about uncontrollable and excessive yawning taking place in many parts of the world – especially the really boring parts, like the Netherlands or even the Midwestern United States," explained WHO Director-General Lee Jong-wook at a press conference Tuesday morning in Geneva. "One report from Mexican officials claims that people across their country are yawning even more often than they would be if they were all at jobs of some sort. So that's how bad it is."

Identified by Malaysian physicians in late July, the hybrid strain of yawn not only passes from one person to another with even more efficiency than a typical yawn, but can also pass from humans to animals and vise-versa, lasts 75 percent longer than a normal yawn and appears to wholly resist the counter-effects of Red Bull.

"Now, we all know how contagious yawns are to begin with," Jong-wook said, 'but this new, more powerful, more communicable strain of yawn threatens to create a mass yawning epidemic unlike anything we've seen before."

The ever-deliberate Jong-wook then paused briefly before qualifying his statement, adding: "Well, except perhaps for when *Zoolander* was in theaters."

According to Jong-wook, WHO officials have not yet been able to isolate the hybrid strain, identify its origin or develop a means of stopping the yawn's spread.

Jong-wook opened his eyes extra-wide, quickly shook his head as if trying to regain his composure, blinked hard four times and then addressed the reporter's question.

"We've had numerous meetings regarding this crisis, but every time we get together somebody ends up letting out a yawn," Jong-wook said. "Sure enough, pretty soon everybody in the room is following suit and we end up voting to take an early lunch. This is part of what's making progress on this matter so difficult."

Although experts agree that this new strain of highly communicable yawn is not life-threatening, Jong-wook cautioned that persons infected with the involuntary muscle reaction will find themselves more susceptible to a number of minor health hazards.

"A person could very easily strain his or her jaw muscles during a violent yawning fit," explained Jong-wook. "Or just imagine how much having your mouth spread wide open all the time because you're yawning would increase your chances of accidentally swallowing a fly. Disgusting."

Asked by a reporter if there was anything a person could do to stop yawning once exposed to the hybrid strain, Jong-wook put his fist in front of his mouth and worked through a very large yawn. He then opened his eyes extra-wide, quickly shook his head as if trying to regain his

see YAWN page 76

Above Citizens of particularly boring areas of the world, such as these Nebraskan men, have been struck hard by the new strain of yawn.

A page from the Recoil handbook...
Golf Tips

Golf has long remained one of the most popular sports throughout the world, played as much for relaxation as for competition. Here are some tips to help sharpen your game:

• Beginners: part of the allure of golf is that the game presents almost unlimited situations that require the player to constantly be making tough choices. Still, for simplicity's sake, you're probably best off picking one end of the club to strike the ball with and sticking with it.

• Your first goal should be developing a good short game. Your second should be getting a cart airborne.

• Many players find that they get more practice and enjoyment out of hitting a bucket of balls if they dump out the balls and hit each one independently.

• You should be trying to hit the ball really, really hard. Also note that direction can be important in some situations.

• Follow through is very important, so if you're going to threaten to kick someone's ass for hitting into you, you better damn well be ready to throw down.

• It is considered bad manners to talk about uninteresting subjects in the middle of other players' swings.

• Despite what you may see on TV, golf is still a good way to avoid minorities, homeless people and homosexuals.

• A lot of golf "pros" will tell you that the key to success is being able to play the fairway, but the cheating way sure sounds a lot easier.

• If you notice that rakes are laid out near all of the sand traps, consider yourself lucky, because you came during the course's Free Rake Day promotion! Free rakes! Whoohoo!

• You can shave strokes off your average by hitting more holes-in-one.

• Hold your feet apart, but not too far apart. Hold your arms stiff, but not too stiff. Basically, do everything perfectly every time.

• This isn't a mini-golf course! Congratulations, son, you just drove a ball into that Amish man's windmill.

• You can avoid having to learn how to chip by simply landing the ball on the green with your longer iron shots.

• Word to the wise: be certain as to the sexual orientation of your foursome before suggesting that the group continue on to the 19th hole.

• Even funnier than giving one of your friends a novelty golf ball that explodes is giving them a novelty golf cart that explodes.

• Face it, buddy, the only way you're ever going to shoot in the 70s is by building a goddamn time machine.

HOROSCOPES

Aquarius (January 20 to February 18)
Aquarius' refusal to pull over for ambulance sirens is racking up negative karma equivalent to the combined cosmic demerits awarded for adultery, stealing from the blind, and teaching your kids to smoke. Sure, selfish driving will get you where you're going a couple of seconds sooner, but you'll pay for it in the afterlife. I understand the stoplights in Hell stay red for 15 billion years at a time.

Capricorn (December 22 to January 19)
The menace of Capricorn's short temper is compounded by the convenience of today's 24-hour superstores, which stock every caliber of ammunition needed for carrying out most liquor-fueled, impromptu acts of violence. No longer does anger have to wait until morning – but frugal Capricorn should at least take the time to check for coupons.

Pisces (February 19 to March 20)
Give God credit for mustering enough ambition to launch His legendary Creator/Supreme Architect monopoly, a venture documented as being six long days of tedious, non-union labor. That's a good example of how much can be accomplished without cable television numbing the creative ambition. Step away from the TV at least long enough to tell time by the position of the sun, rather than by the urgency in Regis' voice.

Aries (March 21 to April 19)
Why in hell do you even own a television if you're not going to spend every free moment watching it? Ignoring the brain-numbing discharge of the tube will invariably spark Aries' ambition and creativity – worthless traits that invariably lead to no good. Television has a designed purpose: to congest the industrious mind, so you won't invent yet another way of destroying the planet, or at least some of the people on it.

Taurus (April 20 to May 20)
Thirsty, trendy Taurus doesn't seem to notice that bottled water companies have brainwashed the public into paying big dollars for a substance that flows readily from a household tap. If you're genuinely convinced you must pay more than the cost of a beer to properly hydrate your body, then you, Taurus, are indeed mentally congruent to 'Evian' spelled backwards.

Gemini (May 21 to June 20)
That classic break-up condolence, "Better to have loved and lost than never to have loved at all," has provided its fair share of comfort during Gemini's woeful times. But considering how bad your last relationship was, perhaps more applicable is the truthful axiom, "Better to have loved and lost than to have to live with a complete goddamned psycho for the rest of your life."

Cancer (June 21 to July 22)
Cancer's self-centered phone diplomacy explains why your telephone rings less than the Voluntary Audit line at the IRS. Hold and Call Waiting are rude, conversation-killing options used by the kind of selfish people who also don't think twice about using someone else's last squeeze of toothpaste on Monday morning. Call Ma Bell and cancel your caller-alienating options at once – they'll put you on hold long enough for you to taste your own medicine.

Leo (July 23 to August 22)
Leo's job search is indeed a difficult endeavor; with your lack of qualifications and job experience, you'll be lucky to land a seasonal gig chalking lines on football fields or mopping up peep-show stalls. Your best angle is the "It's not what you know, it's who you know" theory – more specifically, it's who you know that doesn't know you well enough to think better of hiring you.

Virgo (August 23 to September 22)
Thinking for yourself is an idea that needs to be force-fed into Virgo's malnourished frontal lobes; your willingness to thoughtlessly repeat learned behavior rivals those brain-dead rock pitchers from The Lottery. Don't let society, tradition or television dictate your behavior – do what makes sense to you – but remember that rocking the boat may make everyone else want to throw you overboard.

Libra (September 23 to October 22)
Libra's love of animals contradicts mankind's self-preservation instincts. Remember, no matter how cute chimpanzees may be, any species intellectually capable of sign language, space travel and playing ice hockey is getting way too close to mounting a global takeover. Do whatever you can to hinder the simians' advancements, for it is only a matter of time before apes team with computers to stick us humans in the cages. Won't that be a hoot.

Scorpio (October 23 to November 21)
The way to a father's heart is not through his stomach, it's through leaving him the hell alone while he watches television. Sooner or later, you're bound to have a power outage; when devoid of electronic amusement and faced with family conversation, Scorpio's father naturally resorts to booze, which will loosen his tongue long enough for him to confess his true feelings: "Child, I love you very much – for not bothering me while I watch TV."

Sagittarius (November 22 to December 21)
Sagittarius' blind support of the American military is indicative of someone who's never fired a gun, let alone fired it at complete strangers you've been told to hate. Reconsider your "Die with your boots on" wartime attitude – that's a bloodthirsty phrase most likely penned by some warmonger politician who never had to spoon his own soup, let alone dig one of those shallow graves otherwise known as foxholes.

MUSIC

Above: Members of the probably defunct local band Voice of Translator.

Local band members assume breakup after fourth week without rehearsal

South Bend, Ind. – All four members of Voice of Translator, a local indie rock band recently formed by area musicians, are beginning to suspect that their musical union no longer exists after the passing of a fourth week during which no band rehearsal was suggested, attempted or scheduled by any member.

"For our whole first two months we used to practice at least every Saturday afternoon, no matter what, and usually a whole lot more," said Nick Portman, singer and guitarist for the fledgling rock outfit he co-founded with longtime friend drummer Gary Abbey in January. "I mean, I know [bassist] Jeff [Alexander] had his college midterms somewhere in there and [keyboardist] Joe [Kinney] has been hanging out with his girlfriend a lot and all, but I highly doubt that everyone's been so busy during the last month that we couldn't get together even once. I think maybe we might just be done [as a band]."

Portman said that despite seeing each of his bandmates several times during the past month at unrelated social events, none of the band members, including himself, have even mentioned the band, let alone attempt to schedule a rehearsal.

"It's been really awkward running into one of the guys and neither of us daring to ask the other if he knows why we haven't practiced in weeks," said Portman. "We haven't officially broken up as far as I know, but at this point I'm beginning to suspect that we're pretty much over and done with. And if another month goes by and nobody's called anybody about getting together or booking a show, then we can pretty much forget about it."

According to bassist Jeff Alexander, previous to Voice of Translator's spontaneous hiatus, no member of the band had orally suggested, demanded or otherwise expressed a desire to put band rehearsals on indefinite hold.

"Nobody ever came right out and said anything about breaking up or taking a break or anything – we all just kind of stopped getting together," said Alexander.

> "It's been really awkward running into one of the guys and neither of us daring to ask the other if he knows why we haven't practiced in weeks," said Portman.

So although there's no official word or anything, if I had to put money on it, I'd say we're pretty much broken up."

Alexander said he remembers there being a growing decline in enthusiasm among the band members shortly before they played what is beginning to look like was the band's farewell performance.

"People were missing practices and skipping out on doing flyers and stuff for a couple of weeks before our show at The Never Club last month," said Alexander. "Then, after the show, I remember thinking that it was a bad sign that everybody was taking their equipment home with them instead of running it back to the rehearsal space. For me that's always been a clear sign that an assumed breakup is taking place." ∎

recoilmag.com

page 75

EDITORIAL
Being green is a goddamned cakewalk

By Kermit the Frog

Thirty-some odd years ago, back when I recorded "It's Not Easy Being Green," no words could have been as dead-money true for a singer as were those powerful and emotive lyrics. No matter how corny it may have felt to sing other songs such as "Happy Feet" or "If I Were...," I remember it was always easy to sing "It's Not Easy Being Green" straight from the heart, because whoever wrote that song was obviously coming from the same place as me: being green and hating every second of it. Back in those days there were a lot of prejudices against those of color, and being green certainly was anything but easy. Nowadays, however, I'll be the first one to stand up and agree that being green is a goddamned cakewalk.

Granted, back when I recorded what went on to become my signature tune, I wasn't the same amphibian that I am today. It was the seventies; my worldwide fame was at an all-time high, the pressure of writing for each week's episode of *The Muppet Show* had me compulsively biting my finger webbing, and that obnoxious slut Ms. Piggy was constantly nagging me to put a ring on her hoof both on and off camera. It certainly was not an easy time for me, and walking around with that diseased-looking green skin tone only made my problems that much worse.

Today, however, I find that some of the same situations that caused me to croon that simple melody at show after show with heartfelt conviction – "having to spend each day the color of the leaves" or the fact that "it seems you blend in with so many other ordinary things" – now actually make my life just that much easier! Because with lunatic fans constantly stalking me, paparazzi shooting photos, cops looking for a high-profile bust and everything else that comes with being a staple of the entertainment business, I'll tell you, I thank my lucky stars every day now that I'm "not standing out like flashy sparkles in the water," as the song's lyrics describe, because being green gives me a decided advantage in maintaining my privacy.

For example, whenever I'm doing studio work and for one reason or another suddenly feel that I need a private moment, I can just duck in front of one of the green screens that they shoot against and voila – Kermit has left the building. This also works wonders for hanging around unnoticed to see who is saying what about you. It's like being the invisible man!

Actually, there are a lot of ways that being naturally green helps me in my work as a beloved multimedia entertainer. Your normal Hollywood star, you see, can tend to look a little green in the face when they show up at the set in the morning coked to the gills after an all-night partying binge. Me, I can show up three sheets to the wind, as green as the day is long and nobody can suggest jack shit. And, of course, should anyone ever try, all I have to do is imply that they're a skin-color obsessed racist and that pretty much puts the brakes on that line of questioning in an awful hurry, let me tell you. One thing I know is true: those few people who are still willing to try to play the race card in Hollywood these days usually find that even their straight flushes aren't going to win them too many pots, if you know what I mean.

Also, and mind you, I can't prove this, but personal experience has led me to believe that my green pigment emits a subliminal message that helps me get paid more generously during contract renewal negotiations. Green is, after all, the color of money. And when all of those studio executives sit down and interact with me in all of my green glory, subconsciously they're seeing me as a walking, talking, endless bag of money. Tell me that doesn't come in awful goddamned handy. The idea of making those cheap bastards want to open up their wallets to keep me happy, well, it just makes my green-assed throat swell up to about 10 times its normal size.

So no matter how much I've bitched about it on record or screen over the past half-century, allow me please to just go on the record right here and now and verify the opposite: being green, baby – it's the only way to be. ■

BROAD from page 73

see Queens of the Stone Age because she wanted him to help with a candle party she was hosting or some gay shit like that," said Letchner. "When I naturally called bullshit on that, he gives me this whole heart-to-heart about really liking this broad and wanting to show her his devotion or whatever. And this was *after* we found out that Dave Grohl was going to play drums for Queens at that show. That's when I knew Allen was in trouble – that whether he knew it or not, he was fighting for his life."

Letchner said that while he, Buteyin and other male friends had embraced and enjoyed the bachelor life since graduating college in 2001 – a period in which Letchner insists the foursome "lived life to the fullest" through spontaneous, reckless behavior devoid of responsibility – Buteyin's social agenda underwent significant change once his relationship with Coeling began.

"Back before there was any Sheila, me and Allen, [friend] Warren [Groenendal] and [friend] Nick [Bovenkamp] would spend just about every night hanging out," said Letchner. "We weren't always at the bar getting drunk and chasing tail or anything – a lot of the time we were just sitting around my place, playing video games, jamming some music and generally just wasting time. But the point is that we were doing nothing *together*. Now we're lucky if Allen shows up to drink beer once a week because he's always busy doing God knows what with Sheila. And even when he does go out with us he always has to take off super early to get home and call Sheila. He's like a walking corpse already."

Groenendal, who has known Buteyin since high school, expressed similar frustration regarding his close friend's unfortunate path.

"It's tough to just stand there and do nothing while you watch your friend heaving his entire life into the dumpster all over some chick," said Groenendal. "Eventually Nick and Jeff and I decided to stage an intervention to try to get Allen to realize that no girl is worth trading your life for. We sat him down and told him that if he could see what we see, he wouldn't be doing this to himself. But he just got real defensive and said we were jealous or some insane shit like that and bolted. Didn't even finish his beer – which the old Allen would have considered a capital crime punishable by triple beer bong."

Though Letchner, Groenendal and Bovenkamp said they were disappointed with their inability to convince Buteyin to stop "tossing his life into the gutter for a broad," the trio confirmed that they are resolute in their endeavor to save their friend's life.

"It's frustrating, trying to help someone so intent on destroying their existence by getting mixed up with a chick," said Letchner. "Every time he gets mad at me for trying to stop him from buying himself a first class, one-way ticket to the suburbian death camp, part of me just wants to say, 'Have a nice trip, Dufus.' But another part of me wants to try to save him from going out like that, just like any one of my friends would no doubt do for me if it were my head on the block. I guess I just have to keep in mind that if I succeed, someday Allen will thank me for not letting him throw his life away over a broad." ■

ZOLOFT from page 73

prescribed the drug in 2006.

"It isn't known at this time whether or not there is any connection between Werner's excessive use of antidepressants, his choice of writing device for his suicide note and his decision to take his own life," said Thompson. "It's difficult to place the blame for Werner's suicide solely on Zoloft® just because he used one of their pens to sign his final timecard. Remember, at his time of death he was also wearing a Xanax® t-shirt and carrying an Adderall® keychain."

According to police reports, Werner was found dead on the floor of his San Francisco apartment Wednesday night, having shot himself once with a .45 caliber handgun in the right temple, just below the rim of his complimentary Paxil® visor.

Investigators said that from the looks of Werner's medicine cabinet – as well as his impressive collection of promotional pharmaceutical hats, pens, shirts and other products – doctors had pushed a dazzling array of medications upon Werner in an effort to treat his progressively worsening depression and anxiety.

"Prozac®, Lithium®, Klonopin®, you name it, this guy had it – and that's just looking at his coffee mug collection," Thompson said of Werner's assortment of promotional housewares. "Werner's medicine cabinet had so many pill bottles stacked up in it that there wasn't even any room for a stick of deodorant. His doctor probably wore out ten Zoloft® pens just writing up this guy's prescriptions." ■

YAWN from page 73

composure, blinked hard four times and then addressed the reporter's question.

"Well, exercise is always a great way to keep the oxygen flowing and keep from yawning," Jong-wook said. After receiving blank stares from reporters, photographers, television crew members, caterers, sound engineers, other WHO officials and even the guy who puts the cushy windscreens on the podium microphones, Jong-wook backpedaled, adding: "Yeah, you're right: like that's going to happen. So, no, there's pretty much nothing anyone can do." ■

recoil

RECOILMAG.COM NEWS SATIRE YOU CAN TRUST

Youth football coach spends most of game counting to 11

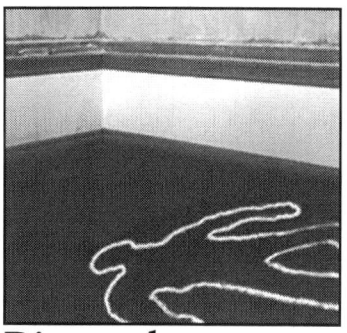

Distraught mathematician jumps from eraser ledge

quikSTAT

What's going to get us in the end?
- Each state's differing age-of-consent law
- Plastic bags
- Those bones getting dug up
- Nothing, because we're just not into that
- Death, hopefully, before the torture continues
- Not the end of cop's broomstick, hopefully

Pervert born into bondage

Miami, Fla. – David Foster, a quiet-mannered, 56-year-old tax attorney who has for decades spent the majority of his money and free time employing fetish-friendly prostitutes to tie him down and berate, spank and whip him, revealed Thursday that his overwhelming fondness for bondage was something he was naturally born into. "I've totally been into bondage for as long as I can remember – it's not like something I acquired a taste for over time – which leads me to believe I was simply born 'into' it."

Widower knows way too much about body disposal techniques

Cleveland, Ohio – Ben Morris, a 38-year-old widower whose wife Rebecca is assumed dead after mysteriously disappearing 18 months ago, knows a bit too much about methods for confidentially disposing of dead bodies, a source close to Morris said Friday. "The other day, and I don't even know how we got on the subject, but Ben was going on and on about how you have to weigh a body down with twice the body's weight in stones or [concrete] blocks to keep it submerged if you dump it into a river or lake, because of bloating," said Jay Bennett, a friend of Morris'. "That doesn't seem like the kind of knowledge a person just happens to carry around with them, you know? It kind of makes me wonder." Bennett acknowledged that in the past Morris has offered his counsel should Bennett ever need instruction as to the best place locally to bury a body. ■

Above: A police surveillance photo of the suspect taken moments before his arrest.

Jobless hippie suspected in brutal killing of time

Oakland, Fla. – Oakland Police Chief Dan Harris told reporters Thursday that authorities have detained a 21-year-old male for questioning in regard to his possible involvement in a rash of merciless time killing that has outraged an otherwise crime-free community during recent weeks.

"Although we can not disclose the identity of our suspect at this time, what we can tell you is that the suspect fits the profile of a serial time killer to a tee: young, single, unemployed and remorseless – like he doesn't have a care in the world," said Harris at a recent press conference. "Thankfully, the people of this community *do* care. We care a lot. And we aren't about to just stand by and watch while someone repeatedly kills time without the slightest hint of guilt."

Harris said the suspect was apprehended Wednesday night inside his brother's suburban home, where investigators believe the suspect carried out a majority of the killings since quitting his part-time job at a local record store and moving into the residence in early March.

"Neighbors reported having seen the suspect for weeks lounging around on the porch drinking beer while they were pulling out of their driveways to go to work or taking their kids to practice or any of the other ten million things that decent, hard-working Americans have to do every day," said Harris. "You can only see a guy sitting around on his ass so many times before you start to suspect that he's a lazy good-for-nothing who's probably thoughtlessly killing more time than anyone can begin to imagine."

Police stormed the residence and

> "Young, single, unemployed and remorseless – like he doesn't have a care in the world," said Harris.

see KILLING page 80

Terrible Christian rock band can't understand why God hasn't blessed them with record contract

Above: Members of God-awful Christian rock band In His Name.

Hollywood, Calif. – Despite their sincere belief in an all-powerful God who blesses those who praise His name with limitless rewards on Earth as well as everlasting life after death, members of the Christian modern rock band In His Name told sources Friday that they can't understand why God has not yet blessed the untalented fivesome with a prestigious, high-paying, multi-album recording contract.

"We love the Lord, but we also love to rock," said Marcus Anthony Tallman, lead vocalist for the religious rock act that has been performing as a unit for more than eight years. "We believe that

see BAND page 80

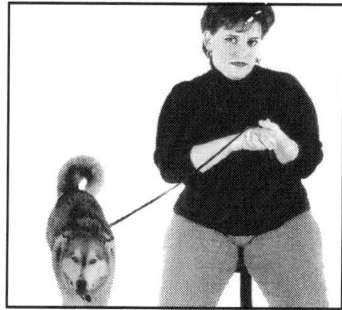

Dog, owner husky

Gambling addict too broke to develop drug addiction

page 77

EDITORIAL
Those crazy fucking neighbors of ours are at it again

Oh my God, you are not going to believe this one. Quick, come and get a look at this – those crazy fucking nextdoor neighbors of ours are at it again.

Remember back around 2003 when those senseless dingbats spent about two

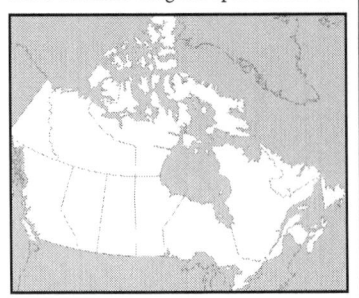

By Canada

months trying to get permission from the entire neighborhood to let them move in on that one property on grounds that the current tenant – the guy with the mustache – was an uncooperative nutbag that needed to be removed from the community? And then when they couldn't get any of us to agree with them, they just went ahead and ran the guy out of town anyway? Now that property is a complete goddamned disaster. The yard's a mess, the power's constantly going in and out, and I don't even think they have running water over there anymore.

Well, you'd think that whole incident would've taught our nextdoor neighbors to mind their own business – but no! Now they're trying to tell those Afghans down the street what they can and can't do in their own backyard. Can you believe the nerve of these people?

I mean, really, who put them in charge of the Neighborhood Watch? I sure as hell don't remember asking them to police the whole community, do you? I guess the cocky bastards think they can just boss everyone else around because nobody dares say anything to the contrary.

What right do *they* have to act like such jackoffs to everybody that doesn't instantly agree with them on everything, you know? It's hard to believe they could really think they're better than everybody else on the block when *their* household seems to have the most problems of anybody. Heck, it seems like every night on the news I see another story about some madman with a gun nextdoor terrorizing the rest of the people that live over there. Is every single person over there armed, for Christ's sake? I tell ya, if it's not one thing it's another with these clowns.

Believe me, if it were up to me, we wouldn't live anywhere near these assholes. It's like everybody else looks at us like we're all buddies with them or something just because we live nextdoor, when the truth is that we can't stand them any more than anybody else can. I'm sure you remember that time at that barbeque when those rude-ass neighbors refused to use the beef we brought because they thought it might be diseased. Jesus, nothing like making us look bad in front of everybody. I was half-expecting them to boycott our beer, too, but I guess all those people living nextdoor like to stay good and loaded so they won't notice what dickheads they're being to the rest of the world.

> Now they're trying to tell those Afghans down the street what they can and can't do in their own backyard. Can you believe the nerve of these people?

Oh boy, I think that's them knocking on our door again. I wonder what insane idea they want our help with this time. Alright, I better get this, I guess. Time to be neighborly. We *do* have to live next to these people. ∎

A page from the Recoil handbook...
Guide To Home Fitness

Studies say as many as 62 percent of all Americans are currently overweight – a condition which puts one at higher risk of developing diabetes, coronary artery disease, osteoarthritis and every other ugly word in the dictionary. Fortunately, getting your body back in shape doesn't have to mean shelling out hundreds of dollars for a gym membership and personal trainer. Below are some helpful tips for developing a low-cost, at-home workout routine.

• Position your refrigerator as far away as possible from the kitchen's entrance, so you'll have to walk a few extra steps each of the 50 times a day you go to get a snack. Also consider getting an extra freezer that you can put all the way out in the garage; the extra walking you'll do during your five or six daily ice cream runs will burn as much as 15 percent of the ice creams' calories.

• Exercising to music can often inspire a more vigorous and enjoyable workout. Buy your most hyperactive child a drum set that he or she can practice on while you work out. (Note: If you live in a crowded apartment complex, make sure the drum kit is no larger than a five-piece.)

• Purchasing a treadmill is one way to guarantee results, as you're certain to burn off some calories hauling that damn contraption first into the exercise area of your family room, then into the storage area of your attic, and finally into the "Free For The Taking" area of your yard sale.

• Meditation can be mood changing – even life altering! Meditation can clear your mind of the cobwebs of worry and doubt that could be causing you to overeat as a form of escape and comfort. Meditation can even free you from the pain of the real world. Oops, wait a sec. Was I saying meditation? I meant medication.

• If a king-size Hersheys bar is eaten in the forest and there's nobody there to see, do the calories count? Most experts say no, so feel free to hit the convenience store right before your nature hike.

• Move in with someone whose table manners are so unfathomably appalling that even catching a mere glimpse of them engaging in gustation will make it quite impossible for you to do the same.

• Excessive calorie intake (pigging out) and a sedentary lifestyle (sitting on your ass all day) can lead to morbid obesity (becoming your mother). Lay terminology (the stuff in parenthesis) was provided by your husband (When's dinner? I'm starving. Did you pick up a six-pack while you were out?).

• Exercise, interestingly enough, rhymes with schmexercise. Coincidence? Highly doubt it.

HOROSCOPES

Sagittarius (November 22 to December 21)
Sexually overactive Sagittarius needs to either lose the pro-life stance or adopt a reliable method of barricading procreation's persistent march. Those not ready for parenting shouldn't gamble with the possibility of pregnancy – one thing is for certain: if you play long enough in the poker game of unprotected sex, you will eventually end up with a full house.

Capricorn (December 22 to January 19)
Your pet needs a reminder of exactly who is in charge. With all the housing, feeding, bathing and other pampering, you're probably both a little confused as to the chain of command. But until domesticated animals upgrade their paws to include an opposable thumb – thus being able to operate the remote control – know that you are definitely calling the shots. Pets are merely your guests; remind them with a rainy night outdoors.

Aquarius (January 20 to February 18)
The rainbow of Life hardly ever leads to a pot of gold - it usually leads to a cesspool of disappointment. Adopting a "money isn't everything, love is the answer" attitude looks good on paper and sounds even better out loud, but in today's materialistic world, money solves problems – whereas love usually just creates them.

Pisces (February 19 to March 20)
The standard Pisces foot fetish stems from the mistaken notion that your own feet are the most adorable stumps ever fused to the end of a set of legs; the general public is quite sick of you unsheathing them for self-admiration. The truth be told, you wouldn't know a good-looking foot if it was shoved up your ass, which, considering your current obsession with procrastination, is gaining in likelihood.

Aries (March 21 to April 19)
Struggling musician Aries should consider pulling your wrinkling face out of your girlfriend's refrigerator long enough to actually work on that glorious rock star career you've been predicting since high school. Remember that a musician's age, when weighed against their success, indicates the difference between a struggling artist and a successful loser.

Taurus (April 20 to May 20)
Mend marital communication breakdowns by reverting to the international human language: chess. Shifting your concentration from emotion to strategy will allow for clearer thinking on the romantic front, where it's important to maintain your sexual proficiency. Remember, ever since IBM's Big Blue outplayed the world's best chess player, battery-powered machinery threatens to pink slip any job normally reserved for humans.

Gemini (May 21 to June 20)
The Internet is the perfect shovel for reclusive Gemini to expand that moat you've constructed between yourself and the rest of the world. Be careful that the impersonal nature of the chat room doesn't atrophy your social skills to a level at which even the simple act of returning videotapes becomes as fearsome as public speaking.

Cancer (June 21 to July 22)
The constant untidiness of Cancer's house can be blamed on physics: the universe's tendency toward chaos dictates that your house will always look like you only clean during the hurricane's eye. Spend the morning cursing Einstein and then take a nap – there's nothing like redirecting blame to wear a person out.

Leo (July 23 to August 22)
When signing a contract, realize that time is money – you'll soon find reading an entire legal document, especially the fine print, an irrelevant waste. Logistically, if whatever's in fine print was of any importance at all, they certainly would have printed it a whole lot bigger. Get in the habit of making no two of your signatures look anywhere near alike, and your legal problems will be negligible.

Virgo (August 23 to September 22)
The innocent, logic-based life insights streaming from the mouths of children are usually dismissed as naïve babble by the jaded adult brain, which has forgotten that the simplest explanation for any situation is usually the correct one. Still, some child philosophies are too advanced for even contemplative Virgo to dissect. Example: what are you eating under there? Under where? Truly baffling.

Libra (September 23 to October 22)
Thinking for yourself is an idea that needs to be force-fed into Libra's malnourished frontal lobes; your willingness to thoughtlessly repeat learned behavior rivals those brain-dead rock pitchers from The Lottery. Don't let society, tradition or television dictate your behavior – do what makes sense to you – but remember that rocking the boat will likely make everyone else want to throw you overboard.

Scorpio (October 23 to November 21)
Martha Stewart may be a subtly sexy little number, but she sure has some whacked ideas; Scorpio would do well to NOT listen to her. Not every household decoration has to be so perfect it makes your friends and neighbors weep openly out of jealousy. And for men, having your house decorated just like Stewart's clues everyone to who's wearing the family pants – you know, those pink ones with the smiley patches sewn onto the ass.

recoilmag.com

FAMILY

Above: A photo from the 2008 Bradbury family reunion.

Stumbling attempt to socialize at family reunion results in commitment to organize next reunion

Piedmont, Ga. – Susan Bradbury, a warmhearted yet reclusive member of the Bradbury family made an ill-conceived and stumbling impromptu attempt to socialize during her family's annual reunion Sunday – a move Bradbury fears may have committed her to organizing the following year's reunion party, a project with which she harbors no desire to be involved.

"I was just trying to make my presence known, so at least people could confirm that I was there before I cut out early," said Bradbury, who admitted to routinely being tongue-tied when it comes to making conversation with relatives in a party atmosphere. "Unfortunately, during my half-hearted attempt to make small talk I apparently blurted out some insane nonsense about how much fun it must be to organize the reunion – you know, doing all of the planning and everything. Before I knew it I had been elected to organize next year's reunion. I was like, 'Okay, what just happened here?'"

Bradbury said that the person most responsible for forcing the reins of next year's reunion into her hands was Sandy O'Donnell, a distant cousin who had been in charge of organizing the reunion for the last four years.

"All I said was that I had once designed some [party] invitations and Sandy was all like, 'Really? Because that's basically all there is to it, and we need somebody to organize next year's reunion. Why don't you give it a try?'" said Bradbury, mimicking O'Donnell's high-pitched voice. "The next thing I know she's standing in front of all of these people asking me if she can e-mail me the list of family members' addresses and the phone numbers of some banquet halls and all sorts of other stuff. Everybody was looking at me. There was nowhere to run. I was completely cornered."

Bradbury claimed that although she doesn't recall ever officially agreeing to organize the 2013 Bradbury Reunion – adamantly insisting that she used the word "maybe" exclusively in her limited responses to O'Donnell's forceful suggestion – she now believes she is committed to spearheading the project.

"I think I'm pretty much screwed because word has gotten around among the family that I'm in charge for next year," said Bradbury. "I've already run into a few relatives that have said, 'So, I hear you're hosting next year's reunion,' or something to that effect. I have no idea how I could get out of doing it now. It's not like someone's going to offer to take the job off my hands."

Bradbury admitted that although she will most likely carry out the organizational duties for the 2013 reunion, she bears no intention of repeating the task for a second year.

"I've already been trying to think of a way of handing off the job to somebody else at next year's party, probably much like the way Sandy did it to me," said Bradbury. "If I can find somebody to volunteer, great, but one way or another, believe me, there's no way in hell I'm getting stuck with this baton for another lap around the track. It's getting shoved into *somebody's* hand, whether they like it or not." ■

SCIENCE

NASA investigation board bursts into flames

Washington, D.C. – NASA officials have confirmed that the Columbia Accident Investigation Board (CAIB) suddenly burst into flames at 2:04 p.m. EST Friday as the five-member crew attempted reentry to an important meeting.

"Members of the investigation board had reported experiencing intermittent communications failures earlier in the meeting," NASA spokesperson Guy Courtland told reporters following the tragedy. "At that point the decision was made to halt forward movement until communications were running adequately. After lunch, the crew attempted to reenter the meeting and moments later were seen breaking up outside their NASA Headquarters conference room. It was a horrific sight."

While many questions remain as to the cause of the explosion, NASA officials said that poor ventilation in the CAIB's meeting room combined with the unseasonably hot and humid weather conditions may have caused the board to burst into flames.

"We've recovered the room's thermostat control unit, which indicates that the temperature in the meeting room approached one hundred and four degrees right before the board broke up," said Courtland. "This would indicate a failure in the ventilation system, as that temperature far exceeds the room's normal operating parameters."

Officials noted that an unusually high level of stress being placed on the CAIB at the time of meeting reentry may have contributed to the board's eruption.

"After being delayed by communications problems this morning, the board knew that they would need to push their agenda or they would risk having to come in over the weekend to finish up our reports," said Courtland. "The amendments were going to be due Monday morning, and [CAIB Chairman] Admiral [Hal] Gehmen said there was no way in hell he was canceling his weekend [sailing trip], so he was really pushing hard for the team to complete the mission. With the board under so much stress, that there was an eruption almost isn't that much of a surprise."

NASA officials were quick to dispatch teams to search arm-to-arm across downtown Washington for remains of the CAIB, in hopes that recovered items may lead to more information about the events that led up to the explosion.

"The truth is that we won't know for sure what caused the accident until all of the recovered evidence is thoroughly analyzed," said Courtland. "But rest assured, just as the CAIB exhaustively investigated the Columbia disaster, NASA will quickly appoint an investigative board to find out what caused the CAIB disaster. NASA has already tentatively named the team the Columbia Accident Investigation Board Accident Investigation Board." ■

Above: The Columbia Accident Investigation Board Accident Investigation Board inspects the recovered remains of the board's meeting room conference table.

BAND from page 77

through God, all things are possible. And even though label reps haven't exactly been banging down the door of our rehearsal studio yet, we're expecting them any time now, as long as we keep spreading the message of God with our music."

According to Tallman, the band has consistently gone out of its way to title and theme its songs in a way that advocates the worship of God, in hopes that God will reward their ministry by bestowing them with international fame and fortune in the rock world.

"It really doesn't say anything in the Bible about *how long* it takes to get your rewards on Earth," added Tallman, whose voice has yet to show promise of developing into a force strong enough to front a major label band. "Still, we're very anxious for our day to come. Jetting around the world to perform sold-out concerts and sing Hallelujah sure sounds a lot more glorified than working weekends and holidays at the Amoco station."

Tallman said that because of each band members' strong faith, the band has the luxury of not needing to fret about the fundamental tasks on which most high-reaching bands must focus so intensely to achieve success in the music industry.

"Unlike non-Christian bands, we don't have to worry about rehearsing much, promoting our shows or building a local fan base because we know that the Lord will soon be plucking us from the pack and putting us on the cover of *Rolling Stone* as reward for our belief and devotion," said Tallman. "As to why that hasn't happened yet, all I can say is that it is not our place to question God's intentions or decisions. And no, I don't think it has anything to do with the fact least one song."

Other members of the band guitarists Mark Hood and Ken Ward, bassist Keith Tap and drummer "Wild" Stevie Barnes – share Tallman's belief that regardless of the band members' technical and artistic shortcomings, In His Name will soon achieve a recording contract because of their devotion to God.

"There's a reason why there are so many Christian rock bands out there: because they know that their secret weapon – their faith – will bring them stardom," said Barnes, who later struggled to identify a Christian act other than P.O.D. that's actually experienced success in the music industry. "It doesn't even matter that I can't play double-bass for more than thirty seconds at a time or if Ken has yet to memorize the notes of the fretboard or even if Manny gets stage fright so bad that he vomits on stage at nearly every show – the Bible assures us that God will reward His followers. It's all made very clear in Leviticus 25:18-19."

Although the band's lackluster songwriting, sub-par instrumentation and infantile stage show has garnered them only harsh press and booing audiences, Tallman and his bandmates have sworn to continue their form of musical praise for as long as it takes for God to reward them with a plush, front-loaded record contract.

"We'll keep playing benefit shows and church picnics for as long as it takes for God to make good on His word and provide us with our untold riches," said Tallman. "Unless, of course, we decide to change over to a devil-worship act in order to speed up the arrival of such worldly fortune. I believe we might actually be having a band vote on that at our next rehearsal." ■

KILLING from page 77

detained the suspect – who was found lying on a couch watching television and eating Doritos right from the bag – after police surveillance confirmed the suspect's suspicious lack of activity. The suspect's brother was cleared of any similar wrongdoing after the 34-year-old was able to present investigators with paycheck stubs, a health club membership card and pictures of his preteen daughters – evidence suggesting that he lacked the opportunity to kill time.

"Our units had to wait outside the residence for nearly four hours while investigators ascertained a warrant," said Harris. "We really weren't too worried about the suspect fleeing, however, because there was a *Big Bang Theory* marathon on TNT at the time."

According to Harris, investigators collected a plethora of valuable evidence from the home, including a hacky sack, an X-Box video game console, several completed crossword puzzles, a small set of bongo drums and a homemade smoking device fashioned from an empty two-liter bottle of Mountain Dew.

The smoking gun in the case, said special investigator Phillip Monroe, is the fact that the suspect's brother's house was outfitted with internet and cable TV.

"A person exposed to such an environment would likely find it very easy to start killing a lot of time," said Monroe. "After becoming comfortable with the thoughtless killing of time, the suspect may have actually started to believe that there wasn't even anything wrong with just killing time instead of finding gainful employment, silly hobbies and pointless busy work to fully occupy his days and turn him into a compliant, faceless citizen. It's enough to make a person sick."

City Prosecutor Jeffery VanZoeren expressed confidence that he could get a conviction should police officially charge the suspect, whom detectives have described as unrepentant and "constantly hungry."

"Let me just remind everyone that the time that has been killed is *gone*. It's gone, and there's nothing that anybody can say or do to bring that time back," VanZoeren told members of the media. "Rest assured that if the suspect is guilty, I'll see to it that he's provided with plenty of time to kill: behind bars."

Kyle Evans, a 42-year-old civil engineer and father of three who lives next door to the suspect's brother, was quick to cast judgment upon the suspect.

"I've seen [the suspect's] type before – they have no respect for time because time has no meaning or value to them," said Evans. "Trust me, this guy is as guilty as guilty gets. He has killed time before, and unless we stop him, he will kill time again." ■

> "He has killed time before, and unless we stop him, he will kill time again."

RECOILMAG.COM   NEWS SATIRE YOU CAN TRUST

recoil

Report: Binge drinking reaches dangerous lows during college breaks

Above: Popular college taverns such as University of Wisconsin hotspot McGruder's Pub (above) struggle to stay in business during college breaks, when binge drinking suffers a significant reduction.

Los Angeles, Calif. – According to a recent 20-college study conducted by researchers at UCLA, binge drinking, which is universally acknowledged as the most serious problem plaguing college campuses, can reach dangerous lows during college breaks.

"While class is in session, as much as forty-four percent of the college population engages regularly in binge drinking, which pretty much everyone agrees is a big number," said Thomas Walters, lead researcher on the two-year study. "But during Christmas or spring breaks, or during the summer, there are considerably less people on campus. So even if, say, seventy or eighty percent of the remaining youths are routinely consuming toxic amounts of alcohol in proportionately small timeframes, that's still a very, very small amount of binge drinking going on."

Results of the study show that a college such as UCLA, with an annual enrollment of approximately 36,000, may have as few as 50 to 60 students actively binge drinking during scheduled breaks in course schedules.

"There are always a few diehards who don't have jobs or anything better to do than remain on campus during breaks and continue to binge drink," said Walters. "The good news here is that often these stragglers will binge drink on an even more regular basis because of their general lack of other commitments such as attending class or studying."

> UCLA may have as few as 50 to 60 students actively binge drinking during scheduled breaks in course schedules.

see BINGE page 83

Accountant's pencil, personality dull

OCTOBER 2002

MARTHA STEWART Living

special prison decorating issue

INSIDE:
MAKE YOUR OWN SHANKS
REMOVING BLOOD STAINS FROM UNDERGARMENTS
HIDEAWAY DRUG STORAGE

PLUS:
SHOWER ETIQUETTE QUIZ
THE ANNUAL BIG HOUSE SURVIVAL GUIDE

Above: The October cover of *Living* magazine. This special prison decrating issue features Stewart demonstrating methods for beautifying your prison cell.

Martha Stewart unveils new line of prison cell housewares

New York, N.Y. – Inspired by the escalating severity of her insider trading allegations, celebrated lifestyle guru Martha Stewart unveiled Thursday a new line of prison cell furnishings designed to compliment the living arrangements of incarcerated yet discerning homemakers.

"The Martha Stewart Big House Living

> "In overseeing the design of these products, I kept in mind what kinds of furnishings I would want to use if I were incarcerated," said Stewart.

line will bring to the American penal system that warm touch of home and essence of finer living for which Living's products are renown," said Stewart during a speech that opened the media event. "In overseeing the design of these products, I kept in mind what kinds of furnishings I would want to

see PRISON page 83

Casey Anthony Fantasy Camp gives participants chance to legally murder someone

Orlando, Fla. – Hoping to capitalize on the overwhelming interest surrounding the trial and subsequent acquittal of Casey Anthony this summer, fantasy baseball camp mogul Randy Hundley announced Monday the opening of the Casey Anthony Fantasy Camp, a purchasable retreat package during which participants are allowed to simulate the experience of brutally murdering a defenseless person without legal repercussion.

"In the same manner that few ever

> Many participants especially enjoy providing police investigators with false information and playing out a series of carefully constructed lies until cornered.

realize their childhood aspirations such as playing Major League Baseball, the Casey Anthony Fantasy Camp affords anyone the opportunity to spend a week living their dream – the only difference being that instead of playing side-by-side with Hall of Fame ballplayers in legendary stadiums, one gets to sidestep the death penalty after experiencing the twisted thrill of snuffing out an innocent

see FANTASY page 84

Right: Anthony enjoying the real-life experience now replicated at the Casey Anthony Fantasy Camp.

page 81

HOROSCOPES

Scorpio (October 23 to November 21)
The romantic sparks should start spewing like a keg party in a fireworks store lacking a no-smoking policy. If you're not looking for a long-term romantic flare-up, shield yourself with a serious relationship's best extinguisher: jealousy. Take on an opposing-sexed roommate – his or her mere presence will stomp out any caller's attempts to build a fiery romance.

Sagittarius (November 22 to December 21)
The rainbow of Life hardly ever leads to a pot of gold – it usually leads to a cesspool of disappointment. Adopting a "money isn't everything, love is the answer" attitude looks good on paper and sounds even better read aloud, but in today's materialistic world, money solves problems – whereas love usually just creates them.

Capricorn (December 22 to January 19)
You don't need to bring gifts to every event to which you're invited. The human resource is in short supply these days, especially on the friendship front – that you take time out of your life to show up at the event is gift enough. If you're planning a party, make your guests aware that while their presents mean nothing, their presence means everything.

Aquarius (January 20 to February 19)
You'd be better off buying a new car than taking your current one to a mechanic, even for something as simple as an oil change; it's hard enough to get mechanics to do a job, let alone do it right. That's because professional gearheads draw the same hourly wage whether they're tearing their hands apart on your bearing assembly or scratching their ass with an oil dipstick, and unfortunately, most of them are even money to botch both jobs.

Pisces (February 18 to March 20)
The interest that others show in Pisces is genuine; they want to know why nothing bothers you. Funny, the only thing that really does bother you is all these people asking you why nothing bothers you. Let them know that just because you can hold your own doesn't make you responsible for holding everyone else's own. They lock people up for that.

Aries (March 21 to April 19)
Aries has all the spontaneity of an atomic clock – shadowing you for an afternoon would bore even Helen Keller into ditching you for something more stimulating. If you're smart, you'll begin combining your lack of spontaneity with your anal tendencies to develop full-blown Obsessive Compulsive Disorder, which will at least be a clinical excuse for being such a freak.

Taurus (April 20 to May 20)
If you think you have a superior mind just because you understand what makes things tick, remember, so did The Unibomber. Over-thinking everything is about as mentally healthy as working full time at a Renaissance Festival; you could easily lose track of what is real and what is fantasy. Thinking is not the same as living; people who think they are capable of working everything out in their head are invariably the same people who believe David Copperfield actually made the Statue of Liberty disappear.

Gemini (May 21 to June 20)
Gemini realizes that mankind was not meant to wake up before noon. There's an old saying that goes, "Morning would be a whole lot better if it came later in the day," which is true, but try explaining that to your boss. Well, as long as you have to get up with the chickens, feel free to curse those foul creatures and taunt them with a sunny-side up reminder of their place on the food chain.

Cancer (June 21 to July 22)
The fire hose of good advice will be blasting you right in the face this week – it'll be hard to ignore, but as always, Cancer will find a way. Sure, you act interested in self-improvement, but the mere act of buying a self-help book doesn't correct anything (except kleptomania). Try to at least thumb the damn book before filing it atop the "ignore" pile, if it will fit – all that unused exercise equipment is chewing up a lot of space.

Leo (July 23 to August 22)
Leo is about to have an encounter with an old flame. Beware; that old flame intends to douse your heart with gasoline and throw a flaming matchbook cover at it. Remember, the term "old flame" is not a misnomer – old flames will burn you just as badly as they did the first time. There's only one way to get rid of a flame: cut off its oxygen supply.

Virgo (August 23 to September 22)
If you're still searching for evidence of a higher power, just mull over this theorem for a few ticks: God is love; love is blind; Ray Charles is blind; therefore, Ray Charles is God. Study the logic. There really isn't much room for argument.

Libra (September 23 to October 22)
Don't trust anyone who speaks more from a spreadsheet than from the heart; would you listen to a preacher who simply read his sermon from a legal pad? Of course not, and you shouldn't listen to me either. Astrologers are the bottom-feeders of the already-corrupt publishing business, and you'd be a fool to take advice from a person like me, who spends his leisure time writing death threats to *Survivor* contestants.

EMPLOYMENT

Applicant more worried about potential employers running credit report than background check

Above: Nervous job applicant Becky Thompson attempts to explain her credit situation to a potential employer's human resources manager.

Buffalo, N.Y. – Becky Thompson, a 38-year-old job applicant at Murphy's Furniture Outlet in downtown Buffalo, is not nearly as worried about the company's human resource department running her social security number through a thorough occupational background check looking for indications of bad references from past employees or signs of a criminal record nearly as much as she fears their acquiring a copy of her personal credit history, Thompson admitted Tuesday.

"My employment record is *fairly* solid, and I don't have any arrests or anything like that, so that sort of investigation doesn't scare me at all. It's just that my credit report probably makes me look like some sort of human Enron, the way my unpaid debts are stacked up," said Thompson. "I don't know how far they go with these checks these days, but if they do look at my credit record I'm sure they'll be sufficiently unimpressed. My credit score can't be more than about four hundred these days, and I'll bet you anything that if those two car repossessions are still on my report, that's going to leave them with a really sour taste in their mouths."

Thompson explained that although her employment records show no considerable gaps or include any fictional information or questionable references, one look at her current credit report would likely cause potential employees to question Thompson's credibility.

"I'm not sure how you get this across to employers on a job application, but a person just doesn't bounce back that quickly from a bankruptcy," said Thompson, who claimed to have recently explained to a number of human resource representatives about the unique circumstances surrounding her 2002 divorce from ex-husband James Reece, which she credited as having directly caused her credit problems. "It'll probably be decades before I can rebuild my credit up to a point where banks and loan officers will even agree to talk to me again, let alone seriously consider my job applications."

Added Thompson: "I just realized that one of my outstanding creditors is also one of my old employers. That can't look good at all."

Thompson noted that she would be more than happy to comply in taking a pre-employment drug test so long as she doesn't have to pay for it. ∎

> "My employment record is *fairly* solid, and I don't have any arrests or anything like that, so that sort of investigation doesn't scare me at all. It's just that my credit report probably makes me look like some sort of human Enron," said Thompson.

A page from the Recoil handbook...
Boating Tips

Setting out upon the open water can be both an exciting and relaxing summer activity. Here are some tips for getting the most from your aquatic experience:

- Men should don a captain's hat, so readers will know right away that this particular MMFF hardcore series has a nautical theme.

- When learning the ropes from an experienced seaman, be sure to ask, "How do you know if it's male or female?" when he point out a buoy. They love that one.

- It is unwritten boater's code that jet skiers are to be treated like the mosquitoes of the aquatic world.

- Yes, believe it or not, some idiot – obviously unschooled in simple physics and spatial-relations concepts – officially decreed that the smaller boat always has the right of way. He or she obviously had no real world experience.

- Use the harbor's buoys to pinpoint exactly where federal law becomes some half-forgotten set of schoolboy guidelines.

- Most gangsters agree that it's bad luck to throw a body over the port side of the boat.

- If you're sailing solo for the first time and somehow find youself seated at Captain Stubing's dinner table, you can expect to fall helplessly in love with an unknown soulmate before reaching Porta Vallarta.

- Trick your brain into confusing lighthouses with whorehouses – that way you'll have a legitimate reason to keep an eye out for them.

- Remember, taking hot chicks out on a rented 100-foot boat outfitted with a live reggae band, two kegs of beer and a punch bowl filled with cocaine will not necessarily guarantee you'll get laid, you ugly son of a bitch.

- Due to recent changes in state and federal laws, houseboats are now only available to middle-aged divorcees and detectives.

- Try to work in a witty joke when encouraging Q to outfit your vessel with extra missiles.

- Though it's considered juvenile to say, "Fine, then I'm not going to work either!" while crossing your arms and turning your back on the outboard motor, sometimes it's the only way to settle things. Besides, the motor's the one that started it.

recoilmag.com
facebook.com/recoilmagazine
@RecoilMagazine

PRISON from page 81

use if I were incarcerated. The results are simply splendid."

Premiering the line at New York's Lincoln Correctional Facility – a chic minimum-security prison in which Stewart has expressed considerable interest as of late – the opening featured an entire block of cells outfitted entirely using Big House Living décor and furnishings.

"This lavish prison shank holder, for instance, is available in an array of colors, each specially chosen to compliment even the dreariest of gray concrete cell walls," said Stweart, modeling the products from inside one of the prison wing's eight-by-eight-foot confinements. Carefully placing four immaculately hand-painted shanks in the holder, Stewart, brandishing her trademark smile, added: "Look at that. It's like a little ray of sunshine, isn't it?"

Stewart maintained a jovial spirit throughout the event despite looming indictments for her timely Dec. 27 sale of 4,000 shares of ImClone stock a day before the FDA denied approval of that company's Ebritux cancer drug.

"I can see how these would come in handy," joked an upbeat Stewart, snatching a crudely sharpened toothbrush from the holder and making several playful stabbing motions, much to media photographers' delight. "With these products, you'll be able to hold your own out in the yard or shower area, and still maintain the Living style."

Also included in Stewart's signature line of housewares are such items as handmade bloodstain-resistant floor coverings and designer drapery and bunk sets equipped with hidden contraband pockets.

"And, of course, those serving considerable amounts of time will also want to pick up a copy of my new prison-oriented arts and crafts book, *Turning The Big House Into A Big Home*," said Stewart. "Also, the October issue of *Living* magazine features a four-page spread outlining many of my secrets to prison cell decorating."

Near the close of the event, media representatives screened several television commercials introducing the new line – part of a $10 million national multimedia advertising campaign – which feature Stewart personally decorating her own minimum-security prison cell with Big House Living furnishings.

"My fans appreciate that, with the Living lines, they can purchase and use the very same lifestyle accessories that I myself use," said Stewart. "And The Big House Living line is no exception. The way things are looking right now, I'll be furnishing my [new] home exclusively with these new products."

Although the new line currently features only housewares, Stewart said the line could easily expand to include other products as she further examines the lifestyle needs of modern incarcerated women.

"I already envision a line of bright orange casual wear, and maybe bed and bath products like medicated tissue and scented sodomy lubricants," said Stewart. "If things work out the way I expect, I'll be getting to know even more about the prison lifestyle and how I can bring to it the Living touch." ∎

BINGE from page 81

Walters said that the dangerously low level of binge drinking during college breaks can have a significantly negative effect on the local economy.

"Taverns, liquor stores and hospital emergency rooms located near campuses suffer significantly decreased business during college breaks," Walters explained. "Obviously, less binge drinking means less beer and liquor sales, and less cases of alcohol poisoning. In many college towns, large numbers of paramedics and ambulance drivers find themselves laid off during summer recess because so few students are recreationally drinking until they pass out and choke to death on their own vomit."

Pete Wagner, owner of McGruder's Pub near the University of Wisconsin in Madison, agreed with the study's findings, saying that summer breaks routinely cause such drastic shortages in binge drinking as to threaten his establishment's ability to stay afloat.

"No doubt about it: without the college kids in here drinking themselves stupid it's hard to make ends meet," said Wagner, who said he prides himself on having served many a U of W student their first drink too many during the last 15 years. "Sure, while college is out of session, there's a lot less scrubbing puke off the floor, and there aren't nearly as many in-booth rape incidents to speak of, but at what price, you know?" ∎

page 83

SPORTS

Ultimate fighters' egos too big to fit in octagon

Los Angeles, Calif. – Ultimate Fighting Championship (UFC) organizers confirmed Tuesday plans to redesign the UFC's trademark octagon, enlarging the fighting cage to nearly twice its original size in an effort to adequately accommodate the enormously inflated egos sidling a vast majority of the league's fighters.

"I don't care if they make the octagon bigger, smaller, wider, upside down or move it to the moon, the fact is that I'm the best fighter alive, and my opponent, I don't care who it is, whatever poor sucker they put on the canvas with me hasn't got a prayer in this world [at winning]," said Tito Ortiz, a 33-year-old American light heavyweight fighter who specializes in submission wrestling. Proudly brandishing the "If you fight Tito Ortiz you lose" t-shirt he first wore after defeating Ken Shamrock in 2006, Ortiz continued: "It's just a plain and simple fact that I'm the most dangerous fighter alive, and I'm going to make sure everybody in the world knows that I am *the best*."

The UFC's decision to increase the size of the octagon follows a recent string of high-profile fights that had to be cancelled or forfeited because of the lack of space in the octagon for both fighters' massive egos.

"The octagon currently in use for UFC bouts, an eight-sided caged enclosure with walls of chain-link fence, provides only 30 feet of space from point to point – hardly enough room for the ungodly mammoth egos these fighters carry around with them," said retired UFC referee Big John McCarthy, who officiated over matches from 1994 until his retirement. "Add in the room taken up by the huge chip each [fighter] has on his shoulder and suddenly there's hardly enough room for these guys to throw a punch let alone wage an epic battle."

UFC officials have admitted that when the octagon was originally conceived and assembled in 1993, designers failed to properly estimate the size of the egos most of their fighters would soon develop.

"We didn't anticipate how much of an effect the act of beating another human half to death can have on a man's ego," said Joe Silva, the UFC's vice-president of talent. "Just look at footage of some of the more successful UFC fighters, like Ortiz, for example. It's a wonder that guy alone can even fit in the octagon, because on top of his Zeus-like ego, the guy walks around like he's got a twelve-foot cock."

"Although *that* might just be because he's dating Jenna Jameson," added Silva. ■

> "Add in the room taken up by the huge chip each [fighter] has on his shoulder and suddenly there's hardly enough room for these guys to throw a punch let alone wage an epic battle," said McCarthy.

Right: Ultimate Fighting Champion Tito Ortiz angrily explains to a referee that the octagon is not large enough to accommodate his wildly inflated ego before a 2006 title fight.

Recoil's Shallow Thoughts

- One shouldn't be too quick to judge a person. For instance, it's wrong to just assume someone is a bad person just because the warden is having him strapped into an electric chair.

- When stepping out for a black-tie event, would Nigel Tufnel of Spinal Tap dress to the nines, tens or elevens?

- I don't think I like the idea of Nihilism. In fact, I don't think I'd like the idea of any religion based on the worship of the Nile River. Basing a religion on the Rhone, of course, would be another story altogether.

- Instead of telling your child to "sit tight," try telling them to "sit taut," because then the child will have been taught to sit tight.

- Why are so many bands on hiatus? It must be good – I'll have to ask my drug dealer about getting some of that.

- I've often attempted to call bullshit on something but, according to my phone book, at least, bullshit's number is unlisted. It's very frustrating, because something like that makes you want to call bullshit even more. It's no wonder I can't sleep.

- The more and more I think about it, I'm starting to feel that I in fact *do* want to be a burden.

- It's common knowledge that 13 is often referred to as a baker's dozen. But how many is in a baker's hundred? How many in a baker's thousand? How many in a baker's million, or billion? MIT probably teaches a class on this calculation alone.

- I've often wondered why cats stretch so much. Are they really that afraid of pulling a muscle during their five-foot mosey to the food bowl?

- Sorry to say, but that often misheard age-old adage is true: in this world, there's no faxed lunch.

FANTASY from page 81

human life," said Hundley, who founded the camp shortly following Anthony's July exoneration of having killed the 25-year-old's infant daughter Caylee Marie Anthony in 2008.

Hundley said that selling reservations for the new camp – an experience which actually takes place in west central Florida, in an area proximate to the actual events surrounding the Anthony ordeal – has been relatively easy despite the hefty price tag of $15,000 and the initial hesitance that sometimes discourages otherwise interested clientele.

"Just like with baseball fantasy camps, where some participants get worried, 'I'm not in shape' or 'I'm not good enough' – fears which melt away as soon as they reach camp – many Casey Anthony campers might worry, 'I don't have what it takes to strangle somebody or hit them in the face with a fire axe or whatnot, let alone bury them in the woods,'" admitted Hundley, who claimed to have already sold-out reservations for the week-long camp through 2014. "But once the participants arrive at camp and start Googling about how to make their own chloroform and such, one's inherent bloodlust or suppressed resentment toward their parents instinctively takes root, and they end of having the time of their lives getting away with murder."

According to Hundley, many participants in the Casey Anthony Fantasy Camp especially enjoy the process of providing police investigators with false information and playing out a series of carefully constructed lies until being cornered and forced to invent new lies – a situation which intuitively brings out a level of spontaneous self-preservation some participants never thought they had in them.

"Included in the cost of the package is the opportunity to lead investigators on a trip through the offices of Universal Studios before finally admitting to not really working there – just like Casey Anthony did," boasted Hundley. "Some participants have remarked that this 'coming clean' moment is every bit as emotionally stimulating as admitting to a spouse about having an affair or coming out of the closet after decades of living a lie in order to keep up appearances."

Recent camp participant Jeff Owosso, 44, said that his favorite part of the seven-day routine – beyond living his dream of killing someone – was mimicking Anthony's nearly imperceptible display of moral fiber throughout the experience.

"Being seen out partying almost immediately after the tragic disappearance of a loved one, being the focus of massive media attention during your trial, and getting a tattoo that says 'Beautiful Life' right after your acquittal – it's everything I've ever dreamed of doing," said Owosso, an insurance adjuster from Kansas City. "And then being provided with a panel of imbecilic jurors who confuse 'reasonable doubt' with 'reason for doubt,' and nonchalantly employing loopholes to stymie our [nation's] substantially flawed legal system when even casual onlookers can immediately see you are guilty – talk about living the dream!" ■

RECOILMAG.COM   NEWS SATIRE YOU CAN TRUST

recoil

Above: Remaining members of the 80s rock band Skid Row have reunited with singer Sebastian Back (middle.)

Original members of Skid Row reunite to record "Middle-Agers Gone Wild"

Toms River, N.J – Twenty-two years following the release of Skid Row's breakthrough debut single "Youth Gone Wild," the rock band's cofounder and bassist Rachel Bolan, 45, confirmed Monday that all five original band members will reunite to record "Middle-Agers Gone Wild," an updated version of the popular anthem from the band's

> "I can barely hold a pen in my hand long enough to write down a single verse of lyrics before my arthritis starts kicking in," said Sabo.

see SKID ROW page 88

Inept cashier cast as host of *The Price Is Wrong*

Liver worst

quikSTAT

Fastest growing jobs in the breakfast cereal industry
- Toast cinnamoner
- Cocoa puffer
- Cookie crisper
- Wheat shredder
- Corn flaker
- Sugar smacker
- Loop fruiter
- Apple jacker

Above: A police mug shot of Derek Piles.

Small-town stalker sets off to try to stalk the big-time in Hollywood

Colfax, Ind. – Twenty-three-year-old pizza delivery driver and reputed stalker Derek Piles will come one step closer to realizing his dream of becoming a high-profile stalker when the small-town youth sets off to try to stalk the big-time celebrities in Hollywood later this month.

"Colfax was a great place to grow up and all, and I've managed to do some decent small-time stalking here and in nearby Indianapolis, but it's time for me to take the next step – hopefully into a celebrity's home," Piles stated flatly. "Moving out to la-la land is absolutely essential if I want to have any hope of making the big-time Hollywood stars have to hire extra security guards to keep me out of their yards."

Piles said that although he has been stalking local men and women seriously for more than eight years, it was not until December of last year – after his most

see STALKER page 87

Marooned U.S. legislator sends clear message to voters: HELP

North Atlantic Ocean – In an attempt to send a clear and focused message to the American voters Thursday, impassioned 68-year-old Congressman Alan Taylor [R-VA] called for nationwide support in his efforts to be rescued from the small, uncharted island on which the Republican lawmaker was marooned five days ago.

"PLEASE HELP – STRANDED ON DESERTED ISLAND SOMEWHERE OFF EAST COAST OF U.S.," wrote an exhausted but determined Taylor, carefully penning the unusually brief proposal on a piece of tree bark pulled from an adult Birch. "IMMEDIATE AID NEEDED. PLEASE SEND HELP!"

Exhibiting some of the early signs of dementia, Taylor read the document aloud to imagined members of an

see HELP page 88

Above: The half-delusional Congressman reads his proposal to an imagined press corps before setting the message adrift on the West side of the deserted island.Hudson's head.

EDITORIAL
Road trip with female friend less sexual than envisioned

Above: Hoffman and a visibly frustrated Kinsler take a short break from their 828-mile journey to not get even remotely intimate at a roadside rest area.

Seikston, Mo. – After stopping for a bathroom break, college sophomore Danny Kinsler announced Monday that his road trip with a female acquaintance is continuing to progress entirely without sexual activity, much to his disbelief and dismay.

Kinsler, who selflessly offered to drive fellow student Natalie Hoffman back to her home for their school's summer break on his way to Florida, is struggling to comprehend how Hoffman has not even suggested the smallest amount of fooling around in the back seat of his Ford Mustang.

"It's like she's never seen a dude before," said Kinsler, who is completely fine with Hoffman 828 miles to not get some. "All I know is that I've taken girls as far as the grocery store in my Mustang and couldn't keep them off of me."

Aside from the obvious sensual environment created by his vehicle, Kinsler had arranged overnight accommodations at a motel to breakup the trip, telling Hoffman he could not drive straight through. He then ensured they shared a room with only one bed, feeling that rampant intercourse would be certain to ensue. Yet, despite setting up the ideal opportunity for Hoffman to discover his penis, the 20-year-old just put her head on his chest and fell asleep watching *The Late Show with David Letterman*.

Based on Hoffman's reputation at school fraternity functions, Kinsler has so far been dumbfounded by the utter lack of promiscuity shown by the sophomore environmental studies major. Also working in Kinsler's favor are his months of built-up trust stemming from his friendship with Hoffman, who did not even have the courtesy to exit the motel bathroom in just a towel after showering, instead appearing fully clothed in sweatpants and a Colorado University hooded sweatshirt.

"That's not right," said Kinsler of the prudish Hoffman, who, upon accepting Johnson's benevolent offer, apparently had no intention of performing even a simple act of oral sex on Kinsler's behalf. "She said some crap about valuing me as a friend."

Kinsler has been attempting to understand the events of the trip, hoping to gain an understanding of why Hoffman has failed to touch his leg knowingly or expose her breasts in a playful manner. He wonders if an opportunity was squandered when he failed to look longingly into Hoffman's eyes after she had playfully punched him in the arm exiting a Wendy's restaurant.

"Man, can you imagine if I had made my move then?" queried Kinsler, who likely now is imagining a graphic fantasy involving the misuse of a chocolate Frosty. "That could have been it, but maybe if I fake car trouble later we can recreate that passion."

Currently 21 hours and 540 miles into their journey to Atlanta, Ga., Hoffman has decided to fall asleep in the passenger seat rather than playfully flirt with and ultimately sexually pleasure the deserving Kinsler. ∎

> Kinsler is struggling to comprehend how Hoffman has not even suggested the smallest amount of fooling around in the back seat of his Ford Mustang.

recoilmag.com

A page from the Recoil handbook...
Becoming Environmentally Conscious

More and more global citizens are becoming personally committed to caring for our fragile environment. Below are some tips for doing your part to protect Mother Earth:

- Recyclables need to be clean to be reused, so seal each item in disposable, polyethylene containers to ensure they make it to the recycling plant unsoiled.

- During the summer months, use a bicycle for transportation until you are no longer able – most likely because you and your 10-speed got run over by a Hummer and you'll never again be able to bend your left knee.

- Be responsible with your used motor oil – plant it nice and deep in the ground so it has the best chance of growing a healthy new oil reserve.

- Think long-term: hold off on outfitting your home with solar panels unless you have it on good authority that the sun will still be able to occasionally poke through the smog in your area five years from now.

- You may be surprised to learn that setting your toaster to "light" instead of "medium" can save .00007 watts of energy per year.

- Use real peanuts instead of Styrofoam peanuts as packaging material. *Note: If, in addition to being environmentally conscious, you're also concerned about world hunger, face it – you're just going to have to pick a side on this one.*

- Find out all you can about the release of Greenhouse Gases. The much anticipated debut CD from this NYC-based garage rock four-piece should be coming out on Lookout! Records within a couple of months.

- Get rid of all of those aerosol cans! In fact, take them out back and spray their contents out right now.

- Reject even those products that have labels bragging "Does not harm the environment" – they aren't specifically doing anything to *help* the environment, now are they?

- Do you know that actress Daryl Hannah has a car that runs on French fry grease? Is that weird or what?

- By purchasing organic fruits and vegetables, you'll be supporting farmers who don't use dangerous pesticides, as well as experiencing the pleasure of biting into a $21 watermelon.

- Find room to plant a tree, even if that means you have to plant it partially on your neighbor's property. Hey, we're trying to be environmentally conscious here, not courteous.

STALKER from page 85

recent work garnered the attention of local news media – that he was struck by the urge to move out west and pursue his stalking full-time.

"When the *Colfax Weekly Review* printed my picture in the paper after my last arrest, it gave me the boost of confidence I needed to try to take my act to the next level," Piles said Monday from Clinton County Jail, where he is currently serving the last week of a 60-day jail sentence for misdemeanor trespassing.

> "I've managed to do some decent small-time stalking here and in nearby Indianapolis, but it's time for me to take the next step," said Piles.

"The way I look at it, if I don't take my shot now while I'm young I could spend the rest of my life watching the news and wondering if it could have been me getting picked up by police for breaking into Renee Zellweger's private yacht."

Piles, a 2000 graduate of Colfax High School, admitted that his parents are less than thrilled with his decision, having for years pressed their son to abandon his stalking ambitions and settle into a more conventional lifestyle.

"Mom and Dad have always wanted me to go to community college and get a square job and stuff, but ever since I was ten years old all I've ever wanted to do is follow people around, invade their privacy and just generally creep them out," said Piles. "I've tried to explain to them that different people want different things out of life. For guys like my dad, that means working a solid job and raising a family; for me it means renting a one-room shithouse in North Hollywood, getting Jennifer Garner's home address and going through her garbage every night. Different strokes, right?"

Despite having amassed a good amount of stalking experience in his rural hometown, Piles has no illusions about the difficult road he will have to travel if he hopes to one day see his name on restraining orders filed by Hollywood's biggest stars.

"I'll bet there are stalkers that have been out in Hollywood for ten years and still haven't even been able to find out where George Clooney gets his hair cut," said Piles, acknowledging the increased focus celebrities put on maintaining their privacy. "All I know is that I've got a lot of ambition and I'm ready to work hard. If it turns out that I end up having to stalk some B-list celebrities for my first few years in order to pay my dues, then by God that's what I'll do. Oddly enough, I've always had this weird obsession with [comedian] Kathy Griffin anyway. Hell, she's probably begging for a tail or two."

Friend Ed May said he is uncertain if Piles has what it takes to make it as a successful stalker in a city rife with competition.

"Derek's got more restraining orders on him than anyone else in Colfax," said May, questioning whether or not Piles will be able to not get noticed as a stalker in Hollywood. "I remember he used to spend a lot of time shadowing our mail carrier Gina a couple of months ago until her boyfriend threatened to kick his ass if he didn't stop. He also used to drive up to Indianapolis to follow that [television news anchor] Mia Robbins around last summer but he quit because he couldn't afford all of the gas money it was costing him. So no, I don't know if Derek has the skills it'll take to outfox Tara Reid's security system or whatnot. I wish him the best, though."

Planning to pack his belongings into his 1990 Chevy pickup and set out for California upon his release from jail, Piles remains cautiously optimistic about his future in stalking.

"I'm excited and nervous, but feeling very alive," said Piles. "I think I'll do alright once I get out there. I actually think the hardest part will be the drive out there. It's almost three thousand miles and I'll be all by myself. It sure would be nice if I could follow somebody." ■

Above: Piles stalks a Shell station cashier in his rural hometown of Colfax, Ind.

HOROSCOPES

Leo (July 23 to August 22)
When signing a contract, realize that time is money – you'll soon find reading an entire legal document, especially the fine print, an irrelevant waste. Logistically, if whatever's in fine print was of any importance at all, they certainly would have printed it a whole lot bigger. Get in the habit of making no two of your signatures look anywhere near alike, and your legal problems will be negligible.

Virgo (August 23 to September 22)
Female Virgo will never be able to communicate with her man until viewing his entire movie collection at least twice. Realize that about 90 percent of male conversation involves quoting lines from *Caddyshack, Fletch* and *Apocalypse Now.* Spend the week wearing out your DVD player – it'll be worth it to see the look of astonishment/arousal on his face when you shout, "Charlie don't surf!" whenever you hear the word "napalm."

Libra (September 23 to October 22)
Redneck Libra's oil-burning truck needs to be traded in before the government fines you as the sole cause of the Ozone problem. Sure, you're attached to that smell of Winstons and Olde Crow that's permanently lining the cabin of your Neapolitan-colored Bondo-bucket, but consider your new truck a fresh tree on which to leave your filthy, stinking, hillbilly scent.

Scorpio (October 23 to November 21)
You'd be better off buying a new car than taking your current one to a mechanic, even for something as simple as an oil change; it's hard enough to get mechanics to actually do a job, let alone do it right. That's because professional gearheads draw the same hourly wage whether they're tearing their hands apart on your bearing assembly or scratching their ass with an oil dipstick, and unfortunately, most of them are even money to botch either job.

Sagittarius (November 22 to December 21)
Lazy Sagittarius, bear in mind that plastic utensils have absolutely no place at catered affairs; don't even think about using them for that feast you're planning. Forcing adults to use plasticware is insulting; even the cavemen had plastic spork technology, but instead opted to manipulate their food using rocks, rather than suffer the embarrassment of using those ridiculous plastic utensils.

Capricorn (December 22 to January 19)
Capricorn should steer clear of drinking and driving – not for legal purposes, but because, quite frankly, you're not very good at either; your typical driving manner rivals a teenager playing NASCAR 2004 while jacked up on Mini Thins. Add that to the little known fact that alcohol impairs judgment (I know, can you believe it?), and drinking and driving sounds like way too fun of an activity to not be sober enough to enjoy.

Aquarius (January 20 to February 18)
Sure it's discomforting that scientists have discovered a black hole in the center of our galaxy that's spiraling the Earth toward doom like a flushed goldfish, but you've got to admit, we had been warned. Yep, those weirdos toting "The End is Near" signs were right all along; I suggest Aquarius strap on a sign, buddy up to those jabbering whackos and to find out what other information to which they alone are privy.

Pisces (February 19 to March 20)
People who still regard shaking hands as the ultimate binding contract between one another have an inordinate amount of blind faith in humanity's common decency. Remember, more often than not the person you're clutching hands with is doing little more than positioning your hand for a closer look at the rings they intend to pry from your cold, dead fingers once they've finally finished you.

Aries (March 21 to April 19)
It is truly a unique blend of poor luck and humorous Karma plaguing you recently; only Aries could be a radio station's "lucky" caller 10, yet receive a "free kick in the groin with purchase of same" as a prize. Don't worry; for once, the law is actually on your side – The Law of Averages, that is, which promises your bad luck will turn around, or at least peter out to a reasonable frequency, by 2020.

Taurus (April 20 to May 20)
In the game of Life, it isn't exactly necessary to win, but you do want to protect from losing completely. Vince Lombardi's football strategy is very applicable in attacking Life: hang tough, avoid mistakes and take no chances. Sure, playing it safe may make for a life that's as boring as the Lions' running game, but at least you'll have a safe seat from which to watch it pass by.

Gemini (May 21 to June 20)
The absorption capability of your brain isn't really comparable to a sponge so much as to a paper towel – it's good for soaking up small puddles of information, but you quickly become saturated when absorbing large quantities. And unlike a sponge, which can be rung out, your brain is basically useless after soaking up its initial info – which somewhat explains your senseless mantra, "I'm not close minded, I'm just right."

Cancer (June 21 to July 22)
People's jealousy often overpowers their moral and ethical values, prompting a desire to destroy that of which they are jealous. And with your snooty social standing being such an easy target, it won't be long before you wake up in a $17-a-night motel room, drugged, moist and obviously tricked, staring balefully as the nightly news shows unflattering pictures of you with your weekly "escort," who apparently moonlights as a photographer.

SKID ROW from page 85

multi-platinum debut album.

"[Guitarist] Dave ["The Snake" Sabo] and I were practically kids when we wrote 'Youth Gone Wild' – hence the song's title," said a weathered-looking Bolan. "Now that we're all in our mid- to late-forties, we thought that rewriting the lyrics for 'Youth Gone Wild' from a more experienced perspective would be a fun and perhaps enlightening experience. And, so far, it has – except for the fact that I can barely hold a pen in my hand long enough to write down a single verse of lyrics before my arthritis starts kicking in."

Bolan said that although the '80s band's current members held no reservations about inviting original drummer Rob Affuso to join the project, agreeing to reunite and collaborate with original vocalist Sebastian Bach prompted a long and somewhat heated debate among the aging group, who are now often grouchy for no reason and taking medication for their high blood-pressure.

"Sebastian was pretty much already in an advanced state of dementia when he was in the band twenty years ago," admitted Bolan. "His behavior on the MTV reality show *Supergroup* a few years ago clearly indicated to us that his mental condition has deteriorated even further, which is a scary thought. Normally, most of [Skid Row's members] wouldn't sit down with that lunatic for a cup of coffee, let alone go into the studio to record with him. Who knows what kind of shit that nutbag is going to pull?"

Sabo, who cofounded the band with Bolan in 1986, echoed Bolan's concern regarding the band's annoyingly grandstanding frontman.

"Did you see that first episode [of *Supergroup*] where that moron was rolling around on the ground like a gorilla after getting to meet Ted Nugent?" asked Sabo, eminently shrugging in sincere bewilderment of the recollection. "[That] dude's wiring is all messed up, man. That's why we booted him in the first place, you know. This is a guy in need of serious psychiatric help."

"Fucking Ken doll-looking douchebag sure can sing, though," Sabo quietly voiced to himself in afterthought.

Sources close to Bach reported that, upon receiving a call from Skid Row's management inquiring as to his interest in the project, the 44-year-old celebrity shouted: "What? Are you shitting me? Abso-fucking-lutely! *I am in!*" Bach then excitedly promised the caller that he would board the first flight to New Jersey – as soon as he attends an upcoming court date regarding his second drug possession charge in the last six months.

Bolan said that despite the stockpile of negatives sidling Bach's short return to the band, he and his bandmates concluded that the recording of "Middle-Agers Gone Wild" unfortunately required Bach's unmistakable voice, high vocal range and dynamic delivery in order to achieve Bolan's vision for the song.

"We decided that even if we forcibly sedate and restrain him in the [studio's] control room until we're ready for his [vocal recording sessions], there's still probably only a ten-to-twenty percent chance that he won't find a way to wreck the entire project," said Bolan. "But the song just won't sound right without [Bach] singing on it, so we eventually decided to go ahead and roll the dice."

"Middle-Agers Gone Wild" will reportedly follow the exact instrumental arrangements and vocal melody line of "Youth Gone Wild" while replacing the outdated lyrics with phrases more indicative of the members' current ages, health conditions and adult-inspired emotions.

"For example, the line 'We walk an endless mile' will be replaced with 'Wearily limp through an endless mile,'" said Bolan. "And instead of 'My nasty reputation takes me everywhere,' we'll say 'My cane and grumpy bitching takes me everywhere.' You know, stuff like that."

Sabo said that should the revamped song become popular enough, he, Bolan, and guitarist Scotti Hill will strongly consider recording and releasing updated versions of other tracks found on their breakthrough self-titled 1989 album – including songs titled "48 And Life," "Can't Stand The Heart Attacks," "Old Pregnant Sister" and "Big Gums," as well as the ballad "I Think I Remember You."

HELP from page 85

international press corps Thursday morning before officially launching his proposal – corking the petition into a haggard wine bottle and heaving it into the tiding waters on the west side of the island.

The thrice-elected Congressman became stranded on the tiny landmass Sunday following the mysterious crash of a chartered overseas airplane en route to Europe in which none of the 12 passengers or crew members were thought to have survived.

> "PLEASE HELP – STRANDED ON DESERTED ISLAND SOMEWHERE OFF EAST COAST OF U.S.," wrote an exhausted but determined Taylor.

Political analyst Peter Randolph said that although Taylor may succeed in sending a pointed message to the American people regarding the need for immediate aid in this remote area of the world, the proposal in its current form stands little chance of facilitating the types of changes Taylor is seeking.

"Even in the unlikely event that this package does manage to land in the hands of a person capable of pushing forward such an initiative, the vague language comprising Taylor's proposal make it practically impossible for anyone to take immediate action with the expectation of success," Randolph argued. "This unfortunate wording not only leaves Taylor's position woefully unclear, it also fails to map out a course of action for getting aid to those who have been displaced. Granted, no one expected Taylor to have listed his exact coordinates, but something a little more precise than 'somewhere off East coast of U.S.' would probably come in handy when the Navy Admiral starts asking where to deploy the search fleet."

Randolph noted that analysts have long criticized Congressman Taylor's unconventional and overdramatic proposals as being nothing more than a means through which to reiterate his longstanding message to the public: that he is in a life-threatening position and will surely die if the situation continues to be ignored.

"I remember a few years back when the Congressman felt compelled to send a message to each and every American taxpayer that he had fallen down a well," Randolph said, recalling the much-publicized 1998 event. "If I remember correctly, he drew up a proposal for emergency relief on the back of a candy bar wrapper, folded it into a paper airplane and managed to fly it up to the surface, where somebody picked it up it and lobbied to get it pushed through."

Randolph argued that Taylor's Please Get Me Out Of This Well Act of 1998 was similar to his current proposal in that it also failed to provide step-by-step instructions about how to successfully liberate the Congressman from his desolate position.

"There wasn't word one on that document that explained how they were supposed to get him out of there," said Randolph. "He didn't even say how deep the well was. Fortunately, while legislators were wasting time arguing the logistics and costs of various rescue operations, Representative John Ellis [R-NY] thought to shout down the well to Taylor and discovered that he was barely more than an arm's length from the surface. Long story short, Congress allocated a fifty-foot ladder and a flashlight for the effort and Taylor was back with us before lunchtime. The point being that if Taylor had included more information or rescue suggestions in his initial proposal, it would have saved the taxpayers a lot of money."

Experts speculate that Congressman Taylor will sit motionless next to one of the deserted island's seven trees and scan the horizon for signs of a rescue effort until as late as noon Saturday, by which time the sight of his proposal washing up on the North shore of the island will convince the Congressman to begin exploring suicide options. ∎

---

headlines every day at
recoilmag.com

recoil

RECOILMAG.COM — NEWS SATIRE YOU CAN TRUST

Electronic highway sign too depressed to talk about traffic right now

Mood swings

Pregnant woman now bitching for two

Exploratory committee to go find out what the hell is going on

Bowels still considering move

Las Vegas, Nev. – Medical experts as well as organs within the gastrointestinal tract of Las Vegas resident Neil Davis reported Tuesday that Davis' bowels – which have been putting off making a firm commitment to relocate waste material for nearly three days – are still considering exactly when will be the appropriate time to move. "The bowels are hard to get a good read on the exact reason for such a hesitation," said Dr. Morgan Armstrong, who consulted Davis regarding his digestive system's indecisiveness to commit to what it knows must eventually happen. "Sure, there are a number of organs that have some say in this matter, but these decisions ultimately come down to the small intestine's willingness to sign off on the order to relax the anal sphincter, so we can just up and move already," said Davis' stomach, which has recently been putting increased pressure on the small intestine to commit to moving as quickly as possible. "Until 'Smalls' is on board the act is kind of 'tied up in committee.' And, of course, it doesn't help that the small intestine has a history of bipolar disorder; it can be a stubborn, procrastinating little bastard one day, and then be real irritable and excitable the next – like you're working with an entirely different organ."

quikSTAT

Worst ship names
- 'Caine Wagon
- U.S.S. Probably Unsinkable
- There's A Tube In The Throat Of The Elderly Man In The Hospital Bed On The Frog In The Log In The Hole Of The Bottom Of The Sea
- H.M.S No Lifeboats
- The Jettison Everything Or We're Doomed
- S.S. Edmund Fitzgerald v2.0
- Titanenburg

Above: A police surveillance photo of the suspect taken moments before his arrest.

Adult ghost going through after-life crisis

Newport, R.I. – An afterlife consultant confirmed Friday that the lingering spirit of Daryl Riley, a deceased neurotic investment banker whose middle years of mortal life had been plagued by a sense of the passing of his youth and the imminence of old age, and regret regarding past career and personal decisions, is currently exhibiting telltale symptoms of experiencing an after-life crisis while haunting his former Newport home.

"Daryl's behavior in the eternal realm suggests that he's been struck by the realization that he's not going to not be alive forever, and is going through what is commonly referred to as an after-life crisis," said Michelle Gatrivani, a medium hired by Riley's widow to communicate with her departed spouse. "It's a phase he'll probably snap out of eventually, but his spirit could be kind of down in the dumps like this for another millennium or two while Daryl faces bouts of dramatic self-doubt regarding his place in the afterworld."

> "His spirit could be kind of down in the dumps like this for another millennium or two while Daryl faces bouts of dramatic self-doubt regarding his place in the afterworld."

Gatrivani's services were contracted after Amanda Riley, Daryl's wife for 42 years, became concerned about recent changes in the behavior of her husband's ghost, who has routinely haunted their family home since dying of brain cancer at age 68 three years ago.

"One thing about Daryl, he was never much of a night owl – except for when he was going through a mid-life crisis in his late forties, when he would often stay up pacing the upstairs hallway until the wee hours, just like his ghost started doing last week," said Amanda Riley, noting that she'd previously only heard the haunting footsteps of her husband's ghost during early evening.

see GHOST page 92

Line between hip-hop videos and soft-core porn continuing to blur

Above: Footage from the music video for the Ron Browz (left) song "Exhibit Harlem," which clearly resembles scenes from numerous soft-core pornography films.

Hollywood, Calif. – Officials charged with governing American television broadcasts voiced their continuing concern that the difference between soft-core pornography and excerpts from many current hip-hop music videos is continuing to become less and less discernable.

"Music video channels such as MTV, BET and FUSE are willingly airing hip-hop videos which contain increasingly strong implied and explicit sexual content – footage which not long ago would have been banned by such organizations," said Deborah Pallas, head of the TV Parental Guidelines Monitoring Board, a group appointed by the Federal Communications Commission (FCC). "If content standards are not more closely monitored, scrutinized and controlled, viewers will soon have trouble telling the difference between an R. Kelly music video and a segment from *Girls Gone Wild*."

> "Viewers will soon have trouble telling the difference between an R. Kelly music video and a segment from *Girls Gone Wild*," said Pallas.

Pallas went on to suggest that many musical acts often resort to creating sexually explicit videos to "make up for weak songwriting."

"Music labels perhaps feel pressured into covering up a poor song by focusing on the visuals of half-naked women getting their rear ends smacked in order to captivate viewer attention," said Pallas. "Just like soft-core pornographic filmmakers do in order to cover up ridiculous plotlines and sterily delivered dialogue."

MTV spokesman Milo Alexander argued Monday that the more controversial

see PORN page 92

page 89

WORLDWIDE HEADLINES

Husband pleads for safe return of wife's sex drive

Atlanta, Ga. – Gary Gerard, 31, pleaded to newspaper and television reporters Friday, asking for the public's help in providing any information that might lead to the safe return of his wife Mia's sex drive, which sources confirmed Gerard had reported missing during early summer. "It's been a nightmare for me, forced to simply wait and wonder, just trying to get through each day to come home in hopes of finding that Mia's sex drive has been returned," said Gerard, who, having been married to Mia for just under two years, admitted to "failing to appreciate what he had while he had it." "Only now, after Mia's sex drive has been removed from my life, am I realizing that I had taken it for granted. I now understand how little time men have with their wives' sex drive, how it should be cherished and enjoyed like you'll never see it again – because it can be suddenly ripped away from you without a moment's notice," said a sobbing Gerard, who then retired to the couple's bedroom to masturbate before his wife returned from the grocery store.

Essence captured

New York, N.Y. – Officials at Calvin Klein announced Friday the successful completion of its three-year effort to capture the essence of spring rain – in a new fragrance called Precipitation. "In this fragrance we've managed to capture the very essence of spring rain," said world-renown fragrance designer Paco Rabanne, who worked with authorities in identifying and capturing the essence. "The capturing of this essence will make the world a more pleasant place." Calvin Klein had previously enlisted Rabanne to spearhead successful efforts to capture the essence of passion, love and longing.

There area nose tackle goes with his 'false start' bullshit again

Janesville, Wis. – Officials, coaches, crowd members and opposing players immediately began complaining about Derek Hounds after the Parker High Vikings varsity nose tackle blamed his third offside infraction of the first quarter on a false start by the offense during the teams' Friday night loss to the Madison Memorial Spartans. "There goes that idiot nose tackle with his 'false start' bullshit again," yelled Spartans' coach Eric Robertson after Hounds' third attempt to sway referee Paul Shremp into believing that the Spartans' center flinched before snapping the football. "False start my ass. Give him a technical [penalty], ref!" Vikings players reported that defensive coordinator David Burns took Hounds aside during halftime and ordered the defensive lineman to count "one apple, two apple, three apple" before rushing in after the snap to prevent further embarrassment to the team.

Great, so now area man is the one who looks like asshole

Tucson, Ariz. – Thanks to your apprehension over complaining about your neighbor's constantly barking dog, great, now area man Fred Banks is the one who looks like a total asshole for complaining to the city about it, Banks said Friday. "You've seriously lived next to that dog for three years and you've never once bitched to anyone about its barking? Oh, great, so now I, the new neighbor, look like a total dink for saying something right away," said an agitated Banks, who noted that he doesn't at all like coming across like such a jerk, despite often doing so. Added Banks: "That's just perfect. Thanks. Thanks a lot."

Disputatious soundmen enter freakishly uninteresting discussion about best way to mix theater

Detroit, Mich. – Jeremy Price and Dale Osborne, sound technicians employed by the sound company Jefferson Audio, entered a mind-numbingly uninteresting debate Tuesday afternoon about the best way to mix the band performing at Fox Theater later that evening. "With the acoustics in this room you've got to roll off the high end and boost the mids on the crossover or the PA will sound like there's a blanket over the speakers," said Price, reiterating an opinion found interesting only by Osborne. "Yeah, but don't forget, frequency response on our new powers amps is ruler-flat from forty-two hertz to twenty kilohertz, with a three decibel down point at forty hertz," countered Osborne. As the two began a spirited debate regarding which frequencies to scoop out of the monitor mix, two stagehands who had been attempting to listen to the conversation began a far more interesting discussion regarding the third season of the HBO show *The Walking Dead*.

Homeless man's problems apparently rectifiable with dime

Denver, Colo. – While seemingly in need of much more to remedy his current situation, an area homeless man announced to passersby Monday that he "only need[ed] ten cents." Several who encountered the vagrant recalled assessing his level of need to require a higher monetary figure. "I took one look at the guy and immediately thought he would need a lot of money, education, and maybe personal counseling to overcome his hardships," said area resident Charles Houska. "I was as shocked as anyone when I found out the only thing between his homelessness and being a productive member of society was a dime." Houska, who gave the unidentified man 58 cents, hopes the street dweller's life has turned around as of one day later. ∎

A page from the Recoil handbook...
First Aid Tips

The ability to administer first aid is one of the most important skills a person can acquire. Here is a basic guide to emergency medical assistance:

• To prevent thievery of your bandages and ointments, affix your first aid kit with a strong lock, then hide the key and tell no one of its location.

• Despite what some people may say, there's nothing "uncool" about playing it safe by carrying marijuana with you at all times in case of a medical emergency.

• In case of poisoning, you may need to induce vomiting; keep a copy of Ashlee Simpson's "Pieces Of Me" video in your first aid kits.

• You can ease the pain of a person who's been cut by reminding them that they just would've had to go to practice every damn day for the next few months had they actually made the football team.

• Puncture wounds can prove incredibly difficult to clean – unless, of course, you're a creative thinker who happens to get injured near a self-serve magic-wand car wash.

• Remember that episode of M*A*S*H when Radar performed an emergency tracheotomy using a pocketknife and ballpoint pen? Yeah, that was a pretty good episode.

• Never, ever attempt to move a person with a serious head or back injury until you've asked their permission.

• You could argue all day about whether a man's burns are second-degree or third-degree, but that's not going to help put out the fire that's quickly engulfing the rest of his body.

• Serious cuts may demand that you apply direct pressure for up to 10 minutes to stop the bleeding – 12 minutes if you're allowing time to show curious people how gross it looks.

• Act quickly to cut out a seizure victim's tongue, so he or she doesn't swallow it.

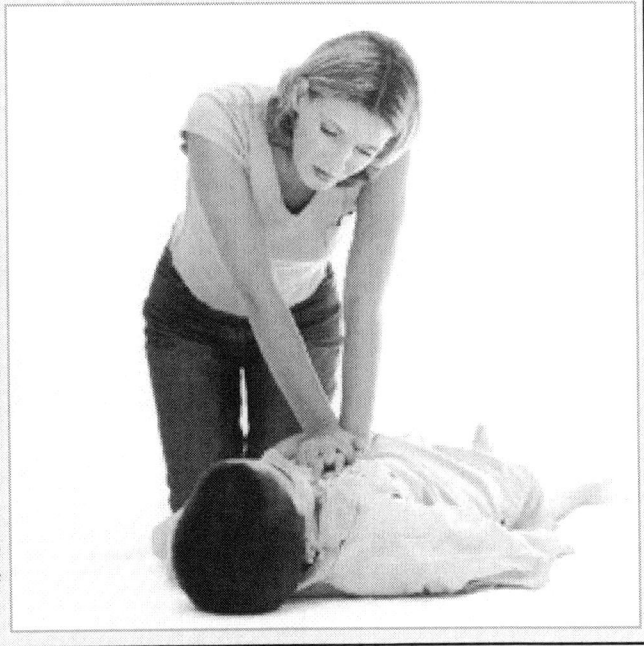

page 90

HOROSCOPES

Gemini (May 21 to June 20)
Your nasty habit of not calling people back is deterring people from calling you at all, and your intimate Internet friendships are doing little more than improving your typing. Life isn't all about e-mail; sooner or later you're going to need real friends – whether for a ride to work or to testify as a character witness on your behalf – so you'd better put out some favors before you have to try to call them back in.

Cancer (June 21 to July 22)
While playing intellectual possum will get you excused from conversations you deem pointless, it could also get you labeled a dullard. Fine. Like they say, "It's better to keep quiet and be thought a fool than to open your mouth and remove all doubt" – something a lot of people should have tattooed on their forearm and be forcibly silenced long enough to read.

Leo (July 23 to August 22)
Your internal emotion suppressor is ready to overload; it's time to open up like the stomach of an Alka-Seltzer fed seagull and spill your guts to whomever's willing to listen – your mom, most likely. Moms are known for wanting to offer lots of advice (whether you ask or not), but if you can exploit the gender gap by discussing your New Age problems, she'll freak and break out the Valium, and soon you'll both feel a whole lot better.

Virgo (August 23 to September 22)
While it is well known that mutual denial is the key to long-lasting marriages, you may also find consistent viewing of today's prime-time television helpful in keeping arguments to a minimum. Granted, weeknight sitcoms are not funny or even mildly entertaining – they're not supposed to be. That programming is for one purpose only: allowing American couples an excuse to not talk to each other.

Libra (September 23 to October 22)
Forget about taking people to court to settle differences; who in hell has the time, money or patience to bribe juries, deal with nitpicking appeals, and suppress the urge to strangle your lawyer? Challenging someone to a duel is a much more efficient and practical method of settling disagreements, provided you don't live in the legally progressive states of Mississippi, Arkansas or Kentucky, which have outlawed dueling, for no good reason.

Scorpio (October 23 to November 21)
Heredity isn't solely responsible for earning you the nickname "Twelve Step" – a lot of your chemical dependency stems from knowing that the crushing pain of modern life is momentarily eased by alcohol. Fear not; denial is the key indicator of clinical alcoholism, so as long as you can admit your drinking problem, you're in the clear.

Capricorn (December 22 to January 19)
You may as well give up on writing those stupid poems – you're just wasting paper, which doesn't exactly grow on trees, you know. If you need a release for those suppressed emotions, try the more contemporary version of self-expression: performance art. Streaking through a Little League baseball diamond may seem like juvenile behavior by a majority of onlookers, but the truly hip will respect it as a form of art.

Aquarius (January 20 to February 18)
Be proud of the power with which your magnetic personality attracts members of the opposite sex, but be careful it doesn't draw any one particular member too close unless you're ready to be re-polarized. A wedding ring may well give your sense of security a positive charge, but it will also repel the remaining members of the opposite sex.

Pisces (February 19 to March 20)
We all enjoy a good cockfight, but you should avoid using one as the main course of entertainment on a date – it tends to inspire bloodlust in the human heart. And with today's Superhardware stores providing such affordable pricing on power equipment, it's too much to expect neither of you to own some, which could turn a romantic nightcap into a bloody de-cap(itation).

Aries (March 21 to April 19)
Your current popularity at work will likely lead to multiple dinner invitations, so you'd better bone up on your table etiquette. The most important thing to remember is that people tend to be offended by the word "puke," even if that is exactly what their dinner tastes like. Just stay quiet and shove the awful stuff into your mouth, even if it does look like it's already been eaten once and has an aroma that would gag a maggot.

Taurus (April 20 to May 20)
Life's first and most important lesson, "the squeaky wheel gets the grease," deserves a little updating – the squeakier of a wheel you are, in direct relation to the general quietness of the room, is critical in how quickly you get greased. It's true; try saying "I gotta hit the can" a little louder than is comfortable when your spouse drags you to an opera, and see how quickly you'll be excused.

Sagittarius (November 22 to December 21)
You need to start shaping up at work. Stop taking the blame for things that are every bit your fault – that's no way to succeed in the business place; being a "go-getter" means going and getting yourself some primitive screwhead from another department to blame everything on. And if there's no avoiding an onus, just say you're colorblind and have Dyslexia – nobody bitches at the handicapped.

MUSIC

Above: The neighborhood-offending garage band The Decent Ascenders.

Neighbors object to garage band's terrible setlist

Madison, Wis. – Residents of the quiet, suburban 800 block of Gold Spring Avenue told reporters Friday that their objections to the teenaged band jamming in the garage of the Jeffries residence are based not on the noise caused by their early evening rehearsals, but by the songs the teens are selecting to cover.

"I'm actually not that opposed to them making all that racket a couple of nights a week, you know – but damn it if they couldn't just learn a couple of descent tunes," said Harold Bishop, 59, who lives across the street from the Jeffries residence, where aspiring 17-year-old drummer Adam Jeffries and his band The Decent Ascenders routinely rehearse.

"Most of the songs I don't even recognize from the radio or from my record collection, which ain't too shabby, I don't mind telling you. But my God, would it kill them to put away the devil music and kick out a nice, foot-tapping [version of Creedence Clearwater Rivival's] 'Proud Mary' once in a while?"

According to reports, although the upstart band has been rehearsing at the Jeffries residence for the past three months, it's been only recently that neighbors have started to complain about the youths' taste in music.

"I guess for the first little while I didn't mind hearing Nirvana's 'Smells Like Teen Spirit' ten times a night, but now it's really starting to wear on me," said Norman Dartmouth, a 38-year-old neighbor. "I know they are [beginners] and they don't know a whole lot of songs, but it sure would be a lot less unpleasant having to listen to them practicing if they could mix it up a bit and maybe learn something off of *In Utero* or even *Bleach*. Imagine, [hearing] those same four chords over and over and over again. It's becoming enough to put me off my eggs."

Opinions of a similar nature have also begun circulating within the Jeffries household.

"I told [Adam] from day one that the first time the police showed up here because of noise complaints, that would be the end of his band rehearsal days in my house," said Henry Jeffries, Adam's father. "Actually, I was kind of counting on that. And here nobody's said shit, can you believe it? Oh, I never hear the end of it, trust me; every last one of my goddamned neighbors complains to me about how bad they are and how the songs they play stink, but nobody will call the damn cops because they're too loud. What the hell is that all about?"

Added Henry Jeffries: "And apparently you can't call the cops on somebody for having bad taste in music, or else they'd be here ten times a day, believe me."

Adam Jeffries admitted that his band members generally harbor a universal disinterest in learning most of the songs that have so far been suggested to them by neighbors.

"Most of the people who live around here are really old, so they are always suggesting that we learn really dumb songs like 'Born to be Wild' or 'White Room' and old crap like that," said Adam Jeffries. "Except, of course, for old misses Higgins next door. She's a Jesus freak, so she's always pokes her head in the garage and saying we should learn some songs that praise Jesus or some shit. We're like, 'Okay, whatever.'"

Commonplace among the neighbors until recently seems to have been a supportive attitude, described by

see SETLIST page 92

COMMUNITY

Area man baffled by friend's remote control units

Above: Tolan struggles to comprehend the remote controls to friend Eric Peterman's entertainment center.

Greenfield, Ill. – Area restaurant manager Greg Tolan experienced complete bafflement Wednesday night while attempting to operate friend Eric Peterman's entertainment center via the console's three remote control units.

"We were hanging out at Eric's place when he ran to the store to get a six-pack; I thought I'd turn off the CD player and maybe cruise channels on the television until he got back," said Tolan, describing the events leading to his confounding technical encounter. "As soon as I looked at the three remotes sitting on the coffee table, though, I realized I didn't have the slightest clue how to operate his system."

Daunted but determined, Tolan said he attacked the situation by first independently studying each remote, hoping for a course of action to "jump out at [him]."

"It seemed like each remote had buttons corresponding to each unit [of the entertainment center]," Tolan explained.

Confronted by multiple controls for Peterson's television, CD player, VCR, DVD player, Blu-Ray player and satellite receiver, Tolan, 30, admitted his initial attempts to operate the system relied more on chance than on educated or calculated movements.

"Really, I just started pointing [the remote units] and pressing buttons, hoping to get lucky," Tolan confirmed. "I tried pressing 'power' on each controller and I swear none of them did anything. I got some lights to flash on the [satellite television] receiver, but that's about it."

Though failing to turn off the CD player, Tolan's barrage of random button pressing did provide power to Peterson's 29-inch Sony Trinitron, which displayed only a blank, blue screen and the words "MUTE ENABLED."

Fearing embarrassment from his failure to grasp the fundamental concepts of navigating Peterson's entertainment center, Tolan eventually sought to conceal evidence of his electronic meddling.

"I didn't want Eric to walk in and see me looking like I didn't know what I was doing, so I just got up and manually turned off the TV using the console," said Tolan. "Then I grabbed his acoustic [guitar] and made it look like I just didn't want to listen to music or watch TV or anything."

Though initially oblivious to Tolan's fumbled attempts at operating the system, Peterson confronted Tolan the following afternoon after finding his satellite receiver's station presets haphazardly reprogrammed and a *Matlock* marathon recorded over the sole VHS recording of Peterson's wedding ceremony.

"He eventually copped to it," said Peterson, a 32-year-old systems analyst.

Though slightly agitated by Tolan's behavior, Peterson has scheduled next Friday evening with Tolan to explain the remote control setup, in hopes of avoiding further incident.

"It's not like [operating the entertainment center] is rocket surgery – the receiver's remote controls the basics of the whole system," said Peterson. "You only use the other remotes for special programming, which I don't see any reason why he'd feel the need to do. Unless he's dead set on taping over *all* the important videotaped events of my life." ■

> Though failing to turn off the CD player, Tolan's barrage of random button pressing did provide power to Peterson's 29-inch Sony Trinitron, which displayed only a blank, blue screen and the words "MUTE ENABLED."

recoilmag.com

PORN from page 89

imagery infused into sexually explicit rap videos is not a deliberate, boundary-pushing attempt to invoke superfluous media attention upon hip-hop artists, but is merely the resulting product of ever-loosening popular cultural and moral constructs.

"Artists such as Akon and T-Pain are simply giving the viewing public exactly what they want to see – the degrading objectification of women in settings such as glorious dance clubs and outlandish swimming pool areas," said Alexander. "Viewer trends are certainly not the artist's fault. It's not like they can help that pretty much everyone on Earth is a perverted sexual deviant who wants to observe as much pelvic thrusting as is humanly possible."

Alexander also contended that the freedom to shoot such erotic content as to make a music video that's almost indistinguishable from a Cinemax *Max After Dark* film often allows hip-hop artists to express themselves more thoroughly.

In retort, Pallus stopped short of implying that such content be "censored," but noted that parents wishing to shield their children from seeing sexually explicit music videos is no longer as simple as utilizing modern television's "channel block" option.

"For example, even though Rihanna's song 'S&M' has been banned from television broadcast in 11 countries for its indecency, I'd bet my nine-year-old son could find it online in about three minutes," said Pallus. "Granted, youtube.com has deemed the 'S&M' video as being 'inappropriate for viewers under the age of eighteen,' what is such content management going to except make underage users want to watch it that much more?" ■

> "Viewer trends are certainly not the artist's fault. It's not like they can help that pretty much everyone on Earth is a perverted sexual deviant who wants to observe as much pelvic thrusting as is humanly possible."

GHOST from page 89

"That's how I knew something was eating at him. I've found that Daryl's spirit is pretty much just as predictable – and as neurotic, apparently – as the real Daryl Riley was, God bless him."

Having visited the Riley home and claimed to have communicated directly with Daryl's spirit through séances, Gatrivani, despite having no formal training in either psychoanalysis or the paranormal, has become convinced that Daryl Riley's spirit is in the throes of a full-fledged after-life crisis.

"At a certain point during a spirit's time in the hereafter, one often becomes obsessively reflective regarding their existence in the immaterial realm, and they often spend a lot of time dwelling how they might better spend the remainder of their supernatural lives," said Gatrivani. "Spirits like Daryl's typically spend this period of their afterlife reevaluating their priorities. Perhaps Daryl's ghost is recognizing the fact that he should be spending more time haunting his family. Or maybe he's wishing his physical apparition was eternally bound to the outdoors instead of being cooped up haunting the inside of a house. He's likely getting tired of only being able to play immature little pranks like hiding his wife's car keys or turning the kitchen sink's faucet on and off once every other day just to try to feel like he's not alive."

Gatrivani insisted that through multiple communications with Daryl Riley, she witnessed firsthand the ghost's descent from sporadic neurosis to chronic after-life crisis. ■

SETLIST from page 91

Dartmouth: "I guess a lot of us felt that even though they make a lot of awful noise with that band of theirs practicing there, at least it keeps them off the streets, gives them something to do other than being out messing around with drugs. Although, at this point, I'll bet a lot of us wouldn't mind so much if they did go hang out in the street and do some drugs, rather than trainwreck their way through [Smash Mouth's] "All Star" for the umpteenth billion freakin' time every night. It could be that they actually *need* some [drugs]." ■

RECOILMAG.COM   NEWS SATIRE YOU CAN TRUST

recoil

CD reviewer channels entire year of pretentiousness into "Best of 2010" wrap-up

Above: Ultra-snooty CD reviewer Dwayne E. Augustine.

Detroit, Mich. – Dwayne E. Augustine, a CD reviewer for the *Metro Times* weekly entertainment magazine, has begun arranging his selections for his "10 Best CDs of The Year," an article Augustine writes annually as a vehicle for showcasing his absolute perfect knowledge and taste in music by listing 10 titles familiar only to music enthusiasts of equal pretentiousness.

"Popularity does nothing but corrupt the emotional impact of the music and the integrity of the artist," said Augustine.

"Any release that gleans any mainstream media attention whatsoever is automatically disqualified – that's rule number one when I pick my top ten discs of the year," said Augustine, attempting to qualify the 28-year-old music critic's reasons for routinely selecting releases by bands that less than five percent of the population has ever even heard of. "The moment a band becomes even moderately popular, I'm sorry, but I won't have anything to do with them.
see REVIEWER page 95

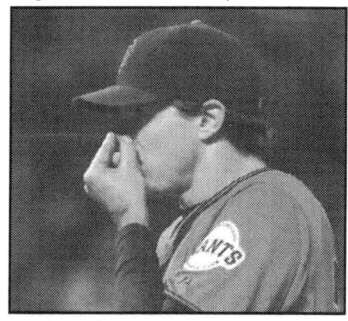

MLB celebrates first snot rocket launched into outer base

quikSTAT

World's least-attended festivals
- Midwestern Agoraphobia Campout
- Lower Oakland Head Lice Swap Meet
- Texas State Jihad Jamboree
- Great Britain Dead Tooth Pull-Off
- Haitian Hoaxfest '05
- Fort Worth Salad Toss Showdown
- Marlboro Country 5K Marathon
- United Steelworkers of America Poetry Jam
- All festivals that contain the words "Insane," "Clown" and "Posse" in any order, singularly or together
- Compton Father-Son Picnic

Above: Jack and Kathy Hudson spend an afternoon giving their flower and vegetable gardens everything they need to mature into healthy, fruitful plants while their unsupervised children play rated M video games indoors.

Parents nurture garden more than children

Madison, Wis. – Suburban homeowners Jack and Kathy Hudson put more time, care and money into the nurturing of their backyard flower and vegetable gardens than that of their two children, a neighbor of the Hudsons reported Sunday.

"Those two may call themselves parents, but from what I've seen they seem more devoted to raising healthy, mature tomato plants than healthy, mature offspring," said Bob Shore, who lives nextdoor to the Hudsons. "They labor away for hours on that little plot like it's the entire family's only source of food. Meanwhile their kids sit alone inside playing Playstation or watching TV instead of getting help with their homework. It pains me to see that kind of neglect, but what can you do, you know? It's not really my place to say anything."

A neighbor of three years, Shore estimated that during the spring and summer months Jack and Kathy Hudson each log at least 25 hours per week watering, weeding and otherwise nurturing their 12' x 15' vegetable garden and three small flower gardens. Comparatively, Shore claimed that the couple – who both work fulltime jobs – appear to spend less than an hour a day interacting with their 12-year-old son, Kyle, and 10-year-old daughter, Anna.

"Jack and Kathy are usually out working their little mini-farms from the minute they get home from work until darkness finally forces them inside, when I'm sure they have to immediately start getting the kids ready for bed," said Shore. "That's not much time to foster your child's interests or work to instill them with solid morals.

> The couple rarely if ever makes an effort to cultivate their children's talents or expose them to religion, art, culture and other nurturing influences.

Heck, that's barely enough time to burn them a Pop Tart for dinner and chase them off to bed."

Shore said that although the Hudsons willfully devote the bulk of their nights and weekends to cultivating their gardens, the couple rarely if ever makes an effort to cultivate their children's
see GARDEN page 95

Wal-Mart visit a perfect argument for birth control

Above: Crazed children begin to overrun every aisle of a local Wal-Mart.

Huntsville, Ala. – After enduring 90 minutes encircled by a plethora of crying babies, screaming toddlers, out-of-control children and frustrated parents at an area Wal-Mart Saturday, patrons Kevin Tyler and longtime girlfriend Julie Slansky unanimously agreed to vigilantly instrument birth control methods in order to prevent pregnancy.

"All those children running through the aisles, hiding in clothes racks, pestering their parents to buy them every goddamn item they see, the crying and yelling – even just thinking about it is giving me a headache," Tyler said, recalling the experience the following morning. "I think all those insane children creating havoc actually bothered Julie more than me, because she loves to shop for hours and hours – but, I swear, she was practically running that cart to the checkout so we could get the hell out of
see WAL-MART page 96

page 93

WORLDWIDE HEADLINES

Landscaping crew plants bushes they will later get high behind

Kalamazoo, Mich. – Sources close to Great Landscaping workers reported Saturday having completed the transplanting of a 15-foot line of mature, view-obstructing Viburnum bushes along the property line of a private homeowner, behind which the employees intend to get high during breaks in the future. "This will be a good spot to sneak off and get into grass cutting-mode next year," said landscaper Mannie Perez while packing sod around the freshly transplanted growths. "Whenever we're scheduled to cut this site next year, I'm sure we'll likely spend the whole day here, driving the lawnmowers in circles and shit."

Overenthusiastic salute leaves soldier unconscious

Fayetteville, N.C. – Officials at Fort Bragg military base reported Tuesday that an enthusiastic young enlistee named Jeremy Dunn, 18, knocked himself unconscious during day one of basic training Monday, suffering a self-administered blow to the head while eagerly saluting drill sergeant Robert T. Bowers. "This little maggot must have *the worst* depth perception I have ever encountered in my twenty-two years in this man's army," barked Bowers, standing over Dunn as base medics worked to revive the Bradford, Minn., native. "Will *somebody* teach this young lady when to stop his arc, for Christ's sake? Or at least issue the poor bastard a goddamn brain bucket before he salutes himself straight into the infirmary. I will give him this, though: the son of a bitch displayed some good upper-body strength there. He'll be king hell in hand-to-hand [combat] – so long as we can get him karate-chopping in the right goddamned direction."

Angus Alert activated in statewide hunt for lost appetite

Sault Saint Marie, Mich. – In accordance with the Angus Alert issued late Thursday night by Michigan State Police officials, area radio and television stations began airing information regarding the lost appetite of local party store owner Alan Peal, which Peal said mysteriously disappeared sometime between the ordering and serving of his medium-rare Angus steak at Outback Steakhouse on James St. early Thursday evening. "We had just finished ordering, because I remember commenting to the waiter about how famished I was," Peal said, recalling the events leading up to his appetite's disappearance. "I got up to go to the men's room and there was somebody in one of the stalls totally puking his guts out. I practically ran back to my table; that's when I noticed that my appetite was gone." State Police officer Jim McNeal told reporters that although a majority of lost appetites end up coming back within 24 hours of their disappearance, some appetites invariably remain lost for days or even weeks. "Last month we initiated the Angus Alert after some guy's girlfriend dumped him," McNeal explained. "The poor guy not only lost his girl that night – he also lost his appetite. From what I hear, he hasn't eaten in weeks. What can I say? It's a tragedy."

Fed typo leads to increase in interest rats

Washington, D.C. – Economists and stock market analysts reacted with confusion Monday on news that the Federal Reserve Board approved a sharp and unexpected increase in interest rats, sources reported. "I don't know what to make of it," said Morgan-Stanley analyst Jeffery Stockard. "The reference to rats is strange. Plus, an increase of a full half-point seems a little extreme. I would have expected a quarter-point raise at most." Board Chairman Alan Greenspan later verified in a news conference that the announcement was actually a typo from the board's meeting minutes, seeking to calm fears that the U.S. was reverting back to the highly unstable rodent-based economy of the 1820s. Greenspan blamed new secretary Melissa Anderson for the mistake, but Anderson defended her action, saying: "It didn't look right, but I thought, you know, maybe the economy involves rats. Interesting rats." After early declines, the market rallied on word the board was considering replacing Anderson with the highly-recommended front desk receptionist from the Occupational Safety and Health Administration.

Merck touts newly released drug that won't kill you

Whitehouse Station, N.J. – On Wednesday, pharmaceutical giant Merck & Co. heralded the development of its new drug, Elemin, a medicine which the company insists does not appear to cause death. Originally developed to treat acid reflux, the drug has so far failed to show benefit in clinical trials and is currently being prescribed by doctors to treat inner ear infections. "We're still tweaking the formula to produce an actual medical benefit, but one thing's for sure: it won't kill you. We're testing for that now," said Michael Stine, Merck's vice president of marketing. Stine confirmed that his company is currently planning a multimillion dollar ad campaign, introducing Elemin as "the drug that won't kill you," with ads featuring a diverse array of people consuming the drug, dancing in fields and not dying. ∎

recoilmag.com

EDITORIAL

Evelyn's orgies are always just such popularity contests

By Eric Crane

I know it's hard to complain about being invited to an orgy; they seem so rare these days that a person really should just feel blessed in the event that they are actually invited to one. But I have to admit, from the moment I recognized the return address on the envelope of this invitation, I was already shaking my head, knowing what I can expect if I decide to show up at another one of Evelyn's semi-annual orgies: the naked adult equivalent of a high school popularity contest.

Yes, if the last three of Evelyn's orgies are any indication, the who and when of the overriding majority of sexual congress that will take place at this affair will be largely dictated by the social status of the people involved. It happens every time: the guys that drive up in the Porsches or are local celebrities or whatever the hell – those are the guys that always get first crack at the party's premium tail. Meanwhile, lowly ol' office managers like myself typically end up sucking on the toes of whoever's left.

Now granted, I'm the quintessential idealist, but wouldn't it be nice to think that a group of 10 or 12 level-headed 30-somethings could simply get together for an evening of no-holds-barred sexual abandon and not have it turn into a petty game of popularity? Personally, I don't think that's too much to ask. And, indeed, sometimes that *can* happen – just not at one of Evelyn's shindigs. Oh, no. No, you could be Dirk fucking Diggler and still barely even get yanked off by the superficial women that Evelyn invites to these things. Unless, of course, you're lucky enough to be one of the

> *Am I the only one who thinks that a four-hour DeSade-O-Rama is simply not the time for more social posturing?*

popular guys – you know the type, those Italian suit-wearing assholes who were obviously born with a silver dildo up their ass.

I ask you, why should the best-looking females at the orgy automatically gravitate toward the males who notoriously own the best wardrobe when you're involved in an activity that specifically refutes the wearing of clothing?

I don't know about you, but where I come from, this popularity issue totally defeats the core spirit of what an orgy is supposed to be: a guilt-free sexathon in which everyone involved is there for the sole purpose of dropping all social convictions and temporarily engaging in otherwise taboo acts of such massive and unreasonable sexual hedonism that it could make Caligula blush. Are we not all on the same page here? Am I the only one who thinks that a four-hour DeSade-O-Rama is simply not the time for more social posturing?

Look, we're supposed to be acting like adults here – I mean isn't that the whole point about participating in improvised

> *We're supposed to be acting like adults here – I mean isn't that the whole point about participating in improvised group sex?*

group sex: getting to act like an adult? I thought I had left this sort of juvenile stuff in the past when I graduated from high school. I guess not.

Well, I can be juvenile too. I'm not going to RSVP. ∎

WAL-MART from page 93

that bedlam."

According to Tyler, 31, as soon as the couple were safely within the quiet confines of Tyler's car, both breathed a loud sigh of relief, sparking a discussion of the events that transpired and their oath to "never, ever, ever have unprotected sex. Ever."

"All those crazed midgets running around screaming completely insane nonsense at the top of their lungs, babies bawling uncontrollably over who knows what – it was overwhelming," said Slansky. "Out of the eight billion kids in that madhouse I don't think I saw a single child that wasn't somehow contributing to that whirlwind nightmare."

Tyler agreed, noting that some of the parents they encountered were either unwilling or unable to control the scene, or have somehow developed a tolerance or ability to block out the continual influx of lawlessness created by their kin.

"About half of them spent more time yelling at their kids and threatening them with every punishment known to man than doing any actually shopping," said Tyler. "You know, somebody ought to open a vasectomy clinic right next door to Wal-Mart. Any right-thinking single male walking through Wal-Mart would immediately go right over there and sign up. They'd make a mint."

Slansky, 29, admitted that she had always considered bearing children at some point in her life until her recent exposure to the onslaught of sugar-upped children overrunning the chaotic supercenter.

"There isn't enough Xanax in the world that could get me through having to deal with that sort of stuff every single day," said Slansky. "So unless there's some way to drop off your newborn at daycare and pick him up about twelve years later – after the child has got all that yelling and crying out of its system – there's no way in hell I'm having a kid, if that's an accurate example of what it's like to parent a child."

REVIEWER from page 93

Popularity does nothing but corrupt the emotional impact of the music and the integrity of the artist."

Coworkers said that Augustine spends every year in excited anticipation of being able to bestow his almighty approval on releases by bands whose names readers won't even recognize let alone be in any position to disagree.

"Last year, for example, Dwayne was so excited to rate DePedro's *DePedro* as his number one [album] for the year," said fellow Metro Times music reviewer Sheila McBride. "Now maybe I'm alone here, but who in the hogfuck Jesus is DePedro? Like he's not just picking that to show off how aware he is of every musician in the universe that maybe twenty other people have even heard of. Myself, I picked Bob Dylan's *Together Through Life* as my number one. At least people have heard of Dylan."

Metro Times editor Chris Farmer said that although he can't agree or disagree with Augustine's Top 10 list, having never heard of any of the artists highlighted in the yearend wrap-up article, he doesn't mind allowing the snobby young critic license to "go nuts with his all-important list."

"We don't pay these writers shit, so if Dwayne's end of the year chest-beating keeps him around writing reviews for peanuts for us year after year, I'm not going to rock the boat," said Farmer. "In fact, now that you've got me thinking about it, I'll bet I could even *charge* Dwayne for printing his big, fancy list every year. I'll have to think about doing that. I'll bet he'd pay it – it's that important to him."

According to fellow writers, Augustine goes so far as to eliminate any release from his Top 10 list if he becomes aware that any other Best Of list includes an album he had originally intended to award with his approval.

"I remember back in 2002, when Wilco's *Yankee Hotel Foxtrot* was cited as the best CD of the year by almost every music critic on Earth, he took them right off his list, even though that album was practically all he listened to all year," said McBride. "Plus, that album went on to sell half a million copies – a fact Dwayne to this day still brings up, insisting that Wilco went too commercial with that record."

An inside source wishing to remain anonymous reported that he or she had gotten a peek at a rough draft of Augustine's 2010 list, confirming that this year's article will indeed be "another of his, 'Hey, everybody, look at me. Look at all the obscure music I know about and how much better it is than what everybody else listens to.'"

"I saw a handwritten list of the albums he's considering," said the source. "At the top, numbered one with a big box drawn around it was Titus Andronicus' 65-minute concept album *The Monitor*, which sold all of about fifteen copies. I might put it in my Top Ten list just to piss him off. That would be a riot. He'd never live it down."

According to the source, written below *The Monitor* were other titles Augustine is considering blessing with a position in his ultra-pretentious list, including Pantha du Prince's *Black Noise*, Oneohtrix Point Never's *Returnal*, Das Racist's *Shut Up Dude*, Liars' *Sisterworld* and Max Richter's *Infra*.

Asked how reviewers such as Augustine earn their credentials as professional music critics, Farmer replied, "Beats me. I don't think it's something you can go to college for or anything like that. I think you just have to say, 'I'm a music critic,' and then you are one. But don't you dare tell Dwayne I said that or I'll have to listen to an endless stream of his bullshit about his being highly regarded in the music community as 'an educated and experienced tastemaker' or some crap." ■

A page from the Recoil handbook...
Winter Driving Tips

Winter weather often presents extremely hazardous driving conditions. Below are some guidelines for negotiating winter's volatile driving environments:

• Putting chains on your car's tires will prevent your tires from escaping.

• Get your car tuned up by a mechanic for the winter season. The car's driver should get tuned up by a bartender before driving anywhere.

• It is very important to check the battery and charging system for your iPod before leaving home.

• Install brand new wipers in place of your old ones that leave streaks or completely miss an area of your windshield. Wow, notice the difference? No? That's because there isn't any.

• Check your tires' pressure. Winter driving puts a lot of pressure on your tires to perform well, and the last thing you want is to rely on tires that are all stressed-out from the constant pressure. Medicate your tires regularly with Xanax if you feel they are right on the verge of exploding.

• During winter you should drive a rear-wheel-drive car if possible. Then you can whip doughnuts and slide around turns and all that cool-ass shit.

• Add a block heater – a small electric engine heater that plugs into your home electricity outlets – to ensure that your car will start even on the coldest of days. Also, you'll need to buy about 250 miles of extension cord.

• If you own an all-wheel-drive vehicle featuring antilock brakes, traction control and stability control, your own a great winter car. If your vehicle is also equipped with a 120mm smoothbore gun and barrel, it's not a car – it's a Merkava Mark IV battle tank, so make sure your auto insurance reflects this difference.

• Buy four brand new snow tires. Surely you have the extra money just laying around, considering the state of the economy.

• Store some basic supplies in your trunk: snowbrush, ice scraper, shovel, bag of sand, jumper cables, flashlight, first aid kit, boots, blanket, change of clothes, shaving kit, shampoo, K rations, metal detector, frag grenade, eight-foot ladder, weightlifting bench, forensics kit, ice cream scooper and cyanide tablet.

• You should shorten the distance you usually allow when following another car. By getting up really, really close, you'll be able to drive in their tracks.

• Stay back at least 15 car lengths from snowplows, unless it's the final lap and a second-place finish simply isn't going to be enough to stay in contention for the 2013 NASCAR Sprint Cup Championship.

recoilmag.com

COMMUNITY

Youth sisters crusading either for world peace or jelly beans

Above: Amy and Denise Daniels.

Denver, Colo. – After having already spent months toiling for their cause, Denise and Amy Daniels of Denver showed determination in continuing their crusade for either world peace or jelly beans by appearing on a local television talk show Tuesday morning and pleading for the donation of more jelly beans.

"We've already got a lot of jelly beans from a lot of great supporters, but we need even more jelly beans – many, many more – in order to meet our goal," said 10-year-old Denise Daniels, who along with her sister Amy, 7, have been going door-to-door around suburban Denver-area neighborhoods collecting their favorite candy in the name of world peace. "Long story short: we need as many jelly beans as people can give us. And, oh, I almost forgot! We want to see world peace."

When prompted by *Good Morning, Denver* host Teresa Williams, Denise went on to explain the sisters' reasoning as to how the collection of overwhelming piles of hard-shelled gummy sweets promotes world peace.

"Well, when you think about it, no matter who you are or where you're from, everybody loves jelly beans," responded Denise after a long period of thought. "So by people of every race and country donating some of their jelly beans [to the Daniels sisters], it shows that all people are generous and that we can all come together and agree on at least one thing: that jelly beans are delicious!"

Williams echoed Denise's sentiment by pointing out that jelly beans are internationally enjoyed by millions of people despite being originally invented in the Middle East.

"Ummmmm… yeah, exactly!" responded an inspired Denise, possibly realizing a new argument for the donation of jelly beans as a means of calling attention to the importance of the end of prejudice and international feuds. "So if people all over the world love jelly beans, and they were originally only eaten in Turkey, it just goes to show that deep down we're all not all that different from each other. So please donate as many jelly beans as you can to me and Amy."

Denise mentioned that even though jelly beans are often associated with the celebration of Easter, people around the world – especially herself and her sister – regardless of their religion, enjoy eating jelly beans year-round.

"It isn't just people who believe in God [who] eat jelly beans," noted Denise, whose family is Catholic. "Almost everybody eats jelly beans, whether or not they are going to end up in Hell for not being Catholic. What's important is that everyone comes together as one by

> Denise Daniels: "What's important is that everyone comes together as one by donating as many jelly beans to us as possible, as soon as possible. Except for the spiced ones. They're disgusting."

donating as many jelly beans to us as possible, as soon as possible."

"Except for the spiced ones," added Denise. "The spiced ones are disgusting."

After noting that the similar confectionary known as jelly babies were originally launched in 1918 in Sheffield, England, as "Peace Babies" to mark the end of World War I, and that production of the candy was forced into suspension during World War II due to wartime shortages, Williams asked if the sisters considered this fact when deciding to use jelly beans as a symbol for promoting world peace.

Williams received only a short nod from Denise regarding her inquiry, as both sisters appeared to be laboriously chewing and unable to verbalize a response.

Denise explained that the idea to collect jelly beans to promote world peace came about during a discussion between the sisters regarding which flavor of jelly bean was their favorite.

"Me and Amy were eating jelly beans and we asked each other which color was our favorite [flavor]," said Denise. "We both could agree that black was our least favorite, but beside that, neither of us could pick a favorite. We kind of like them all equally. That's when we got the idea to do a jelly bean drive, because it's kind of the same with people. We shouldn't like one color [of] people more than another, we should like them all thee same – just like with jelly beans. At least that's what my mom and dad say."

Williams closed the interview by telling viewers that jelly bean donations could be dropped in the Daniels' family mailbox at 2103 Orlando Avenue and encouraged Denver residents to help promote world peace by donating jelly beans to the Daniels sisters.

"Or Skittles!" added Amy Daniels. ∎

SCORES		
Boeing	747 AR	15
Somebody call!	**911 M**	**16**

GARDEN from page 93

talents or expose them to religion, art, culture and other nurturing influences.

"The other night I overheard Kyle telling his dad about how he was interested in learning to play ice hockey, but then Jack just responded by going on and on about how expensive all of the equipment is," said Shore. "This right after he just dished out five hundred bucks on a new irrigation system for his plants last week. It's like they'd rather give their azaleas a better opportunity to blossom than their kids. Talk about having your priorities messed up."

"But, hey, that's just my opinion," added Shore. "Who knows, maybe it's worth undermining your kid's ability to reach his full potential if that means you get to eat fresh green beans two weeks out of the year."

According to Shore, the Hudsons routinely convey the impression that they are more concerned about the general wellbeing of their approximately 75 tomato, cucumber, zucchini, bean, cabbage, radish and carrot plants than the wellbeing of their two children.

"Last summer when Jack found deer tracks in his precious garden he went right out to Menard's that very day and bought a new fence to put up," recalled Shore. "Yet when I asked him yesterday about how his son was feeling after listening to the kid hack up a lung the night before and Jack says, 'Oh yeah, Kyle's got a cold or something, we think. We're going to take him to a doctor if he doesn't get better by the end of the week.' Poor kid, he'll probably have to turn green and start sprouting corn out of his ears in order to get their attention."

In addition to appearing more anxious to talk with Shore about their garden than their children, Jack and Kathy Hudson also take more pride in their gardening achievements than in their children's scholastic accomplishments.

"The Hudsons had me over for dinner last year to 'celebrate the harvest,' as they put it," said Shore, who admitted he is rarely invited into the Hudson residence. "As Kathy served each vegetable she and Jack had to give me the whole who-ha on how well the respective plant had grown, how big their vegetables had gotten and all that jazz. They were ear to ear teeth when they paraded out last year's prized cucumber and sliced it into the salad. After the whole production, on my way out the door, I happened to notice Anna's report card sitting on a desk. She had gotten straight As. You'd think that's what we would have been celebrating, but no. That didn't even warrant a mention."

Shore predicted that his neighbors' tendency to nurture their garden more than their children will cause irreparable damage to Kyle and Anna.

"Let's face it, all children tend to compete for their parents' attention, but Kyle and Anna are up against a dozen asparagus plants – and losing," said Shore. "I bet it won't be more than a couple of years before one of those kids comes home with a tattoo just to get mom and dad to take notice of them. Maybe a nice, big tat of a zucchini in tears hanging from a noose on Anna's arm will get her parents' attention." ∎

> "It's like they'd rather give their azaleas a better opportunity to blossom than their kids," neighbor Bob Shore said.

RECOILMAG.COM   NEWS SATIRE YOU CAN TRUST

recoil

Major League Baseball slowly, ever so slowly reaches completion

Buck stopped

Report: pornography instills teenagers with false image of librarians

Little Rock, Ark. – The universally held suspicion among male youths that all female librarians transform from polite, repressed spinsters into coquettish, aggressive sexpots upon the removal of glasses and hair pins is unrealistic, or at least exaggerated, Cornell University researchers announced Monday. "Most males carry this cruel myth well into adulthood," explained UCLA professor Harvey Paris. "Creative shortcomings among adult film and magazine producers are largely to blame, since they overuse the time-tested library scene with such regularity that it ingrains a false image of librarians into the minds of impressionable youths. Sadly, in real life, most librarians do not turn out to be the hot little sex kittens that use their esteemed position to seduce young men into becoming their love slaves, undressing slowly atop their desks…" Paris then excused himself and retired to the men's room for more than 10 minutes. ■

'This won't hurt a bit,' claim nation's mean, lying nurses

New York, N.Y. – America's no-good, deceptive nurses once again falsely announced this week that children would barely feel a thing moments before agonizingly puncturing their skins with razor-sharp needles.

"This won't hurt a bit," declared a nation of misleading and callous

see NURSES page 100

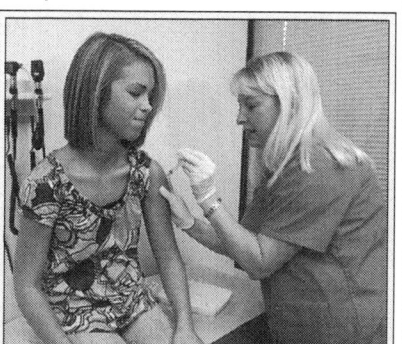

Above: Psychologically unstable ex-Navy seal Neil Quinn (right) cleans his weaponry, unbothered by the presence of the physical apparition of Gale Roberts' spirit.

House's ghost more scared of psycho new tenant than vice versa

Charleston, S.C. – Sources reported Thursday that the physical apparition of the spirit of a deceased, well-liked Charleston woman now haunting her former Trentwood Avenue home seems unable to scare the house's newest tenant to nearly the same degree that the psycho ex-Navy seal's unorthodox day-to-day behavior scares her.

Gale Roberts, an unmarried 37-year-old woman with no children who was very active in her community and highly regarded by her neighbors, died mysteriously in her sleep Aug. 14. Because Roberts had lived alone and never formally generated a will, the house she had bought and lived in for nearly two decades was sold at a public auction to Neil Quinn, a psychologically unstable loner who immediately stripped the home of all of Roberts' possessions,

see GHOST page 100

New study reveals lack of new subjects to study

New York, N.Y. – Results from a recent study conducted by a group of researchers at Columbia University's School of Academic Sciences demonstrates conclusively the absence of any new subjects available for scientific research.

"I'm afraid that after thorough investigation, it has been determined that there are no longer any health issues to research, no environmental links to correlate, in fact no topics *at all* that warrant thorough

Dr. Nosworth: "We've blown our whole wad. There's just nothing left to study. Zero. Squat. Nada."

study," said Columbia researcher Dr. Irwin Nosworth, dropping his shoulders in despair during a press conference Monday afternoon. "Apparently, the researchers of this and past generations have simply gone and studied everything that can be studied. We've blown our whole wad. There's just nothing left to study. Zero. Squat. Nada."

According to Nosworth, the study's results merely confirmed a situation

see STUDY page 100

Left: Researchers sit around trying to think of something to study.

page 97

DEFENSE

F-29 Crowdsmasher making huge impacts at airshows

Above: A publicity photo of the F-29 Crowdsmasher in action.

Andrews Air Force Base, Md. – Despite having only recently been cleared to participate in both military combat and public airshows, the new Lockheed Martin F-29 Crowdsmasher fighter jet has already made huge impacts with airshow audiences, having twice during June demonstrations abandoned its scripted flight plan and produced spectacular ground collisions, fully engaging large numbers of surprised spectators in the process.

"When the Crowdsmasher goes up for its demonstration, it literally just seems to drive each and every [airshow] audience member right to the very edge of their seat," said Fredrick Airshow promotions director Natalie Clearing. "Everyone from the paying customers to members of the emergency response team to the typically oblivious peanut vendors simply refuse to take their eyes off the plane for a single moment while it's in the air – they're that captivated. It's exciting to see that they seem to have a real vested interest in the jet's performance."

The F-29 Crowdsmasher – assigned its foreboding moniker for its notable tendency to veer out of control and crash into large contingencies of airshow onlookers – has brought widespread attention to military aerial demonstrations, but has yet to translate to increased airshow ticket sales.

"We're hoping that what the glorification of multi-car crashes has done for NASCAR's popularity, the Crowdsmasher can do for airshows," said Clearing, confirming the dramatic increase in airshow press coverage since the F-29's fantastic crashes. "There's a real buzz being generated by the prospect of the Crowdsmasher's dual Pratt & Whitney® engines using a combined 70,000 pounds of thrust to send the craft cart-wheeling into scores of screaming spectators."

Clearing suggested that the F-29's unique ability to intimately interact with airshow audiences is driving the jet's unprecedented popularity.

"The steady decline in attendance at public airshows during the last decade to me indicates that the lure of a simple mid-air collision has not been enough to attract interest in today's hands-on market," said David Moore, former pilot for the legendary stunt aviator squad the Blue Angels, who also consulted on the design of the F-29. "The Crowdsmasher is building a reputation as being able to consistently deliver a truly interactive experience for a good percentage of an airshow's audience."

Added Moore: "If being able to see and feel a sixteen million dollar jet up close while it's actually in the air, even if only for a split second, doesn't draw audiences, I'm not sure what will."

Clearing agreed with Moore's sentiments, saying that airshow planning committees have been unable to envision an attraction capable of drawing as much attention to aerial demonstrations as the crashing of an airshow's star component into paying attendees.

"The Crowdsmasher is a guaranteed showstopper, that's for sure," Clearing said. ■

> "The steady decline in attendance at public airshows during the last decade to me indicates that the lure of a simple mid-air collision has not been enough to attract interest in today's hands-on market," said David Moore.

A page from the Recoil handbook...
Going to the Beach

Nothing spells summer fun like a day at the beach. Here are some tips to help you enjoy your day in the sun:

• Remember, we each must share the beach with others. That means you should let the most needy-looking persons have first dibs on the discarded syringes.

• It is said that extract from the herb St. John's Wort can relieve the effects of sunburn. It is also said that if you kiss your sunburn three times right before you go to bed, the Sunburn Fairy will visit during the night and magically heal you.

• When swimming, beware of rip tides, sneaker waves, undertows and other cowardly terrorist ploys.

• Diving headfirst into unfamiliar waters will let you know right away if the area is safe for diving or not.

• Rendezvous at the beach seawall at the base of the cliff, which will offer some safety from the Germans' stationary guns. As Navy Destroyers storm in, scale the cliff in small groups and take out the resistance nests using small arms and grenades. (This tip provided by U.S. Lieutenant General Omar Bradley, Omaha Beach, Normandy, circa 1944.)

• Never, ever swim alone. If you don't have anyone to swim with, try placing a personal ad that says you're looking for someone to get wet with.

• Be considerate: don't almost drown until after the lifeguard at least finishes his or her cigarette.

• Clerics and magic-users (third-level or higher) can use their Protection From Energy spell to combat the effects of the sun. The rest of you peasants will either need to find a Scroll of Protection or cough up enough platinum pieces to buy some sunscreen.

• If you have been dreaming of saying "Enough!" and finally drawing a line in the sand once and for all, during your trip to the beach would be an opportune time.

• Keep in mind that littering is not permitted on most beaches until 5 p.m.

• If you encounter a Sand Witch, ask her to cast a spell and make you one of those things with bread and bologna and ketchup that you can eat.

• While you're out scouring the beach day and night with that metal detector, you may want to see if that machine can help you dig up a goddamned life, too.

• Alcohol dehydrates the body, which is why it's such a good idea to drink beer at the beach – there's nothing like a good swim to hydrate the body after you've drank yourself stupid.

• After eating, you should hold your breath for at least one hour before swimming. [NOTE TO FACT-CHECKER: CAN YOU RECHECK THIS ONE? SOMETHING JUST DOESN'T SOUND RIGHT ABOUT IT. EDITOR.]

page 98

EYE ON DICK

GROCERY DAY 2012

Standing in direct conflict with bar scene observers' oft-stated presumption that party juggernaut and cultural icon Dick Bill "seems more machine now than man," is the fact that despite his stern reluctance, Dick does actually force himself to consume some fort of non-liquid provision that possesses legitimate levels of nutritional value at least once every third day. Securing such provisions, of course, requires that Dick journey North once per month from his underground sanctuary before the stroke of midnight – an unnatural hour for Dick that routinely finds his mood at truly its most foul. Below are items of interest regarding Dick and his encounters with supermarkets, perishables and other treacherous buy-two-get-one-free incidents:

FREE SAMPLES
In a Wal-Mart parking lot, Dick was once firmly informed by policemen that the toaster oven used to prepare the pizza rolls is not considered part of the free sample, and was forced to return the uneaten portions of both the roll and the oven.

COUPONS
Dick has refused to use coupons of any kind ever since a 2001 incident at a local D&W Foods location, in which Dick accidentally presented a cashier with a coupon for "One free kick in the balls with purchase of same" during double-coupon Tuesday.

MEATS
In perhaps one of the worst calls ever, Dick Bill's four-yard-reception of an English roast was ruled incomplete by an on-staff butcher, who argued that Dick got only one foot down before going headfirst into a floor cooler full of frozen corn.

STORAGE
Dick usually manages to jam all of his groceries into his modified keg-refrigerator even though his half-barrel takes up 75 percent of all available fridge space. Also note that the freezer area iced over years ago, but Dick refuses to thaw it out because of some insane global warming theory, which friends agree makes absolutely no sense unless it's explained after ingesting two hits of LSD.

WAR

Above: GI Joe forces storm the Cobra-controlled entertainment center located in the family room of the Holthup residence.

GI Joe establishes beachhead on entertainment center

Gainesville, Fla. – An elite team of 12-inch tall GI Joe action figures, acting under the command of Lieutenant Major Jonnie Holthup, 10, stormed the entertainment center of the Holthup residence Saturday morning, seizing control of the resistance encampment and pushing the enemy back as far as the kitchen refrigerator, sources said.

"Reconnaissance missions had indicated the presence of a large cell of enemy Cobras that was using the entertainment center as its base camp," said Holthup in a press conference that followed the confrontation. "This morning our forces conducted a full-scale invasion of the stronghold, which drove the outnumbered and overpowered Cobra soldiers into retreat. I'm happy to say that our forces reported zero casualties and are now fully occupying the position – just in time for *SpongeBob SquarePants*."

According to Holthup, GI Joe forces attacked the enemy-infested entertainment center – which normally just houses the Holthup family's television, DVD player and stereo – shortly after breakfast, despite conditions that were far from optimal.

"The strike was made more tactically difficult by the fact that my mom decided to clean the whole living room right when I was trying to attack," said Holthup. "So here I am trying to coordinate my air support while moving a convoy of AFVs (Armored Fighting Vehicles) into attack position from the west flank when all of a sudden my stupid mom makes me pick up all of my infantry soldiers so she can vacuum. I tried to explain to her that this was mostly a ground invasion and that the foot soldiers' position was absolutely pivotal, but she didn't care."

> "Here I am trying to coordinate my air support while moving a convoy of AFVs into attack position from the west flank when all of a sudden my stupid mom makes me pick up all of my infantry soldiers so she can vacuum," said Holthup.

Forced to improvise, Holthup ordered the infantry soldiers to double back, assume sniper positions atop the coffee table and provide covering fire for a pair of spy ninja troopers riding twin Ranger attack cycles. After approaching the base silently in Stealth Mode, the ninjas ditched their bikes at the foot of the entertainment center and scaled its east wall using a grappling hook and rappel rope – all without being spotted by Cobra scouts or waking up Molly,

see BEACHHEAD page 100

BEACHHEAD from page 99

the Holthups' cat, which lay asleep on a nearby armchair.

Holthup dispatched two Humvee convoys to construct blockades at the living room's two main exits in order to prevent ground escape of Cobra forces. A lone GI Joe Frogman diver with harpoon gun was also deployed to the 15-gallon fish tank that stands adjacent to the entertainment center in the unlikely event of an attempted water escape.

Once atop the enemy base, the Special Ops ninjas slit the throat of a Cobraviper guard before rappelling down onto the television just as friendly air strikes took out a machine gun nest located next to the DVD player. At the same time, snipers fired fatal head shots at will from the coffee table as ground vehicles encroached on the entertainment center's perimeter and began launching a seemingly endless string of missiles until all of the approximately 15 Cobra soldiers were dead.

Annexation of the Holthup entertainment center knocks a huge hole in Cobra's military stranglehold on the downstairs rooms of the house and firmly establishes GI Joe's presence in the highly volatile but strategically critical "family area" of the three-bedroom dwelling.

"Controlling the living room is a significant step toward occupation and control of the entire house," said Holthup. "Using the entertainment center as our beachhead, we will now be able to set up and protect a supply line that will stretch from my bedroom all the way into the living room. We'll also be much closer to the front line when we assemble and ready troops for our siege on the kitchen later this afternoon."

"And now that we control the entertainment center, we can watch whatever we want on TV or even play the stereo," added Holthup. "Under Cobra's evil rule the TV was always set on CNN. Getting that channel changed may very well have shifted the entire momentum of the war to our side."

Holthup said that his troops are unlikely to see combat again until just before bedtime, when a small group of Special Ops soldiers will stage a nighttime raid on the Cobra-controlled downstairs bathtub – a strike expected to be almost entirely amphibious. ∎

> "Controlling the living room is a significant step toward occupation and control of the entire house," said Holthup.

STUDY from page 97

"For months we had been having increased difficulty formulating study topics that hadn't already been tackled by some team of researchers somewhere in the world," said Nosworth, who himself has led numerous studies ranging from the mating habits of the three-toed sloth to how the use of aerosol hairspray affects the growth rate of human fingernails. "For a brief period last month we thought that perhaps nobody had yet studied a possible correlation between domestic violence and the amount of leftover ham in a couple's refrigerator, but, believe it or not, some UCLA students appear to have already explored that in 2004."

Added Nosworth: "We began to wonder, if studies as uncommon as *that* have already been done, what could possibly be left? We couldn't come up with anything. However, by studying the decreasing productivity of research teams around the world, we've been able to confirm that it isn't only Columbia researchers who are drawing a blank – the scientific community as a whole has become unable to think of anything new to study."

In a lengthy article written for the December issue of *Science*, Nosworth explains in great detail the results of the three-month study. The exhaustingly thorough piece, entitled "No More Stones to Turn," is expected to occupy almost the entirety of what is likely to be the peer-reviewed journal's final issue.

The researchers' techniques and findings occupying the magazine's first five pages, while the rest of the article focuses on reminiscing about previous studies, analyzing spreadsheets of information regarding the social lives of Columbia researchers and presenting assorted doodles the researchers drew on leftover sheets of graph paper, for which they admitted to being unable to imagine having any future use.

"I have a feeling grant money is going to be awfully hard to come by in 2014," Nosworth told reporters. "I guess it's time to ask my brother about a job at his oil change shop. So long, science. Hello, dirty air filters."

However, not all academics are so ready to throw in the towel on scientific inquiry. Dr. Tamara Allens of the University of California at Berkeley is currently seeking funds from the National Academy of Sciences for a new research project entitled "The Decline of Available Research Topics and Correlating Rise of Home Breweries Among Scientific Researchers."

"The grant application may not be the strongest ever," said Dr. Allens. "But given the lack of competition this year, I think we've got a good shot." ∎

NURSES from page 97

health professionals as they heartlessly inflicted pain on various regions of patients' epidermises.

Though young victims made their feelings known through shouts of "ouch," winces and an abundance of tears, the maniacal nurses, who seemed reluctant to show any remorse, issued a statement asserting that the horrific needle-inflicted pain "wasn't so bad, was it?"

"This is just another scare tactic," said a wounded eight-year-old Tyler Crowder, who is never going to the doctor's office again. "I think parents may be working with the stupid nurses to propagate this fabrication."

Meanwhile, nurses, who seem to have a particular hatred of children's shoulders, deny any such alliance and maintain their long-held stance that shots only sting for a moment at the most.

"The atrocities of shots rank next to the torture inflicted by evil dentists," Crowder said. "At the dentist, you can at least bite the doctor's fingers, but many nurses are too crafty to expose themselves to retaliation."

In addition to suspicion of deceiving children about the looming pain of skin-destroying needles, nurses have also been implicated in malicious lies regarding waiting times and the abundance of suckers.

"The last time I was [at the doctor's office] the nurse told me if I was brave during the shot I would get a sucker when I left," recalled Kayla Saffel, a seven-year-old dollhouse manager. "Then they were out of suckers and so they gave me an eraser that fits on top of a pencil."

"And that medicine in the plastic spoon did not taste like cherry," added Crowder. "How long will we continue to fall for their lies?" ∎

GHOST from page 97

redecorated to suit his personal taste and moved into the house on Oct. 15.

"Gale's soul has been in a state of unrest ever since she crossed over to the other side," said Valerie Fitoussi, a neighbor and professional medium who claimed to have been able to communicate with Roberts' spirit ever since her death. "It is not uncommon for a person's spirit to 'haunt' the home to which their mortal body was so attached. It is believed that spirits often show themselves or somehow make their presence felt in order to try to scare new residents and persuade them to leave so the spirit can have the house all to itself. However, in this case it seems that Gale's spirit is actually more scared of the person living in her house than he is of the ghost."

Added Fitoussi: "And let me tell you, after living near the guy for the last few months, I can totally understand why."

According to Fitoussi, although Roberts will occasionally perform minor supernatural acts in attempts to unnerve Quinn – acts such as flicking the porch light on and off, turning on the kitchen sink faucet or oven, or stomping the upstairs floor when it is otherwise unoccupied – the 34-year-old seems completely unalarmed by the specter's continuous presence.

In describing some of the abnormal behavior exhibited by Quinn, neighbor Bernard Ross offered some insight as to why even the supernatural incantation of Roberts could feel frightened sharing living space with Quinn.

"Sometimes at night I can see [Quinn] through the window, sitting in his chair in almost complete darkness, staring off into space, mumbling something to himself while he rubs a huge hunting knife against a sharpening stone over and over until dawn," said Ross. "Now I'm no psychiatrist, but to me that's a sign that something just ain't right with the guy's wiring, if you know what I mean. It makes me feel sorry for the ghost of Gale, that she has to haunt the same house that [Quinn] lives in. Only God knows what crazy shit he does in there all day. I'd be scared to live in the same house with the guy, too."

Other neighbors confirmed that on more than one occasion local police have come to Quinn's house in response to a neighbor's call about loud screaming in the middle of the night, only to find Quinn locked in his bathroom and calling out military commands to imaginary recruits at the top of his lungs.

Neighbors agreed that, considering the disturbing behavior exhibited by Quinn – such as his Saturday afternoon ritual of cleaning his sniper rifle collection while sitting atop his roof, his placing armed bear traps at various locations in his front yard or his tendency to don camouflage fatigues and deploy smoke grenades for cover when venturing across the street to retrieve his mail – they would be more afraid to live with the dishonorably discharged veteran than with the supernatural apparition of the spirit of the pleasant, well-mannered neighbor they had in Roberts.

"I can sense that Gale's spirit is growing more and more frustrated – and scared," said Fitoussi. "During a recent séance she said she fears that she'll never be able to generate anything nearly as scary as whatever is already going on in Neil's mind, so the odds of him moving out and her maybe getting the house all to herself, or even sharing it with a nice, quiet family, are slim. And Gale says she's afraid to go to sleep, fearing that Neil will kill himself just so that his ghost can come and kill her ghost. Who knew ghosts could be so paranoid?" ∎

> "It makes me feel sorry for the ghost of Gale, that she has to haunt the same house that [Quinn] lives in. Only God knows what crazy shit he does in there all day. I'd be scared to live in the same house with the guy, too," said Fitoussi.

recoil

RECOILMAG.COM — NEWS SATIRE YOU CAN TRUST

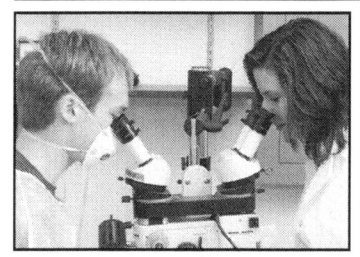

XX marries XY

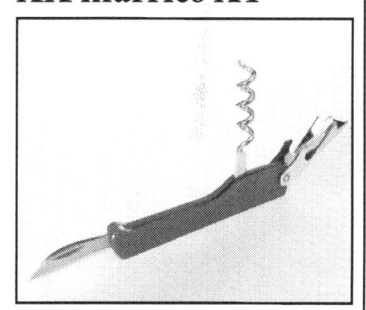

Irish Army Knife only useful for getting drunk

Nook in cranny

recoilmag.com

Barn razed, raised

St. Joseph, Mich. – Confusion ran rampant among the gathering of approximately 60 Amish community residents pitching in to raze and then raise a barn for River Country's Jones family Saturday. The confusion began promptly at 8 a.m., when every ablebodied man, woman and children arrived at the Jones property to begin the dismantling of the family's aged and tattered barn. "I don't get it. I thought we were here to raise a barn today, not take one apart," said a bewildered Adam Crane, 18. After the men razed the barn and the children toiled spiritedly in hauling away and burning the ancient lumber, the entire workforce gathered together at noon for what many thought was a job-finished celebratory lunch prepared by the women. "We all partook heartily at mealtime, most of us believing that we were done for the day," said Cane Barger, 42. "Then, after dessert, David [Jones] rose from his seat and said, 'Well, I guess we better get moving if we're going to raise this barn before sundown.' Everyone just sat there in total silence, probably all thinking the same thing that I was: 'Didn't we just get done doing that?' As almost all of us learned that day, the words 'raze' and 'raise' are separate words that sound the exact same but have different spellings and completely opposite meanings." Questioning one another throughout the exhaustive effort of raising a completely new barn, workers eventually traced the root of the misunderstanding, attributing it to David Jones' occasional vocal stutter. "David often stutters or repeats the same word a couple of times when speaking – hence the miscommunication when he asked the community to 'help raze, raise a barn.'" ■

Family ripped apart by bitter divorce, bear

Above: The Stevens family, shortly before being ripped apart by a bitter divorce and a wild bear (left).

Denver, Colo. – Sources close to the Robert Stevens family – a seemingly stable unit universally lauded throughout the neighborhood for nearly a decade as the absolute perfect model of a solid, modern suburban family – said Saturday morning that the family has been completely ripped apart by both Robert and Rebecca Stevens' sudden and reportedly bitter divorce, as well as by the bear that had entered the family's residence and ripped both parents, the couple's three children and the family dog to pieces Friday night.

"It's really just a god-awful tragedy when a family is ripped apart by divorce and the children start getting used as bargaining tools for a settlement," said Bernard Longer, a neighbor and close family friend. "In my opinion, nothing tears a family apart limb by limb quicker and more painfully than a spiteful divorce involving custody battles. Well, except in this case, for that huge bear they found in their kitchen. Those are some mean, angry bastards."

> Neighbor Bernard Longer: "[It] looks like they're definitely split apart for good now."

Added Longer: "Bears, I meant, are mean bastards. Not Robert and Rebecca – at least not in my experience with them. They always presented themselves as the perfect couple, but they must have been very unhappy if they were filing for divorce. Who knows what finally did it – abuse, infidelity, bickering, lying, wild bear in the kitchen – but [it] looks like they're definitely split apart for good now."

According to Denver Police Officer James Knight, who was first on the scene after responding to a domestic violence complaint, situations such as what occurred to the Stevens family are becoming more and more common in

see **BEAR** page 104

Local band singers demand more vocal in stage monitors

Above: Six representatives of the 97-member coalition of singers demanding louder vocal monitors.

Austin, Texas – Singers for all of Austin's unsigned original bands sternly demanded an increase in the volume of the vocals in the front stage monitor speakers at every live music venue across Austin Friday night.

"I'm gonna need more vocal in the monitors up here," David Teller, singer for the local rock band Mein Cough, told soundman Brian Waltz through the center stage microphone at Emo's nightclub immediately following the band's first song. "Seriously, man – I can't hear myself at all onstage."

Similar scenes played out simultaneously throughout the city's nightclubs as the

> "I'm gonna need more vocal in the monitors up here," David Teller told soundman Brian Waltz.

entire coalition of local band singers continued to present its unified front in demand of louder vocals in the monitors.

"Dude, I can only hear myself [singing] through the main [house speakers]," said Tyrannosaurus Sex singer John Sanders, demanding that The Parish nightclub's sound technician Mike Authier increase the volume of the vocal monitors. Though fully aware that the monitor system would be unable to provide sufficient headroom to adequately compete with the band's stage volume, Authier attempted to meet the singer's demand for increased volume,

see **MONITORS** page 104

WAR ON DRUGS

Pablo Escobar adorns first Drug War commemorative plate

The first Drug War commemorative plate (above) will be available for $39.95 on Jan. 1, 2013.

Tucson, Ariz. – Reports issued from executives at the collectable memorabilia manufacturing company W.C. Bunting said Thursday that the image of the late Pablo Escobar, the most ambitious and ruthless drug lord in history, will grace the first of a series of collector's plates commemorating the American Drug War.

"As the most recognizable name and face associated with the Drug War, Escobar was the obvious choice to adorn the debut plate of this powerful, must-have collection," said Gary Albright, spokesperson for W.C Bunting, which in the past has issued commemorative plate series honoring figures from the Civil War and World War II. "No other figure in history encapsulates the efforts of the war on drugs quite like Pablo Escobar, who was estimated have earned at least twenty-five billion dollars per year during his glory years – back before he was shot behind the ear and killed, of course."

Made from only the finest imported china, the series of collectables will feature six plates – one to be released every two months beginning with the Escobar plate on Jan. 1, 2013 – each sporting the image of a famous drug-affiliated figure and available for $39.95 plus shipping. With the Escobar plate already in production in New Zealand, Albright excitedly discussed his company's plans for the five remaining plates.

"The March plate will feature the image and signature of George Jung, or 'Boston George,' as they called him," said Albright. "Jung was the fellow portrayed by Johnny Depp in the major motion picture *Blow*. That Jung is still alive makes this plate very special, since we were able to obtain a recent signature for this plate's production. What's really exciting is that Jung is scheduled to be released from prison in 2015, so people will definitely want to get their hands on these plates and possibly plan on meeting him at the prison gate to get it signed when he is released. The value of a personally signed George Jung Drug War commemorative plate will no doubt be substantial."

Albright said that although there was mild controversy among W.C. Bunting department heads regarding whether it should be Escobar or Jung appearing on the first plate, in the end it was clear that Escobar deserved the honor.

"Really, it shouldn't have been any contest who was the most significant Drug War figure, considering that Escobar is credited with having ordered the killing of at least six hundred police officials before a specially designed task force finally took him down," said Albright. "Sure, maybe George Jung is more popular because of the movie *Blow*, but I believe it is Escobar's contribution to the Drug War that will ultimately stand the test of time and be remembered as something special."

Having unanimously decided to dedicate two of the four remaining plates to Columbian Cali Cartel founder Gilberto Rodriguez Orejuela, a.k.a. "The Chess Player," and Rayful Edmond, the motivated youngster credited with introducing crack cocaine to Washington, D.C., in the 1980s, Albright and company ran into problems when attempting to bestow one of the final two plates to the dope-fueled comedy team of Cheech and Chong.

"Cheech and Chong firmly objected to appearing together on one of the last plates, as those two simply aren't having anything to do with each other anymore," said David G. Mears, a legal consultant to the W.C. Bunting company. "So rather

> "Sure, maybe George Jung is more popular because of the movie *Blow*, but I believe it is Escobar's contribution to the Drug War that will ultimately stand the test of time and be remembered as something special," said Albright.

than having both Cheech and Chong together on one plate and having one left over for Timothy Leary, we had to put Cheech on one plate and Chong on the last one. No disrespect to Mister Leary, who definitely deserves the honor, but mathematically we were kind of stuck. We couldn't just put Cheech *or* Chong on one plate and leave the other out, you know? Really, in retrospect, we should probably have extended the series to a seventh plate, but the executives get real nervous when you start messing with the 'limited' part of a limited edition. As if anyone's going to care." ■

HEALTH

Harrah's opens new hospital on Vegas strip

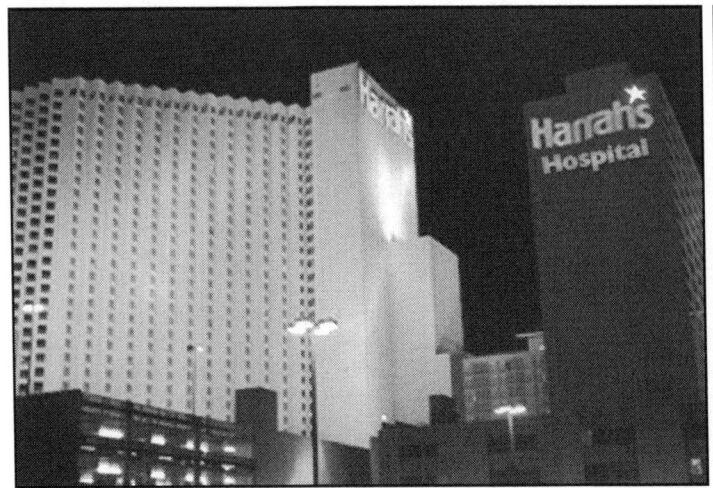

Above: The luxurious 39-story medical facility is located next to the MGM Grand on the famous Las Vegas strip.

Las Vegas, Nev. – Harrah's Entertainment, the world's largest gaming company and owner of 40 casinos worldwide, officially branched out into the medical industry Monday when company executives cut the ribbon at the opening of Harrah's Hospital, the first five-star medical center located on the famous Las Vegas strip.

The lavish 39-story high-rise represents a new breed of lodging facility that merges the glamour of high-stakes gaming with the necessity of life-saving medical treatment.

"Until now, a tourist suffering a heart attack at the craps tables at one of our Vegas resorts meant one less active gambler in the city, at least for that night," said Gary W. Loveman, CEO of Harrah's Entertainment, Inc., at the hospital's opening. "Now, through the miracles of modern science and technology, that patient could be playing video poker that very evening in the privacy of his or her recovery room – provided he or she survived the emergency operation, of course."

Harrah's Hospital differs from typical medical centers not only in location but in the range of services offered. In addition to a first-rate emergency room, surgical staff and long-term care facilities, the hospital also offers slot machines and video poker in patients' rooms as well as a full range of table games in waiting rooms and other areas of the hospital.

"Next to each nurse's station is a table games pit where patients and visitors can try their luck at blackjack, roulette, craps, baccarat and other popular games of chance," said Loveman. "Those feelings of mourning and grief that often accompany hospital visits could now

see HARRAH'S page 104

HEALTH

Nine-year-old Tamra Wilcox (above) prefers the chewable contraceptive tablets to conventional "swallow pills." (Inset) The recent approval of Ortho-Novum 1/12 by the FDA is expected to significantly lessen the amount of preteen pregnancies reported yearly in the U.S.

New chewable birth control pill aims to combat preteen pregnancy

New York, N.Y. – Green-lighted by last month's Food and Drug Administration approval, drug manufacturer Ortho-McNeil Pharmaceuticals unveiled Monday the company's newest oral contraceptive: Ortho-Novum 1/12 – the world's first chewable birth control pill.

Designed to target the ever-growing demographic of at-risk preteen females, the edible Ortho-Novum 1/12 tablet boasts an easier ingestion process than its orally administered predecessors or competitors.

"Mommy was always making me take those icky-tasting swallow pills," said Tamra Wilcox, the blossoming, nubile nine-year-old daughter of Pensicola, Fla., pro-choicers Daniel and Rita Wilcox. "This new pill I eat with my Flintstones®; they're fun and taste good, and Mommy says they will help keep me from growing up too fast. I'm really not sure what Mommy means by that, but she says I'll probably understand pretty soon because I'm extra-cute and have the body of a twelve-year-old."

Ortho-McNeil CEO Blaine Monroe says his company's breakthrough chewable tablet form – presented in shapes of bears and other adorable wildlife animals – was simply a necessary evolution for a company that has for many years been monitoring the gradual drop in the median age of sexually active youths – a number which studies show is quickly approaching the single-digit mark.

"Obviously, our company has survived because of its ability to fill a demand, and the ability to adapt as that demand changes," explained Monroe of Ortho-McNeil's history. "Today, the American parent's demand is for a fun-to-take chewable that inhibits the ability of their precious darling's eggs to travel through the fallopian tubes, alters their cutie-pie's cervical mucus to block sperm, and partially inhibits implantation in Daddy's little angel's uterine wall."

The drug's $50 million promotional campaign is a clear indication of Ortho-McNeil's firm belief in the magnitude of the chewable contraceptive's targeted demographic. Having already negotiated an exclusive three-year promotional contract with teen pop sensation Britney Spears, Ortho-Novum appears poised to stake claim as the industry standard among today's sexually liberated preteen female.

"We contracted Spears not only because of her weighty role in creating our target market, but because she can also help us *sell to* that market," explained Monroe, outlining Ortho-McNeil's promotional campaign for the drug. "As Spears continues to negatively influence the moral standards of our nation, the average age of our sexually active youth is expected to drop to a point where a chewable oral contraceptive will become an absolute necessity for concerned parents who don't want their babies having babies before at least reaching their teens."

By mid-summer, parents can expect to find Ortho-Novum 1/12 in the new pharmacy departments of Toys-R-Us and Kay-Bee Toy retailers. ∎

> The edible Ortho-Novum 1/12 tablet boasts an easier ingestion process than its orally administered predecessors or competitors.

HOROSCOPES

Libra (September 23 to October 22)
Police will continue to pull you over until you remove those anti-establishment bumper stickers. Hassling you boat rockers is simply a stitch-in-time, bud-nipping police tactic; intelligent, thought-provoking bumper stickers often prod people into thinking for themselves – effectively loosening Big Brother's chokehold and leading to anti-government riots the police will have to work through weekends to control.

Scorpio (October 23 to November 21)
Although Scorpio's quick-witted humor often pumps life into light-hearted social events, your sarcastic quips won't go over with uppity dinner party cliques; those superficial snobs sold their senses of humor long ago. Be warned, high society table etiquette suggests you refrain from slinging such zingers as, "Which of these three forks do you people use for stabbing each other in the back?" They won't be amused.

Sagittarius (November 22 to December 21)
Sexually overactive Sagittarius needs to either lose the pro-life stance or adopt a reliable method of barricading procreation's persistent march. Those not ready for parenting shouldn't gamble with the possibility of pregnancy – one thing is for certain: if you play long enough in the poker game of unprotected sex, you will eventually end up with a full house.

Capricorn (December 22 to January 19)
Don't kid yourself into thinking the culmination of your child's video game obsession will be a high-paying job in the computer field – few companies are willing to hire someone whose computer knowledge is limited to the location of the secret warp boards in *Super Mario Brothers*.

Aquarius (January 20 to February 18)
Broken-hearted Aquarius' pleading letters to the ex read like applications to an insane asylum; "I can change" and "that wasn't the real me" are the confused babblings of a person who either has multiple personalities or is so internally malleable that there isn't even a solid person inside to be attracted to, let alone love.

Pisces (February 19 to March 20)
Garage sale-deprived Pisces will continue to suffer Saturday morning withdrawals until next spring revitalizes the entrepreneurial spirit in suburban homeowners. Maybe you should use this down time to ponder the rationale behind sifting through the useless garbage that seemingly well-to-do families feel compelled to peddle for 10 cents, rather than throw away.

Aries (March 21 to April 19)
Aries is plagued by a fatal compulsion to accept secondhand hearsay as sworn fact. Beware; the rumor mill is a factory of fiction and exaggeration where employees eagerly work overtime to meet demand for their prime product: truthless gossip. Remember, just because someone says your ex turned gay doesn't necessarily make it so – no matter how probable it may seem.

Taurus (April 20 to May 20)
Letting your heart be your guide is as surefire a way of ending up in the wrong place as carpooling with Ray Charles; half the time your heart's fickle emotional compass leads you in the wrong direction. For efficiency's sake, ignore your blood-pumper's misguiding influence; focus instead on approaching life's decisions with the meticulous, disciplined logic of a Vulcan mathematician with OCD.

Gemini (May 21 to June 20)
Entertaining your mate's late-night hypothetical questions will serve no other purpose than undermining the foundation of your relationship. When pillow talk begins drifting into "What if?" territory, Gemini would be wise to play possum – deep rhythmical breathing coupled with three or four sporadic arm twitches should convince your bedmate you're a bit too asleep to field their wormcan-opening inquiries.

Cancer (June 21 to July 22)
Cancer's typical conversation topics are as predictable as a power slant on second and one; you need to inject some creativity into your discussion subjects. Weather-, *Seinfeld*-, and government-based conversations are the trademark of people who are either afraid to say what they are really thinking about or really are thinking about those dull things they talk about – either way, not a good stigma to have.

Leo (July 23 to August 22)
Leo can expect a long week of dodging the particularly violent mood swings of your overworked, stress-filled mate. From the cuddling affection of a freshly fed kitten to the raging hostility of a wounded wild boar, the physical and vocal byproducts of your mate's emotional pendulum may seem oddly familiar. Look in a mirror.

Virgo (August 23 to September 22)
Removing your chest's weighty burden is a job requiring an independent contractor – namely, a priest; two minutes in the big, wooden penalty box confessing your crimes to a Divinity Engineer will work wonders for wringing out your conscience. But while using God's personal intercom will jettison your guilt, the legal consequences of your sinful behavior could make a move to Mexico Virgo's top priority.

page 103

HARRAH'S from page 102

quite possibly be replaced by the thrill and exhilaration of hitting it big on one of the hard ways [playing craps] or hitting a thirty-six-to-one bet at roulette. No doubt, the patient or visitor will feel a whole lot better about their hospital experience if that happens."

According to Loveman, the hospital also shares other features common to many Harrah's properties such as an indoor pool and exercise center, mostly used for physical therapy and rehabilitation, plus a buffet-style cafeteria capable of feeding more than 3,000 guests and visitors per day.

"There's no reason that a hospital has to just serve 'hospital food,'" said Loveman. "Harrah's Hospital's buffet features fresh seafood, prime rib and other specialty foods, plus a full salad and dessert bar. Of course, those patients on restricted diets will have to abide by limitations, but for the most part, if you're staying at Harrah's Hospital and not being fed through a tube, then rest assured you're eating as good as any hospital patient can possibly eat."

According to Loveman, each of Harrah's casinos' guests will now automatically be registered at Harrah's Hospital, where they will be transferred should they incur an accident or require medical attention during their stay. Loveman said that while guests' medical insurance will typically cover the cost of their hospital stay, Harrah's Hospital will also offer payment options that will appeal to the gambling nature of its guests.

"We expect our double-or-nothing bill payment option to be very popular," said Loveman, referring to the hospital's policy of letting patients attempt to zero-out their account by betting the entire cost of their bill on a single hand of blackjack. "We've also made a point of positioning some of our loosest slot machines inside the Intensive Care Unit, so anyone who is looking like they will have an expensive medical bill can start trying to recoup some of that cost right away during their stay." ■

MONITORS from page 101

resulting in a long, loud blast of high-pitched feedback erupting from the stage speakers. A temporarily deafened Authier eventually rebuffed Sanders' demands, telling the singer that the vocal monitor volume was at its limit.

"During soundcheck I suggested that the band's guitarists and bassist turn down their amplifiers so the singer would be able to hear himself in the monitors," reasoned Authier, 34. "Oh, you can't hear your vocals in the monitors? Well, maybe – just maybe – that has something to do with your guitarist having his Marshall [amplifier's] volume set on ten [for] the entire set.'"

Authier noted that the relatively small size of the venue dictates that musicians' amplifiers be set on a lower volume in order for the vocals to be heard clearly in the stage monitors.

"This isn't an arena, for Christ's sake – turn your damn amps down. Is that so hard to understand?" Authier questioned.

> "Seriously, man – I can't hear myself at all onstage," announced Teller.

Joining Teller and Sanders in the heroic stance were lead singers from unsigned Austin bands from every genre, although rock and metal singers bore the largest responsibility for getting the message across to area soundmen.

"Metal bands always play the loudest, and their singers are always bitching about not being able to hear themselves [sing]," said Waltz. "Most of the heavy bands have terrible, terrible singers – so much so that you'd think that the singer not being able to hear how awful he sounds would be a *good* thing. But instead they blame the 'shitty monitors' for their poor performance. I hear it every night: 'Need more vocal in the monitors. Still need more vocal in the monitors.' Sometimes I think singers just think they're almost obligated to say that in between songs because they see everyone else doing it. Fucking babies." ■

BEAR from page 101

Denver's suburban areas.

"The stress of two parents working full-time while also trying to maintain their household often causes couples to build up resentments toward one another," said Knight. "And it certainly doesn't help that wild bears are capable of opening doors that have levers instead of doorknobs, or that mountain lions have learned to enter houses through the flaps of dog doors. The combination of divorce and coming home to find a bear looting your refrigerator often lead right to what we're seeing here today. I mean, just look at this mess of blood and body parts. This all–"

Knight then suddenly excused himself before vomiting into the kitchen sink.

Colorado Governor Bill Ritter, concerned about the increasing frequency of these situations, encouraged a two-prong approach to limiting similar future tragedies.

"Couples experiencing problems in their relationship should try working with an experienced marriage counselor," said Ritter. "And every citizen in the area should always be carrying a loaded shotgun." ■

A page from the Recoil handbook...
Writing Your Resume

Securing gainful employment during a weak job market is no mean task. Here are some tips for creating a resume that's guaranteed to stand out from the rest:

- If you're seeking full-time employment as a writer or photographer, save yourself some time by throwing your completed resume in the trash.

- Keep in mind that most resumes are scanned these days, so you will need to attach one of your eyes to the resume for the retinal scanner to read.

- A word about choosing your resume format: use a Chronological format if you are staying in the same job field; use a Functional format if you are changing fields; and use a Crank-up-the-Funktional format if your primary skill is performing twenty-minute slap-bass solos.

- Instead of typing your resume, cut words out of magazines and paste them on a sheet like you would a ransom note. This shows you are creative and willing to go that extra mile.

- Lengthy, unexplained gaps in your work history will create an aura of mystery around you, arousing intrigue in employers who will no doubt want to interview you and learn more about this human enigma who's seeking work.

- Resumes can be impersonal; consider dropping by your prospective employer's house unannounced for an impromptu interview. Go late at night, so you know someone will be home.

- If you're lacking job experience, say you worked at companies that nobody would want to call: Sodomy Superstore, Satanic Charitable Missions, Old Navy, etc.

- List the following as your objective: "To avoid being discriminated against for being a gay minority and the inevitable protracted legal battle that would result."

- Pay a street thug to "endorse" your resume with a T-ball bat after-hours. Hey, you have to spend money to make money.

- When applying for an office job, include your desired office layout and window preference, so it can be ready for you at the time of hire.

- Modern times require additional references from every coworker you've had an affair with over the last five years.

- To show your ability to recycle and save money, print your resume on the backs of old flyers you find at the post office, city hall and public entertainment venues.

- If your resume manages to score you an interview, demonstrate your positive attitude towards teamwork by dressing up as a cheerleader for the interview.

SPECIAL THANKS

A.J. Tarachanowicz, Aaron Bezeau, Aaron Harraman, Aaron J. Klamer, Aaron Sandy, Aaron Schaut, Abbey Lou Leonard, Adam Beasley, Adam Duck, Adam Forrest, Adam Murphy, Adam Rossell, Adam Savas, Addison Wolford, Al Brede, Al Jourgensen, Al McAvoy, Aladin Kadic, Alan Bashara, Alana Eve, Alex Van Portfiet, Alicia Deven Clark, Alicia Hoffman Beyer, Alicia Menninga, Alison Joy, Alyx Dawson, Amalie Endland, Ambassador Augustine Strindberg Frantz, Amy Cochran, Amy Endres-Bercher, Amy Jones Bloom, Amy Mayes-Keegan, Amy Rose Gasper-Burke, Amy Tabor, Amy Weber Gonzalez, Andi Serocke, Andrew John, Andy Drasiewski, Andy O'Riley, Andy Westmoreland, Andy Willey, Angela Austin, Angela Diesel, Angie Fry DeCamp, Anita Norberg, Ann Kirkendall, Anna Ward, Annamarie Buller, Anne Marie Sands-Smith, Anthony Nowack, Anthony Squiers, Aris Hampers, Ashleigh Rose Hinzmann, Ashley Tanner, Ashley Wellman, Avalon Jewell, Aziza Pogi, Barb Hoogerhyde Griffin Hayes, Barbara Dzienski, Barbara McGrath, Barbara Weatherhead, Barbara White, Barry Price, Becky Seguin, Ben Allen, Ben Klebba, Benjamin Leonard, Bernie Kersten, Beth Anne Miller, Beth Brace, Beth Potter-Brown, Bill Fahl, Bill Vits, Bill Walters, Blue Michael Ellis, Bo James, Bob Beale, Bobby Trayer, Bob Niece, Bob Schader, Brad Franck, Brad Grockowski, Brandee Krumske, Brandon Ward, Brenda Hazen Bierens, Brenda McBrian, Brenda Mertz Wodek, Brent Findley, Brent Velting, Brett Alward, Brett VanTil, Brian Carmer, Brian Cousineau, Brian Edwards, Brian Gerrity, Brian Hobbs, Brian Hoekstra, Brian J. Bowe, Brian Jones, Brian Kozminski, Brian Myers, Brian Page, Brian Stauffer, Brian Vander Ark, Brian Vanderbos, Bridget Nicole Rose, Brooke Berry, Bruce Bellgraph, Bruce Evans, Bruce Hillman, Bruce Madden, Bruce Vanderkooi, Bryan Bristol, Bryan Dangremond, Bryan Wilder, Cameron Murray, Carl Kelly, Carol Kang, Carol Manos, Carolyn Matheson, Carrie Northup Page, Cassie Truskowski, Chad Carlisle, Chad Cherrie, Chad James, Chad Verwey, Charles Colegrove, Charles Dillman, Charles W. Runyan, Charley VanPortfliet, Cheryl Stevens Piippo, Chika Pena-Potter, Chris Bond, Chris Brown, Chris Burns, Chris Cole, Chris Fehsenfeld, Chris Haner, Chris Johnson, Chris Knoll, Chris Marshall, Chris Miller, Chris Ozment, Chris Protas, Chris Randall, Chris Surfus, Christie Manardie-Yokom, Christina Bivins, Christina McDonald, Christina Radisauskas, Christine Kelso, Christine Rzemek Hill, Christy Mack, Chyna Dawn, Cindy Moroney Krzykwa, CJ Gardineer, Clare Metz, Clay Stauffer, Cliff Julien, Compucraft, Connie Cunningham, Corey Anton, Corey Ruffin, Corey Scott, Cortney Erndt, Cory Hart, Craig Hill, Craig Nelson, Curt Wiser, Curt Wozniak, Cynthia Black Hosner, Dahna Zaske Burrone, Dale Zalaoras, Damien Thompson, Dan Banker, Dannelle Shultz, Dan Toth, Dan VanderKooi, Daniel Ellcey, Daniel McCoy, Danielle Kangas, Danny Eatmon, Danny Smash, Danny Thompson, Darin Estep, Daryl Mintox Minton, Dave Battjes, Dave Deaver, Dave Draugalis, Dave Enger, Dave French, Dave Holland, David Abbott, David Burns, David Dodde, David Farrell, David Hardin, David Letterman, Dave Nowack, David Platte, David Smigelski, David Winick, Dawn Dodge, Denise Bravata Bohay, Denise Kae Van Nuil-Nordhof, Denise Pastor, Dennis Cassiday, Dezy Magbi, Diamond Deschaine, Diane Witt Isler, Diane S. Stine-Schmidt, Diane Wolford, Dino Signore, Dolly Hunter, Don Clark, Don Dorshimer, Don Hunderman, Don Meixner, Donna Jo Durbin Wagnitz, Doug Saunders, Drew Nikodem, Drew Whitz, Dr. John Scott, Dustin Anderson, Dustin Cook, Dusty Lee Elliston, Dusty Scheuerman, Dusty Taylor, Edward Bolda, Edward Jay Nelson, Eileen Frantz, Elaine Sterrett Isely, Elijah Watson, Elsbeth Hussey, Emilee Petersmark, Emily Hunter, Emily Jamieson, Emily Leuenberger, Emily Stavrou Schaefer, Eric Kincaid, Eric Pobojewski, Erica Vance, Erin O'Kelly, Erin Straley Wieschowski, Erin Wilson, Erwin Erkfitz, Eve Dragstra, Fallon Briggs, Francesca Amari Sajtar, Frank Black, Frank Duron, Frank Lehnen, Frank Werner, Fred Bivins, Fred Bregman, Fred Bueltmann, Fred DeVries, Garret Michael Felix, Garrett Zack, Garry Boyd, Gary Grice, Gary Hollingsworth, Gary L. Smith, Gary Mavis, Gary Zalewski, Geoff Schalow, Georgia Abbott Spicer, GiGi Julien, Gina Wagner, Gordon LeTourneau, Grace Wolbrink, Grant Carlson, Greg Endres-Bercher, Greg Giles, Greg Towery, Haralson, Heathcliff Berru, Heather Allegrina, Heather Miller-Giebel, Heather Van Dyke, Heidi Bloom Person, Helium Frantz, Henry Forrest, Heidi Ellen Robinson-Fitzgerald, Herm Baker, Homer L. Smith, Ian Bruce, Ian Dodge, Isaac Hartman, J. Oscar Bittinger, Jackie Jackson, Jackie Sirianni, Jacob Taykowski, James Adado, James Brown, James Fleck, James R. Murphy, James Y. Watson, Jamie Springer, Jamey Authier, Jan Lewis Griffith, Janet Shelby, Jason Cunningham, Jason Drost, Jason Eakins, Jason Eller, Jason Hill, Jason Malenfant, Jason Pardieke, Jason Roth, Jason Swanson, Jay Deacon, Jay Lawrence, Jayne Scott, Jeanna Smith, Jeff Armstrong, Jeff Avink, Jeff England, Jeff Faria, Jeff LaCross, Jeff Martin, Jeff VandenBerg, Jeff Wiser, Jeffery McGrath, Jeffery Rings, Jeffrey Mcfarland, Jeffrey Scott Stevens, Jen Beers, Jen Christner Hain, Jenine Sparks Carey, Jen Petrovich, Jenn Reynhout, Jenn Schaub, Jennifer Heitz, Jennifer A. Pope, Jennifer LaDuke Williams, Jennifer Whiting Mitts, Jenny Jonas Chaffin, Jeremy Holloway, Jeremy Kosmicki, Jeremy M. Ensley, Jerry Beute, Jerry Cabrera, Jerry Evers, Jere Hinman, Jess Hamberg, Jesse James Miles, Jessica Albert, Jessica Lawson, Jessica Scheuerman, Jessie Beveridge, Jessika Wright, Jevon Dismuke, Jim Ballmer, Jim Burns, Jim Hayden, Jim Mitchell, Jim Rodery, Jim Tomaszweski, Jobot, Joe Basch, Joe McCargar, Joe Sarnicola, Joel Ferguson, Jo Tanis, John Gonzalez, John Kowalko, John LaCross, John Lippi, John Masnari, John Moy, John Rich, John Sanger, John Serba, John Shortt, John Sinkevics, Jolana Manino, Joleen Rumsey, Jon Dunn, Jon Trelfa, Jonathan Beatty, Jonathan Mullin, Jonny Bruha, Joseph Fox, Josh Nueman, Josh Vanity Giebel, Joy Watson Jr. Jr.Jr., Juan Lopez, Juanita Shamp Velez, Judson Brood, Judy Silverman, Julia Meixner, Julie Kurylowicz, Juliet Bennet-Rylah, Justin Rutkauskas, Justin Swiderski, Kara Apodaca, Karen McPhee, Karen Shortt, Karen VanTil, Kari Stewart Pasma, Karisa Wilson, Karrie LeFevre Schaedig, Kathy Brokus, Katie Seguin, Katy Batdorff, Keith Golinski, Keli Utecht Werda, Kellee Alcook, Kellie Beyer-Meyers, Ken Bierschbach, Ken Dzienski, Ken Hoyt, Ken Lotterman, Kenneth R. Adams, Kermit Harris, Kevin Ballmer, Kevin Cole, Keith Hosner, Kevin Howard, Kevin Matthews, Kevin Nunn, Kevin Rice, Kim Kibby, Kiowa Kirchoff, Kirk Krzykwa, Kirstyn Schwartz, Kolene Allen, Krista LaTulip, Kristin Nicole Barone, Kristi Stratton Simmons, Kristy Ryan, Kurt Isler, Ky Henderson, Kyle Fletcher Alward, Lance Hendrickson, Lando Frantz, Larry Bate, Larry Niece, Larry Wardino, Laura A. Dillivan, Laura Haig, Laura Johnson, Laura Kennedy, Laura Maslanka, Laura Mason, Laura Sage, Lauran Hardin, Lee Vandersloot, Leelan H. Smith, Les Jared, Lesley Kozminski, Lewda Leveller, Linda R. Stuba, Lisa Badder Goodall, Lisa Lin Olsen, Lisa Schrotenboer, Little T, Liz Snavely, Liz Viernes, Lord Byron Frantz, Loreine Fitzgerald-Webber, Loretta Cipta, Lori D. Talo, Lorna Wilson Reece, Louie Cantu, Lou Musa, Lucia Vaccaro Bierschbach, Lucy Ernst, Luke Smith, Lyle Fales, Lyndi Charles, Marcus Malone, Marcus Taylor, Mardie Hammond, Mario Castillo, Mario Leon, Mariposa Stoddard, Marjorie Pierson Yost, Mark Alan Daves, Mark Berry, Mark Cooper, Mark Dorich, Mark Kenny, Mark Kroll, Mark Landauer, Mark London, Mark Rozema, Mark Rumsey, Mark Sellers, Mark Simmons, Mark Stegeman, Mark Steven Post, Marly Mary Green, Marshall Yoder, Mary Cohen, Mary Elizabeth Koepnick, Mary Goodblood Rivera, Mary Habermehl, Mary Morsman, Maryanne Saladino, Matt Chewie Wade, Matt Dowdy, Matt Gullo, Matt Moser, Matt Seguin, Matt Simpson Siegel, Matt Southwell, Matt Wyatt, Matthew Dolinar, Matthew Scott, Max Primm, Megan Cornell, Megan Dooley, Megan LaSorsa, Melanie See, Melissa Koziej Kolenda, Melissa Metivier, Melissa Prezelowski-Smith, Melissa Stewart Kurek, Melissa Woodely, Michael Aiko Leavell, Michael Coleman, Michael Crittenden, Michael Dordan, Michael Frederick Cunningham, Michael Landon, Michael McIntosh, Michael Merchut, Michael Miller, Michael Packer, Michael Pfleghaar, Michael Redding, Michael Sheneman, Michelle Donk, Michelle London, Michele Morgan Myers, Mick Force, Mick Nasty, Mike Barkhuff, Mike Bowe, Mike Charbonneau, Mike Dodge, Mike F. Meyers, Mike Gagliardo, Mike Hall, Mike Kerr, Mike Luxford, Mike Naughton, Mike Nedwick, Mike Raaymakers, Mike Randazzo, Mike Raymond, Mike Redding, Mike Roland, Mike Stevens, Mike Walsh, Mikel Moore, Milissa Taylor Patow, Mimi Cummings, Missy Stalter-Mills, Misty Eakins, Mitchell Cousineau, Mitchell Hayes, Molly Tate Sanger, Mona Eddy, Moryah Nordhof, Nancy Bouwkamp, Nancy Rabideau, Nancy Serba, Nancy Struski, Nate Juett, Nathan Bartrum, Nathan Christopher Jean, Natron Clements, Neil Rajala, Neil Vaughn, Nesa Fab, Nicholas James Thomasma, Nick Cavanaugh, Nick Monoyios, Nick Washburn, Nick Weave, Nick Williams, Nicole Brimmy Spess, Nicole Cave, Nicole Jean Murphy, Nicole Leedy, Nikki Mol, Nita Pineiro, Norm Mcfaden, Novia Doyle Moser, Pamela Jansen, Pat LaBreque, Patrick McClinchy, Patrick Minnick, Patrick Talsma, Patty Rekeny, Paul Hunter, Paul Pastalaniec, Paul Jendrasiak, Paul Ward, Paula Dixon, Pete Bass, Pete Dunning, Phil Beckwith, Phil Kulas, Phylis Bergmen, Poppy Frantz, Preston Smith, Rachael Partridge, Rachel Flowers, Rachel Ruiz, Randy A. Springer, Randy DeBoer, Randy Dzienski, Ravyn Christine, Rebecca Gohl, Rebecca Palmer, Rebecca Witt, Regina Greenway, Renee Kay Gardner, Ric Nelson, Rich Burkholder, Rich Davis, Rich Hunker, Rich LeTourneau, Rich T. Anderson, Richard Kelly, Richie Lampani, Rick Carroll, Rick Frantz, Rick Hayes, Rick Tipton, Rob Bruce, Rob Costley, Rob Dodge, Rob Savage, Robert Adgate, Robert Frantz, Robert Ryan, Roberta King, Robin Costley, Robin Nicole, Robin Petersen, Rodney Johnson, Rodney Lane, Ron Boot, Ron Clause, Ron Hurd, Ron Parker, Ron Schalow, Ron Whitemyer Jr., Rosalynn Bliss, Rose McKay, Rose O'Brien, Rosie Kozminski, Ross Morgan, Roy Wallace, Russell Gorton, Russell Olmstead, Ruth Kelly, Ryan Lieske, Ryan Michael O'Neill, Ryan Mulder, Ryan Trogden, Sam Kenny, Sam Rodriguez, Samantha Gronemeyer, Sandra Tempesti, Sandy K. Coonan, Sarah Anne Harrier, Sarah C. Myers, Sarah Dordan, Sarah Fifelski, Sarah Hale, Sarah Jean Anderson, Sarah Howard, Sarah Smith, Sarah Stump, Sarai Worsham, Saul Williams, Scott Hammontree, Scott Hickock, Scott Korringa, Scott Minkley, Scott Partain, Scott Sanford, Scott Stefanski, Scott Waddell, Screamy Frantz, Sean Maitner, Sean Michael O'Connor, Sean Quashnie, Sean Smith, Shalonda Mitchell, Shane Rawlings, Shanee Laurent, Shannon Gould Skowronek, Shannon Sweet, Shannon Williams, Shannon Wolford, Shantel Hesser, Shar Briggs England, Shawn Bergsma, Shawn Melton, Shawn Saylor, Shawn Utecht, Sheila Premo Brophy, Shelly Klein, Shelly Spears Wilson, Shepard Fairey, Sheri Garbrecht Sheneman, Sherry DeHaan Williams, Shona Painter Hughes, Sierra Britton, Skip Koepnick, Skip Petrovich, Skye Schader, Staci Stauffer, Stephanie Rosen, Stephen Grow, Steve Albini, Steve Garner, Steve Lubbinge, Steve Shultz, Steve Williamson, Steven Shehori, Stew Matz, Stu McCallister, Stuba, Sue Swanson, Susan Bartz, Susan Brubacher, Susan Evangelista, Susanna Edwards Bond, Suzanne M. Beveridge, Tad Tafelsky, Tami Vandenberg, Tammy De Vries Kretowicz, Tammy Fuller, Tanya Lee, Ted Gillis, Ted R. Reidsma, Ted Smith, Teri Lynne Peterson, Terina Greenway, Terri Ann Bird, Terri Deboer, Terri Walma White, Terri Wood Spivey, Terry Garlets, Terry Johnston, Tessa Perry, Theresa Gillis, Karen Briggs Kirkland, Theresa Milanowski, Thomas DeWitt, Thomas Gregory Bliss, Thomas J. Kretowicz, Thomas Snyder, Thomas Wolford, Thomas Wolford Jr., Tia Maria, Tiffani Duck, Tim Carpenter, Tim De Groot, Tim Motley, Tim Pratt, Timm Vanderhill, Tina Tufts, Todd A. Dietlin, Todd A. Stewart, Todd Ernst, Todd Hort, Tommy Allen, Tommy Brann, Tommy Davis, Tommy Schichtel, Tom Smolinski, Toni Addington, Tony Lubenow, Tonya Mashue, Tracey Nowinski, Tracy Olmsted, Tree Frie, Trevor Reidsma, Tricia Woolfenden Boot, Trina Dunning, Trish Hale, Tylene Caldwell Cooley, Valerie Peterson, Vaughn Jurgens, Veronica Kandl, Vickie Van Otteren, Vicky Johnson Azman, Victor Ward, Victoria Upton, Wayne McGuire, Wayne Pickard, Wendi Watts Lewis, Wendy Petersen, Wil Lucy, William Case, William Gronemeyer, William Willemstyn, Yoshima Frantz, Zach Kitt Bruursema, Oderus Urungus and the staff of Holland Hospital.

Made in the USA
Charleston, SC
07 May 2013